THE
COMPLETE
IDIOT'S
GUIDE® TO

Understanding
Ethics

by David Bruce Ingram, Ph.D.,
and Jennifer A. Parks, Ph.D.

ALPHA

A member of Penguin Group (USA) Inc.

We dedicate this book to our loving parents, Betty Nixon, Richard Ingram, and Lauretta Parks. Through them we have learned the meaning of moral excellence.

ALPHA BOOKS

Published by the Penguin Group

Penguin Group (USA) Inc., 375 Hudson Street, New York, New York 10014, U.S.A.

Penguin Group (Canada), 10 Alcorn Avenue, Toronto, Ontario, Canada M4V 3B2 (a division of Pearson Penguin Canada Inc.)

Penguin Books Ltd, 80 Strand, London WC2R 0RL, England

Penguin Ireland, 25 St Stephen's Green, Dublin 2, Ireland (a division of Penguin Books Ltd)

Penguin Group (Australia), 250 Camberwell Road, Camberwell, Victoria 3124, Australia (a division of Pearson Australia Group Pty Ltd)

Penguin Books India Pvt Ltd, 11 Community Centre, Panchsheel Park, New Delhi—10 017, India

Penguin Group (NZ), cnr Airborne and Rosedale Roads, Albany, Auckland 1310, New Zealand (a division of Pearson New Zealand Ltd)

Penguin Books (South Africa) (Pty) Ltd, 24 Sturdee Avenue, Rosebank, Johannesburg 2196, South Africa

Penguin Books Ltd, Registered Offices: 80 Strand, London WC2R 0RL, England

International Standard Book Number: 0-02-864325-9
Library of Congress Catalog Card Number: 2001099415

12 11 10   13 12 11

Interpretation of the printing code: The rightmost number of the first series of numbers is the year of the book's printing; the rightmost number of the second series of numbers is the number of the book's printing. For example, a printing code of 02-1 shows that the first printing occurred in 2002.

Printed in the United States of America

Note: This publication contains the opinions and ideas of its authors. It is intended to provide helpful and informative material on the subject matter covered. It is sold with the understanding that the authors and publisher are not engaged in rendering professional services in the book. If the reader requires personal assistance or advice, a competent professional should be consulted.

The authors and publisher specifically disclaim any responsibility for any liability, loss, or risk, personal or otherwise, which is incurred as a consequence, directly or indirectly, of the use and application of any of the contents of this book.

Most Alpha books are available at special quantity discounts for bulk purchases for sales promotions, premiums, fundraising, or educational use. Special books, or book excerpts, can also be created to fit specific needs.

For details, write: Special Markets, Alpha Books, 375 Hudson Street, New York, NY 10014.

Publisher: *Marie Butler-Knight*
Product Manager: *Phil Kitchel*
Managing Editor: *Jennifer Chisholm*
Acquisitions Editor: *Gary Goldstein*
Development Editor: *Joan D. Paterson*
Production Editor: *Billy Fields*

Copy Editor: *Drew Patty*
Illustrator: *Chris Eliopoulos*
Cover/Book Designer: *Trina Wurst*
Indexer: *Angie Bess*
Layout/Proofreading: *Svetlana Dominguez, Susan Geiselman, Michelle Mitchell*

Contents at a Glance

Contents

Foreword

People have a keen interest in doing things *right*. When a friend of mine threw her first formal dinner party a couple of months ago, she consulted a book on etiquette to make sure that her place settings were just as they should be. Granted, not everybody shares her level of concern for the finer points of table manners, but the kind of problem my friend faced is common in everyday life. That's why we constantly look to others (usually the people around us) for advice on the right way to live, and why a few people, like Martha Stewart and Miss Manners, are able to make a living advising and instructing others on these points. *The Complete Idiot's Guide to Understanding Ethics* is an excellent vantage point from which to survey the array of moral choices in the course of life; it offers sage advice about how to develop a sense of ethical intuition.

Ethics, too, is about doing things right, although ethics is different from etiquette or fashion or grammar in at least one important respect. Flouting one of these other social codes can make you a target of criticism, but only of a limited kind. Others might call you uncouth, or badly dressed, or inarticulate, but hardly anybody will say that you're a *bad person* because of how you set the table. Ethical choices matter more than other choices do. The ordinary choices somebody makes about how to dress or how to talk reflect that person's personality; ethical choices reflect a person's character. That's why ethics—unlike the other systems of social rules we live by—isn't really optional. Ethical choices define who you are, whether you want them to or not. And that's also why ethics is a much harder subject than etiquette and why most people aren't content to resolve an ethical dilemma by looking up the answer in a book.

Making ethical choices is difficult enough, but spotting an ethical question can sometimes be a challenge, too. With many of the moral dilemmas you'll read about, in this book and elsewhere, it will be pretty obvious that a lot is at stake. We all know that ethicists disagree on life-or-death, "hot button" issues like abortion or the death penalty. And there are plenty of smaller, less controversial ethical decisions that each of us makes every day, often without noticing them. The decision whether to buy leather shoes raises a bunch of ethical issues—even though to many people it may not seem too different from the decision whether to wear brown shoes with a blue suit. The choice between "I'm sorry" and "I regret what happened" has an ethical dimension to it, even if on the surface it looks like the choice between "who" or "whom."

Although this book is called *The Complete Idiot's Guide to Understanding Ethics*, it's hard to imagine that anybody who reads it will really be a complete idiot on the topic. Getting by in the world requires you to have ethical *intuitions*, even if you never stop to think about them or try to spell them out. Understanding ethics is about making, and spotting, ethical choices, but it's also about understanding our intuitions—how they hang together (or don't), where they come from, and how they motivate us.

Gerardo Vildostegui

Gerardo Vildostegui is a Ph.D. student in ethics at the University of California, Berkeley. He has a law degree and an undergraduate degree in philosophy from Yale University and is a former Editor-in-Chief of *The Yale Law Journal*.

Introduction

We talk about ethics all the time in our day-to-day lives. We say that John Smith is not an ethical person or that Sally Smith has a good business ethic. But did you ever wonder what ties together all this talk about ethics? If you did, then this book is for you.

The Complete Idiot's Guide to Understanding Ethics provides the most accessible introduction possible to the most important philosophies about right and wrong, good and bad (you don't need a college degree to understand this book). Reading this guide, you'll also learn about the most important philosophers and their ideas about ethics—ideas that have deeply shaped us all, whether we know it or not. Most important of all, you'll learn how to think about ethical problems more clearly. This guide will help you lead a more ethical life and, hopefully, a more enriched and happier life.

This book is divided into five parts. Here's what they cover:

Part 1, "Doing Ethics Right and Doing the Right Ethics," explains why ethics is so important to well-being. It shows why thinking about our values and norms rationally and impartially is key to solving moral dilemmas that we face in everyday life, and it shows how science and religion can aid us in that endeavor.

Part 2, "What Does It All Mean? The Nature of Ethics," raises tough challenges to ethics. Chief among them is the fact that almost everything we do seems to be driven by self-interest. Another is the idea that selfishness (putting yourself first) is itself a duty, according to the prevailing wisdom of our competitive age. Finally, there's the problem that people disagree about what's right and wrong in ways that mirror deep religious and cultural differences. Together, these challenges to ethics encourage profound cynicism about ethics.

Part 3, "General Recipes for Guiding Ethical Decision-Making," discusses seven major strategies or approaches to solving ethics problems that arise in everyday life. These approaches include strategies that appeal to virtues and vices, divine commands, mutual benefits, absolute duties, consequences for all, caring for and about others, and various combinations of the above.

Part 4, "Applied Ethics," shows how the general moral recipes discussed in Part 3 can be applied to moral problems that occur in the following areas: medicine and healthcare, business, the treatment of animals, and the environment. Topics discussed include physician-assisted suicide, abortion, genetic technology, whistle-blowing, animal rights and animal experimentation, deep ecology, and protecting the environment for its own sake.

Part 5, "Beyond the Personal: The Ethics of Social Justice," shows why personal morality requires political engagement in making social, economic, and political institutions more fair than they are now. We address problems of social justice and welfare, economic and political justice, and race and gender justice. Topics discussed include: liberalism, capitalism, socialism, immigration, democracy, race, affirmative action, multiculturalism, equal pay for equal work, pornography, and sexual harassment.

Interspersed throughout each chapter of the book are helpful sidebars that contain pithy bits of useful information and advice.

Do the Right Thing!

This sidebar warns the reader to be on the lookout for dangerous pitfalls and other urgent responsibilities that need to be attended to.

Tried and True

Handy tips for moral thinking and acting are featured in this sidebar.

Ethically Speaking

This sidebar defines terms or clarifies important concepts.

Moral Musings

Interesting facts about ethics not covered in the main body of the text are set forth here.

Acknowledgments

In closing, we'd like to acknowledge Lauretta Parks for her willingness to read and provide useful criticism of earlier drafts of the guide. We'd also like to thank Jacky Sach for arranging our collaboration with Penguin Group (USA), Inc. Our development editor, Joan Paterson, gave us cheerful advice on improving the format of our chapters for which we are grateful. Last but not least, we'd like to thank our students for being such gracious guinea pigs in classroom laboratories!

Trademarks

Part 1

Doing Ethics Right and Doing the Right Ethics

So you think you're a wise guy, huh? Well, I did, too, until I read my first ethics book! I didn't have a clue about why "doing the right thing" was so important. And I never gave a second thought about the reasons justifying my actions. In fact, when somebody demanded an explanation from me, I'd spin around like a greased wheel, all blow and bluster. Hardly the picture of cool, dispassionate reflection.

Well, in this part we'll learn something about what it means to be a responsible moral adult. We'll learn about the proper way of thinking things through with others (impartiality and reasonableness being key). And we'll see how much science and religion can help us out here. Above all, we'll come to understand what "being true to yourself" really means.

Chapter 1

So, What's Your Philosophy of Life?

In This Chapter

- ◆ Ethics in everyday life
- ◆ Do's and don'ts of ethical conversation
- ◆ Ethical norms and why they matter
- ◆ The ethical ingredients of a good life

Socrates, one of the world's great moral philosophers, said that ethics concerns "no small matter, but how we ought to live." That is what this book is about. It's probably what you are interested in if you bought it: What is ethics, and what does it have to do with you?

This chapter will start with the basics, like what is ethics? And how can I tell ethical from nonethical issues?

We'll start with looking at ethics in your everyday life. Of course, how you behave—and should behave—is the most important part of your ethical life. But not far behind is how you talk and think about your ethical life. After all, when you're not sure what you ought to do, you typically do think it over with someone else whose opinion you trust—someone hopefully like us! So put on your thinking cap and let's get started.

Ethics in Everyday Life

To begin at the beginning, you need to think about ethics in your everyday life. While you might think that ethical issues only come in big packages, or arise only in situations involving matters of life and death, the truth is that your life is infused with issues and dilemmas of a moral nature.

Let's go through an average morning from the very beginning and see where ethical issues arise: First, you get out of bed, put your feet on the floor, and go to the bathroom to get ready for work. You take your shower, do your toiletries and go to the closet to pick out your wardrobe. Then it's breakfast (glug a quick cup of coffee) and time to run out the door to get to work. Hey, you might say, where are the ethical issues in all of this? Sounds pretty mundane and uncontroversial, doesn't it?

But rewind the tape for a minute: you're back in the bathroom getting ready to have your shower. You step into the warm stream of water and … WHOOPS! What kind of products are you using to wash with? Have they been tested on animals? Has the towel you dry yourself with been washed with detergents that pollute the environment? And do you splash on cologne or perfume after your shower? What about cosmetics? If the video tape of your morning ritual shows you putting on makeup, then is that makeup cruelty-free?

> ### Moral Musings
>
> Many ethical issues don't involve life-and-death matters. Should I tell a lie to avoid hurting someone's feelings? Should I be loyal to family and friends even when they do bad things? Should I sacrifice happiness for devotion to others?

> ### Do the Right Thing!
>
> You shouldn't feel guilty for the choices you are making on a daily basis; just be aware of how filled with ethical issues your life really is.

Things get worse as you go to the closet to pick out your clothes. Because consider: what label is in the collar of your shirt? Does the manufacturer run sweatshops, where workers piece together your shirt for slave wages? Same applies to your dress, jacket, or pants. Do you put a leather belt around your waist? And what about your shoes? (Oh, no, you might be saying, not the shoes, too!) Are you concerned about whether your belt or shoes are made of leather, whether you should wear wool or silk, or whether (heaven forbid!) it is ethical to own that glorious fox fur coat that your mother gave you as a gift a few years back?

Finally, you stumble to the kitchen with ethical dilemmas spinning in your head, and you pour yourself a cup of coffee. But wait! Where does your coffee come from? Were poor native Guatemalans exploited so that you could have that rich, nutty beverage? If you cook an egg, is it free-range, or is it the product of a factory farm chicken?

Stomach churning after consuming this breakfast of champions, you head out the door in a fog of uncertainties. Do you (1) get into your brand new SUV and turn your Bob Marley music up loud to clear your head? or (2) walk to the bus stop or subway platform to wait for public transportation. Which choice is the most ethically sound?

Our Daily Rituals

What is important to note here is that you probably don't consider these mundane activities to *be* ethically problematic: they are habitual, mechanical responses to the sounding of the alarm clock. And so they should be: if you did have to think through each and every ethical step in your morning rituals, you would probably stay in bed, curled up in a ball, with the shades pulled down.

Ethics is an everyday aspect of human life, and in order to live the ethical life, and avoid retreating to our safe little beds, we have certain commitments and beliefs on which we act. For example, if you are committed to animal and environmental rights, your morning rituals might be different from someone who is not: you will use certain products (environmentally friendly) and avoid others (animal-tested); wear certain materials (cotton) while shunning others (leather); and consume certain foods (faux bacon) while eschewing others (real bacon).

Your ethical commitment means that your environment is stocked with materials that you find ethically acceptable for use; and this means that you no longer have to think about the ethics of your morning routine! By the same token, you might not be particularly concerned about animal rights, or the leather belt you put on in the morning. In either case, the point is that the ethical issues are present, but you have worked out your beliefs and commitments, and are leading the best, most consistent ethical life that you can.

Tried and True

As a starting point, consider some of your common habits and practices. When starting to think about ethics, it helps to be self-aware: Where did your habit/practice come from? Do you still agree with your reasons for doing it? If not, it might be time to rethink that practice and make a change!

Back to Basics

But this doesn't answer the most basic question: what *is* ethics? You can't continue very far in thinking about it without first asking what it is. To get to the point, *ethics* involves asking questions about the good life; it requires examining right and wrong conduct, good and bad values.

Now that you've considered ethics in your everyday life, think about how we *use* ethics in everyday conversation. It isn't uncommon for people to ask your opinion about a certain topic. You know what they mean by asking: They want to know what you stand for, or what matters to you, or what your beliefs are. So the question "What do you think about …?" is really an attempt to categorize and understand you—"She's pro-life" or "He's against capital punishment."

Thinking about how we use ethics—and how it gets talked about and acted on—leads to the issue of ethical language. When starting to think about ethics, you should think about the importance of the words you use: it's important to be aware of how they affect your thinking about an ethical dilemma.

Ethically Speaking

Ethics is a sub-field of philosophy that aims at clarifying the nature of right and wrong, good and bad. Besides clarifying the meaning and justification of ethical ideas, ethics tells us how we ought to behave.

Why Terminology Matters

Consider ways that people talk about some pretty hot ethical issues:

1. Abortion as "killing the innocent fetus."
2. Abortion as removing an "insignificant scrap of tissue."
3. Prisoners "getting what they deserve" when they face the death penalty.
4. Talking about people with disabilities as "invalids."
5. Businesswomen "taking jobs away from men."

These are all examples of ways in which the speakers have emotionally loaded their language. Emotionally loading your speech involves using provocative language to get people on your side, or using language to turn people off of beliefs that oppose your own. A person who speaks of abortion as "killing the innocent fetus," like a person who talks about it as "removing an insignificant scrap of tissue," is using emotionally and ethically loaded language ("killing," "innocent," "insignificant," "scrap of tissue") to sway others to their way of thinking.

Do the Right Thing!

Try not to manipulate others into doing what you want them to do. Instead of playing on people's emotions, appeal to their reason. Don't say, "You're a disloyal American if you criticize the government." Say "Your criticism of the government is wrong for this reason," and then give the reason.

Part of the problem here is that emotionally loaded language also assumes that you already know what is right and wrong. For example, if you are talking about the death penalty and prisoners "getting what they deserve," then you have already decided that it is morally correct to put them to death. Likewise, "taking jobs away from men" assumes that they are men's jobs in the first place. The whole point of talking about capital punishment or affirmative action for women is to question what ought to be done; making the above assumptions is putting the cart before the horse.

Circular Reasoning

Really, this is a point about circular reasoning. The term *circular reasoning* means that you have already decided the correctness of your statement: for example, the statement "Prisoners are getting what they deserve when they face the death penalty." The problem here is that whether or not they are getting what they deserve is exactly the moral question up for grabs! This statement offers no argument as to *why* prisoners deserve the death penalty, and is a good example of circular reasoning.

Ethically Speaking

The term **circular reasoning** is any train of argument in which the conclusion you're arguing for has already been stated—implicitly or explicitly—in the supporting reasons given for that conclusion. In other words, circular reasoning has the following form: P is true because of P. If I argue that it's wrong to kill animals because they're persons, by which I mean any living thing that has a right to life, then I've argued in a circle. I've tried to convince you that it's wrong to kill animals by saying that they have a right to life, which is just another way of saying that it's wrong to kill them!

Labels and Loaded Language

You should also think about other uses of language and how they relate to ethics. Consider why people care about which labels you apply to them. For example, labeling disabled people as "invalids" or "vegetables" not only demeans them, but carries negative implications that can affect how we view and treat them. The old saying, "Sticks and stones may break my bones, but names can never hurt me" is not true: names *can* hurt, beyond causing hurt feelings!

Your thinking about ethical terminology can be directly related to the headlines you read or news reports you hear. Consider this billboard campaign about paternity tests, and what it ethically suggests:

IS IT YOURS? FIND OUT FOR SURE! CALL 1-800-PATRNTY

What impact does such a billboard have on our ethical thinking? Here are some things to keep in mind:

◆ It is trying to elicit some kind of behavior.

◆ It suggests that your wife/girlfriend is dishonest.

◆ It implies that your wife/girlfriend may have been having an affair.

◆ It suggests that you should only support children who are your genetic relations.

◆ It encourages suspicion.

Tried and True

To be as clear and honest as possible in your ethical speech, you should always use the words you mean and mean the words you use.

You can apply this same kind of questioning to just about anything that you read or hear. The point isn't to be a super sleuth, always on guard against loaded language: it is to make you think about what you read and hear.

It's Not Just a Fact, It's Your Life

Okay, so we talk and walk the ethical line all the time. But did you ever wonder why? Couldn't we just live without ethics? Maybe perfect little angels could, but none of us is perfect. And since we don't live our life on our own blissful clouds, removed from all earthly cares, we have to learn to get along with one another. But because I'm busy getting my earthly needs met, I don't really have time to think about you. So maybe my needs conflict with yours (after all, there's only so much water to drink from in the communal trough). Bingo! We have a conflict.

Now, we could just duke it out to see who gets the prize. But a life of playing "Who gets to be King of the Hill?" gets pretty tedious after a while. Life under these conditions would be, as the great philosopher Thomas Hobbes once said, "solitary, poor, nasty, brutish, and short." Very short indeed. What to do?

Moral Musings

Do you ever wonder what it would be like if we never grew up? A world full of juvenile adults would be like the baby ward of a hospital, with every baby crying to get fed first. Growing up is learning to put aside the immediate satisfaction of your own needs for the sake of satisfying others' needs.

We could begin by calling a truce and agreeing to some common rules so that we could live free from worries about what our neighbour might do to us. And of course we should have some way of enforcing the rules we agree on. But however we decide to solve that problem, the main point is that we need to regulate our interaction according to some common rules of the road, rules that enable you to predict what I'm likely to do in some typical situation, so you can go about efficiently pursuing your life without any surprises from me.

Ethicists call these rules *norms*. Norms are just regular ways of doing things that everybody agrees on. Some norms are not ethical per se. Take traffic regulations, for instance. Is driving on the right side of the road morally better than driving on the left side? In most of the world it is—otherwise there would be a lot of road kill out there—but not in Merry Old England.

However, the real point is that we could switch driving conventions from left-side to right-side (or vice versa) without committing a moral outrage. After all, who cares if the Brits decide to drive on the left side? For that matter, who cares if they drive at all?

It's an entirely different matter when it comes to norms against stealing, killing, and raping. These norms, which are enforced by heavy penalties in every country of the world, are not ones we could choose to live without. Here the rule is: No Norm, No Society. Period.

Ethically Speaking

Norms are regular ways of doing things that everybody agrees on. Unlike other conventions, **ethical norms** regulate all aspects of our lives in ways that are crucial for the existence of society. They are also a core part of who we are.

So *ethical norms* are different from run-of-the-mill conventional norms that keep things running well, like preventing cars from crashing. That's not to say that all ethical norms are so crucial to the existence of society that they must all be put into law. Telling the truth is a pretty darn important norm: You would have a pretty hard time living full time with people whose word you couldn't trust. Still, you might not want the "truth police" forcing you to be honest 100 percent of the time. At least not in all situations, and not if you want to have friends! We do make exceptions, however: Truthfulness in advertising must be enforced, since our very survival sometimes depends on it. More about this in Chapter 19, "Business Ethics."

Come to think of it, there are lots of ethical norms we wouldn't want put into law. A law against cheating on your lover is one of them. In a society like ours, where individual freedom is highly valued, the right to screw up your private life is a given (otherwise, how would all those divorce attorneys make a living?). Not so in Saudi Arabia, though. There, where conservative Muslim clerics teach otherwise, sexual infidelity can cost you your head. Ouch!

This raises an interesting question: Which ethical norms should be put into law? Ah, this is the fun of doing ethics! We're not always sure, so we get to spend lots of time and energy debating each other on whether such-and-such a norm ought to be legally enforced. Hey, here's a neat little game you can try out at your next party: just ask your guests which of the following ethical norms ought to be made into law and then stand back and watch the sparks fly!

 ♦ No hate speech allowed! Should there be laws against talking down people because of their race, sexual orientation, nationality, or religious background?

◆ No public drunkenness allowed! Should there be laws against drunken behavior in public spaces? (This is a really good one to ask at a party where you're serving alcohol.)

◆ No sex with animals allowed! Should there be laws against beastiality? (This should *really* get them going!)

◆ No topless women in public! Should there be laws regulating what women—or for that matter, men—wear in public? (Guys, be careful when you debate this with a feminist!)

◆ Insert the norm of your choice. Remember to pick one that most everyone thinks is a good ethical norm.

Had some fun? Okay, getting back to our main point, we need norms in order to interact with one another in predictable ways. Ethical norms, however, are especially important. For unlike mere conventions, they regulate all aspects of our lives in ways that are crucial to the very existence of society. But they are also crucial to our sense of who we are.

Norms, Social Cooperation, and Life's Purpose

So far, we've seen how ethical norms make possible social cooperation. Conventional norms make interaction possible, but they aren't crucial to social cooperation. In trusting others ethically, you not only feel confident in predicting how they'll behave, you also feel confident that they'll think of you as something more than just an object in their way. In other words, you assume they will regard you as a person worthy of consideration.

Why consideration? After all, when it comes to trust, isn't it enough that you can predict that I won't stab you when you turn your back? Well, not entirely. Suppose, for all you know, I haven't done so all these years because I have never had the opportunity. You may predict with almost 100 percent certainty that I won't stab you in the back now, but you still shouldn't trust me. In order for you to trust me fully, you would have to believe that I hadn't stabbed you in the back for the *right reasons*. In a nutshell, you would have to believe that I hadn't done so because I sincerely thought it was wrong, not because I worried about getting caught!

What I'm getting at is the idea of relating to others in the right attitude, what philosophers call the "moral attitude." The moral attitude is simply a kind of mental projection, a putting yourself in the shoes of the other. It's a way of mentally registering the fact that the needs of others matter as much to them as your needs matter to you. Having registered this fact, the moral person concludes that each person's needs deserve to be weighed equally, and that pursuing one's goals at the expense of others' is wrong.

Tried and True _____

Remember what mom or pop used to say to you (after you pulled Sally's hair): "Imagine how you'd feel if Sally pulled *your* hair?"—and you laughed because you had a crew cut. Imagining what it's like to trade places with someone else is still the most tried-and-true method for thinking about our moral duties toward others. Even if it doesn't lead to a clear answer to the question: How should I behave toward Sally (or what do I owe Sally)?—at least it gets us to think that we might have some duties to Sally.

Now, much has been written about how this attitude—more familiarly known as moral conscience—gets instilled in people. According to some psychologists, it happens during early childhood. Sigmund Freud claimed that good potty training was essential to developing it. Sociopaths seem to lack moral conscience (maybe they didn't get good potty training!). However it arises, one thing seems evident: Moral conscience consists of the ability to almost automatically empathize with others, to identify yourself with them, and to feel their pain as if it were your own.

In other words, what we have been calling ethical norms are not just rules that we choose to follow. They are also an important part of our identity—who we, in the deepest depths of our hearts, are. So when we do a "no-no," we not only experience the pain of others' wrath, we experience the pain of our own wrath. Hmmm … that might explain all the guilt and self-loathing we feel when we forget to call our mothers on their birthdays!

Shame, guilt, self-loathing—why dwell on the downside of ethical norms? In fact, there's an upside that I almost forgot to mention. It's this: Ethical norms also give our life meaning. Without them, our lives would not only be "nasty, brutish, and short"; they'd be without purpose and hope.

Let me explain. Take your typical "me-first" sort of person—you know, the guy or gal at the office who stops at nothing short of murder to get that coveted promotion. This person (let's call him Sal) goes through life paying lip-service to norms of decency whenever it suits him and shrugs them off whenever it doesn't. What does Sal have to show for himself at the end of his life? Money. Fame. Power (if he's lucky and plays his cards right). But no respect from others, just fear. No love from them. And nothing great that others will remember him by. Zilch.

Worst of all, Sal doesn't have an answer to that frequently asked question: What does your life mean? Lives are like great novels. They unfold a plot; they have consistency and direction. There are moments of crisis, defeat and triumph. And then there's the big climax that comes toward the end. When Sal looks back on his life, he'll see lots of the same empty striving after money, power, and fame repeated over and over again. Increases in wealth, fame, and power, however, do not make a richer, more complex, and more integrated life. Sal's been spinning his wheels, when he should have been pedalling toward the final goal: an ethically fulfilled life.

Now compare Sal to his ethical counterpart. Hal is devoted to something beyond himself—his family, friends, neighbors, needy strangers, and maybe future generations. Despite all the ups and downs, twists and turns, his life has some constants and, more important, some underlying values that have guided it. The ethical code he lives by includes a vision of goodness and justice. He can measure his life by the fight to realize that vision. He has something to hope for. In the end, he has lived the adventure of a full life. He can respect himself, and rest certain in the knowledge that others do likewise.

In sum, living a life according to ethical norms is not simply living a life of self-loathing and guilt. True, ethically conscientious people may experience guilt when they stray from these ethical norms. But living an ethical life is also the chief way to give our lives deeper meaning and purpose. And if that's what it takes to be truly happy, then as Socrates taught, happiness and moral virtue might just be inseparable. So Socrates *was* on to something when he said that "The unexamined life is not worth living."

Okay, so we need to live by ethical norms in order to lead happy lives. Does that mean that we have to try to be as normal by our society's standards as possible? Not exactly. Sure, we're trained from childhood to follow common norms of conduct. But most of these norms are pretty general and allow for some creative flexibility on our part. Also, we are *more* than our training, more than standardized products stamped from the same ethical mold. With age comes maturity and the freedom to make decisions according to our own moral dictates. We don't have to conform like sheep to every commonly accepted rule. If, after exercising moral reflection we feel that the rule is deeply wrong, we have a moral duty to not accept it. So there's no virtue in striving to be normal. To the contrary. No one ever came up with a new and better idea who wasn't cut from a slightly different mold.

The Least You Need to Know

- Ethical issues arise in your everyday life.
- Be mindful of the different ways an action might be described.
- Avoid the trap of circular reasoning.
- Adopt the moral attitude in your dealings with others.
- Try to live by some ethical ideals; they give life meaning.
- Don't make conformity your ethical ideal.

Chapter 2

The Inevitability of Ethical Dilemmas

In This Chapter

- ◆ Making sense of ethical dilemmas
- ◆ Conflicts over values
- ◆ Ways of clarifying values
- ◆ Taking responsibility for ethical choices

When I was a kid I used to *hate* eating brussels sprouts. If I didn't eat them, my mom would take away my dinner and, what's worse, my television privileges! Ah, what to do? I'd agonize over this choice for half an hour sometimes. I'd ask myself: What's worse—the indescribably yucky taste, and aftertaste, of those little green heads (not to mention all the subsequent gas) or the pain of not seeing my favorite TV shows?

You might say I was stuck between a rock and a hard place, what we sometimes refer to as a dilemma. A dilemma arises whenever a choice has to be made in which something good has to be given up or something bad has to be suffered no matter what is chosen. In confronting those little green time bombs, I was faced with both types of dilemmas. I had to pick between the lesser of two evils, eating brussels sprouts or watching no TV, and between the greater of two goods, watching TV or feeling that my taste buds and bowels hadn't been defiled.

This chapter is about another kind of dilemma. Specifically, it's about ethical dilemmas and other moral conflicts. Why ethical dilemmas? Well, it turns out that ethical dilemmas are what give life to ethics in the first place. We'll begin by talking about ethical dilemmas that we're all familiar with and then move on to discussing the ways we try to resolve them. This discussion will then lead us to consider conflicting beliefs about what's right and wrong, good and bad. These beliefs are about values, so we'll need to be clear about them. What are values? How are they different from personal preferences? Can (and should) we try to clarify them? If so, how? And how does all this relate to taking responsibility for your life as an ethical person?

Making Sense of Ethical Dilemmas

Okay, let's begin with a real *ethical dilemma*. Some years ago I worked with organizers in California who were struggling to improve the wages and working conditions of farm workers. The bad conditions on the farms were caused by a combination of two factors: the greed of farm owners and the huge supply of workers. Because of their number, many workers were desperate enough to hire themselves out for whatever wages the owners were willing to pay. After a while, I came to believe that the only way to force farm owners to raise wages was by restricting immigration to reduce excess workers. With a smaller labor pool, I thought, workers would be more valuable and wages would go up. So far so good. But then I discovered an ugly fact: many of the foreign farm workers—Central Americans mostly—were escaping from bad governments and terrible poverty that was partly caused by my own country's foreign policy!

I was now caught in a moral dilemma: If I was against allowing Central Americans entry to the United States, I would be condemning them to possible torture or even death in their own countries. But if I supported their immigration, I would be condemning those workers already living in the United States to awful wages and misery because of the over-supply of labor. The moral obligation to aid people at risk pushed me to support immigration, but the moral obligation to improve conditions for workers already in the United States pushed me to restrict it.

Ethically Speaking

An **ethical dilemma** forces us to choose in a way that involves breaking some ethical norm or contradicting some ethical value.

In case you were wondering, ethical dilemmas happen all the time. Every day, in fact. Here are some examples:

◆ Should I be honest and tell my best friend something that will hurt her feelings, or should I spare her feelings?

- Should I respect my teenager by allowing him to make an adult decision about something risky, or should I protect him by denying him this choice?
- Should I buy disposable plastic diapers that aren't biodegradable, or should I hire a cloth diaper service that uses up scarce water and electricity sources?
- Should I give birth to my potential child, despite the likelihood of its being born with serious, life-threatening, painful, and disabling defects, or should I abort it?
- Should I commit my mentally incompetent parent to a care home where she will get the best medical treatment, or should I follow her advance directive to get care at home, despite the hardship this imposes on her, me, and other family members?
- Should we spend our savings now on buying some needed home improvements, or should we spend it later on our kid's college education?
- Should I extend the life of my beloved pet, or should I put an end to its increasing suffering by having it put to sleep?

So, far from being unusual, ethical dilemmas are pretty common. In fact, I bet that you can think of some ethical dilemmas you're facing now (or have recently faced). An ethical dilemma forces us to choose in a way that involves breaking some ethical norm or contradicting some cherished moral value. How does this happen?

Some ethical dilemmas come about because we're torn between conflicting moral duties—for example, doing good for others and not interfering in their lives. Sometimes doing good for people requires that we *do* interfere with their lives! Normally, we have duties connected with the many different ethical norms we follow. Although these norms and duties do not always conflict with each other, they may conflict in certain situations.

To clarify, think back to the first dilemma: Do I tell my friend the unpleasant truth, her boyfriend is cheating on her, or do I refrain from telling her out of concern for her feelings? Let's suppose that I feel I must tell her the truth because I follow the principle: "Always tell the truth." Let's further suppose that I feel I shouldn't tell her the truth because I also follow the principle: "Never cause harm to anybody." Now these two principles do not always contradict each other. There are plenty of times when telling the truth will not result in harming people. In fact, sometimes the best way to not harm someone is by telling the truth. Think about your own case: By telling the dentist the truth ("I have a toothache on the left side") you avoid greater harm to yourself. No problem there!

So principles of telling the truth and not causing harm only conflict some of the time. In the

Tried and True _____

Ethical dilemmas are hardly the sorts of things that only happen once every blue moon. They happen all the time; every day, in fact. Watch for them: sometimes they come in smaller packages!

example stated, the truth I tell my friend just happens to be a painful one: "Your boyfriend is cheating on you."

Do all ethical dilemmas arise from conflicting norms or principles? Reconsider the final example on our list of ethical dilemmas: Do I extend the life of my beloved pet or put him to sleep to spare his pain? While it might look like two principles are at work here—extend life or end it—there is really only one principle with two crummy options. Both of the conflicting alternatives are driven by the same principle: Do good for (or, at least, do no harm to) any creature that can feel pain. The conflict, or dilemma, stems from having to choose between two actions that are really sad, unwanted choices.

But we're not done with our lesson just yet. There's another important thing: What might at first appear to be a dilemma may not be. The hitch is this: Ethical dilemmas leave us with no happy choices because sometimes there are none. Still, in many cases when we're asked to choose between the jagged horns of a dilemma, there's a softer option that's been left out of the picture.

Take my earlier dilemma about the farm workers and their wages. Are there really only two alternatives in this case—to support or oppose immigration? Well, no. Actually, there are a number of "softer" alternatives that could help both groups in this case. Consider:

- We could give the immigrant workers other kinds of jobs so there's less competition between farm workers.
- We could create better laws to support decent wages and benefits for farm workers.
- We could restrict immigration but change the United States' foreign policies so that we don't create the need for people to leave their countries.
- We could adopt any combination of these options.

> **Moral Musings**
>
> Not all ethical dilemmas involve choosing between two happy options. Sometimes an ethical dilemma involves having to choose between two actions, both of which are undesirable options.

> **Do the Right Thing!**
>
> Remember that what on first glance seems to be an ethical dilemma with no happy solution might not be. Always assume that there are more options than just two. Then, try to think of all the factors that bear on the issue at hand. Make a list! For example, in the case of immigration, ask yourself what causes people to immigrate (inform yourself of the causes); what causes low wages in a particular economic sector, and so.

Much of our ethical life is pretty straightforward. In most situations, our duty is clear and there's no dilemma. This raises an interesting question: could we imagine a better world in which ethical dilemmas no longer existed?

Maybe such a world could exist for angels who are never confronted with pain, death, or human frailties. Many ethical dilemmas are caused by scarcity of resources—when there just isn't enough goodies to go around. This is something angels never have to worry about! For humans, good things normally come with a price. We have to put up with a lot of painful things (like going to work Monday mornings) in order to survive. Again, perfect angels are never tempted to do wrong, and because they know perfectly well what's good for them and what's right for the world, they never fight about anything.

Then again, there's the flip side. If you're immortal, perfect, and all-knowing, your choices won't matter to you (after all, when you live forever nothing really matters). In fact, you won't need to worry about ethics, doing the right thing, or living the good life. Why go out of your way to help someone when there's no one around who needs help? So maybe the ancient Greek poet Homer got it right when he pictured the Olympian gods as terribly bored with their lives!

In sum, ethical life is the life of imperfect mortal beings. But being imperfect and mortal is what makes life so interesting! You've got only so much time to live, so your choices matter to you. Because your choices matter to you, you have to give them purpose and meaning. That involves making hard choices, and balancing conflicting duties, goals, and values. In that sense, life is one dilemma after another. Finally, because you're you and not Joe or Jill, you've got your own ideas about right and wrong, good and bad. So yes, moral conflict is unavoidable. As the wise ones say, "Get over it!"

In short, we can't imagine a human world without ethical dilemmas, or without moral conflicts between ourselves and others. This is the topic of our next section.

Tried and True

Ethical life is the life of imperfect mortal beings. Because your choices matter to you, you have to give them purpose and meaning. That involves making hard choices, and balancing conflicting duties, goals, and values.

Moral Conflicts

The ancient and wise Socrates got it right when he said that ethical conflict is just part of the human condition. He and his student Plato weren't particularly happy about it, which led them to dream about a more perfect and ideal world—a utopia in fact—where people would live in perfect harmony.

The ancient Greek city of Athens that Socrates and Plato called home (about 2,400 years ago) was a pretty swingin' place. It had lots of business people in addition to writers, artists, and—you guessed it—philosophers. Come to think of it, Athens was a lot like our society. Where people are free to develop their own ideas and share them with others, conflicts—including ethical conflicts—are bound to arise. Enter Socrates. He took note of the intensity of ethical disagreements and—voilà!—he invented what we today call ethics.

Moral Musings

Socrates was the first to discover that ethics is born of human conflict. One of my favorite examples of such a conflict comes from a dialogue Socrates supposedly had with a young man named Euthyphro. In the dialogue (recounted by Plato in the *Euthyphro*), Euthyphro is going to court to charge his father with having murdered a slave. While it might seem that Euthyphro is being a good citizen in doing this, he is also being disloyal to his father (who, it turns out, only accidentally contributed to the slave's death).

Let me explain. Socrates understood that ethical problems come from human conflict and disagreement. Usually, we don't notice our ethical norms at work: When we're not challenged, ethical problems just don't bubble up to the surface. It's when we're confronted by other folks who challenge our ethical decisions that we first begin to think about them. And thinking about our ethical decisions most often involves justifying and being clear about them to ourselves and others.

Tried and True

In thinking through ethical conflicts, remember that they typically have their source in the contradictory ethical demands placed upon us by our societies.

Socrates contributed something else to our understanding of ethics. He claimed that ethical conflicts are often caused by society itself. Society can hold us to certain duties that may conflict: for example, the duty for women to be full-time breadwinners and full-time moms. It is impossible for women to fulfill both duties, and as a result, conflict arises (both conflict within women—"What should I do?"—and conflict between people—"You belong at home with your children!").

Consider the following conversation. See if you can tell what ethical norm or principle is being questioned. How does the questioning expose ethical contradictions on a social level?

Jill: Affirmative action for blacks is only just, because without it blacks would still be discriminated against in hiring, promoting, and educational placement.

Jake: But affirmative action is unfair, because it discriminates against deserving whites just because of their race. And laws should be color-blind, right?

Jill: Who says whites are deserving? After all, for generations white families have reaped the economic and educational advantages from over three centuries of slavery and legal discrimination against blacks. You can't pretend that the current distribution of educational and economic opportunities is "color-blind."

Jake: But you can't penalize innocent people for the sins of their ancestors.

(Hint: If you're having a tough time figuring out what ethical norm Jill and Jake are disagreeing about and what social contradictions are being exposed, go to Chapter 26, "Affirmative Action and Multiculturalism.")

To recap, ethics is a kind of philosophical thinking that gets us clear about the role of norms in ethical dilemmas. These dilemmas first become noticeable when we meet folks who disagree with our ethical beliefs or actions. Such disagreements, in turn, usually have their basis in the contradictory demands placed on us by our societies. When someone tells a woman "You should be at home taking care of your kids!" this is an example of the contradictory demands: Go to work and be at home.

Preferences Versus Value Choices

To begin with, what precisely is a value? A *value* is something that has worth, at least for some people. It points out a good that we should go after either because it is valuable in itself (what ethicists call an "intrinsic" value) or because it is a way to reach some other value or good (what ethicists call an "instrumental" value).

That's a mouthful to chew on, so let's break it down into the following parts:

- A value is something that has worth …
- For some persons …
- And points out a good that we should go after …
- Either because it is valuable in itself …
- Or because it is a way to reach some other value or good.

First, a value is something that has worth. Values are the result of evaluations, or value judgments. Evaluations judge things, situations, and actions along a scale ranging from good to bad. When we say that so-and-so is good or bad, better or worse, we say this in relation to some other value that it is being compared with. Although evaluations don't always involve value judgments—think of "color values" arranged along a color spectrum or the "numerical values" inserted in mathematical equations—in ethics they always do.

Ethically Speaking

A **value** is a standard—typically shared by others in a given community—for judging the goodness or badness of some thing or some action. A person who has values is someone who has standards; weak values correspond to weak standards; strong values correspond to strong standards.

Moral Musings

Ethical values always imply standards of worth. They are the standards by which we measure the goodness of our lives.

Second, a value is held by some group of persons. This is crucial, because it shows how values are different from personal preferences. Personal preferences are just that—personal. We would never think to change somebody's mind about their personal likes and dislikes. Suppose I like tutti frutti ice cream and you like chocolate. It would be pointless and stupid for me to try to convince you that your preference for chocolate is wrong and my preference for tutti frutti is right.

Not so with values. Just compare these two lists:

List One

> I prefer blondes to brunettes.
>
> In a game between the Dodgers and the Yankees, I root for the Dodgers.
>
> I like pugs more than poodles.
>
> Green is my favorite color.

List Two

> Better to have loved and suffered than not to have loved at all.
>
> Money can't buy happiness.
>
> A mind is a terrible thing to waste.
>
> Better to be Socrates dissatisfied than a pig satisfied.

Tried and True

Did you ever hear the saying "One person's principle is another person's preference"? It's not always easy to figure out whether a judgment is about principles or preferences. My mom, for instance, sometimes argues with me about matters of etiquette—like holding the door open for somebody else—as if they were matters of moral principle; in this case, it's a matter of being considerate towards others. However, I tell her that this ritual is simply a matter of preference for me.

Notice that list one refers to just one person—me—and describes my likes and dislikes. But list two refers to no one in particular, because it applies to all or most persons. List two has value judgments that we make when trying to change people's behavior or lifestyle. The values they uphold—love, education, spiritual happiness, and the dignity of a thoughtful and sensitive life—are shared by many (if not most) people. And they are held so highly by us that, in supporting them, we're urging that all people accept them. (I ask you: who doesn't need a little love, education, and spiritual happiness?) Unlike personal preferences—like the saying goes, "There's no disputing taste!"—we argue over the meaning and truth of value judgments. Yes, we all agree that love and spiritual happiness are important ethical values, but what exactly do they mean, and how valuable are they in comparison to other goods? How do these values fit into the total mix of values?

Third, what follows is that values are different from facts. When I state a personal preference, I'm describing a fact about myself; I'm not saying that you or anyone else ought to have the same preference. But when stating a value, although it might seem that I'm just stating a fact (e.g., "love is good"), I'm really saying something more. Because to say that something is good is also to recommend it to others as something they ought to want, too.

Before taking up points four and five, note that not all value judgments are ethical judgments. Some value judgments are judgments about taste, not ethics. Check out the following list:

- beauty
- strength
- justice
- courage
- integrity (standing by one's principles)

- equality
- freedom
- happiness
- health
- respect for nature

The first two values, beauty and strength, are not ethical values, because they are not how we judge the *ethical* worth of a person. Ugly weaklings may be just as morally good as beautiful, brawny people. In fact, ugly weaklings stand a chance of being morally better people because they're not spending huge amounts of time on their looks or their physique—they're developing their moral traits! However, beauty and strength involve judgments of taste that appeal to shared standards in art criticism, athletic assessment, and so forth. The next five values, by contrast, are ethical. They are part and parcel of the necessary ingredients for living an ethical life and living in a just society. Imagine a moral life or a just society that didn't seek justice, freedom or equality—who'd want it?

It's not so clear whether or not happiness, health, and respect for nature are ethical values. For example, is happiness really necessary for living an ethical life? As we shall see, the ancient ethicists thought it was, but others did not. Health is also tricky. You need to meet minimal standards of health in order to do anything, let alone to act ethically. It's pretty hard to live the good life when you're busy coughing up a lung. And what about respect for nature? If this is an important value, is it because being respectful of nature makes our lives beautiful, or fulfills an ethical obligation of some sort?

Fourth, some values possess *intrinsic* worth. This means they are pursued for their own sake, whether anything good comes from them or not. For Socrates and the ancient Greek ethicists, happiness filled this bill. All other values and goods were only considered worthwhile if they brought about happiness. So the question "What is happiness good for?" made no sense to them. After all, why be happy at all, if not in order to be, well, happy!

Ethically Speaking

Some values and goods possess **intrinsic** worth. Happiness, for example, is an intrinsic good, and so too are self-respect, health, and moral virtue (as in the expression "Virtue is its own reward"). This means they are pursued for their own sake, regardless of their consequences for achieving anything else. Other values and goods only possess **instrumental** worth. Money is valued for what it can buy but not for itself. And money can't buy health, self-respect, or moral virtue. Intrinsic goods, of course, are also instrumental for obtaining other goods, but unlike money, they are first of all valued for their own sake.

Fifth, some values and goods are only *instrumentally* valuable. They are not valuable for their own sake but only because they let us achieve other values. Take courage, for instance. By itself, courage is neither good nor bad. When a really bad seed is courageous—well, look out! I'd hate to meet him. Still, it's hard to imagine living a truly ethical life without having the courage to make sacrifices or do the right thing; so courage is an instrumental ethical value.

One last point before moving on. As you've found out, ethical values come in degrees from less to more. They are yardsticks for measuring progress. For example, you can always become a more courageous person. But not all values fit this model: others are "all or nothing," which means that you either have them or you don't. An example of this is respect for the rights of other people ... it's all or nothing, baby! What would it mean to have "some" or "a little" respect for them? Aretha Franklin was wrong—"just a little respect" just ain't enough!

Tried and True

Although you should sometimes compromise with others on how best to act, never compromise your values. Compromising your values means lessening your concern for what's good and right. Concern for what's good and right is the very stuff of ethical life.

To recap: Values and personal preferences are two entirely different sorts of critters. Talk about ice cream, beer, or peanut butter is just talk about personal preferences. But talk about courage, justice, and equality is talk about values, which are judgments that go beyond personal tastes.

True Blue: Be True to Yourself

Socrates once said "The unexamined life is not worth living." His point is that the highest form of loyalty to others is loyalty to your own moral conscience. Socrates' goal was to raise the moral awareness of Athenian citizens about the contradictions and confusions of their ethical traditions. He walked around Athens, starting discussions about things like justice, freedom, and truth, trying to get people to think about what they mean. This got Socrates into trouble: he was eventually arrested for "causing trouble." But rather than being a "troublemaker," Socrates showed the highest form of patriotism. To paraphrase a popular TV Army recruitment ad, true patriotism means encouraging your country to "be all that it can be" (ethically speaking). That's what Socrates was all about.

Sadly, the price Socrates paid for his courageous patriotism was the death penalty. I mention this fact because he refused to cave on his moral beliefs. If Socrates had agreed to stop philosophizing with people on the streets of Athens, it might have saved his skin. But in his opinion, betraying his moral conscience would be equivalent to killing his very soul—a much worse fate than dying for something that really mattered.

Why did he feel this way? Recall what I said earlier about ethical norms: they are a part of your very identity, your sense of self. The same can be said of ethical values. Shared values link our personal lives up with our fellow human beings. They are the solid bedrock that anchors the otherwise shifting sands of personal preference. Values give purpose to our lives, and make possible a personal identity that stretches across a lifetime. They make up your moral character, and make you a unique individual. Think about this: People identify you as an individual through the values that you stand for.

So being ethical is being true to your deepest beliefs, which means being true to yourself. But is it enough to stick by your guns? Is there anything more to being true to yourself?

> ### Moral Musings
>
> The nineteenth century French poet Charles Baudelaire thought that basic values such as truth, moral goodness, and beauty sometimes clashed. Truth can sometimes be ugly; beauty can tempt us into vice; moral goodness can seem to demand sacrifice and austerity. In today's world, it often seems as if moral goodness is sacrificed for the sake of acquiring knowledge (science and technology) and sensuous pleasure (material consumption). Do you agree?

Critical Reason and the Moral Agent

Socrates thought so. After all, he warned us to continually re-examine our beliefs rather than just sticking by them in some unchanging way. Put simply, for Socrates, it is not enough for you to do the right thing. You also have to take time to think about *why* it is the right thing. In short, you have to examine the meaning of your behavior and your reasons for it.

In the next chapter, you'll see what Socrates meant by examining your life in this way. For now, consider this thought: To the extent that you don't examine your life, you don't "own" it. It's not yours, but someone else's. It means that you do something because that's what everyone else does, because you've always done it that way, or because Joe Schmoe the big expert tells you to. But doing something for these reasons is not taking responsibility for your own life.

You heard me right. Being morally responsible means you must think deeply about the meaning of your values and the norms you hold dear. If you don't do that, you're not being adult. Being adult means that you freely—voluntarily and with forethought—take control over the values that otherwise would stay hidden. So dig 'em up and examine 'em!

The Least You Need to Know

◆ Know when decisions involve ethical dilemmas and beware of false dilemmas.

◆ Be careful to distinguish values from preferences.

◆ Ethical conflict is the spice of life—don't avoid it.

◆ Take responsibility for your ethical life by examining your values.

Chapter 3

Convince Me That I'm Wrong

In This Chapter

- ◆ Why reasons matter
- ◆ The role of authority figures
- ◆ The importance of impartiality
- ◆ Being a skeptic

A recent Gallup poll shows the following statistics about Americans: 52 percent believe in astrology; 22 percent believe that aliens have visited the earth; 67 percent claim they had a psychic experience; and 33 percent believe there was once a lost continent called Atlantis.

These high numbers are surprising and, while not directly ethical issues, do relate to this chapter on reasons in ethics. The above statistics should make you ask: What reasons do people have for believing these things? Are there good reasons for such beliefs? That is exactly what we will talk about in this chapter. You will consider things like: Why do reasons matter in ethics? What do good and bad reasons look like? To think clearly about ethics, and to build toward your own consistent and well-reasoned set of ethical beliefs, you need to consider these questions and apply them to your currently held views.

Give Me One Good Reason

Let's start by examining that riddle we've all heard: Why did the chicken cross the road? To get to the other side. It's a silly riddle precisely because the chicken has *no* good reasons for doing so; but, then again, chickens probably don't have good reasons for doing much of anything! If we can learn anything from such a dumb riddle, it's that not all reasons were created equally, some are better than others. You don't want to be like that chicken, crossing the road to get to the other side, then once you get there having no idea why you're there, do you? Of course not! While we don't expect chickens to give reasoned accounts of why they do things, we do expect it of people. That's why reasons matter.

Reasons have everything to do with ethics: If you have no good reasons for an act or a belief, then you can't have thought it through very well and maybe you shouldn't be doing it or believing it at all. It's quite scary to think that there are people out there who are voting, protesting, financing causes, or running campaigns without any clear idea of why they are doing it. Each and every one of us should be clear about our reasons for our values, beliefs, and behaviors, and we should each be able to give a reasoned account of them to others.

But it's not true in every case that we need to give a reasoned account of our choices. For example, people may ask why you give money to a certain charity, and you should be able to provide some reasons. It may be none of their business, but you should at least in principle be able to give reasons for your choice. You might respond that it's a good charity, or the cause really matters to you, or you want to give something back to society. If someone asks why you like beer, though … well, that's a different story. You don't need a reasoned account in that case. Why not? Because, as Chapter 2 explained, there is a difference between preferences and values; and you don't have to give a long-winded, reasoned account of why you have a preference for beer, unless you want to bore everyone to death! So we have two lessons so far:

Tried and True

If someone asks you why you believe or act as you do, don't just say, "Because I believe (or act) that way." Give them a reason why. But before you give a reason why, ask yourself why—and keep on asking yourself why. Only then will your life become meaningful to you.

1. Not all reasons are created equally.

2. We don't need to have, or give, reasons for everything.

Basically, you don't need any reason at all for drinking beer. The fact that you like it is reason enough for drinking it. Nobody really cares. Not so for those charities, however. Giving reasons is important to *ethical* life, but isn't so important in the nonethical domain where questions about personal preferences come up. In short, no one really cares why you like beer, but people do care about what charities you support and why.

Giving reasons for our actions is important socially, too. It either connects us to others or divides us from them. So much of our social life depends on a shared understanding of what's true, right, and appropriate. When this understanding breaks down, the only way to restore it is by asking the reason why we disagree with one another.

For Example ...

To clarify things, let's use pornography as an example. We know that different groups oppose pornography, and sometimes for different reasons. Fundamentalist Christians, for example, are against pornography because it goes against traditional family values. Some feminist groups are also against it, but because they believe it treats women as objects and promotes violence against women. While both groups are anti-pornography, their *reasons* may be different, and those reasons divide them up into different social groups. So it's important to know not just what people believe but why they hold those beliefs!

The point in reading this book and in doing ethics isn't to get you to change your mind about things, or to think about ethics in one particular way. It's to get you to think about why you value certain things—like charity—and why you think it's right to practice them. To take a popular example, if you are opposed to abortion, examining your reasons for your opposition won't necessarily change your position (though it may!); it *will* make clear your reasons for holding that view, though. I teach ethics to university students every semester, and rarely do I change their minds about the ethical issues we study. Students who start class as pro-life usually finish that way, too. But students do clarify their thinking and think through their reasons for their ethical beliefs.

> ### Moral Musings
>
> The saying "birds of a feather flock together" helps to understand why reasons are socially important. People who have similar reasons for their beliefs and actions tend to gravitate toward one another. Our reasons for believing X and Y connect us with others who have the same reasons. They set us apart from people who dispute our reasons.

Changing Your Mind?

But—and this is a big but!—sometimes thinking through your beliefs and your reasons for having them will lead you to conclude that you were wrong, that you don't agree with the reasons, and that maybe you need to change your beliefs and actions. If, to use the abortion example again, you examined your reasons for believing that abortion is wrong and realized that you just don't agree with them anymore, then it would be pretty hard to continue picketing outside abortion clinics and lobbying the government for stronger laws against abortion. Or, if you did the same thing as a pro-choice advocate and discovered that the arguments against abortion were persuasive, you would be pretty ethically inconsistent if you continued to lobby for more liberal abortion laws.

Ethically Speaking

Dogmatism is the stubborn refusal to consider challenges to your own ethical point-of-view. It is also the out-of-hand rejection of competing ethical theories or explanations. You might know some dogmatic people … you probably call them "pig-headed"!

While changing your mind isn't the end goal of doing ethics, it is certainly a possibility that you have to leave yourself open to; otherwise, you are being dogmatic. *Dogmatism* is a real problem because it means that you have slapped on your blinders, and are refusing to consider challenges to your beliefs, values, and actions.

It's Your Decision

There's another thing to keep in mind about our reasons for doing things: we have to come to them by our own lights, and not be manipulated into accepting them by someone else. This is why children aren't held to the same moral and legal standards that adults are, because they often can't give their own, well-thought-out reasons for doing or believing something. To put it bluntly, parents hold the purse-strings; they have the authority and control. (As I said in Chapter 2, parents can make us eat brussels sprouts against our will!) There's an important distinction here between being convinced of someone's reasons through a sound argument and being manipulated into accepting their reasons. In the one case, you are resting on your convictions. In the other, you are being held hostage to that other person's belief.

To recap, we've settled the following issues so far:

1. Where ethics is concerned, you must have reasons for your beliefs.
2. Reasons can either socially bind people together or divide them.
3. By thinking about your ethical reasons for believing something, you need to be open to the possibility of revising them.
4. There is a difference between being convinced by someone's reasons and being manipulated into accepting them.

But now let's get back to a point that was raised earlier in this chapter: Not all reasons are created equally.

Because My Parents Said So

Consider the following list of reasons you might have for believing that abortion is morally wrong:

◆ Because your parents said so

◆ Because your pastor/rabbi/priest said so

 ◆ Because your best friend said so

 ◆ Because you read it in the paper

 ◆ Because the organization you belong to is against it

 ◆ Because God said so (see Chapter 4, "God Made Me Do It," for more on this!)

 ◆ Because you flipped a coin

 ◆ Because your doctor said so

Guess which of these reasons are good reasons for being anti-abortion? You got it ... none of them! Why? First, appeals to authority—"It must be right because my parents/minister/ doctor said so"—are a real problem. What makes your parents, minister, or doctor moral authorities on this subject? You can't appeal to their positions as parents, ministers, or doctors, since there's no reason to think those positions make them authorities on the ethics of abortion. (They might be authorities on other things—biblical interpretation, the flu, or whether to wear a coat in winter—but not on abortion in particular.)

Second, believing something because someone told you so is no reason at all for accepting it. As I said before, you need to *reflectively* accept or reject a belief. The classic example is when kids go to their parents to ask "Why should I do this?" and their parents say "Because I said so." Power mongers! Fascists! The kids who go off and do as they're told are acting on authority alone, without any good reasons being offered. Poor little tykes!

Third, you don't have to accept *all* the beliefs of an organization that you belong to: ethics isn't a package deal, or an all-or-nothing enterprise. So to say "I believe X because the Society for the Promotion of Pug Ownership believes it" is a cop out. (Okay, you got me—I love pugs!) The Pug Society may have some things right, and on reflection you may decide that you agree with them—that's why we join organizations, after all. But by joining a group, you don't automatically buy into all that they stand for, there should be room for disagreement. Some Pug Society members might believe that black pugs are better than fawn ones; I happen to disagree, and should be free to do so. Organizations that dictate a strict party line and that don't allow you to question, disagree, or reject ideas are called cults, and should be avoided.

But, you might ask, isn't it legitimate to take on the beliefs of people that you highly respect and care about? It only makes sense to follow in the footsteps of people that are your moral role models. So if you see Gandhi as an excellent person, then why not just adopt his beliefs and values without question?

> **Do the Right Thing!**
>
> Think for yourself! Letting others do the thinking for you is tantamount to letting yourself become a slave to their thoughts and desires. That's dangerous, because once we let others do our thinking for us, we lose our freedom to resist evil— just look at the Nazis! So remember: Don't be a thoughtless follower!

There is something to this idea. As Chapter 9, "Ancient Greek Virtue Ethics," will show, ancient philosophers thought that having moral role models was crucial to leading and learning to lead an ethically good life. We learn to be good, just as we learn to read and ride a bike, with the help of other people. And just like reading and riding a bike, it takes practice to get really good at it. But we can't cop out by just picking our moral role models and doing what they do ... we need to find out *why* they do what they do (their reasons) and then figure out if we agree with them. If so, after reflecting on it, then we may adopt their ethical viewpoint. If not, we should reject it, even if the person we most admire believes it.

> **Moral Musings**
>
> Ancient philosophers thought that having moral role models was crucial to leading and learning to lead an ethically good life. But we can't cop out by just picking our moral role models and doing what they do ... we need to find out *why* they do what they do and then figure out if we agree with them.

You might think this sounds like a lot of work and a lot of trouble, well, maybe it is. If we want to practice ethics in a serious-minded way, though, we can't be lazy about it and cut corners. Like I said in Chapter 1, "So, What's Your Philosophy of Life?" we don't have to be super sleuths, always on guard, but we do have to take a hard look at our reasons for our beliefs.

All Reasons Are Not Created Equal

Okay, so not all reasons are equally good. You've learned that appeals to authority and other blind acceptance of beliefs are ethically problematic. Basically, as some experts on ethics put it, your reasons for believing or doing something must be based on impartial reasons. Let's look at this concept, find out what it means, and see why ethicists argue for impartiality.

First, consider the following ethical dilemma. I learned it in my Introduction to Ethics class!

You are standing outside a burning building. The flames and smoke are getting denser, but there is still one way of entering the building. Trapped inside it are the following beings:

- ◆ Your beloved mother.
- ◆ A Nobel-prize–winning scientist that is close to discovering a cure for cancer.
- ◆ A highly intelligent ape that may unlock the secrets of the missing link.

You only have time to save one being, and each is equally distant from where you are standing. Given that you could save any one of them, which one would you choose, and why?

Well, what is your answer to this one? I don't know about you, but my first instinct was to run in and save dear old mom. After all, she changed my smelly diapers, fixed my boo-boos, got me through my terrible teens, and loaned me money when I needed it! But my professor corrected us on that one: "Wrong!" he said, "because your response is based on *partial reasons*, and ethical choices should be made impartially." Wrong to save mom? How is that possible?

Ethically Speaking

Partial reasons are reasons that show our biases for or against persons based on our relationships with them. A partial reason against Johnny becoming mayor of Doodleville might be that he forgot to send me a Valentine last February, which hurt my feelings.

Partial Reasons Matter

Here's how: because when we make any choice based on the fact of another person's relationship to us, we make it based on partial reasons—whether or not we like or love them, whether they have done anything for us, whether they are our lovers or enemies. It's like assuming that some people are more worthy just because we know and love them. But as I pointed out in Chapter 1, the moral attitude requires you to see that each persons' needs deserve to be weighed equally. Sure, your mom's needs and goals count just as much as the scientist's and the ape's—but the point is that they are not supposed to count *more* just because she's your mom. You are supposed to consider the other beings as your mom's moral equals, leaving aside your particular feelings for her and deciding objectively what do to.

This is a controversial claim. I still think that the morally right thing to do is save your mother—in fact, as I pointed out to my professor, anyone who could coldly stand outside that burning building and calculate who to save when his mother is inside is one cold fish! It *should* matter that your mom is your mom; that she changed your diapers and soothed your feverish brow. As you will see in Chapter 14, "Using the 'F' Word: Feminist Ethics," feminist ethics argues for the ethical importance of personal relationships … they do matter. But my professor's claim does make sense: we shouldn't just go around deciding how to behave toward others based on our particular relationships and feelings for them. Sometimes being impartial—having impartial reasons for doing something—is very important.

Impartiality Is Important

Consider a couple of quick examples, and you'll see why impartiality matters. The first example is nepotism … you know, when someone gives a job to one of his family members, whether or not the person is qualified and well-trained for the job. This really makes people mad (especially when they are stuck working with the incompetent person!), but why? It is because we expect people to be hired based on objective considerations like education, job training, talent, and so on. When Uncle Bunny hires his nephew, Peter, as Assistant Director at the firm it is a direct violation of such objectivity. The second example is a nurse on a busy ward. Suppose this nurse has some favorite patients and some he just can't stand. Would it be right for that nurse to run in response to the call bell every time dear old Mrs. Smith rang it, but ignore the bell because that old curmudgeon Mr. Jones was ringing it again? Certainly not! Nurses should care equally and impartially for their patients, and not "play favorites"; doing so is a violation of professional objectivity, and implies that some patients are better than others.

So where does this leave us? You could say that impartiality requires that we don't make subjective decisions in our dealings with other people. As a rule, it means that we'd better have a darned good reason for treating people differently. The racist, who violates impartiality by refusing to hire people of color, lacks good reasons for his hiring practices because he can give no good reasons for refusing them jobs. (The reasons are going to be bad ones that aren't based on any good evidence!) But when you give a box of chocolates to your dear friend, you aren't violating the rule of impartiality, since you probably do have good reasons for giving the chocolates to her rather than someone else. As for mom … well, I still think there are good reasons for rushing in to save her from the burning building. Assuming she hasn't recently cut you out of her will!

Tried and True

We shouldn't just go around deciding how to behave toward others based on our particular relationships and feelings for them. Sometimes being impartial—having impartial reasons for doing something—is very important.

Ethically Speaking

Skepticism refers to both a philosophical stance and an everyday attitude of doubting—but not necessarily denying—the truth of commonly held beliefs. For instance, a skeptic might doubt that we can ever know with absolute certainty whether there is a world outside our mental perceptions of it.

The Importance of Skepticism

You can't really understand the importance of skepticism if you don't first know what it is. Skepticism is an attitude rather than a belief about something. It is what you might call the willing suspension of belief, and requires us to apply reason to all ideas that we are presented with. You could probably best sum up the skeptic's position in two words: "prove it."

Modern skeptics appeal to science and scientific method as ways of determining what is true: Basically, if a claim is supported by reliable scientific studies, and respectable scientists support it, then it is far more believable than a claim that is supported by quacks who practice pseudo-science. Still, a good skeptic will admit that even scientific claims are provisional and subject to challenge. This is because science is open-ended, so it is always possible that something we now think is true could some day be discovered to be false. Remember, Chris Columbus set out to determine whether the world was really flat! The idea that the earth was flat was just one of the many beliefs that has been corrected over time.

But what about skepticism where ethics is concerned? We can't very well appeal to science and scientific experts to determine when or whether ethical claims are valid. It's not like a scientist can test for the morality of eating meat the way that she can test for the existence of sub-atomic particles, is it? So you might think skepticism is useless when it comes to ethics.

I don't think so. If you think of skepticism as an attitude, and you can apply attitudes to all kinds of areas, then skepticism works in ethics. A skeptical attitude toward ethical claims would require the "prove it" mentality that I just mentioned.

As a skeptic, you would require that people provide *good* reasons, and strong arguments, for the moral claims they make. You would suspend belief, at least until you could mull over the issue and decide if the reasons are any good.

An example might help here. Suppose you are talking to an acquaintance who says he thinks that homosexuality is wrong because it is unnatural. If this were a scientific claim you could run out, do some research, and then come up with your own conclusions. But this is a moral claim, not a scientific one: Homosexuality is "wrong" (bad, immoral) because it is unnatural. If you were to respond as a skeptic to this moral claim, what would you do?

 Do the Right Thing! _____

Don't accept any moral judgment at face value! Think of ethical questioning as a kind of legal proceeding, where nothing is accepted without supporting evidence. The evidence doesn't always have to be conclusive or provide certain knowledge. But it does have to provide enough supporting reasons to reach a verdict that can withstand reasonable doubt. Often, no single item of evidence will establish a sufficient reason to exonerate or convict, but all of the items taken together will. So take a tip from the legal profession: Don't accept the truth of any moral judgment unless it withstands the test of reasonable doubt!

Well, you would need to think critically about this claim, and resist the urge (if you had it!) to just accept it at face value. Getting back to reasons, your job would be to consider your acquaintance's claim and his reasons for making it. For example, you might try to determine if homosexual activity is present in the natural world—are animals doing it? If so, this leads you to reject the "unnatural" claim. So much for what is factually provable in ethics … the rest comes back to reasoned judgment! All that skepticism in ethics requires is that you treat ethical claims with some doubt, avoiding the dogmatism that I mentioned earlier, and being open to all people's views and their reasons for holding those views. The key to skepticism is to suspend your belief in others' ethical judgments until you've had the chance to work out your own judgments through rational, impartial deliberation.

The point of skepticism is to avoid the kinds of traps you have read about in this chapter. A skeptical attitude will help you in the following ways:

- ◆ You will demand a reasoned account of others' ethical claims.
- ◆ You will avoid appeals to authority.
- ◆ You will consider all points of view.
- ◆ You will not be swayed by partial considerations (friendship, for example).

One last thing. Skepticism has been given a bad rap, and outside philosophy has been largely misunderstood. Some people think it means the same thing as cynicism—the view that we can never come to an appropriate understanding of what is right and wrong. This isn't what skepticism is about … and if it were, I couldn't support it because there would be no point in doing ethics! If there will never be an appropriate understanding of what is right and wrong, then ethics is just a waste of time. No, skepticism isn't cynicism; and it isn't the refusal to accept beliefs that upset the status quo, either. Skeptics are always questioning, so they aren't hung up on the way things are, or holding on to the status quo.

Having this skeptical attitude is really important to doing ethics well; its importance is further emphasized in the next chapter, where we will consider the role that God and the Bible play in ethics.

The Least You Need to Know

- ◆ Make sure you have reasons supporting your beliefs and actions.
- ◆ Avoid appeals to authority in making your ethical judgments.
- ◆ Have moral role models, but still think for yourself.
- ◆ Don't be manipulated by others into their beliefs.
- ◆ Take a skeptical attitude to ethical claims.
- ◆ Be impartial, unless you have a good reason for treating people different.

Chapter 4

God Made Me Do It

In This Chapter

- ◆ Can a nonbeliever be ethical?
- ◆ For the true believer, is God's command the standard of right?
- ◆ Pluses and minuses of a Divine Command Theory of right
- ◆ How far can the Bible guide ethical decision-making?
- ◆ Why believers should take responsibility for their ethics

Recent polls show that about 9 out of every 10 Americans (90 percent) believe in God. Judging by the number of priests, rabbis, and ministers on ethics panels, you have to conclude that lots of folks take God seriously as a moral heavyweight. And why shouldn't they? If God exists, God must be all-powerful, all-knowing, and perfectly good, right? Not to mention: Eternal Creator of the Universe and Divine Legislator Over All That Exists. So God must be the one who determines right from wrong, good from bad. From here it's only a short step to the idea that something is automatically good because God says it is, and something else is automatically bad because God condemns it.

This view of ethics—called the Divine Command Theory—stems from a belief in God's existence. So it would seem that virtually all 90 percent of believing Americans should hold this theory. But should they?

In this chapter we're going to look at the pluses and minuses of the theory; you may be in for some real surprises! I'm going to try my darnedest to convince you that this theory is a bad one. But don't despair. I think I have a better ethical theory that goes along just fine with both God's existence as moral ruler and—as nonbelievers will be happy to hear—the importance of reason to ethical decision-making.

Can a Nonbeliever Be Ethical?

Okay, so not *all* Americans believe in God. Does that make them naughty little girls and boys who can't be trusted to do the right thing?

A quick look at some famous atheists and agnostics (people who aren't sure whether God exists) might provide an answer to this question. For starters, there is no evidence that Socrates believed in a moral law-giving type of God. Yet he seems to be one of the most morally upright people who has ever lived, acknowledged by most philosophers to be the very founder of ethics, and praised by almost all great ethical minds.

"All right," you say, "Socrates was a great guy. But not everyone is Socrates." Is it possible that most of us lesser beings can't be persuaded to do the right thing unless God's looking over our shoulders? If you don't think so, just listen to what Mary has to say to Sue in their little tête-a-tête:

> **Mary:** You know as well as I do that most people are just looking out for Numero Uno. They'd be killing each other if there weren't something beyond them directing their lives, you know, some universal commandments, like "Thou shalt not kill." And where do these commandments come from, if not from God?

> **Sue:** I agree that we need rules against killing each other. I mean, who wants chaos? But people don't have to believe in God in order to come up with plenty of good reasons to not snuff each other. Hey, I might only be looking out for Numero Uno, but I'm also not crazy about getting caught stealing or murdering. And neither is anyone else.

> **Mary:** That's just my point! Common sense says that you shouldn't break the law or do anything morally wrong because you might get caught and suffer the consequences. But what's preventing you from breaking the law if you think you can get away with it? Not common sense, that's for sure! So try the fear of God out for size. Heaven or Hell, you pick 'em.

> **Sue:** Hey, I never said I'd break the law if I could! You make it sound like my only reason for obeying the law is because I'm afraid of being caught breaking it. What if I told you that my real reason for being ethical is that I care about furthering the cause of humanity. Now that's a heck of a lot better reason for being moral than fearing the flames of ... uh ... hell!

Well, were you persuaded by Mary's reasoning? It's a little complex, so let's break it down into two parts. The first part of her argument goes something like this:

1. Acting ethically involves obeying some ethical norm. (Remember, we talked about ethical norms in Chapter 1, "So What's Your Philosophy of Life?")

2. Ethical norms are a set of general commands that are supposed to be true for everyone, at all times and all places.

3. Humans can't be the authors of such commands, because then the commands would not be true for everyone, at all times and places. (Humans aren't in the position to do this, since we're all mere mortals.)

4. Whoever makes these commands must be eternal and exist everywhere at all times.

5. So it follows from 1 through 4 that acting ethically involves obeying God's law.

All right, take a deep breath and let's take a closer look at this argument. It assumes that ethical norms are true for all times and places. Does this mean that such norms are inflexible, and never take into account changing circumstances? Not at all. Take the norm: "Thou shalt not kill." Virtually all societies have lived by this norm, even if they have understood it to mean different things (for example, as either allowing or ruling out capital punishment). Does this prove that the norm is not true for all times and places? No. It only shows that different circumstances—times and places—affect the way the norm is applied. The general meaning of "Thou shalt not kill" remains unchanged throughout its different applications. So the mere fact of ethical differences across space and time does not show that there are no universal and eternal rules commanded by God.

Got that straight? Now, here's the second argument:

1. Most people would act unethically if they could get away with it.

2. Fear of punishment and desire for reward are what keep people in check.

3. Earthly punishment and reward are not good enough incentives, because people know that they can sometimes act unethically without getting caught and that much ethical behavior goes unrewarded.

4. What keeps most people in check is punishment and reward in a life hereafter.

5. So most people would act unethically unless they believed in getting their just desserts from God.

Notice what this argument *doesn't* say. It doesn't say that *all* people would act unethically if they were atheists or agnostics, only that *most* would. It

> ### Moral Musings
>
> The ethical argument for belief in God doesn't say that all people would act unethically if they were atheists or agnostics, only that most would.

doesn't say that some goody two-shoes nonbeliever like Socrates is a threat to the general argument that (in the famous words of the great Russian novelist Fyodor Dostoyevsky) "if God did not exist, everything would be permitted."

So, does Mary's argument settle the case for believing in God? Well, not quite. After all, there's still Sue's counterargument lying on the back burner. Maybe we don't need to appeal to God in order to explain the near universal acceptance of norms like "Do not kill." And maybe we're not as cold-bloodedly calculating and self-interested as Mary says we are. If we're not so bad, then maybe fear of God's punishment and reward isn't necessary for ethical life after all. In fact, maybe the best reasons for being ethical have nothing whatsoever to do with God!

Because God Said So: Divine Command Theory

For now, let's give Mary the benefit of the doubt and say that ethical life requires belief in God. As we saw earlier, it's a short hop, skip, and jump from that idea to the idea that God's commanding or condemning something is what makes it right or wrong. This idea—the *Divine Command Theory*—seems to have certain advantages: it tells us in no uncertain terms what's right and wrong and provides a powerful incentive for good behavior, that is, fear of punishment and hope of reward in the afterlife.

Ethically Speaking

Divine Command Theory says that something is right or good just because God commands it and that something is wrong or bad just because God condemns it.

Examples of Divine moral commands come right out of the Bible.

The Ten Commandments (Deuteronomy 5:16–20) are familiar to almost everyone. Here's a few of them, just to remind you:

- Honor your father and your mother.
- You shall not murder.
- Neither shall you commit adultery.
- Neither shall you steal.
- Neither shall you bear false witness against your neighbor.

Christians and Muslims also appeal to the New Testament and Koran, respectively, in clarifying these commands. Jesus tells us, for example, that the second greatest commandment (besides loving God) is loving your neighbor as yourself (Matthew 22:36–40). In the Koran, Mohammed tells us to "Give to the near of kin their due, and also to the destitute and wayfarers" (The Night Journey).

Now that we all have some idea how the Divine Command Theory is supposed to work, let's see how useful it is. It goes without saying that atheists and agnostics will have a hard time accepting God as *the* moral authority. They might accept the commands in the Bible and Koran all right, but not because God commanded them; if nonbelievers accept them, it will be for other reasons. So right off the bat, we see one important limitation with appealing to God's will in settling moral disputes, it only works with true believers.

No surprise there. So we say that the Divine Command Theory is the perfect theory for believers only. No big deal, right? Wrong. It turns out that the Divine Command Theory is not a good ethical theory, even for believers.

I can just hear you muttering: "Okay smarty-pants, you better come up with one heck of a good explanation!" Well, I certainly intend to do just that. But it's going to require a lot of concentration and patience on your part. So take what I have to say nice and easy. Pull up a chair. Open a brewsky. And chill down a bit. Now, where was I? Oh yeah, the problems with the Divine Command Theory. Did I forget to mention that there are three problems? They are …

Tried and True

The Divine Command Theory is not a good ethical theory, even for believers. It leaves open the possibility that immoral acts might not be wrong, if God says they're not.

- It leaves open the possibility that immoral acts (like murder) might not be wrong, if God says they're not.
- It makes God's power over us the basis for what is right, when the whole point of morality is to avoid the "might makes right" mentality.
- It does not provide sufficient ethical guidance.

Each of these three objections is pretty darn subtle, so let's examine them slowly, one at a time.

Objection #1

The first objection is that the Divine Command Theory leaves open the possibility that immoral acts (like murder) might not be wrong. This point was argued by one of the greatest Christian philosophers who ever lived, Soren Kierkegaard. Kierkegaard didn't have to go very far to dig up damning evidence. The Old Testament story about Abraham and Isaac was all he needed.

Are All Immoral Acts Wrong?

In the story (Genesis 22:1–24), God tests Abraham's love by commanding him to sacrifice his son, Isaac. Although the story has a happy ending—an angel speaks just in the nick of time to stop the killing—there's no doubt that Abraham would have murdered his son had the angel not stopped him.

According to Divine Command Theory, if God hadn't sent the angel to stop the killing, Abraham's murdering his son would have been the ethically right thing to do because God said so. But that would contradict our belief that murder is always wrong. So Divine Command Theory leaves open the possibility that things *we* find unethical might not be so to God.

Now, back to Kierkegaard's take on the Abraham/Isaac story. (This is where things start to get heavy, as in *very intense*.) Kierkegaard says that absolute commitment to God (like Abraham's) is precisely what makes religious faith such a wonderfully passionate affair. Abraham did not know that God would intervene at the last moment: He was willing to risk the very thing he loved most for the sake of proving his love for God.

But that's not all he was willing to sacrifice—and here's where Kierkegaard's commentary becomes very interesting (even downright uncomfortable). You see, Abraham was willing to sacrifice ethics. If God is the supreme authority, then nothing—not even our ethical qualms—should stand in the way of honoring His will. I guess this explains why legion after legion of fanatical believers have learned to suspend their ethical convictions when serving God. When the end justifies the means, and the end is God, well … you get the picture. If you sincerely believed that God commanded you to kill innocent children, you'd do it, wouldn't you? Just as Moses and his soldiers slaughtered the men, women, and children of the kingdoms of Heshbon and Og on God's command (Deuteronomy 3:6). Just as Christian Crusaders in the Middle Ages killed innocent Muslims and Jews. Just as extreme followers of Osama Bin Laden's fundamentalist brand of Islam obliterated the lives of 5,000 innocent men, women, and children of all ethnicities and creeds in the unforgettable terrorist attacks of September 11, 2001.

Well, what's a decent law-abiding defender of the Divine Command Theory supposed to do? Hmmm. Try a fall-back position? Okay, let's try this one on for size. The defender could save the theory by saying that God, being perfect, would never command anything immoral. As for God's ordering Abraham to kill Isaac, well, God reversed himself. (No harm done, right? Just put the scare into ola' Abe for a while.)

> **CAUTION**
>
> ## Do the Right Thing!
>
> If God's will is absolute, then nothing—not even ethical norms—should stand in the way of honoring it. Not surprisingly, legions of fanatical believers have put their ethical beliefs in a state of suspended animation when it comes to serving that will.

Problem is, God *did* command Moses to kill innocent babes, and that's not right. Oh, maybe it was a one-time thing, an exception to God's general rule against killing innocent babes. Who knows, maybe God knew something about the children of Heshbon and Og that we don't (like, maybe they weren't children after all, or they were children but would soon grow up to be truly evil dudes). Maybe his order to kill them was a way of avoiding bigger trouble down the road.

Okay, I personally like this fall-back position, although it's not 100 percent perfect. For one thing, God's perfection would limit what God could do. If you're perfect, you just can't make mistakes, right? Your perfect nature won't let you. But isn't God supposed to be so all-powerful that he's not limited by anything, not even by His own nature? I mean, if God created Himself, He could alter His nature at the wink of an eye. So if God can do that, God can surely redefine the terms of His perfection to allow for the moral killing of innocent babes! So, at the risk of repeating myself, don't we have at least a teensy weensy problem trying to reconcile the two thoughts that (a) God couldn't command the killing of innocent babes because he's restrained from doing so by His perfect nature and (b) God, being all powerful, is not limited by His nature, and so could command it?

Well, maybe that fall-back position wasn't so hot after all. Let's forget about God's perfect nature limiting what He can desire. God is all-powerful and can will whatever he wants, including the killing of innocent babes. Now, does anyone else have a brilliant idea for saving the Divine Command Theory?

Who's in Charge?

You're in luck! Turns out that there's another fall-back position. A supporter of the Divine Command Theory can say that we've got it all backwards. If God's command is the only standard of right and wrong, then who are we to say if what He commands is ever immoral? When we question the morality of God's decision to command the slaughter of innocent babes, aren't we holding God to our standards of right and wrong, when it should be the other way around? In other words, as the saying goes, "Speak whereof ye know" or otherwise shut up!

So the proper response to God's commanding things that seem immoral is to just remind ourselves who's in charge here. Take a page from the Book of Job in the Old Testament (you remember ol' Job, don't you? He was God's most devoted servant who was reduced to sitting on a dung-heap because of a wager between God and the Devil). We need to remind ourselves that whenever God seems to command immoral things, or when he seems to allow evil things to happen that he could have prevented (such as horrible diseases that kill innocent babes), that just goes to show how utterly mistaken our perceptions of right and wrong are! After all, who are we to question God's ways? God's knowledge is infinite in comparison to our own measly gnat-brained understanding of the world. So we shouldn't be terribly surprised to discover that God's ways are mysterious to us. So, too, we shouldn't doubt for a moment that the suffering of innocent babes at God's command serves a higher good.

Sound like a good defense of the Divine Command Theory? Well, think again. This fall-back position undermines our belief that we can know with any certainty what God thinks is right or wrong, good or bad. If we just look around us, we see that God is allowing lots of bad things to happen right in front of our very noses! God must have a very good reason for allowing all these things to happen—after all, God has the knowledge and power to stop them. So maybe they aren't really bad after all! Maybe we should feel happy when awful diseases strike down innocent babes (it's God's will, after all, and His will is good).

Tried and True

One way to live with the idea that God might command something that goes against our ethical norms is to say that God's ways are mysterious to us. But if God's ways are that mysterious to us, we can't ever discover what He really commands.

And what about things that seem morally horrible to us? God allows them to happen, too. God even commands them sometimes. And these commands are supposed to give us insight into God's moral mind? So, to repeat my earlier plea, what is a decent, law-abiding defender of the Divine Command Theory supposed to do?

Put On Your Thinking Cap

I've been arguing away here and haven't been giving you a shot at doing a little philosophy. Okay, now's your chance. Imagine for a moment that you're a supporter of the Divine Command Theory and you want to save it from the objection that it allows acts that contradict moral reason. Remember, you've already rejected two possible counter-responses, the God-is-perfect and the God-is-mysterious responses. How would you go about defending it now? Think long and hard about this before reading the next paragraph.

Time's up! So, do you really want to see how we might save the theory? If so, read on at your own peril. Because the next set of arguments are real brain-teasers and are not intended for the lazy reader.

Let's go back in time for a moment to ancient Greece. During this time, Plato wrote a piece called the *Euthyphro*. The book's narrative consists of a conversation between Socrates and Euthyphro in which Socrates is questioning him about the meaning of loyalty and, most important for our purposes, respect for holiness. The question naturally arises: What makes something holy? The answer is that what is holy is whatever the Almighty likes. Notice the similarity with the Divine Command Theory: X is right (holy) because commanded (liked) by God. Unfortunately, as we have seen (and as Socrates himself points out), this answer allows that anything might be right (holy), so long as the Almighty commands (likes) it.

But Socrates suggests an intriguing way to avoid this consequence. His proposal is very subtle, so read very carefully! Ready? Suppose that something being morally right has nothing whatsoever to do with it being commanded by the Almighty. But of course, the Almighty commands what is right—I mean, He's perfect, right? But *why* does God like or command something? Obviously, because it's right.

Step back and take a very deep breath. We've just made the following change in the Divine Command Theory: Instead of saying that something is right or wrong because God commands it, we're saying that God commands it because it's right or wrong. Yeah, and so what? What's the big deal about that?

Just this: We're now saying that God commands things because they are in line with some standard of right and wrong. And why would God choose to match his will to this standard? If the standard were identical to his will, it would make no sense for Him to conform His will to it. It would be like God obeying Himself, or choosing to be Himself—not very meaningful, right? So the standard of right and wrong can't be identical to God's will. It has to exist independently of God's will, limiting that will rather than being defined by it.

And notice something else. Putting things this way places God in the same situation as us. We freely match our behavior to an independent standard of right and wrong—a standard we discover rather than just make up. So does God. And you know what's really neat? There's no reason why the standard of right and wrong can't be the same for us as it is for God. We've solved our problem with the Divine Command Theory allowing immoral acts. Whatever God commands conforms to the same standards of right and wrong that we live by, so He would never command something that violated our sense of right and wrong!

Defining Different Standards

So have we saved the Divine Command Theory? Well, if you've followed the discussion very carefully up to this point, you're probably smelling a fish. Remember our earlier problem when we tried to guarantee that God would conform to morality by saying that it was required by His own perfect nature? Yep. The same problem crops up

> **Moral Musings**
>
> We can reformulate the Divine Command Theory by saying that God commands something because it's right. But then what makes something right is not God's commanding it, but standards of right and wrong that exist independently of God's will. This contradicts the view that God's will is absolute and unlimited, and amounts to abandoning the Divine Command Theory.

here. In short, in the God-commands-X-because-it's-right version of the theory, God's will is no longer the absolute source of all meaning and being. There's a standard of right and wrong that exists independently of God's will. As such, that standard limits what God can do no less than if it were a part of his irresistible nature. But the idea that God's will can be limited in this way runs smack in the face of God's being all-powerful, the creator of Himself and all that exists. If God is truly all-powerful, is there any doubt that He created all that there is, and could change Himself and all of creation at a moment's notice?

Whew! Wasn't that a gnarly brain burner? Stand up and take another deep breath. Okay. Ready for the next assault on the Divine Command Theory?

Objection #2

Problem number two on our list can be formulated this way: If right and wrong is whatever God commands, then God's might makes moral right. But in ethics the whole point is to limit "might." Godzilla had power over Japanese people because he could squish them with one step—but this didn't mean that Godzilla was always right. There's a difference between scaring the pants off people—having power over them—and being right.

Let's clarify. If someone were to ask why God's will should be obeyed, there can be only one answer. God created us and God can destroy us. God's power, either as a creative force of love or as a destructive force of vengeance, is what obligates us to obey Him.

Consider two different images of God, both of which come from the Bible itself. The first image is that of a loving mother who commands obedience from her children because she is their source of life and knows what's best for them. The second is that of an angry father, who commands obedience from his children because he can hurt them if they disobey.

Is Dad's Way Right?

Neither image provides a good model for an ethical authority that we should obey. Let's start with the second image, that of the angry father. The angry father model works relatively well in explaining why very young children obey their parents. Because you can't explain to children why something is right or wrong, you must order them to do it, backed by appropriate rewards and penalties. The angry father model also works well with some adults, namely criminals, who need the punishing power of the state to keep them in line.

But the angry father model doesn't work well in explaining why we follow laws; and it doesn't explain why we follow the dictates of moral conscience. Take our obedience to laws. We obey laws, at least in part, because we think they're necessary for protecting us from the unrestrained actions of bullies. And speaking of bullies, why should it matter if the bully just happens to be God? If the argument against bullying is good for the goose then it's good for the gander! Just because someone is a big bully—stronger and smarter than we are—doesn't give them the right to push us around. No, siree! That applies to government, which is beholden to us, and exists in order to protect the powerless and weak against the powerful and strong. And it applies to God.

So we obey out of a sense of moral obligation not because we feel forced to by threats, but because we feel in our heart of hearts that something is right. Similar reasons show that obeying ethical norms for fear of divine retaliation is also wrong.

> **Do the Right Thing!**
>
> If the main reason you're obeying God's commands is out of fear of punishment or desire for reward, then you're not behaving ethically. Might does not make right, and our reasons for doing right can't be reduced to the child's desires for heavenly delights rather than hellish torments.

Is Mom's Way Righter?

Good-bye Bad Daddy, hello Sweet Mama! Should we obey a loving, nurturing God? Answering in the affirmative assumes that we are God's children, and that we owe obedience to Her because She knows what's in our best interests better than we do. The problem with this model of divine moral authority is that truly loving mothers are supposed to raise their children so that they can grow up to be responsible adults capable of making their own moral decisions! As we saw in Chapters 2, "The Inevitability of Ethical Dilemmas," and 3, "Convince Me That I'm Wrong," the key to leading an adult ethical life is not just doing the right thing because someone else tells you to do it.

Well, I hope all this philosophical hair-splitting hasn't totally fried your brain. Because we have one more objection to the Divine Command Theory to look at.

Objection #3

The third and final objection is that it doesn't provide the kind of certainty about right and wrong that it promises. For starters, there are lots of religions out there claiming to speak for God. How do you know which one is the true faith? By listening to voice of God ringing inside your head? Good! Just make sure it's not the Devil deceiving you into thinking that it's God.

Does the Bible Tell Us So?

Let's suppose you're a Christian (and if you're not, just pretend for a moment). Is there a list of clear Do's and Don'ts in the Bible that can answer your deepest ethical concerns about abortion, homosexuality, capital punishment, and social justice?

The main problem we face is determining how much of the Bible is really God's word. The different versions of the Bible that currently circulate today are the product of almost 3000 years of transcribing oral stories into written languages of antiquity (Aramaic, Hebrew, Greek, Latin, etc.), translating accounts originally written in one or more of these languages into accounts written in modern languages, and editing out and adding portions of different written accounts. Whatever language Moses spoke, we know with 100 percent certainty that it wasn't late twentieth-century English!

Most importantly, we don't have any of the original sources that our current translations of the Bible are taken from. We can't, for example, compare a modern translation of the Ten Commandments with the version written on the original stone tablets given to Moses by God on Mount Sinai!

Unless we have complete faith that each and every step of the compilation process—transcribing, translating, and editing—was guided by the hand of God, there's no reason to assume that what the Bible asserts as God's word really *is* God's word. Even if we assume that no human arbitrariness played any role in this process, the mere act of translation alone raises serious doubts about whether the various versions of the Bible circulating today are exact replicas of the originals, true to their every word.

Let me explain. *Translation* is not like copying something mechanically. It involves a certain amount of creative interpretation. Take word order. In Greek and Latin, nouns that function as the subject, object, and indirect object can appear anywhere in a sentence. We know which nouns are what by their case endings. In English, by contrast, word order serves this function. The translation of an English Bible into Mandarin Chinese is even more difficult, since Chinese is nonalphabetic. Leaving aside differences in grammatical structure, things said one way in one language often have to be said differently in another language in order to preserve any of their original meaning. This is especially the case with figurative speech.

For example, if I tell a bunch of Americans that John is an apple-pie sort of guy, the meaning is probably clear enough (John is an ordinary kind of guy). But if I said that to a bunch of Australian Aborigines, they wouldn't understand me. I'd have to say instead (in their

> **Moral Musings**
>
> The oldest remnants of the Old Testament currently known to us (from the Book of Isaiah)—the so-called Dead Sea Scrolls—date back to around the time of Jesus; and the oldest complete Latin version of the Bible (the Vulgate used by the Catholic Church) dates back to the eleventh century.

language of course) something different in order to convey the same meaning—like "John is an emu-egg-omelette sort of guy!" In general, then, translators do not translate literally but creatively, so as to bridge the sometimes huge gap between languages and cultural frames of understanding. Something always gets altered or lost in the best of translations!

Ethically Speaking

Translation involves transferring a thought expressed in one language into another language. However, languages have different ways of saying the same thing, partly because of differences in their grammatical structure. For instance, hieroglyphic languages convey complete ideas through images, whereas alphabetic languages convey them through combinations of letters arranged to form words, which in turn are arranged to form sentences. No matter how much meaning is preserved, something always gets lost (and added on) in the translation!

Clarity

Let's assume for the sake of argument that all of the above concerns about your Bible's accuracy are shelved. Does your Bible provide clear guidance in charting today's rough moral waters?

Think again about the moral conflicts raised by abortion, homosexuality, capital punishment, and social justice. The Bible does not talk about abortion at all, and it only addresses homosexuality, capital punishment, and social justice in the context of dealing with specific problems and issues. Furthermore, although the most well-known ethical commands in the Bible are highly relevant to our ethical concerns, such as the commands to not murder and to love our neighbor, they are too general and broad in scope in nature to provide much guidance.

Of course, that's part of their charm. As we saw at the beginning of this chapter, what makes them true for all times and places is that they can be used by virtually everyone! Both advocates and opponents of capital punishment can cite the commandment against murdering in support of their positions. The same applies to abortion. By regarding the fetus as something less than a person, or by treating it as a person whose existence is endangering the life of a pregnant woman, the defender of abortion rights can regard abortion as killing in self-defense rather than as murder, and so can also accept the commandment.

Citing scripture to narrow the range of ethical options can be tricky. Take abortion. In the first chapter of Jeremiah, God tells the prophet Jeremiah that "Before I formed you in the womb I knew you, and before you were born I consecrated you: I appointed you a prophet to the nations." An opponent of abortion might cite this passage as evidence in support of the idea that God regards all unborn fetuses and embryos as sacred.

However, that's not what God is literally saying here. Indeed, a closer reading of the whole passage shows that it's Jeremiah who is relating what God said to *him*, in order to convince possible skeptics of his (Jeremiah's) moral authority to lead them, not in order to convince them of the sanctity of unborn life. Again, the abortion foe might cite the 21st chapter of Exodus, which details the ancient laws of Israel. One law punishes anyone who causes a pregnant woman to miscarry. Problem is, the punishment prescribed for this infraction is a fine, payable to the husband, which suggests that killing a fetus was not regarded as an act of murder under this law.

Tried and True

Using the Bible for ethical guidance can be tricky because it doesn't address today's pressing ethical conflicts in any straightforward way. Even when Biblical commandments are relevant to contemporary moral issues, their sheer generality frequently enables them to be cited by both sides in a dispute.

Don't get me wrong here—I'm not saying that abortion is okay. In fact, a reading of different passages of the Bible might just tip the balance in favor of an anti-abortion view. What I am saying, however, is that the Bible doesn't say clearly and in no uncertain terms that abortion is right or wrong.

Consistency

As if vagueness of meaning weren't enough of a problem, the Bible's ethical pronouncements might not even be entirely consistent with one another. For instance, Jesus insists that rigidly obeying all the old Jewish Laws is unnecessary and contrary to God's love. He refers to a higher commandment of God, of loving your neighbor and turning the other cheek (cf. Matthew 19:21–24). The old law of Moses commanded that adulterers be stoned to death, but Jesus offers forgiveness instead (John 8:1–11). The old law certainly supports capital punishment. But does the new law? And does Jesus' saying "Render unto Caesar what is Caesar's" allow governments the ethical right to establish whatever laws and penalties they feel are necessary?

As for social justice, Jesus says "How hardly shall they that have riches enter the kingdom of God! For it is easier for a camel to go through a needle's eye, than for a rich man to enter into the kingdom of God" (Luke 18:24–25). Combined with his command for his disciples to throw away their earthly possessions, do claims like this support the view that large inequalities in wealth are immoral? If so, how would they be squared with the fact that, in the Old Testament, God rewards some of his most faithful believers with riches aplenty? Hey, even poor ol' Job (you remember him) was eventually rewarded for being God's guinea pig with more wealth and children than God took from him!

To recap: Even if we were convinced that the current translation of the Bible contained the original, eternal, and unchanged commandments of God, anyone using them would still have to interpret them. To put it a bit more controversially, whatever guidance we might draw from the Bible would be guidance heavily larded with our own sense of right and wrong. Is there a bit of irony in that or what?

Do the Right Thing!

People who claim their interpretation of the Bible is the only right one commit the sin of pride. It really makes you wonder about the audacity of all those televangelists—and the gullibility of those who blindly follow them. Anyone who claims to have a pipeline to God's ear is as likely to be inspired by the devil, or some other evil demon (maybe their own), as by the Good Creator.

There's an important moral to be learned here. If someone tells you that God or the Bible clearly commands (or condemns) something, take it with a grain of salt. Most people decide on their own what they think is right or wrong and then go looking in the Bible for whatever scrap of Scripture seems to support their views. They might feel that their reading of the Bible can't be wrong because they're true believers whom God wouldn't possibly lead astray. But when you think about it, proclaiming your own perfect knowledge as God's chosen mouthpiece is really conceited. To put yourself at the same level with God amounts to committing the worst possible sin of pride—playing God!

Difference Between Faith and Reason

Well, it looks like we're stuck with the heavy responsibility of figuring out where our moral duty lies. We can appeal to holy books, holy prophets, and holy messiahs all we want to in gaining insight into our duty. That's fine and dandy. But when push comes to shove, we're the one's who are left holding the bag. It is we who must do the heavy work of divining the divine, so to speak, of drawing clear moral guidance from the empty well of Biblical scripture.

Does this mean that God plays no ethical role in guiding the believer's life? If Kierkegaard is right, the answer would seem to be yes. According to him, ethics is a branch of reason, or common sense. And reason, he reminds us, is really opposed to faith.

How so? To have faith in God is to take a risky leap. The risk is what makes it all worthwhile. Without it, you can't explain the intense passion that fervent believers bring to their faith. Indeed, if passion is your cup of tea, it follows that the riskier the faith, the more intense the passion. Indeed, in Kierkegaard's estimation, Christianity is the highest and most passion-filled religion because it requires a greater leap of faith than all other religions. It assumes a willingness to suspend the very rules of logic in affirming that a mortal human being (Jesus of Nazareth) is the Son of God, identical to Him in Spirit. Now, you can't beat that—a true contradiction in terms—for being a risky proposition!

If, on the other hand, belief in God were as safe and secure as any other reasonable belief—as certain, say, as the ground you walk on—then it wouldn't inspire much passion. So Kierkegaard's recommendation: let science and reason deal with the tried and true facts of daily life; let faith and passion deal with the sublime mysteries of creation.

The only problem with this view of the relationship between reason and faith is that it seems to make religious (or faith) commitments essentially irrational. And making them irrational opens the door to religious fanaticism, with all its suspension of reasonable ethical limitations. So is there a less risky way of thinking of the relationship between reason and faith?

Some important Christian philosophers have certainly thought so. Philosophers like St. Augustine and St. Thomas Aquinas believed that reason alone—without the aid of faith—was an adequate guide to knowing right and wrong. According to them, even atheists can know the difference between right and wrong, so long as they use reason. This was their way of sneaking God into ethics through the back door: because God creates reason! They believed that human reason was just an expression of divine will. More on this in Chapter 10, "Middle Age Virtues."

> **Moral Musings**
>
> The difference between faith and knowledge is the difference between having an intense feeling of love, yearning, and hope for something beyond anything we can really imagine, and having a correct and proven belief about some fact. Facts are safer—passion is often indistinguishable from delusion (and some crazy people sincerely believe that the voice they hear is God speaking to them). And yet it is faith, not fact, that moves mountains.

When you think about it, this is a nifty way of getting around the problems associated with the Divine Command Theory. At the outset of this chapter, it seemed that if God were the source of ethical right and wrong, then we would have to conform our behavior to whatever God commands. But now we see that there's another option. We can conform our behavior to God's will—as responsibly determined by our own reasoning. In other words, we can just let the divine light of reason be our guide!

The Least You Need to Know

- ◆ Even nonbelievers can be ethically upright.
- ◆ Conforming your behavior to God's commands is not the best God-based approach to ethical guidance.
- ◆ Holy books require responsible interpretation in order to function as ethical guides.
- ◆ Ethical reason and faith need not conflict with one another.

Let Science Be Your Guide

In This Chapter

- ◆ When science replaces religion as moral guide
- ◆ Scientists as moral gurus, good or bad?
- ◆ When science replaces morality (period)
- ◆ Science and ethics, different strokes for the same folks
- ◆ Of moral engineers and other monsters

Extra! Extra! Read all about it! Scientist discovers gene that causes criminal behavior! Sound far-fetched? Well, I've got news for you. As you read this, scientists are isolating genes that they think cause criminal behavior. In 20 years, they say, we'll be able to eliminate the genes responsible for lots of bad characters. Other scientists have jumped on the genetic engineering band-wagon as well: this one claims to have discovered the gene that causes homo-sexuality; that one claims to have discovered the gene that causes selfishness. And so it goes.

There was once a time when religion ruled the roost. But no longer. Nature has long replaced God as the top of the moral pyramid. But how and why did this happen? That's what we're going to find out in this chapter. Along the way we're going to ask—and hopefully answer—some pressing questions: Can moral problems be reduced to scientific problems? Is moral reasoning identical to logical and scientific reasoning? And, does the scientific picture of the world collide with the moral one?

Pretty heady questions. And my take? I hope to convince you that, despite all the bad stuff you may have heard about science and genetic engineering, ethics needs science as much as science needs ethics. That doesn't mean, however, that science should be our guide in all things. After all, science isn't everything, and can't provide all of life's answers.

If Not God, Then Nature

So how did we get to the point where we are today, with scientist Smith telling us that in the future dear old Aunt Sally's hairy chin will no longer be a problem for future generations of women in your family? I mean, was science always this big a deal?

Well, no. Roll back the clock 400 years and gaze into your crystal ball. What do you see? (For the sake of simplicity, keep your focus on Europe.) Lots of people being hassled because of their religious views? Bingo! Lots of people being burned at the stake for being suspected of witchcraft? Right again! Lots of people living in misery because the Church pooh-poohed progress and put to death scientists like Galileo? You bet.

Do the Right Thing! _____

Many, if not most, ethical disagreements are disagreements about facts. For instance, people who disagree about the morality of capital punishment often have differing ideas about how the criminal justice system operates. When it became known that many prisoners on death row in Illinois were wrongly convicted because of bad legal representation, prosecutorial misconduct (often verging on criminal behavior), and so, many people who were supporters of capital punishment in principle came to accept an indefinite moratorium on executions. The lesson here is obvious: Informing yourself about how the world really is—which is what any good scientist tries to do—is also indispensable for making sound moral judgments. So inform yourself!

Why this history of suppression? Well, recall what I said in Chapter 4, "God Made Me Do It," about religious fanatics who are all too willing to chuck out ethical common sense in favor of obeying what they think is God's absolute command. If you think that your eternal life depends on obeying God's command, and you think, like the witch hunters, that God commands you to "burn the heathen," then you'll do it, right?

In order to nip this sort of fanaticism in the bud, we need a couple of things. First, we need a strong dose of common sense. Witch hunters and other fanatics have to get off their high horses and make a few inquiries of the sort we made in Chapter 4. Where in the Bible does it say that you absolutely have to believe that the earth is flat and that it's the center of the universe? And how does the witch hunter know beyond a reasonable doubt that his human hotdog—the poor soul burning at the stake—is a witch?

Second, once this much doubt about human knowledge has crept into our brains, we become a little more hesitant to risk eternal fire and brimstone by accidentally killing innocent people. In other words, we realize that fanatical devotion to God's command isn't going to get us through the pearly gates unless we're pretty sure that we've got all the facts right. So a life of risky fanaticism begins to look less attractive in comparison to a more peaceful life of tolerance and—need I say it?—material comfort. The kind of comfort that science and technology provide.

Tried and True

To nip religious fanaticism in the bud you need two things: a strong dose of common sense and a higher estimation of the mundane pleasures of earthly life. The terrorists who attacked the World Trade Center towers and the Pentagon on September 11, 2001, were religious fanatics. Inspired by an extreme and probably false interpretation of the Koran, their brand of Islamic fundamentalism immunized them against any fear of death and made it easier for them to discount the immense suffering they were inflicting on thousands of people. In fact, their contempt for their victims may have partly mirrored their supreme resentment against and demonization of a culture they perceived to be too materialistic and decadent.

Ah yes, material comfort. You know—food, clothing, shelter, a new VCR, a DVD player, and ... oops, getting carried away there. Anyway, the point is this: Religion isn't going to get you material comfort. You need industry, technology, and, last but not least, science. Yes, we *all* need a little science to avoid lives that are miserable—imagine life without medicine, technology, and (awk!) television!

And so it was that science came to gradually nudge out religion. Oh, it didn't happen overnight. And science never completely snuffed out those religious yearnings. In fact, many of us still prefer religion to science. And maybe that's as it should be. After all, science was not a gracious winner.

Roll that tape forward, please! Here we are, surrounded by all this wonderful tolerance and material comfort! All thanks to the almighty power of modern science, our new God. Now, about that chin of Aunt Sally's ....

Moral Musings

Science declared the old religious picture of the universe dead. No more nice nature with little birdies trying to fulfill God's appointed purposes. Just mean and nasty nature, raw matter colliding blindly with raw matter, little birdies being eaten by bigger birdies!

The Good Scientist as Moral Guru

Scientists playing God, you say? You betcha. We're talking genetic engineering, here. The potential elimination of genetic diseases and disabilities. The creation of a master race of strong, beautiful, and morally upright humans. The creation of new and improved foods and energy sources. The elimination of Aunt Sally's chin hair. In short, we have turned the scientist into a divine creator and benefactor of humanity.

Did someone mention something about mad scientists out of control? Dr. Frankenstein and his monster? Our moral qualms abound. How can we be sure that scientists won't use their power through technical expertise to take total control over our lives? Even if we manage to hold on to our freedom, how can we be sure that we won't abuse the power that science has bestowed on us? Who knows, we might start cloning a race of look-alike organ donors and slaves. We might create a few horrific monsters along the way, and some really gnarly viruses. And those of us who still rely on private health insurance (if we can afford it) may right now be under scrutiny for genetic health risks; this could be used against us to deny benefits. The parade of horrors goes on and on ….

We'll have time to talk about the ethics of genetic engineering and screening in more detail in Chapter 18, "Biomedical Ethics." For the time being, let's leave these two polar images of science—as divine benefactor and evil monster—aside for a moment and look at why one of the greatest philosophers who ever lived claimed that scientists are moral gurus.

Tried and True

When you need technical advice, seek an expert for guidance. But when you need moral advice, seek out a trusted friend. After talking with your friend you'll be in a better position to take responsibility for your decision.

In his book, the Republic—regarded by many as the greatest book of philosophy ever written—Plato argued that all knowledge is technical expertise, including knowledge of right and wrong. If you're an ordinary Joe or Jill, you don't mess with technical expertise. For example, if you have chest pains, you don't check it out by slicing yourself open with that old rusty knife you have in the kitchen. No, you go to a doctor, preferably a heart specialist.

Knowledge Versus Belief

Why did Plato think that all knowledge was technical expertise? Basically, he thought that *really knowing* something to be true was different from merely *believing* it to be so. To have real knowledge means not only having a true belief, but being able to back up your belief with good reasons. You wouldn't trust a weatherman who rolled dice to predict the weather, even if he did happen to get it right most of the time! And for Plato, as for many scientists today, good reasons have to be reached according to a special method that guarantees a very high degree of certainty. For Plato, this method was mathematics and philosophical insight, plus years of studying different areas of science; for today's scientists, it's mathematics and the experimental method, plus—you got it—years of studying different areas of science.

Plato's dream of placing ethics on a firm, scientific basis has enchanted various philosophers throughout the ages. There was Jeremy Bentham (about whom I'll have more to say in Chapter 13, "Consequentialist Theories"), who thought that you could reduce ethics to a mathematical, pain/pleasure, cost/benefit calculus. John Dewey, judged by many as America's greatest philosopher, believed that the experimental method in science was the one and only true method for any kind of problem-solving, ethical problem-solving being no exception. And then there's Henry Sidgwick, who saw ethics as a science, and who wanted to "attain systematic and precise general knowledge of what ought to be."

Ask the Expert

The point—in case you missed it—is that we look up to scientifically trained experts in all fields of life to solve our moral dilemmas, and not just our scientific questions. For example, we may think that researchers not only have the answer to whether we can use embryonic stem cells for medical purposes, but whether we ought to use them. Asking whether something is scientifically possible is different from asking whether we should do it. And scientists don't have these moral answers!

I'll return to this point at the end of this chapter, because it has pretty grave implications for our faith in democracy. What I'd like us to do now is examine a more extreme position along the let-science-be-your-guide spectrum. This view is not the view that ethics should be founded on and reduced to scientific expertise; it's the view that ethics should be eliminated and replaced by science, period.

Moral Musings

My students constantly ask me: "What's the right thing to do in this (fill in your favorite moral dilemma) situation?" Well, I got news for them. Philosophers like me who teach ethics don't have privileged access to the moral truth. Philosophy is not like science, and moral knowledge isn't like scientific knowledge. We philosophers are in the same boat as everyone else, except that we are a little more attuned to the complexities of moral questions and the difficulties involved in knowing how to answer them. For that reason, we're less likely to think that we know all the answers (as Socrates famously said, philosophical wisdom consists in knowing that you're ignorant).

Hello Science, Good-Bye Ethics

Remember what I said about science not being a gracious winner in beating out religion for first place in our heart of hearts? Well, not being satisfied with merely putting religion in its proper (second) place, some scientists and philosophers went further. They argued that religious talk of God and other things invisible to the microscope or telescope was a bunch of baloney. As if that wasn't bad enough, they then claimed the same thing about ethics. Geez … is any thing sacred?

I understand that some scientists might be a little dubious about God-talk. As I noted in Chapter 4, it's hard to talk meaningfully about God, since He's not a physical being. Few people see God as a man with a big beard who walks around waving to us with a flashing smile. At best, God is a big mystery to us. So there probably isn't much we can meaningfully say about Him.

But doubts about ethics? Come on … you must be kidding! Well, think again, my friend. Some of the same reasons why scientists and philosophers said that God-talk is meaningless apply to "Good-talk" as well. For beginners, let's look at problems with the ways we talk about God.

The problem lays out like this: Ever ask yourself how words get their meaning? Take the following sentence: "The cat is on the mat." How do you know what "cat" means? Well, when you were just a baby your family would read you books with pictures of cats and they would point out cats to you in passing, each time saying something like, "Oh, see the pretty cat!" Same thing happened with other words, like "mat" and "on." In other words, you learned the meanings of words by matching them up with some observable thing or event. Conclusion: Sentences as a whole have meaning only to the degree that they match up with observable facts.

Can You See, Taste, Feel It?

Well, can you see where this is all leading? If sentences have meaning only if they can be matched with observable facts, and sentences about God are about nonobservable facts (I mean, you never see, feel, smell, or hear God directly with your own eyes, hands, nose, or ears), then sentences about God are meaningless!

And, it would appear, a lot of other things we talk about are meaningless, too. Sentences with words like "good," "right," and "ought" in them are also a problem because you can't see or touch them. Compare the following sentences:

- You should not hit George.
- You are not hitting George.

The first sentence—"You should not hit George"—makes an ethical command, and is not asserting an observable fact as is the second sentence. It's not saying that something *is* the case (there's no "are" or "is" in the sentence); rather, it's commanding or ordering that something be done.

This distinction between "is" and "ought" is one of the big differences between language that describes a situation and that states facts on one side, and language that evaluates or commands, on the other. Evaluative uses of language, such as value judgments and moral commands, are about values, not facts. The statement "Eating meat is morally wrong because animals have the right to life" is not stating a fact about the world; rather, it is making a judgment about how we should behave. Evaluative language recommends or commands that something be done.

The distinction between stating facts and making evaluations isn't always clear. For instance, a lot of sentences that make moral evaluations contain the word "is" in them. For example, I could substitute the sentence "It is wrong (bad) for you to hit George" for "You ought not hit George" without changing anything. So don't be misled by the "is." "It is wrong (bad) to hit George" is not describing a fact: it's warning you to not do something, whether or not you're actually doing it.

Tried and True

When you're thinking about what to do, don't automatically conclude that the way people actually think and behave is necessarily right. The way things ought to be isn't necessarily the way they actually are.

Word Play

And one more thing, while we're on the topic. Some words in our language do double duty: They can be used to either describe (state a fact) or evaluate (recommend a value). Look at the following two sentences with "good" in them:

- This is a good battery.
- This is a good action.

Both sentences contain "good" in them in what appear to be identical sentence structures. But notice that what we mean when we say "This is a good battery" is that this battery produces enough of a charge to do its thing. In saying this, we might mean to recommend the battery to someone, but not necessarily. We could also just be describing the difference between a good and bad battery to a bunch of students interested in how batteries work. But when we say, "This is a good action," we're not *describing* the action at all, but *recommending* it.

Now where were we? Ah yes, the argument that the language of ethics is as nonsensical as the language of religion. I've said that ethics-talk makes evaluations and gives commands rather than stating facts or describing things. But according to this argument, language is only meaningful if it is describing observable facts. So God-talk and Good-talk are both equally meaningless.

But surely, you say, we must be saying something meaningful whenever we engage in God-talk or Good-talk! Granted. A less extreme advocate of science might agree. But she wouldn't agree with the most important point that religious and moral claims are as verifiable as scientific ones. Sure, we can confirm that certain religious and moral beliefs are *held* to be true by some people. Sociologists and pollsters confirm this all the time. But there's no way of confirming that these religious and moral beliefs are *in fact* true. Even if everyone happened to believe that the world was flat (which they once did), that wouldn't make them right.

That leaves science—the highest authority on observing facts—as the sole authority in our lives. Sure, scientific facts are meaningful. Without them, a huge part of our lives wouldn't make sense. But if that's all the meaning there is, then why bother? If there's nothing higher—ethical or religious goals—directing our lives and giving it meaning, then why not cash it all in now, and save ourselves the trouble of living out an empty life?

Is Choice Possible?

Things look even worse when we see what the scientific picture of the world tells us about ourselves. It says that there's only matter and energy. What we call the soul—mind or spirit—is nothing more than brain activity, a particular mix of matter and electro-chemical energy, and nothing more. When we die, it's lights out for good. And nothing happens in our brain without a cause. One chemical firing in the brain leads to another, in an unending chain of connections. So, according to this scientific view, there are causal connections that necessarily make us think in certain ways.

Philosophers call this scientific view of the world *determinism*. It's just a high-fallutin' way of saying that there's no such thing as free will. Oh, we might think that we're in complete control over all our thought processes. We deliberate about options before we choose and that sort of thing. But if we take the scientific view of things seriously, our sense of being the first, uncaused initiator of our thoughts and volitions is as much of a delusion as the idea of a God who caused Himself into existence.

Ethically Speaking

Determinism says that everything was predetermined to happen just the way it actually happened, including our thoughts and desires. Our willing something is the inevitable effect of some prior cause. Although we think we're responsible for our actions, the truth is that what we experience as our volition is really an electrochemical event in our brain that is mechanically caused like any other physical process.

And now for the really bad news. If determinism is true and we aren't really free to act differently than we do, then we can't be held responsible for what we do. It's like saying that if, without your knowing it, someone implanted a device in your brain that made you kill, it wouldn't be your fault that you killed. The device makes you do it, so you can't be blamed. But in a world where no one can be blamed and everything that happens is determined from the beginning of time, ethics talk seems silly. I mean, to tell someone that he ought to have done something he didn't do assumes that he could have chosen different, but determinism says that's impossible. Bye-bye ethics.

> **Moral Musings**
>
> A less extreme advocate of science might concede that the languages of religion and ethics are meaningful. But she wouldn't concede the most important point: that religious and moral claims are as verifiable as scientific ones.

Having Your Cake And Eating It, Too

So science rules your head but ethics rules your heart. How do you reconcile them? Darn good question; I'm glad you asked. The way to reconcile them is to say that science and ethics (and maybe religion) are different, but equally necessary, perspectives for viewing the world. And two people can have radically different perspectives on something and both be right. The important thing to remember about a *perspective* is that it's limited. By definition, it's only one point of view among many. So it doesn't give you the whole picture. Science, religion and ethics are each like that.

And here's something else you should know: The usefulness of a perspective depends upon what you're trying to explain. Take religion. It leaves the small, mundane problems of everyday existence to science and instead addresses the big, spiritual mysteries of life. Mysteries like who (or what) created the universe? Or, what's the ultimate end of life? Science can't answer these questions. And it doesn't try to, really. By their very nature, these questions assume the workings of God in nature.

Now take science. It addresses the mundane workings of cause and effect in the material world. Its primary purpose is to make life easier for us by providing us with knowledge of how things work. By viewing the world as based on determined and predictable laws, science gives us great power. We can use knowledge of cause and effect to bring about endless improvements in our lives—or endless death and destruction!

 Ethically Speaking

A **perspective** is a partial point of view. It's like the Chinese tale about the elephant and the blind mice. Each mouse had a different notion of what the elephant was like based on its own limited exposure to a particular part of the elephant's anatomy. Each notion was correct—but gave only one side of the whole truth.

And ethics? Ethics doesn't address the great mysteries of life and it doesn't give us the technical know-how to re-engineer nature in conformity to our material needs. What it gives us is clear thinking about the proper rules that guide our relationships. By viewing human behavior as action *voluntarily* chosen to meet certain goals, ethics assumes the fact of moral responsibility in our lives.

> **CAUTION**
>
> ### Do the Right Thing!
>
> So you're looking for an authority figure to tell you what to do: the scientist, the philosopher, the minister/priest/rabbi/imam, the great leader, or some other parental substitute. Well, for God's sake, buck up and take some responsibility! There are no moral experts! Let your informed conscience be your guide!

I think we're now in a position to challenge science as the exclusive authority on meaning and truth. The scientist who rejects religion and ethics is guilty of treating science as if it were the only game in town. But science isn't absolute. It provides meaning and truth about some things, but not *all* things.

Meaning is what we ultimately hope for, and what we highly value. Of course, you can't gain spiritual wisdom and moral insight in the same way you gain scientific knowledge. There are no hard "facts" that we can compare moral and religious truth against. We gain spiritual wisdom and moral insight through hard experience and, most important, by talking to one another.

Can We Talk?

Why talking to one another? Well, remember what I said earlier about the importance of examining your life and being able to justify your moral beliefs with good reasons. This process—what we call reflection, or gazing inward on yourself as if gazing at a reflection in a mirror—involves sorting through your values and beliefs in order to make them consistent with one another. It's almost as if you were having a conversation with yourself, making sure that all parts agree with each other. And the conversation never ends, because every time you think you have agreement, new contradictions crop up. It's like reading a good novel—only it's your life, your autobiography. Understanding the parts as parts of the whole changes the meaning of the whole as well, which in turn leads you to read the parts differently and then the whole differently, without end.

So, unlike the scientific method, which stops the buck where the cold facts begin, the method of moral reflection has no end. It's like a conversation that goes back and forth between the voices that make up my life and the whole "me", and between the "me" that gets reflected on and the "I" that does the reflecting. But what gets this inner dialogue going is talking to *others*, reflecting my ideas off of them while they reflect their ideas off of me. And like that inner dialogue, this outer conversation is never-ending.

And truth? Although there are points in our outer conversation where all voices temporarily agree and (as we saw in Chapter 3, "Convince Me That I'm Wrong") shared norms come into play, moral truths are never fully grasped and defined, once and for all.

For once discovered, they grow like seeds into trees, branching out into ever more complex systems!

Two Sides of the Coin

Let's recap, shall we? Contrary to the extreme view that science is all there is, we really do need religion (faith and hope) and ethics (value and moral rule) to give our lives meaning and purpose. Remember, science can tell us what the most efficient means are for achieving our ends, but it can't tell us which ends are the right ones. That's a question of value, not a question of fact.

Flipping to the other side of the coin, ethics and religion need science. There's an old saying in ethics that "ought implies can." We can't be morally obligated to do things that aren't within our power to do. Science tells us what's within our power now, and what might be within our power in the future. Hey, it's even sort of reassuring to know that there's a predictable world of causes and effects out there that act as a reliable backdrop to our moral actions!

Tried and True

We live in a crazy world where science and technology lend themselves to any purpose, be it good or evil. Meanwhile, people allow all sorts of weird mystical beliefs—and extremely dangerous religious ideals—to guide their conduct. If only people—scientists and lay persons—would heed the voice of moral common sense!

Of Moral Engineers and Other Monsters

There's just one more thing that has to be said before concluding this chapter: that we're continually tempted to think that science can solve all of our problems for us. But we seldom think of what the implications would be if that were true.

Who said anything about letting scientists solve all our problems? Well, consider the following cases.

◆ Pro-life activist Phyllis says that scientific evidence shows that a fertilized egg has a much greater chance than an unfertilized egg of growing into an adult human being. She says this proves that the fertilized egg is a person with a full right to life. Pro-choice activist Gloria says that scientific evidence shows that a fetus lacks a sophisticated brain, and that this proves it isn't a person with a full right to life.

◆ The President appoints an economist to head the Federal Reserve Board, thinking that economics is all about scientifically managing an economy. The head of the board raises and lowers interest rates in order to raise and lower rates of borrowing, investment, employment, and consumption. The idea behind all of this is that a growing economy is good for everyone.

Here we have two instances in which people appeal to *scientific* expertise in trying to solve their *moral* problems. In the first case, opponents in the abortion debate both appeal to biology to justify their view of the fetus' personhood. Ah, if only the determining personhood were that simple! Clearly, Phyllis and Gloria could accept each other's scientific evidence and still not accept each other's conclusions. The reason is simple. Saying that something is a person—which in this context means "ought to be given a right to life"—is a moral, not a scientific question.

In the second case, the Chair of the Federal Reserve Board and the President assume that economics is only about ensuring a constant growth of the total pie, not about dividing the pie fairly. But why assume that economic growth is necessarily a good thing? After all, with growth comes greater pollution, environmental degradation, and a host of other quality of life problems.

And even if one assumes that economic growth is a good thing, it can't be managed apart from addressing another moral question: Who should get the added surplus? (Darn! I was short-changed again by the IRS!) For example, when the Fed Chair decides that the economy is growing too fast (say, because demand for scarce labor and goods is driving up wages and prices too high), he raises interest rates. Raising interest rates, in turn, decreases investment and employment. So, some people—often the poorest—get laid off (maybe you're one of them) so that others (bankers and investors) can get a full return on their loans and investments.

There are countless other times when we reduce moral questions to scientific expertise. None is more blatant than when we shirk our political duties as citizens on the grounds that we're incapable of making informed decisions about "technical" matters pertaining to the management of the economy, the national defense, the environment, and so on. Why should I bother informing myself about technical matters beyond my understanding? Better to let the experts decide for me!

And they would be only too happy to do so! Plato spoke for all technocratic experts when he said that the masses can't know what is in their best interests. You want real law and order, real prosperity? Then junk democracy—endless talk never resolves anything!

The Least You Need to Know

- Avoid both religious fanaticism and scientific extremism.
- Appreciate how science, religion, and ethics make different contributions to life.
- Remember that science needs ethics as much as ethics needs science.
- Learn to value democracy as a public process of moral conversation and reflection.
- Beware the pitfalls of letting science solve your moral problems.

Part

What Does It All Mean? The Nature of Ethics

No guide to ethics would be complete without presenting the other side of the coin. I'm talking about dissing ethics. You see, a lot of people are down on ethics. Some folks think that everything boils down to looking out for *numero uno*—you know what I'm talking about, the "me first" mind set. Other folks say that everything's relative, as in "It's okay if the X people want to eat their children and the Y people don't, because who's to say what's right or wrong?" And if the Doubting Thomases weren't bad enough, there are the cynics who scoff at all moral talk, as if it were all a bunch of hypocrisy.

In this part we examine the strengths and weaknesses of the anti-ethics stance. Is it true that everything we do is driven by self-interest? Is it true that everything we do is relative to the shifting sands of time and place? Is it true that ethics is just a ruse to hoodwink us into following the unhealthy and altogether partisan wishes of the most numerous or the most powerful?

Chapter **6**

"Me First" Ethics

In This Chapter

- ◆ Do human beings always put themselves first?
- ◆ Should human beings always put themselves first?
- ◆ The claim that altruism is impossible
- ◆ Dispelling the myths of egoism

Two friends, Jane and Susan, are talking as they eat lunch in the cafeteria. Jane says "You know, I really admire Mother Theresa … she was such a kind, unselfish person, giving her whole life over to other people." "Baloney!" Susan says in response. "Mother Theresa only did what we all do. She did what made her happy, what made her feel good about herself. Her work with the poor wasn't unselfish: it was done for totally selfish reasons! She was just like the rest of us."

In this chapter we will consider the "me first" ethics expressed by Susan. Some people think that no matter what we do, we always act out of self-interest: That even if we think we are acting for charitable reasons, we are just plain wrong. We will also consider the separate claim that we should always act on our own self-interest—that this is the best moral approach to ethical life. So first get your elbow out of the face of the person behind you, and then let's consider whether unselfishness is possible or desirable!

Psychological Egoism

Psychological egoists are not making a claim about how we *ought to* behave—that is the claim of Ethical Egoists. No, psychological egoists are making an assertion about how we *do* behave: that in everything we do, we always act out of self-interested motives.

Self-Interested or Selfish?

This may sound right to you; for others, it may seem a very odd claim. People generally think that we do all kinds of things on a daily basis that show genuine care and concern for others. For example …

- Helping little old ladies with their heavy grocery bags.
- Putting coins in other peoples' meters so they don't get parking tickets.
- Giving money to homeless people on the street.
- Grabbing a dog before it runs out into the traffic.
- Raking up your neighbor's leaves.
- Giving an acquaintance a ride downtown.

Ethically Speaking

There's a big difference between acting out of **self-interest** and acting **selfishly**, and you shouldn't mix them up. A person can act out of self-interest and not be selfish: For example, if I go to the dentist to fill a throbbing cavity, it is in my self-interest (no more pain!), but you couldn't say it is a selfish thing to do.

So how does the psychological egoist respond to such examples of altruistic behavior? Well, she denies that they are done from selfless motives. She claims that what really motivates these kindnesses is self-interest. How so?

Psychological Egoism is a theory of human nature, and not an ethical theory. There's a difference. Ethical theories tell us how we ought to behave (usually they tell us we should be unselfish!); theories of human nature tell us how we do behave.

And psychological egoists claim that it's only human nature to act out of self-interest: We can't help it; it's hard-wired, just like dogs sniffing each other. So with regard to every example listed above, psychological egoists will give an explanation from self-interest. We help little old ladies because it makes us feel good; we give money to homeless people on the street because it makes us look good to other people; we rake up neighbor's leaves so the neighbor will owe us a favor down the road; we grab the dog to prevent it from running into the street because it would upset us if the dog were hit; and so on. And you thought they were just nice things to do? *Wrongo!*

So much for being oriented toward caring about other people. But let's look at this theory a little harder: If we do, I think you'll agree that it starts to unravel.

Okay, so far we've established that psychological egoists believe all moral acts are motivated by self-interest. These folks have a great trick: They can take any kind, caring act you can name (go on, think of one!) and turn it into a self-interested act. Think about how, in a couple of sentences, Susan turned Mother Theresa from a saint into a self-serving, "me first" kind of gal. Pretty neat trick, huh? How did Susan do this? She offered some standard arguments in favor of psychological egoism. They are …

- In all cases, where people do things both good and bad, they are only doing what they really want to do. So we can't praise Mother Theresa for her acts of kindness because, after all, she was only doing what she really wanted!

- Doing good acts makes us feel really good about ourselves; our brain releases pheromones, we feel a sense of self-worth, and it makes us happy. This is what Susan was getting at when she said that Mother Theresa "did what made her happy; what made her feel good." What this means is that acts that appear unselfish are really done for the sake of that good feeling—we want those pheromones, darn it! Think again about the person who pulls the doggie back from the street, he goes home feeling kind of "high"—feeling good about himself for doing a good deed. He avoided the "yuck" feeling that comes with watching doggie intestines get splashed across the road!

> **Moral Musings**
>
> Thomas Hobbes was a famous philosopher from the seventeenth century. Hobbes supported psychological egoism; he said this about acts of charity: "There can be no greater argument to a man, of his own power, than to find himself able not only to accomplish his own desires, but also to assist other men in theirs; and this is that conception wherein consisteth charity."

> **Do the Right Thing!**
>
> Psychological egoists claim that (1) we only do things because we really want to, so we shouldn't be praised for doing good acts and (2) we want the good feelings that come with doing good things, so doing good acts is really self-serving. Do you see anything wrong with these claims?

This is really depressing, you might be thinking. No more faith in the cup of human kindness! But wait a minute. Is Susan—and the other psychological egoists—right?

Psychological Egoism: Objection One

No, they aren't, and here's why. First, Susan claimed that people only do things because they really want to. But is that true? I'll bet you really dig getting up at 6 A.M. on Saturday mornings to get downtown in time to teach English as a Second Language. And I'll bet the guy who jumps into the freezing cold waters of Lake Michigan to save a drowning kid really wants to make that plunge! And I suppose that you just love visiting your deaf, elderly grandpa with Alzheimer's disease at the nursing home on Sundays. The point here is that all the time we do things we don't really want to do; we do them out of a sense of obligation—because we promised to, or because we think it's our duty.

Tried and True

If everything we did was something we wanted to do, then saying that John did something because he wanted to do it wouldn't be very informative. But then neither would psychological egoism. The assertion, "Everything we do is done because we want to," would be true by definition: To do something is to do something we choose to do; and to choose to do something is to want to do it. So, "Everything that is done is done because we want to do it," would mean nothing more than the empty claim that "everything that is done is done because its done." Not a very interesting claim, don't you agree?

Also, Susan would need to explain this: If we always do what we really want to do in our heart of hearts, then why do we sometimes feel that inner struggle to get off our butts and do it? If you really wanted to do the 6 A.M. ESL lesson, then why do you feel that pull some Saturday mornings to stay in bed and skip it? Those inner struggles—doing what we promised, even when we don't want to—means that Susan can't be right. If we always really wanted to do the things we do, there wouldn't *be* any internal struggle, right? We'd merrily roll along, with our sense of obligation and our desires completely on board with one another.

Objection Two

There's another problem related to Susan's first point. She said that, whether or not an act is good, it is always done because the actor wants to do it. The problem is that we suddenly can't distinguish between good people and bad people, since we're all just in it for ourselves, no matter what we do. But this is absurd, since that wipes out the very thing that makes one guy good and the next guy bad. Mother Theresa no different than an axe murderer? Let's be serious! The very thing that made Mother Theresa an unselfish, caring woman was the kinds of things that she desired: she wanted people to not starve to death, die of horrible diseases, live on the streets, and so on. The axe murderer wants others to die at the blade of his axe. Enough said.

Objection Three

So the psychological egoists' little empire is starting to crumble. Let's pull another brick out from under them! Susan's second argument was that doing good acts makes us feel really good about ourselves, and it's that good feeling we're going for when we are kind to others. Sound okay? I don't think so, Susan! For consider this: which comes first, wanting that "oooh, aaahh" feeling, or wanting to do good for others? Susan says it's the good feeling ... but actually, the good feeling follows from doing good acts. It's not the other way around: it's not as though we scout around for things we can do to get the "oooh, aaahh" feeling—rather, we do the good acts and then the pheromones kick in. So there's no reason to think that Susan is telling the story the right way.

Anyway, even if we do derive good feelings from doing good things for people, so what? There should be some benefits to being a good person, shouldn't there? The fact that doing good acts makes us feel good is irrelevant here. In fact, if anything, getting that good feeling from doing kind acts is just another thing that sets Mother Theresa apart from the axe murderer. Morally good people feel good about being of service to others; morally bad people don't. Mother Theresa, bless her sainted heart, did the right things for the right reasons; the bloodthirsty axe murderer does not!

Now we know what's wrong with Psychological Egoism—there are some pretty serious flaws with it as a theory of human nature. It doesn't do a good job at all of describing why we do things, and can't sustain its main claims. But this isn't the end of the story, because just when you thought you'd won the war, it turns out you only won the battle! That's right ... along comes another egoist theory to consider—this time Ethical Egoism.

Ethical Egoism

Psychological egoists claim that we always act from self-interested motives—we can't help it; it's built right into our psychology. Ethical egoists don't make claims about human nature like that; they make claims about how we ought to behave. It's important to get this distinction, or else you will

Do the Right Thing!

If the psychological egoist is right, then mothers only take care of their infants for self-interested reasons. Is this a good explanation for the huge sacrifices that mothers make for their children? Do you think mothers care for their babies in order to ensure the continuation of their gene pools, or is there something more going on?

Ethically Speaking

There's an important difference between Psychological Egoism and Ethical Egoism. **Psychological Egoism** makes claims about how we *do* behave: We act from self-interested motives. **Ethical Egoism** makes claims about how we *should* behave: We should always act on our own self-interest.

be confused right from the start. *Psychological Egoism* makes claims about how we *do* behave; *Ethical Egoism* makes claims about how we *should* behave.

Ethical egoists tell you that, no matter what, you should always act on your own self-interests. So rather than saying that we have duties to other people—something that most ethical theories tell us—ethical egoists say that we only have one duty, and that is to ourselves. Later in Chapter 22, "The Immigration Controversy," we will talk about different approaches to ethics—individualist versus communitarian approaches. But for now all you need to know is that ethical egoism is an individualist theory: It starts with the importance of the individual, and her rights and freedoms.

If individuals really matter, ethical egoists say, then we shouldn't force them to sacrifice their own lives, and their own goals, for the sake of the "common good." Promoting altruism in humans is bad because it recommends that individuals give themselves over; it means that the individual doesn't matter any more, and that we only care about the good of society.

Whoa, you might be saying. Is there really a theory that says we should never do anything for other people? Well, you would be confused if you thought that's what Ethical Egoism means—because as an ethical egoist, you might very well do things for other people. But the *reason* you would do for others would be because it is in your own best interests, not because it's good for them!

Let's go back to the list of good things that you could do for other people. It included things like carrying heavy groceries for little old ladies, putting coins in the meter so other people don't get parking tickets, and raking up your neighbor's leaves. Ethical egoists wouldn't tell you not to do these things, but they would tell you to only do them if you would benefit yourself. And you could imagine lots of ways in which you could benefit from helping little old ladies, or raking up neighbors' leaves; people might see you, and give you praise—you would look good in front of others for doing these things. Or you might know you are going away for two weeks and need someone to rake your leaves while you're gone, so raking for your neighbor is putting him in your debt! Whatever the case, what makes these acts morally right isn't that it helps other people, but that it advances your own interests.

> **Moral Musings**
>
> If you think ethical egoism means you should never do anything for other people, you're wrong. You might do nice things for others, so long as it's beneficial to you in the long run. Would ethical egoism endorse parental nurturing? How can any parent know whether the rewards of parenting down the road will ever be worth the hassles of raising a teenager here and now!

> **Moral Musings**
>
> Ethical egoism isn't the same as hedonism, or the moral doctrine that identifies moral goodness with pleasure. Some ethical egoists, like Friedrich Nietzsche (whom we'll discuss in Chapter 8, "Cynical About Ethics?") have actually equated self-interest with self-mastery, which generally requires forsaking pleasure for power.

Another thing: Ethical Egoism isn't a hedonistic moral theory. *Hedonism* is the pursuit of only and all things that make you feel good—sex, drugs, and rock 'n' roll! Ethical egoists aren't saying that you should only go after those things that make you feel good; the theory is about your self-interests, and sometimes things that feel really great aren't in our interests at all! For example, I love sweets—I could eat them all day—but it isn't in my best interests to have a steady diet of cakes and pies. And we all know by now that, no matter how good it makes you feel, smoking is really bad for you. Ditto for drinking too much. In fact, Ethical Egoism may require you to *not* indulge yourself in these feel-good activities just because it isn't in your self-interest. It also means you might have to do painful things, like going to the doctor or dentist, because it's in your interests, even though they aren't pleasant activities!

Ethical Egoism Defended

Now that we're clear on what Ethical Egoism isn't saying, let's take a harder look at what it *is* proposing. Then you can decide if it's a theory worth holding on to. To be honest, I hope you decide that it isn't: such a moral point-of-view can do a lot of damage, and the "me first!" mentality challenges what it means to live in a community with other people. But in any case, here are some positive arguments that ethical egoists have put forward in support of their theory:

◆ Ethical Egoism is morally right because it encourages individuals to look out for themselves. Since we each know best what is in our self-interests, Ethical Egoism is better than theories that encourage us to "do for others." When we try to do for others, we are likely to get it wrong; it's better to let people do for themselves!

◆ Promoting altruism and charity is bad because it places the individual at the mercy of society. If we want a society that is really all it can be, we need to encourage individuals to be great, and not sacrifice themselves for the common good. Great societies are born of great individuals.

It's enough to look at these two arguments to see if the ethical egoist is right. The first claim is that it's always better to have individuals look out for their own good rather than having others do it for them. Most people don't appreciate paternalism—having other people deciding what's best for them—and want the freedom to act for themselves. According to this view, altruism and charity are offensive and paternalistic because they suggest that you can't "do for yourself" and that you need others to look out for you. For the betterment of society, then, we should adopt Ethical Egoism.

> ### Moral Musings
>
> "I have come here to say that I do not recognize anyone's right to one minute of my life. … It had to be said. The world is perishing from an orgy of self-sacrificing."
>
> —Ayn Rand, *The Fountainhead*

Whoops! Do you see the slip that ethical egoists make when they say that it's better for society if each person looks out for herself? Suddenly they have slipped from a concern with the individual to concern for the good of all. It sounds pretty unegoistic to say that it's better for society if we all act as egoists. Now the concern is with society, and not the individual.

Ethical Egoism Refuted

There's another problem here, too. Ethical egoists are saying that it's an insult to interfere in the lives of individuals, and that as good ethical egoists we just shouldn't do it. It's insulting and intrudes into people's lives too much. But apply this thinking to a person receiving unemployment benefits or welfare. Would that person be likely to say he finds it "offensive" that he is receiving this help? Or do people in the Third World really find it insulting that North Americans send aid to their countries? I seriously doubt it.

> **CAUTION**
>
> ### Do the Right Thing!
>
> Ethical egoism says that we should only look out for ourselves. But where would we be if everyone did that? Children, elderly, and other dependent people need others to look out for their interests. And guess what—we all have been (or will become) those dependent people.

> ### Moral Musings
>
> Volunteerism (giving up personal time for service in the community) is increasingly required as part of college studies. But there are groups that are completely against this move. Critics say it is forcing the individual student into servitude against her will, and that it should not be allowed. Do you think volunteerism is morally wrong?

Let's look at the second claim: that promoting altruism and charity is bad because it abandons the individual to society. One of the greatest proponents of this view was philosopher Ayn Rand. Rand wrote popular novels touting the absolute value of the individual; her novels, *The Fountainhead* and *Atlas Shrugged*, are international best sellers. Maybe you've read them! Rand is dead, but her legacy of individualism—she called her theory "Objectivism"—lives on.

According to Rand and her supporters, the individual is the unit of supreme importance, and anything we do to make him sacrifice his own goals and intellect is absolutely wrong. This means, of course, that encouraging individuals to be self-sacrificing, altruistic, or charitable is totally wrong. Why? Because, as Rand says, by promoting altruism we suggest that the individual is of no value, and that any demands other people make on him must be fulfilled.

Here's where you can build on what you've read so far. Remember in Chapter 2, "The Inevitability of Ethical Dilemmas," how you read about thinking of other alternatives? I said that "in many instances when we're asked to choose between the jagged horns of a dilemma, there's a softer one that's been left out of the picture." Bingo! That's exactly what ethical egoists are failing to do here … consider another alternative.

The way ethical egoists tell the story, our only choice is between absolute individualism—putting the interests of the individual first—or total altruism/collectivism—putting the good of society before the individual. But altruism and individualism aren't black and white; there are shades of gray in between. For example, altruism doesn't require us to fulfill any and all demands that other people make of us; some will just be ridiculous and we shouldn't accept them. Sometimes we should give up our own plans for the sake of others, but not always. Rand and other ethical egoists make it sound as if the total submission of the individual to the collective good is the only choice!

Altruism? No Way!

So now you have the whole, dirty story. Egoists—whether psychological or ethical egoists—claim that altruism is either impossible or morally bad. Whichever way you slice it, altruism is out the door. Bye-bye.

What does this mean? In both cases of egoism it means that we should not hold people up to an altruistic standard, since it's either impossible to be altruistic or it's immoral to do so. Going back to the list of good acts you could do for others, it wouldn't mean that you shouldn't do them anymore. But what it *would* mean is that when you heft those heavy grocery sacks for little old ladies, either your motive is self-serving (to make yourself feel good) or it should be self-serving (to want to impress people with how thoughtful you are).

Egoism of these two varieties has been supported by philosophers across time, and has certainly invaded our thinking at the social level. Many people have read William Golding's *Lord of the Flies* about the group of British schoolboys who are stranded together on a desert island and end up killing each other off. We now have popular shows that promote the ideas of psychological and ethical egoism: *Survivor, Big Brother,* and *The Weakest Link.* More and more I hear students say that we are all just out for ourselves, and that you shouldn't trust anybody. And so on. Ethical and Psychological Egoism permeate our culture; it doesn't need much encouragement given our current social trends.

Before you ride the egoism hobbyhorse, too, remember this: Charity and altruism aren't just for wimps and suckers. We all require charity now and again; and if it weren't for our parents' altruism, none of us would have survived past babyhood!

Altruism doesn't require the kind of total selflessness that ethical egoists depict. Being altruistic shouldn't mean that we totally give up our own life goals, plans, or dreams for the sake of other

Tried and True

The Bible contains a bit of wisdom that we should all keep in mind, especially when we're thinking about egoism. It's "love thy neighbor as thy self." Whether or not you're religious, it's a decent piece of ethical advice!

people. It does mean that the motto "I'm number one!" isn't always true, though. Self-interest can be a good thing—it can lead to self-preservation, which is important—but it isn't the only game in town.

Finally, you should consider this: There will always be those of us who think they are better than others, that they don't need other people, that lesser people drain their energies and their creative juices, and that society is a burden on the individual. They may be ethical egoists, and are likely to think that they are the great ones who shouldn't be burdened by altruism and charity! Such people should ask themselves: what is it about them that makes them better than others? Are their lives more enjoyable than the next person's? Are they so much smarter, or creative, or worthy that they should be in a separate ethical category from the rest of us slobs? Probably not, since truly great people know their human limitations, and know that society helped, not hindered, their greatness!

The Least You Need to Know

- Don't assign greater weight to your own interests than to the interests of other people.
- Question theories of human nature that suggest we are inherently self-interested.
- Feel good about doing morally good acts for other people. It's just one of the benefits of leading an ethical life!
- Remember that at one time or another, each and every one of us will benefit from others' charity and altruism.
- You should be self-interested; you shouldn't be selfish.

Chapter 7

"Us First" Ethics

In This Chapter

- ◆ Rethinking "I'm okay, you're okay"
- ◆ Why tolerating differences can be an ethical problem
- ◆ The distinction between facts and value judgments
- ◆ Are ethical values universal?

This chapter will treat the whole question of difference: How do we respond to different ethical beliefs and practices that arise between individuals and between cultures? Some people think that tolerance is an ethical ideal: that above all else, we should each be respectful and tolerant of other peoples' and other cultures' beliefs and practices. In China, the government allows couples to have only one child each; a second or third child results in heavy penalties, such as huge fines or jail sentences.

We will consider this claim and others in this chapter. You will decide for yourself: Is the rightness or wrongness of an act dependent on each person or culture?

Ethical Subjectivism

Let's start with differences between individuals' moral beliefs and then work our way out to differences in cultural beliefs. You might think, to keep things clear and simple, that we should just write off our different individual ethical beliefs to a difference of opinion—"I'm okay, you're okay." For the sake of not having to listen to colleagues bicker at work, and so you don't have to be challenged by people who dispute your ethical beliefs, you might be tempted to take the view that "it's all relative." This would mean that, when the guy in the cubicle next to you says "George Bush is a redneck and I hate his guts!" you would calmly reply "That's your opinion, and you're entitled to it."

Ethically Speaking

Ethical subjectivism isn't a moral theory that tells us what's right or wrong, good or bad. It's a claim about the nature of moral judgments: that moral judgments are nothing more than expressions of personal opinion. That's all, folks!

Ahhh ... sounds good (and nonconfrontational), doesn't it? What a nice, peaceful world this would be if only everyone took that view. Philosophers have debated this point, and have even come up with a name for it: ethical subjectivism. Ethical subjectivism, like psychological egoism, isn't a moral theory: it's a claim about the nature of moral judgments. *Ethical subjectivism* isn't telling us what is good or bad, right or wrong. It's telling us that what moral judgments come down to is an expression of opinion, nothing more nor less.

People who are ethical subjectivists don't argue for "moral truths" or "moral absolutes." According to subjectivists, people who use words like "truth" and "moral absolute" are barking up the wrong tree, since all moral claims come down to nothing more than personal opinions, expressions of feeling. Give an ethical subjectivist just about any moral claim you can imagine—"abortion is wrong"; "physician-assisted suicide is morally good"; "what Hitler did was evil"—and the subjectivist will tell you that your statements aren't appealing to some truth that exists out there independent of your thoughts ... they are just expressions of your own point of view.

Okey dokey. Just to make sure this is crystal clear, let's set up a little dialogue so we can figure out what an ethical subjectivist would say about it. Let's listen in on a conversation between Oliver and Fred:

> **Oliver:** I think it's a good thing that scientists are developing genetic engineering. It would be great if some day we could prevent babies from being born with horrible diseases.
>
> **Fred:** Well, I think you're wrong. Once genetic engineering becomes possible, insurance companies will get their hands on our health files and have all kinds of genetic information about us. That info can be used to deny us jobs and medical treatment!

Oliver: But you can't use the possibility that engineering can be used for bad purposes as an argument against developing genetic engineering. Think about babies born with cystic fibrosis and cerebral palsy, and how hard their lives can be. Genetic technology can prevent those diseases from happening!

Fred: We're better off keeping things the way they are; besides, what's wrong with having cerebral palsy or cystic fibrosis?

What's going on between Oliver and Fred? Is it a disagreement about the truth of whether genetic technology is morally good or bad? According to the ethical subjectivist, all Fred and Oliver are doing is expressing a difference of opinion: there is no "fact of the matter," and these two guys can debate genetic engineering until they're blue in the face, but nothing will be settled. All this dialogue shows us is that Oliver and Fred have different opinions—and never the two shall meet!

Tried and True

Ethical subjectivism makes you a moral expert on all issues. Because, according to this view, if you believe something is morally right then it is right for you, and that's the end of the story. The next guy may believe something different, and that would be true for him. So there are no disagreements possible according to ethical subjectivists!

There's an additional point to keep in mind about ethical subjectivism here: whatever an individual believes is right and wrong *is* right and wrong for that individual. Look at it this way: since we are each the moral expert about what we believe, then we each determine right and wrong for ourselves. There is no "higher" court of appeal. So all along you've been a moral expert and you didn't even know it! If Fred and Oliver are each presenting their viewpoints truthfully, then they are each right: Fred thinks that genetic engineering is bad, and Oliver thinks it's good.

You can see why ethical subjectivism is appealing to people, at least initially. What could be better than a calm, peaceful world where individuals just agree to disagree? The idea of being tolerant of others is surely a good one … we know that people have hurt and killed each other over their opposing moral beliefs, and this is a pretty bad state of affairs.

Ethical subjectivists make the following claims in favor of their position:

1. **Ethical beliefs come down to feelings.** Different people have different feelings about things; and feelings are entirely subjective. So ethical beliefs, because they are based on our feelings, are subjective, too.

2. **Individuals just don't agree on what is right and wrong.** So there is no objective "right" or "wrong" about things—there is only opinion.

3. **Ethical beliefs aren't objectively provable.** They aren't like facts that we can point to. (For example, if someone claims that "the world is flat," we can show them that they're wrong; the same is not true about ethical claims!)

What are we to do with these claims? They seem to be right, and may be appealing to you. Let's take a closer look.

When the Feeling's Just Not There

Is it true that ethical beliefs are only based on individual feelings (i.e., I feel something is bad; you feel it's good)? There's more to your beliefs than just that, isn't there?

Most of us base our beliefs on a variety of things, including reason, experience, and imagination. For example, through experience of causing emotional pain to others, we learn to be considerate of their needs. Or from seeing others cause pain to people we care about, we learn that it is wrong to do so. And at least some of us (I hope!) have come to our moral beliefs through reason—we figured out for ourselves that something is right or wrong. We may have learned a great number of our moral beliefs from our families, religious leaders, and friends. If you were taught from birth that stealing is always wrong, then that isn't a belief based on feelings alone. So while feelings may play some role in our ethical beliefs, they aren't the whole story.

Moral Musings

Feeling shame, guilt or anger is a warning sign that something we did or something someone else did might be wrong. But feelings can be misguided when based on false beliefs. Think, for instance, of the anger incited in a white mob by a race baiter. Here the proper antidote is cool dispassionate reason. Most racist diatribes are filled with logical gaps, contradictions, and false generalizations.

To Believe or Not to Believe

Second, individuals' different beliefs don't disprove the existence of moral truths. The fact that you and I might have different beliefs about a moral issue doesn't mean that there is no truth of the matter. We might both be wrong; or one of us could be right. We will consider this in more detail when we talk about cultural relativism later in this chapter.

Convince Me That I'm Wrong

Third, while ethical beliefs may not be directly observable facts about the world, it isn't true that there is no way of determining if one ethical belief is better than another. We have some pretty good ways, including weighing the arguments for and against something. If someone is seriously trying to argue the moral correctness of hurting animals against someone who is arguing that it is wrong, we can look at the reasons they give and determine which position holds the most water. (You can pretty much bet the person who is arguing in favor of hurting animals will have some rather sketchy arguments in their favor!)

So when it comes to ethical beliefs, it isn't just "anything goes" the way the ethical subjectivist seems to suggest.

There are some other weird and logically unacceptable things that follow from ethical subjectivism. If you and I have different ethical beliefs about something, subjectivists claim that we are both right. Take pornography as an example again. The ethical subjectivist would have to hold the following two beliefs at the same time:

◆ Pornography is immoral.

◆ Pornography is not immoral.

Why would the subjectivist hold both positions? Because if you and I each take one of these positions, and it is true for each of us, then subjectivists would have to say it is true that pornography is both moral and immoral. But this is a logical contradiction: Pornography can't be both moral and immoral at the same time. (It's like saying "it's raining" and "it's not raining" at the same time—that's impossible!)

Here's another weird thing about ethical subjectivism: you couldn't really say that people who support ethical subjectivism have any moral beliefs at all. Think about it for a minute.

When I say that something is the right thing to do, I'm recommending that others should do it, too. Ethical subjectivism says that moral judgments like this are on a par with assertions like: "Tutti frutti ice cream tastes good to me." But notice what's wrong with the ethical subjectivist's comparision: It makes no sense to recommend that other people change their taste buds to conform to your own. "It's right to like tutti frutti ice cream" and "you should like tutti frutti ice cream, too" aren't reasonable recommendations.

And yet another strange implication of ethical subjectivism: according to this account, it doesn't matter how you came to hold a belief; all that matters is that you believe it. You could flip a coin or draw straws to come to your ethical beliefs, and it wouldn't matter one whit. All ethical subjectivists consider is that you have a moral belief and that you really believe it ... not how you came to have the belief. Yet as we know from Chapter 3,

Do the Right Thing!

Can you be said to have moral beliefs at all if you don't think they are true for everyone? If you think kicking cute, fluffy little puppies is wrong, then is it only wrong for you, or is it wrong for everyone to do it? Think about this: People who are anti-abortion think abortion is wrong for everyone to practice. Period. End of story. That's what it means to have an ethical belief!

"Convince Me That I'm Wrong," it really *does* matter how you came to your belief, whether you have good reasons or not.

Now We're Getting Somewhere

Think about this: Do you believe in *moral progress?* Do you believe that, over time and with some thought, we can revise our beliefs to improve them? Take slavery as an example. Do you think it's a moral improvement that Americans practiced slavery into the 1800s and then stopped? Most people would call that "moral progress": Through reason, public debate, and our ability to learn, we moved from slavery to anti-slavery beliefs (well, most of us did).

Ethically Speaking

If you believe in **moral progress**—that over time and with some thought we can revise and improve our moral beliefs— then you can't accept ethical subjectivism. Because if you are right about your beliefs and I'm right about mine, then there's no room for improvement, is there? No room for improvement means no moral progress.

If you'd like to hold on to that belief in moral improvement then you can't be an ethical subjectivist. Why? Because subjectivists hold that what *you* think is right and wrong *is* right and wrong. You can't be mistaken about your own moral beliefs; so there's no room for changing, improving, or correcting your beliefs. Sickos who believe that kicking cute, fluffy little puppies is morally acceptable have no motivation to revise that belief at all—after all, they can't make a moral mistake because right and wrong come down to what they believe is right and wrong. So if a puppy-kicking type thinks it's okay to do that ... well, there's no way to change his mind about it. Think about that for a minute or two.

Believing Isn't Knowing

Finally, ethical subjectivism makes the crucial mistake of collapsing the difference between believing something is true and something actually being true. To recap: If I believe something is true, then it's true for me. If you believe something different, then that's true for you. But ethical subjectivism leaves no room for the possibility that what you believe might be wrong. And this is pretty important for ethics: finding out you're wrong, fixing up your beliefs, and learning from the whole experience. So ethical subjectivism takes away a pretty fundamental part of doing ethics—making mistakes, learning from them, and moving on!

Maybe you're convinced that ethical subjectivism isn't for you ... maybe after thinking about this, you've decided that it has far too many flaws to be of ethical value. But tolerance—and being respectful of other people—is such a good thing! Maybe we could hold onto it at the cultural level and say that different cultures should respect one another and their different moral beliefs/practices. Wouldn't this be an improvement? That way we wouldn't have individuals running around, each being moral experts, and we could hold on to our notion of moral progress. Well, as you will see, cultural relativism suffers from many of the same problems as ethical subjectivism, just on a larger scale. Let's consider it now.

Cultural Relativism

So much for ethical subjectivism. But what about cultural relativism? Most people think tolerance is good; especially tolerance of different people from different cultures—"We're okay, they're okay." Why do you suppose we have that old saying "When in Rome, do as the Romans"? It's telling us that, when you visit another culture, you should be respectful and follow their beliefs and practices. For example, I visited Turkey once, and before I was allowed to enter a mosque, I had to wrap a piece of fabric around my shorts because bare legs are not allowed in their places of worship. It would have been disrespectful of me to object or complain about it, since it was their culture and I was their guest!

Cultural relativism takes a variety of forms, but we'll consider a simple one here. It's like ethical subjectivism taken to a higher level: instead of claiming that ethical beliefs are relative from individual to individual, it's the claim that ethical beliefs are relative from culture to culture. You might think by moving out to the larger scene, the problems with ethical subjectivism get solved. After all, now you're not saying that what each individual thinks is right is right: you're saying that whatever each culture thinks is right is right. Unfortunately, this doesn't solve the problems of subjectivism at all—the difficulties are just taken to a higher level.

Cultural relativists are concerned—with good justification—about giving absolute moral authority to moral claims. This is because throughout history human beings have used moral authority to interfere with different cultures and force beliefs on them. For example, when white people moved into the northern territories of Canada, they encountered Native Canadians with very different beliefs and practices. White people forced their ways on the Natives, and as a result Native culture has been largely stripped away. Native Canadians are still suffering the fallout of white people's domination.

> **Moral Musings**
>
> The famous sociologist William Graham Sumner (1840–1910) said, "In the folkways, whatever is, is right." He meant that whatever customs, beliefs, or traditions are at work in a culture are right, just because they belong to that culture.

And consider what might have happened if Hitler hadn't been stopped in his attempt to push his moral beliefs … if he'd had his way, all cultures would look like his Aryan ideal,

Ethically Speaking

Moral objectivism is the belief that morality is universal, eternal, and unchanging. For example, murder is always wrong, for all times and places. **Cultural relativism** (also called "moral relativism") is the belief that morality is relative to each individual culture, and that we can't make universal moral claims like "murder is always wrong."

and millions more people would have died. Let's face it, he managed to kill enough people before he was stopped! Cultural relativists point to such examples and say "See? See how awful *moral objectivism* is?"

So now we know what motivates cultural relativists: it's the reasonable concern that if we practice moral objectivism, we'll stomp all over other cultures. But cultural relativists have more to say in favor of their theory; consider the following claims they make:

♦ Different societies have different moral beliefs/practices, and we have no way of judging one culture's beliefs/practices to be better than another's. Where ethics is concerned, right and wrong are matters of opinion, and opinion differs from culture to culture. (This should look familiar if you recall the claim of ethical subjectivists!)

♦ You find huge cultural differences in views of right and wrong, so there is vast disagreement between cultures about moral values.

♦ Individuals should conform to the moral code of their society, and people visiting other cultures should conform to those moral codes, too.

Cultural relativists share the view with ethical subjectivists that there is no objective right and wrong in ethics; it comes down to what the culture thinks is right and wrong. If something is practiced in a culture, then it is right and cannot be criticized by outsiders. Well boy, does this raise some major issues! Consider some of these different cultural practices:

♦ In Northern Native cultures, the elderly are put out on ice floes and sent off to die.

♦ Some nonwestern cultures practice "female circumcision," which involves either cutting off a girl's clitoris or sewing her vulva shut, leaving only a small opening to urinate and maybe another for menstrual flow, so that she cannot experience sexual pleasure when she grows to adulthood.

♦ In Afghanistan, the Taliban (a fundamentalist Islamic group) have denied women education, forced them to wear burqas—wraps that cover their entire bodies and faces, leaving only a slit to see through—and have confined them at at home, out of the public eye.

Cultural relativists would say: These practices are no better or worse than North American practices—they are just different.

But is that true? In cultures where bride burning is acceptable (i.e. setting a woman on fire because her family can't give a big enough dowry for her), do we really want to say "we're okay, they're okay"? In North America, most of us think that women should have the same basic rights as men—but do we mean that only North American women have these same rights, or do we mean *all* women should have these rights? If we think that forming a family is a basic freedom that everyone should have, do we mean to exclude couples in China, who are only allowed to have one child each? Like we discussed previously, when people say that "burning women alive is morally wrong," they aren't just stating a personal or cultural opinion. It's a universal claim that they are making: No one should ever do it!

This raises another problem with cultural relativism: it leaves you powerless to say anything about ethics. The claim "X is wrong" reduces to the claim "in this culture, X is wrong," which isn't saying much of anything at all. In connection to this, cultural relativists are assuming that everybody in a culture agrees on the moral code of that society. But look at the United States—we don't have agreement on what is right or wrong, even *within* our country! Fundamentalist Christians, feminists, Ku Klux Klan members, and Mormons do not all agree on our moral code. So the claim "Americans believe X" could only mean something like "the majority of Americans believe X." This is a kind of "majority rules" viewpoint: that what the majority thinks is right must be right.

But should we accept the "majority rules" viewpoint? No we shouldn't, and here's why: the majority gets it wrong sometimes! Not that long ago, a majority of Americans supported segregationism—keeping blacks out of so-called "white" schools, restaurants, neighborhoods, pools, and so on. Just because a majority supported it doesn't mean it was right, does it? As Chapter 1, "So, What's Your Philosophy of Life?" pointed out, disagreeing with the majority has to be possible if moral change and improvement is going to happen.

Anyway, consider people from other cultures who disagree with their culture's practices. Should we really say to a woman who doesn't want her clitoris cut away "too bad, it's your cultural practice"? Most people don't think so; usually, we provide amnesty for people who are

Do the Right Thing!

If we say that standards of right and wrong extend no further than the standards upheld by any given culture, then how could abolitionists have argued against slavery in the Old South? According to antebellum Southern culture, blacks were inferior to whites, so much so that enslaving them seemed no worse than working draft animals.

Tried and True

Don't accept the "majority rules" approach to ethics: that what the majority thinks is right must be right. This cuts out the possibility of dissent and abandons individuals to their societies. Besides, sometimes the majority is wrong about things!

fleeing things like that! If we take cultural relativism, or "majority rules," seriously, then we'd have no grounds for supporting individuals who flee their governments.

Besides, we can make objective claims like "bride burning is wrong"; we do make such claims all the time. There *are* objective grounds for judging cultural practices. For example, what about this one? "An act is morally wrong if it causes physical or emotional harm to people." Hurting people is bad, and any cultural practice that does this is morally wrong.

Do the Right Thing!

We do know with objective certainty that some actions are morally wrong. All cultures agree, for instance, that murder is wrong. The problem, however, is that not all agree about which actions count as murder. Even within the United States, people disagree about whether a particular act of abortion is right or wrong. There might be an objectively right answer to this question; but how can anyone know it with enough certainty to convince everyone else?

Just because two cultures disagree about something doesn't mean that there is no truth of the matter. It could be that we just haven't discovered the truth yet; or it could be that one culture is right and the other is wrong. Different beliefs do not mean that there is no truth to be found. Cultures can just be wrong—hey, we were wrong about lots of things, like slavery, refusing women the right to vote, and segregationism!

Finally, let's consider the claim that there are huge differences between cultural practices which means that cultures vastly disagree about moral values. If you look closely, you'll see that there might actually be agreement about values, so that differences in practices are driven by non-value considerations, such as differences in cultural values and differences in factual beliefs.

"It's All Relative: Facts vs. Value Judgments"

Sometimes what look like totally opposing value judgments are just different interpretations of facts or different responses to the environment. Take the Northern Native practice of putting the elderly on ice floes. Here's how you might see the difference between our values and Native values:

◆ We respect our elderly and hold respect for life dear.

◆ Natives who put their elderly out to die show no respect for their elderly and have no respect for life.

But is this true? What if I told you that northern Native people respect their elderly just as much as we do—and maybe even more than we do, since they don't allow them to die lonely and undignified deaths in dismal institutions—and hold respect for life highly? Under different environmental conditions (freezing cold, scarcity of food, worries about contagious disease, inability to take care of everybody) people could express the same values in a different way. Native people respect life, and want to protect the lives of their children as much as possible. The Native elderly consider it a dignified way to die—that is, being altruistic so the younger generation can survive to old age, too. So what looks like a basic difference in values is really just different life circumstances dictating different interpretations of "respect for elders" and "respect for life"!

Sometimes, too, we're talking about different interpretations of the facts, and not a big difference in values. All cultures might agree that "equals should be treated as equals." But while the Taliban might agree about the fact that women are men's equals, they dispute that women should be treated in the same way as men. By wearing burqas and staying out of the public eye and not being allowed to go to school, for example, they think they are protecting women, not failing to respect them as equals.

There's an important lesson here, then: don't automatically assume that totally different cultural practices show a totally different system of values. We might have the same values and just have different ways of expressing them. The lesson is that cultures may not have such different values—that there is more commonalities between cultures than we initially thought.

All of this isn't to say that cultural relativism has nothing to recommend it. As I said at the beginning, there is much that is good in the theory. For example, tolerance of cultural differences is a good thing: we shouldn't try to change the way people in other cultures farm, worship, eat, speak, or dress. Throughout history we've tried changing other cultures, "modernizing" them, and sometimes to disastrous effect. We don't really want a boring world where everyone looks, acts, and thinks the same way.

Cultural relativism also recommends a dose of humility, which is a good thing for each and every one of us. We folks in North America can tend to get a pretty inflated view of ourselves, so theories like ethical subjectivism and cultural relativism that make us question ourselves can't be all that bad.

The problem is, if these theories were right then the book would just end here. Because what more could there possibly be to say about ethics once we all agree to just disagree? There have been some pretty persuasive moral absolutists, philosophers who claim that there is an objective, universal morality that we are all bound to follow. We'll hear more about these philosophers and their theories in Part 3, "General Recipes for Guiding Ethical Decision-Making." But next we'll consider a doctrine that really does spell the end of ethics: nihilism, the view that ethics is meaningless and, worse, a kind of sickness.

The Least You Need to Know

- Don't accept ethical subjectivism. Just because you believe something doesn't mean it's right!
- Be respectful of cultural differences, but be willing to criticize different cultural practices that do harm to people.
- Don't reduce different cultural practices to opposing moral values—it may just be a different expression of the same values.
- Avoid a "majority rules" approach to ethics: sometimes the majority is just plain wrong!

Chapter 8

Cynical About Ethics?

In This Chapter

- Is ethics just a sham to keep the poor and powerless—or rich and powerful—down?
- Is ethics bad for your health?
- Must moral prophets sometimes put themselves above ethics?
- When is it good to be a little cynical about ethics?

Not too long ago I got into an argument with my friend over whether to vote on Election Day. The argument went something like this: "Bill," I screamed, "I'm ashamed to hear that you're not going to vote! It's your duty as a citizen! Voting is the heart and soul of democracy, and democracy is the way we common folk tell our elected officials to do what's right for the whole country!"

Staring at me in utter amazement, Bill coolly replied: "Democracy is just a con-game. The rich and powerful control the mass media and buy off all the candidates. Whoever gets elected has to return the favor, so our laws favor the rich and powerful. And please don't talk to me about rights and the common good of the people. What you call the common good is really just the good of some special interest, and talk of rights is nothing but empty rhetoric: Rights are just so-many blank checks to be filled and cashed according to the partisan whims of judges and legislators."

Ouch! Boy, did that ever hurt! For all my pompous moral sermonizing all I got back in return was a cold blast of cynicism. Okay, maybe I overdid the screaming bit. And maybe, just maybe, Bill had a point. Sometimes there are reasons to be cynical about ethical norms and values, especially when people and institutions are falsely masquerading in them. Sometimes we need to look at ethics from the standpoint of a spectator looking from the outside in. And sometimes too much ethics—worrying about right and wrong, feeling guilty and shame about something we did—is unhealthy. But wholesale cynicism about ethics is hard to maintain without being dishonest with yourself and others. So the lesson here is: Be suspicious of existing norms and institutions, but always do it ethically!

Ripping Off the Masses

Okay, we've all had our cynical moments, right? Mine often come after Congress passes a new tax law or spending bill. (Let's see now. Who'd ever think there was any pork buried in a defense budget that authorized the payment of $50,000 per toilet seat to company X, and who'd dare suggest that the tax exemption for hairy elephant farms without hairy elephants is not in the national interest?) Come to think of it, all that stuff about psychological egoism and ethical relativism that you *should* have read by now (you did read it, right?) provides plenty of grist for the ol' cynicism mill. After all, if we can't help being selfish or narrowly biased in favor of our own group's values, interests, and beliefs, then we can't really be blamed for not living up to the ethical ideal of moral impartiality.

Ethically Speaking

Cynicism is an attitude of doubt directed against moral beliefs, practices, and institutions. Listening to self-appointed, self-righteous hypocrites who masquerade as moral gurus makes us become cynical. But cynicism isn't necessarily bad if you do something constructive with it. So just go ahead and channel that anger and disgust into a moral crusade in defense of honesty and truth!

The problem is, we pretend to live up to that ideal. We talk the game of ethics—you know, "the good of all," the "rights of humanity." So a certain dose of *cynicism* would seem entirely appropriate. For what is cynicism, really, but seeing through false pretense?

Now, you ask, when does that happen? Well, it happens when you stop taking what people say at face value. Normally, of course, we *do* take what people say at face value because we want—and often need—to trust them. (I mean, can you imagine a society without trust?)

Our trust is shaken, however, when words and actions don't quite match up. What we observe doesn't match what others tell us and even what we tell ourselves!

Going Cynical

Here's another way to think about it. Normally we're too busy playing life's little games to actually have the time to stand back and cast a critical eye on them. It's only when we see somebody getting wrongfully shafted by the law, or—bringing it closer to home—when we begin to wonder why we're losing so much and the other guy is winning so much that we start to examine it critically. We become, dare I say, amateur social scientists observing our own life from a more detached, spectator point of view—sort of like looking in from the outside!

When you shift perspective—from player to spectator—you begin to see things that you weren't aware of before. Maybe (like in a game of tennis) you notice that the linesman responsible for calling foul balls seems to be favoring your opponent! Or maybe, you notice for the first time how even the very rules of the game—which allow your opponent to serve while you receive—give your opponent a distinct advantage!

Tried and True _____

When you're playing the game of life, you seldom have any opportunity to step outside the game and question its ground rules. Hey, being a spectator can sometimes be more interesting than playing the game. The trick is being able to do both at the same time!

Looking In from Outside

Let's take another example. Suppose you attend a church. After a while, you begin to notice something strange. Preacher Bill is getting very rich off you and the other poor parishioners. You begin to question the sincerity of his preachings about the poor being blessed. One day, you stand up in church and challenge him. He says, "Don't seek your reward here on earth, but in heaven! Anyway, how dare you challenge God's justice! God has created a perfect world, and if it so happens that you are poor and I am rich, it is because God has willed it to be so!"

Bingo! Something goes off in your head. All that stuff about the poor receiving their reward in heaven and God's willing it to be so is hard to deny, given your church's teachings. Ah, but maybe your church is not the sole messenger of God's eternal truth, as preacher Bill claims it is. You begin to look around—outside the narrow confines of the church community—and you notice that there are other churches. Some of these churches seem to teach a different Gospel, about elevating the poor and doing justice here on earth. But other churches also have rich preachers and poor parishioners. Something smells fishy here. You begin to make deeper inquiries into these church's origins and find out an uncomfortable truth: Many of these churches were recently set up by the Mafia! Others have older links to shady politicians and businessmen going back generations!

Bam! You begin to think to yourself: Gee, these churches all claim to be the sole messenger of God's truth, but they all have shady origins that suggest otherwise. Hmmmm … and come to think of it, all of the things those preachers are saying sound awfully self-serving! Could all that stuff about the poor getting their just reward in the hereafter and

God's willing the rich to be rich and the poor to be poor just be a con-game that the preachers use to rip off the poor? And just to think! I used to take religion seriously!

Now don't get me wrong here. I'm not saying that religion—or at least most religions—are like this. I'm merely showing how true believers can be converted into cynical critics once they begin to scratch beneath the surface of empty rhetoric and see hypocrisy staring them in the face. Religion's an easy target, because we all know that there are lot's of fly-by-night charlatans out there ready to rip off the unwitting and naive. But what about ethics?

Marx's Critique of Moral Ideas

Well, one of the philosophers who warned us about being on the lookout for religious con-games like the one above also warned us about ethical con-games. His name was Karl Marx. Marx is often credited with being the founder of Marxism in the same way that Jesus is often credited with being the founder of Christianity: In both cases, the belief systems were really set up by other folks who borrowed from—often loosely—and added to, the so-called founder's teachings. People have done lots of bad things in the name of Marxism (like setting up totalitarian Communist governments) just as people have done lots of bad things in the name of Christianity (like persecuting Jews). So, just as you shouldn't blame Jesus for things that were done in his name, so you shouldn't blame Marx for things done in his name, either. In fact, Jesus and Marx were a lot alike in their concern for the poor, their dislike of greed and hypocrisy, and their suspicion of rigid and inflexible laws.

Moral Musings

Karl Marx's ideas had more in common with the teachings of Jesus than with the communist governments that were erected in his name. Some Catholic clergy in Central and South America have argued that Jesus was something of a social revolutionary who preached the virtues of simple communal equality and condemned the vices of wealth, status, and power. This wedding of Christianity and Marxism—sometimes referred to as Liberation Theology—was hotly debated among Christians and Marxists during the '70s and '80s. However, it's not so far-fetched—Jesus himself once said that it was easier for a camel to pass through the eye of a needle than for a rich man to enter the Kingdom of God!

Marx thought that ethics, like religion, was often used by the wealthy and powerful hypocritically to keep the hard-working poor in their place. True, Marx respected the ideas of liberation, community, equality, and justice he found in the Bible—he had to, because they were the very ideas that inspired his own quest for a perfect ethical community. But he also warned that these ideas could, and generally were, manipulated by the ruling classes in order to *deny* liberation, community, equality, and justice.

Community as Empty Slogan

How so? Well, take the idea of community. Our leaders and preachers talk a good game of community. We are all a part of this wonderful community, rich and poor alike. But, for Marx, the rich and poor are really at war. Looking at our own capitalist society, he observed that the wages paid to the workers come out of the owners' profits. So higher profits mean lower wages and higher wages mean lower profits. Bingo! You got class warfare, not community. And to talk as if there were community under these conditions is to deceive yourself into thinking that loyalty to "the nation" or to "the company" is more important than loyalty to those with whom you earn your daily bread and butter.

Equality as Empty Slogan

Again, take equality. Our leaders all talk about how we are all "equal before the law" and possess "equal rights." Well, in some sense that's right. The rich as well as the poor are equally forbidden to beg in the streets and sleep on park benches at night. And we all—rich and poor alike—have an equal right to have health insurance. And we all have an equal right to contribute virtually endless amounts of money to our favorite political causes.

But then again, Marx says, what's a right mean to me if I don't have the resources (education, wealth, health, etc.) to exercise it? The freedom that comes with enjoying a right depends on the capacity and opportunity for exercising it. Having an equal permission (right) to do X or being equally prohibited from doing X (not having a right to X) says nothing about having that capacity. So if there's no job, welfare check, or charity for me, I am not free to refrain from begging. If my income won't allow me to buy health insurance, then I'm not free to do so, and my so-called equal right is a sham.

Tried and True

Our leaders tell us that we have equal rights, and in one sense that's true. But then again, Marx reminds us that a right doesn't mean very much to persons who don't have the capacities or opportunities for exercising it. So let's take a tip from Marx and strive to make our society one in which each person has as much equal opportunity to exercise his or her rights as anyone else.

Imaginary Freedom, Imaginary Equality

Then there's freedom. Ah, sweet freedom! We talk about how we live in a free nation. No one forces us to do anything we don't want to do. Hey, every contract we enter into is of our own free will, right? Well, not exactly. A bunch of workers who are given the choice of accepting pay and benefit cuts or seeing their jobs go south of the border are being extorted by the company (or so Marx would say). The company is unaffected one way or the other—it will get its lower wage and benefit bill no matter what the workers say. Its hands are not tied, it's free to move or stay. The workers don't have this sort of freedom, because the option of losing their jobs and not working is not a real option. Come to think of it, loss of income and benefits almost always means a loss of freedom, because now you're dependent on the government, charitable institutions, or some loaning institution for your existence.

Justice as Empty Slogan

Last but not least, there's justice. Everybody gets just what they work for, right? Well, Marx says, think again. Jimmy inherits five mil, Joey inherits zilch. Is that fair? Jimmy buys an ax and some wood for a buck, hires Joey for two bucks, flies off to Monte Carlo for a playboy fling, and makes six bucks off the wood Joey cuts. Hey, is that fair? I mean, who's done all the work around here anyway?

I think you get the picture: From Marx's perspective, ethical values and norms are just so much smoke and mirrors designed to keep the masses enthralled to the great powers that be. The working poor come to accept the justice of their own exploitation, just like they accept their imaginary freedom and equality with the rich. No wonder Marx was so cynical about ethics! In his opinion, the only way to penetrate this charade of brotherly love is to question our ethical ideas: stop taking them for granted as if they were timeless truths for everyone and start looking to see who benefits from them and who doesn't. Once we got that figured out, we can begin to transform our society into a truly just community, composed of people who are truly free and equal.

Hey, wait a minute! Isn't Marx contradicting himself here? I mean, one moment he's dissing ethics, another moment he's sounding, well, awfully ethical—especially with all this hype about equality, freedom, community, and individuality.

Truth is, Marx may have been cynical about how far our social institutions really live up to their ethical

> ### Moral Musings
>
> "The communists do not preach morality at all ... They do not put to people the moral demand: love one another, do not be egoists, etc; on the contrary, they are very well aware that egoism, just as much as self-sacrifice, is in definite circumstances a necessary form of the self-assertion of individuals.
>
> —Karl Marx, *The German Ideology*

billing, but he never really abandoned ethical ideals. In fact, he felt confident that history would prove him right in the end. Workers all over the world would unite, throw off the chains of class domination and economic exploitation, and set up a perfectly harmonious community in which everyone would grow up to be a complete and caring person. Not only the state (law and order) but even norms of right and wrong would gradually disappear, because everyone would have what they needed!

No more fighting, just an orgy of good fellowship. Wow, sounds great! When do we begin?

Sick to Death of Ethics

Now that's just one point of view. People like Ayn Rand (you remember her from Chapter 6, "'Me First' Ethics," right?) would be suspicious of religion and ethics for just the opposite reason. In the opinion of these critics, religion and ethics are con-games that oppress—guess who?—the rich and the powerful! And why the rich and powerful, you ask? Well, those who are rich and powerful got to be rich and powerful for a reason. According to Rand, they got that way by excelling in strength, intelligence, inventiveness, ambition, and industriousness. But ethics and religion don't extol these virtues. Uh-uh. They teach us to be meek and humble and self-sacrificing for the sake of God, country, and humanity.

Preaching a Gospel of equality and brotherly/sisterly love may make for peaceful co-existence, but—say critics like Rand—it goes against what makes human beings individuals rather than herd animals. And what makes us individuals is our desire to excel and stand out from the crowd. Competitiveness and domination, not cooperation and equal respect, is the true mark of human distinction. Religion and ethics aim to limit—nay, punish—this noble striving for excellence by requiring that the talented few give up their power and wealth and limit their creativity for the sake of kow-towing to the herdish laziness, stupidity, and conformity of the lowly masses. And the masses? Because they are naturally envious of the achievers, they'll do anything they can to drag them down to their own level of mediocrity.

Friedrich Nietzsche's Affirmative Nihilism

Maybe the most extreme defender of this sort of anti-ethics was Friedrich Nietzsche (pronounced *neechah*). Nietzsche opposed familiar ethical ideals, but like Jesus and Marx before him, he reserved much of his anger for ethical hypocrisy. In fact, Nietzsche's philosophy is a good place to test my theory that every philosopher—no matter how morally repugnant his or her philosophy might be—has something worthwhile to say. So, you ask, what *did* Nietzsche have to say that is worthwhile?

Freedom's Not All What It's Cracked Up to Be

Well, for one thing, Nietzsche like Marx pointed out how much hypocrisy there is in all our ethical boasting. For instance, as we noted in Chapter 5, "Let Science Be Your Guide," we think that freedom of choice is a great moral thing, because it enables us to hold people responsible for what they do. Yet Nietzsche points out the dark side of this idea. Holding people responsible for what they do, we blame them for what they don't (but should) do. But blame leads to punishment, which, when you get down to it, is mainly motivated by a desire for vengeance—a most ignoble aim if there ever was one!

So for Nietzsche our ethical ideas, like freedom and responsibility, are really—to put it somewhat ironically—not all that ethical! In theory they sound good, but in practice they feed our more vicious instincts for cruelty. And they ignore the truly tragic fact that much of what we think is done freely is not done freely. According to Nietzsche, people who behave nicely were trained to behave that way. Because they were lucky enough to be raised in a loving and supportive environment, they developed a moral conscience. Not so the unfortunate psychopath! But why blame the psychopath for being born into bad circumstances? It just doesn't make sense!

Ethics as Sickness

Now for the real kicker. While unmasking the darker motives underlying our ethical beliefs, Nietzsche noticed something else important: ethics can lead to a serious sickness of the soul! Ethics demands that we sacrifice our instinctual needs for the sake of living together peaceably. You've heard of Sigmund Freud, haven't you? Freud—who was very much taken with Nietzsche's ideas—said that we have to sacrifice sexual and other forms of pleasure for the sake of work and, most important, for the sake of living an ethical life. By denying the free and full expression of our natural instincts, we end up making ourselves psychologically and even physically sick.

Ethical Self-Annihilation

Nietzsche had a special word for this form of ethical self-denial: *nihilism*. Today, ethicists use "nihilism" (which comes from the Latin word *nihil*, or *nothing*) in a somewhat different sense to refer to Nietzsche's own view that ethical codes as such are bad because they deny life itself—or at least, what is most vital about life. For Nietzsche, the instinctual striving to excel beyond conventional ethical limits is what is most vital to human life. This "will to power," as Nietzsche dubbed it, is not really a will to dominate others, but a will to create new ideas and values that challenge old ideas and values.

Ethically Speaking

Nihilism is the term coined by Nietzsche to express the way in which ethical norms deny what is most vital about human life—the will to power. Some contemporary philosophers (notably Ayn Rand, whom we discussed in Chapter 6) develop a variation of Nietzsche's critique of ethical nihilism. They argue that moral altruism demands self-sacrifice and feeds a kind of resentment against those who stand out from the crowd. The end result of this concern for moral equality is a suppression of those possessing superior genius.

Of Sheep and Supermen

Unfortunately, the vast majority of average folk don't like to upset the ol' apple cart, as the saying goes. Most of us prefer the secure comfort of familiar routines to the exciting risk of new experiments. In Nietzsche's opinion, this just gets it all backward. Life is risky, so why not embrace the danger of something new and different? Instead of worshipping ethical norms that stifle creative genius, we should be worshipping the creative genius that, well, creates ethical norms!

You heard me right—it's bold scientists and artsy-fartsy types who should be leading the way, not stale preachy types. That's not to say that some of those preachy types weren't creative geniuses. Even Nietzsche admitted that no less an ethicist than Jesus himself was a creative genius. According to Nietzsche, Jesus took the old Jewish law and qualitatively transformed it into a new set of values.

This raises a very interesting question: Are the ethical revolutionaries (those who create new ethical values) above ethics? Think for a moment about what we said about God in Chapter 4, "God Made Me Do It." If God creates ethical standards, then they do not exist as a prior limit on His creativity. On the contrary, it's God who limits and defines these standards. Now, let's assume for the sake of argument that God doesn't exist (for Nietzsche, God is as good as "dead"!) In other words, let's assume that ethical revolutionaries are the ones who really create ethical standards. Wouldn't these mavericks be as unconstrained by the ethical standards they create as God would be by the standards He creates?

Nietzsche thought so. Being unconstrained by their own creations, ethical revolutionaries would be "above" ethics—not only the old ethics that they discard but the new ethics that they themselves create! In short, they would be (in his words) "supermen" living "beyond good and evil."

Let's see now, if the value creators are above the ethics they create for us, the followers, then it seems like we have a two-level theory of ethics. In other words, one kind of conduct would be appropriate for the value creators and another kind would be appropriate for us. Value creators would be free to violate the ethical standards they create for us in their pursuit of excellence. We followers, by contrast, would not be free to violate these standards.

An Ounce of Cynicism Is Worth a Pound of Nihilism

Take the idea of value creation. Maybe Nietzsche's point in talking about value creators is to get us average folk to accept full responsibility for our own value judgments. As we've seen over and over again, the temptation to hand over responsibility for judging right and wrong to so-called authorities—be they scientists, clergy, political dictators, or philosophers—is very great. We need to affirm our own freedom and responsibility to judge and, if need be, reinvent (or reinterpret) ethical values according to our own lights.

Furthermore, if refusing to accept any ethical authority outside of one's own moral conscience is nihilistic, then at least it is nihilistic in a positive, life-affirming sense. Anyway, we're not talking about inventing the ethical wheel all over again. Even Nietzsche admitted that it's impossible for us to be Gods, as if we could just create values out of sheer nothing. No, we're talking about taking full responsibility for our critical—and at times creative—use and interpretation of values already in circulation.

So it seems that we can't live without some ethical values after all! Absolute nihilism—or the attempt to live outside of a community of shared values—is virtually impossible for us to imagine. As we said in Chapter 2, "The Inevitability of Ethical Dilemmas," values are what give our life meaning and purpose. Oh, sure, we could imagine some lonely superman heroically eking out an existence devoid of any meaning and purpose beyond his empty act of creation. But what good is there in that sort of life?

And cynicism? Ditto! It's virtually impossible for us to imagine what it would be like to live outside of a community of trust. We can't live our lives constantly suspecting every ethical norm or institution. We can't live our ethical lives as full-time spectators and critics, constantly looking for the least shred of hypocrisy, insincerity, and inauthenticity on which to impale our norms. Nor can we hold up every aspect of our ethical identity to microscopic analysis, as if that identity were somehow detachable from us. No we can't. Because we live our lives as participants in a game whose rules

CAUTION

Do the Right Thing!

Questioning the moral status quo is the very heart of a mature philosophically enlightened ethics. But radical questioning has its limits, too. Why? Because questioning doesn't happen in a vacuum. When you question something, you always do so from a point of view that is itself unquestioned. So be humble about the limits of your own radical questioning!

demand mutual trust and respect, we can scarcely imagine anyone radically questioning all such rules—unless, of course, that person were a hermit!

The Least You Need to Know

- Learn to question authority and unmask hypocrisy.
- Appreciate the fact that actions are shaped by both circumstances and choices.
- Accept responsibility for your values.
- Ethical sacrifices are sometimes unavoidable; but a life of self-sacrifice is unhealthy and contrary to human excellence.

Part  General Recipes for Guiding Ethical Decision-Making

Are you ready for some fun? So far, we've sort of circled the wagons. We've talked about the generalities of ethics. Now we're going to get down to brass tacks. We're going to look at some very specific recipes for solving moral problems—finally something you can use!

But which recipe? Ah, that's the beauty of it. There's so many to choose from! Just pick 'em: virtues and vices; divine commands; contracts for mutual benefit; absolute duties and rights of reason; consequences for increasing overall happiness; caring relationships—you name it. In this part, we'll look at the strengths and weaknesses of each one of these recipes, using real-life situations to illustrate our discussion. Then we'll throw them together into one big casserole. Along the way, we'll learn about some heavy-weight philosophers, like Aristotle, St. Thomas Aquinas, Thomas Hobbes, Immanuel Kant, and John Stuart Mill.

9

Ancient Greek Virtue Ethics

In This Chapter

- ◆ What are virtues and vices and why do they matter?
- ◆ Virtuous living and its relationship to true happiness
- ◆ The importance of developing a strong character
- ◆ When moderation counts
- ◆ Are there different virtues for different sorts of people?

Hey, did you ever wonder why there are vice squads? You know, those teams of police officers who bust people for prostitution, drugs, and kiddie porn? If you think about it, a lot of the stuff that gets counted as "vice" doesn't really hurt anybody. Take prostitution. Sure, the women and men involved in it might be exploited by their pimps and exposed to dangerous situations. But there are lots of other jobs where workers get exploited and hurt even worse, so there's got to be another reason. Maybe it has to do with the immorality of extra-marital sex: but extra-marital sex isn't punished by law. So what is it that makes prostitution a vice, and one that is outlawed in most states in the United States?

I think I know the answer. Many citizens feel that prostitution eats away at the "moral fiber of society." Maybe it's the combination of selling your body (which reminds us of slavery), tempting others into infidelity (which undermines basic trust and commitment), and—last but not least—degrading your very person (which the "john" also degrades while degrading himself).

We recognize vice. It's all around us. But what is it exactly and, just as importantly, what is its opposite, virtue? In this chapter, we're going to explore what makes a virtue a virtue and what makes a vice a vice. I won't be giving away the story by telling you right now that virtues and vices are an important part of ethical life. They are what link ethical life to other important values, like happiness and strength of character. Ah, sweet happiness! If only we knew what it is! Well, hold on, because you're going to find out.

The Virtue of Vice Squads

Back to our prostitute. You'll recall that she isn't necessarily doing any harm to anybody—just trying to earn a living like the rest of us. No wonder she's legit in many countries. After all, the prostitute isn't necessarily violating any big moral rules like, "don't kill," "don't steal," and "don't lie." But there's something ethically fishy going on here, because even in places that legalize prostitution it's commonly thought to be a vice.

I've suggested that it has something to do with undermining the moral fabric of society.

Now, there are lots of ways to undermine the moral fabric of society, like tempting people into infidelity. People who are unfaithful to their spouses and lovers might make it a habit in their dealings with others. And infidelity encourages other vices, not the least of which is dishonesty. Okay, I guess a world of dishonest and disloyal jerks wouldn't be as bad as a world of thieves and murderers, but it would be pretty bad nonetheless. Ditto the degradation of the prostitute. If you're willing to lower yourself into doing … that … well then, who knows how far you might go? Today's down-and-dirty prostitute is tomorrow's child abuser—or worse.

So, to sum up it all up: what's bad about prostitution is not the bare act of sex for sale, which in and of itself might not harm anyone. What's bad about it is that it corrupts moral character. And a corrupt moral character is bad, because people who have it can't be trusted. But then it's just a short hop, skip, and jump from being a lousy character (morally speaking) to being a vicious criminal. And voilà! Society goes to hell in a handbasket.

Virtues and vices. We're talking moral character here, folks, not moral rules. You can have a perfect society with perfect moral rules and all the high-powered surveillance equipment money can buy. But if people are rotten at the core, no amount of rule-enforcing is really going to save society. Uh-uh. No way, José!

Tried and True

We all know that we're judged by the company we keep. Well, it makes sense. We can pick up nasty habits by hanging around the wrong sort of people. So the lesson here is: Be sure to keep company with good people.

Now, where were we? Ah, yes—vices. Let's just take a gander at some of them:

- selfishness
- cowardice
- mean-spiritedness
- thoughtlessness

- rudeness
- malevolence
- dishonesty
- infidelity

You Are Your Character

The first thing to notice about these vices is that they are character traits. A character trait is not your occasional behavior that can be turned on or off. No, it's an ingrained part of your identity that habitually—indeed, almost mechanically—influences almost everything you do. The second thing to notice is that having any one bad character trait doesn't make you a criminal or a rule breaker. You could, I suppose, be a mean-spirited but law-abiding, trustworthy (perhaps even polite!) citizen. Still, you'd be a bad kind of guy for all that. You'd take glee in watching poor homeless folks shivering on cold winter nights. And you'd be a bad person. Enough characters like that and society would be unbearable. I'd head straight for the hills and become a hermit.

Moral Musings

Your character traits are so deeply embedded in your personality that you can't really control their expression. That's not surprising. After all, what you are is a product of many years of training, experience, and, yes, habit formation. Although we can control some of our habits (we can retrain ourselves by consciously relearning new routines), we can't control all of them. Why not, you ask? Because even the simplest action, like raising your arm, involves countless reflexes and habits that we're not even aware of—and can't be aware of, otherwise nothing would come natural to us, not even raising an arm!

Same thing applies to virtues. Check these out:

- generosity
- courage
- kindness
- thoughtfulness

- politeness
- benevolence (doing good for others)
- honesty
- loyalty

The Virtue of Virtues

Again notice that these virtues—all mirror opposites of the vices I listed above—are character traits just like vices, except they're good traits. The more virtuous you are in terms of generosity, the less vicious you are in terms of selfishness; and the more selfish you are, the less generous you are as well. And notice that having them says nothing about whether you're law-abiding or stick to moral rules. Robin Hood was generous to a fault! Still, it's safe to say that the more people who possess one or more of these virtues, the better the society. And if they happen to be honest to a fault, they'll never think of stealing!

It's Good to Be Good

Good people—people who are virtuous—aren't necessarily good rule followers, although they're likely to be so. No, their goodness consists in their characteristic (shall we say habitual?) tendency to do good things that are not required by law. No one says you have to be nice or generous. Fact is, you can be perfectly selfish and mean and still not violate anyone's basic rights. Heck, you can follow the Ten Commandments and still be a mean son-of-a-gun.

All of which gets back to the $60,000 question: Why be virtuous? Glad you asked, because it gives me an opportunity to talk about Ancient Greek ethics, which shares twin billing in this chapter. The great old heavyweights—Socrates, Plato, and Aristotle—and all of their followers agreed that a life without *virtue* was an unhappy life. But what, then, is happiness?

Amazingly, almost all the Greeks agreed on the basic distinction between pleasure and happiness. Pleasures and pains, they noted, are fleeting states of mind, referring mainly to sensations and feelings. Happiness, by contrast, is a more enduring state of fulfillment and well-being. According to Aristotle, it's the be-all and end-all of life itself! If you don't believe me, just ask yourself why you do anything that you do. Why is money, health, family, friends, God, or virtue itself desired by you? Because they're good for you. And why are they good for you? Because they make you happy by some measure of material or spiritual fulfillment.

Ethically Speaking

A **character trait** is a deeply engrained feature of a person's personality. Here are some excellent character traits to have: honesty, generosity, integrity, kindness, and courage.

Okay, granted that we're all pursuing the big state of bliss at the end of the rainbow. In fact, Aristotle says that happiness only comes at the end of a life well lived, when you can say to yourself, "Gee, I had it all!" Not until you've reached the end of your life can you say for sure that it's been a good one. After all, some calamity or misfortune might strike you. Or you might become a different person. You begin to indulge your vices and suddenly you're untrustworthy and nobody likes you anymore.

Okay, I can see how illness, financial ruin, and family tragedy can forever wreck a person's life. But why would we ever think that vice is always bad for us? I mean, why can't master criminals who never get caught be happy? They have wealth. They have power. What don't they have?

> ### Moral Musings
>
> Unlike momentary feelings of pleasure, happiness is a state of overall spiritual well-being and fulfillment. As such it's the ultimate end underlying all of our strivings. According to Aristotle, it can only come at the end of a life well-lived in accordance with virtue.

A Life of Vice

Well, to begin with, they don't have friends they can trust. Master criminals who surround themselves with lackeys and henchman who are a lot like themselves have a lot to worry about. And lots of worry makes for lots of unhappiness. Lacking essential non-criminal virtues, like honesty—I mean, have you ever heard of an honest criminal?—our master criminal and his gang of thugs will have a hard time trusting each other. And bad company is as bad company does.

Ah, maybe you're thinking that the only thing this example shows is that vices are bad, not that virtues are good. Well, you're wrong. You see, as I mentioned above, for every virtue there's a corresponding vice. That means, the only way to get rid of vice—and get happy—is by becoming virtuous. If dishonesty is what's corroding your relationships and making you unhappy, then what you need to do is become honest.

Okay, so being virtuous is sometimes painful. But the person who dies a painful death for the sake of being good (think of Jesus) isn't necessarily unhappy, or unfulfilled. Because remember, happiness is a state of spiritual contentment, not a momentary feeling of pleasure. Heroes and heroines die with the inner satisfaction that they've been true to themselves and others (and to God). They've achieved moral excellence, and that's what really counts.

Virtue and the Good Life

What I'm driving at here is the idea that virtues—good character traits—are good for the soul, or make for the soul's happiness—because they are directly linked to things that are, well, good for us! What's good for us? Friends are good for us. And how do you get friends? By being—you guessed it—friendly (and kind, polite, and so on and so forth). Again, being honored and loved is good for us. And we gain honor and love through being honorable and loving.

In short, virtues are universally recognized by almost all societies as human excellences. And the goods that they bring us are the most important of all, because they give our lives meaning and purpose. We pursue excellence and virtue for their own sake, not simply because they're a way to achieve money, power, and fame. Virtue and excellence are a necessary part of the good life. Sure, you need a little health and wealth to achieve excellence, but the excellence of a virtuous character is worth much more than money, fame, and power.

Hey, even a staunch opponent of moral rules like Nietzsche (whose nihilistic anti-ethic we discussed in Chapter 8, "Cynical About Ethics?") admitted that human excellence and virtue is something worth striving for! Being virtuous has its rewards. I mean, I could think of worse things than being loved and admired for being a superior human being!

Tried and True

Virtues are the most important goods of all. A life without virtue is a life devoid of character and constancy of purpose. We're not talking flaky, we're talking corrupt, degenerate, vicious, psychopathic, or just plain evil!

Please Don't Kill Me with Kindness

Let's assume that being a good person is really where it's at. Now, I said that goodness (or virtue) is a matter of character. What I mean is just this: When we talk about a person's character we mean something that is constant and predictable about that person's behavior. Character is not something that we can just turn on or off by simply choosing to do so. It's so much a part of who we are—our very identity—that we could act out of character about as easily as acting out of our skin.

Character in Training

And here's why. Character is something that's formed by years of training. But it's not something that we deliberately choose to have and then methodically practice. No, it's something that comes to us as a gift from others. It begins to take shape in us when we're kids. As kids we more or less automatically—without even thinking about it—copy the behavior of our parents and other people we look up to as role models. If the role models whose behavior we're mimicking are virtuous types, then we'll grow up to be virtuous as well. If not, well then, we'll turn out to be rotten apples. It's as simple as that! (We all know how hard it is to reform a bad character.)

And notice, too, that we're not just shaping our behavior when we learn by imitating our elders. We're also shaping our wants, or the things we desire to do. That's very important, because what's the point of ethical conduct, if you don't *want* to do it? So, character is like an anchor that shapes your wants as well as your conduct, and that's why it's so important for ethics. Because if you don't want to be ethical, then you'll succumb to the temptation to do wrong.

Weakness of the will (weakness of character) is just another way of saying that you lack *moral integrity*. Integrity means constancy, but it also means harmony. A person whose character is stamped by moral integrity has a harmonious set of good wants and good habits. Persons who lack integrity are constantly fighting with themselves, wanting one thing but doing another, often simply out of habit.

So are we just a product of our childhood training? Not entirely. We can become aware of our bad tendencies and try to reprogram our behavior. But what should we be aiming for when we do it?

> **Ethically Speaking**
>
> **Integrity** is a virtuous character trait that is closely connected to reliability, trustworthiness, honesty, and having principles. A person who has moral integrity can be counted on to behave in a way that is constant and harmonious. Persons who lack integrity are fickle because their wants and habits are constantly at war with one another.

Staying Balanced

Aristotle thought he had an answer. He said that we have to have the right balance of virtue—the *Golden Mean*. Right balance of virtue, you ask? Aren't we supposed to have all the virtue we can get?

Well, yes. But the way you get the biggest bang for your buck—the most overall virtue—is to know when enough is enough! Sound crazy? Then consider Jane. Jane is virtuous. Jane's stellar virtue is caring for others. In fact, she's so caring that she ends up neglecting her own needs. Worse, she's so afraid of hurting anyone's feelings that she never interrupts them when they do bad things to her—like physically abuse her!

Now, wouldn't you say that Jane has carried the caring routine a bit too far? Then there's Jim. His particular excellence is tolerance. Unfortunately, he goes overboard tolerating jerks who are intolerant—neo-Nazi's and hate-mongers who prey on minorities. Jill, on the other hand, is generous—to a fault. She gives up all her family's wealth to a charity, leaving them with zilch.

As the old saying goes, you really can kill someone with kindness! (At least that's what I tell my mom when she's trying to push another serving of her homemade lasagna on me.) Your virtues can become your vices. So the lesson here is: Act in moderation. In order to really lead a virtuous life, don't go overboard with any one virtue!

Do the Right Thing!

Parents beware! As the old saying goes, you really can kill your children with kindness. Being too protective of your children can prevent them from taking reasonable risks and growing up to be adults (you know, folks who use their freedom responsibly in order to take risks). Excessively pandering to their interests can spoil them rotten and turn them into selfish brats. So remember, your virtues can become vices; always act in moderation; but when it comes to *loving* your children, forget about moderation and pour it on!

So, once again, what is moderation? In case you still didn't get it, I'll leave you with this nifty example—taken straight from the horse's mouth! The wise Aristotle observed that if you happen to be a foot soldier, too much courage can make you reckless to the point of endangering your fellow soldiers. Too little courage—fear and hesitancy—can make you do the same. So, I guess Aristotle is telling us that there's just one right standard of moderation that we should all be shooting for, right?

Different Strokes for Different Folks

Wrong! One of Aristotle's brilliant strokes was to see that different sorts of undertakings call for different standards of virtue. Suppose you're part of a line of infantry marching up a hill. This situation calls for cold courage. You can't recklessly charge ahead, because breaking ranks weakens the entire line, making everyone vulnerable.

But suppose instead that you're a part of a special suicide mission. You've volunteered to run up the hill all by yourself as a diversionary tactic so that your comrades can sneak around the back side of the enemy. Here, courage really does call for behaving with reckless abandon.

Tried and True

The proper exercise of virtue is not the sort of thing that can be learned from reading a "How to Be Virtuous" manual. There isn't a simple recipe that anyone can consult for guidance in life, because life is full of surprises, and unique situations call for unique responses. For instance, being an honest person doesn't mean that you always have to tell the truth. If a bad guy wants to know where innocent sweet Sally is, you'd lie, right? Would that little act of discretion make you a dishonest person? No, but it just might make you a hero.

So the exercise of courage according to the proper mean doesn't always mean acting somewhere between fearful hesitancy and recklessness. In one kind of situation, a little fearful hesitancy can be just the ticket to keeping ranks together; while in another, it would be totally inappropriate. So the proper mean for exercising courage varies from situation to situation.

Again, some situations call for more of one kind of virtue than another. Military combat always calls for a high level of courage. Nursing, by contrast, calls for lots of kindness and caring. A military that cared too much for the enemy's feelings would be a bad military, just as a hospital that encouraged bold maneuvers that ignored hospital procedures would be a bad hospital.

Exercising virtue is a lot more like performing a balancing act artfully—you know, instinctively and intuitively—than rigidly obeying a command (like "never lie!") or a set of rules. But don't get me wrong here. Love may be blind, but not virtue. It does require a kind of practical reasoning, or wisdom—the ability to size up a situation quickly and measure one's response accordingly.

Virtue and Evil

Before concluding this chapter, I'm going to make things perversely interesting by throwing you a few curves. You'll recall that virtues are what define moral strength of character. Now—for the million dollar question—Can evil people, or at any rate people who are committing immoral acts, be virtuous? Take our Robin Hood, the guy who steals from average innocent folk simply in order to help poor, homeless people. He breaks a moral rule against stealing because he cares too much for the poor. Granted, he's not acting moderately. He's not being as completely virtuous as he could be. But is he being virtuous at all? Could you describe his stealing as morally wrong, but ethically caring?

Or take the white Southern slave owner who braves all sorts of dangers in hunting down fugitive slaves—mainly women and their children. Could we say that he was acting courageously? To make the question more interesting, suppose he braves the same dangers (poisonous snakes, crocodiles, and quicksand) as the fearless woman from the Underground Railroad who's helping these run-away slaves escape their masters. We wouldn't hesitate to say that she was acting courageously, would we? But would we say the same about the slave owner?

You can see the problem. Doing nasty things like running down women and children escaping from slavery is definitely unethical, but doing it courageously is doing it well, in a way that expresses ethical virtue. So, what do you think? Is the slave owner ethical? Is he even courageous? If courage is exercised through an evil act, is it a vice?

These are all disturbing questions, because they suggest that any virtue can become a vice when in the service of evil. Even more disturbing, they suggest that a person who excels in all the virtues—a truly virtuous person—can still commit horrible crimes out of sheer ignorance of what they're doing. Sound implausible? Well, just remember that some "good" ordinary people like you and me were once brainwashed by Nazi propaganda into thinking that Jews were out to destroy humanity.

What this shows is that something more besides ethical virtue is needed in order to live a morally upright life. Other virtues—of a more intellectual nature—must also be cultivated. To be more exact, you can't be fully ethical unless you're willing to question authority and think critically about what other people tell you. So parents, the next time your kids question your authority, just smile and pat them on the back!

We've seen that the most important aim underlying all other aims is happiness, or complete spiritual fulfillment. We know that living a life of virtue is important (indeed, necessary) to achieving this. But what, really, is happiness, and is it the same for everyone?

Take Jimmy, for instance. His parents are both professors and he's had ample opportunity to develop his brains. But he's also fallen in love with mud wrestling, which has been a long-standing obsession with him. And he's good at it. His parents, however, disapprove, telling him that the highest form of satisfaction in life comes from using his brains, not his brawn. And anyway, what kind of life is that, slinging mud out in the trenches with a bunch of over-sized men wearing thongs? Shouldn't Jimmy give it up and start hitting the books?

Our earlier discussion of how virtue is relative to circumstances should key us into the right answer. Clearly, what makes a soldier happy is not what makes a nurse happy. What makes Jimmy's intellectual parents happy may not be what makes Jimmy happy.

In fact, Aristotle recognized that we're all uniquely different from one another in capacities and circumstances, so that the proper model of happiness for one person won't necessarily fit another person.

The Least You Need to Know

- Being virtuous is a large part of living ethically.
- It's important that children model the virtuous behavior of their elders.
- Living virtuously is necessary for attaining true fulfillment in life.
- Exercise virtue wisely—remember the Golden Mean!
- Remember that what makes for true fulfillment differs from person to person!

Chapter

10

Middle Age Virtues

In This Chapter

- ◆ Nature as a moral order
- ◆ A Christian view of natural morality
- ◆ How to tell unnatural from natural acts
- ◆ When nature's command is higher than the law of the land

Talk about your weird habits. Lenny likes his dog Joey. So much so that he copies everything Joey does, more or less exactly. He gets down on all fours whenever he eats his meals from a bowl on the floor—mostly kibble with a few liver treats thrown in. He likes to chew on furniture and sticks as well. And talk about your licking! Whenever Joey licks him, Lenny returns the favor. Then there are some nasty habits we won't get into (like the yummy treats that Joey finds in the alley behind the garage). But Lenny is private about all this. He likes to do his Joey routine while watching *I Love Lucy* re-runs on TV! Outside his house he's a successful, if somewhat barkative, CEO for a major firm that makes dog houses.

Well, I don't know about you, but I find Lenny's behavior a little perverse. Why, you ask? Well, it's just not natural. I mean, it's okay for Joey to act like a dog because, well, he's a dog. But it's just not right for a human being! Lenny has a legal right to his perversions—after all, it's all done in the privacy of his own home. But that still doesn't make it morally right. I mean, isn't it degrading to act that way?

We all draw the line somewhere when it comes to behavior that we find excessively unnatural and degrading. Some of you think that homosexuality is wrong for this reason. If you do, you might also find masturbation and oral sex immoral. Sex, of course, is a lightening rod for our feelings about what's natural and unnatural, so our discussion of nature and morality will frequently return to this, er, touchy topic. We'll see that nature's determining what's right and wrong is an idea that fits well with Aristotle's virtue ethics (which I talked about in Chapter 9, "Ancient Greek Virtue Ethics"). And although we'll discuss some of the difficulties in knowing what's natural and unnatural, we'll see that the idea of human nature plays an important role in justifying basic rights that are universally valid for all human society.

Nature as a Moral Order

Okay, let's begin with nature. Everyone agrees that nature is orderly. Natural events happen in a way that's pretty predictable—regular and normal. The laws of physics tell us that certain sorts of things can be expected to happen with perfect certainty. I drop a ball from a tree and I know it will fall. Other norms are less certain in their operation than gravity. I know with a high degree of probability that my dog will give birth to fewer than ten puppies, because it's very rare—though not totally unknown—for my breed of dog to have more.

Much of the normal behavior of living things is also like that. There's a range of behavior that can be predicted with a degree of probability, from very normal (like eating and sleeping) to very abnormal (like giving birth to 15 puppies). But notice something else: In some instances when a living thing behaves abnormally, we also attach a value judgment. We say, for instance, that it's sick or defective.

Normally, when we say that something is defective we have in mind something that was made to perform a certain function, like a hammer. The hammer's identity is virtually identical to its hammering function, so that if it serves this purpose poorly, we say it's defective.

> **Moral Musings**
>
> Our everyday talk about living things is laden with references to purposes. Aristotle went even further, saying that you couldn't explain the falling of a rock without referring to the rock's desire to achieve a state of peaceful rest!

Same thing applies to living nature. We say, for instance, that a person has a bad eye when the eye isn't fulfilling its main purpose, which is to see. Or, we say that a person is sick when her body is not performing up to par, which is to allow normal daily functioning.

In fact, it's virtually impossible to talk about nature without at least tacitly thinking about purposes and functions. For instance, when we ask, "Why do animals have eyes?" we answer "In order to see." And if we ask, "Why do they see?" we answer "In order to catch food, avoid predators, and—most basically—to live better." The phrase "in order to" keys us into the idea that there is some purpose or end that the behavior (seeing) and organ (eyes) serve.

So our everyday way of talking about living things is full of references to purposes in a way that our talking about purely physical events—such as the falling of a ball—is not. In fact, there was a time, before modern science came on the scene 500 years ago, when people thought that all natural events could be explained in terms of purposes. Aristotle, for example, thought that you couldn't explain the falling of a rock without referring to the rock's desire to achieve a state of peaceful rest!

But, come to think of it, the idea that everything that happens in nature happens for a purpose is not at all foreign to someone who believes that nature is created by God and mirrors divine purposes. Aristotle, incidentally, didn't believe that nature was created by God in accordance with divine purposes. However, he did believe that every kind of thing has it's own nature, and that this nature prescribed a standard of perfection and purpose. For instance, he said that the single thing that distinguished humans from all other animals was the ability to reason and communicate rationally. So human nature refers to just those innate potentials for rational speech and behavior that human beings develop over the course of their lives.

Notice that our nature as human beings refers to a fact about ourselves—that we do have the in-born biological potential to develop rational speech and behavior—and a norm, or purpose. That is, people can develop their humanity more or less well. We think rational speech and behavior is an excellence that people *ought* to try to cultivate within themselves. So people like Lenny who fall below a normal range of rational speech and behavior are not only considered to be abnormal, they're considered to be defective, disabled, or lacking full humanity.

Okay, so nobody today really buys Aristotle's explanation for why rocks fall (although my pet rock really does like to rest all day—lazy thing!) But we do buy into two of his less outdated ideas. First, we do think that different sorts of things have different natures. Remember Lenny? Well, Lenny seems to have forgotten this very important point. Dogs are innately different than human beings. Second, we agree with Aristotle that innate natures dictate standards of normal and—most important—good functioning. Although it sounds kind of weird, we can say that for every kind of thing there is a standard of well-being, excellence, and virtue.

Tried and True

Our distinctive human nature consists in possessing an innate biological potential to develop rational speech and behavior. This potential is our distinctive excellence and virtue, and can be cultivated with greater or lesser success. People who fall below a normal range of rationality are thus thought to suffer from some kid of lack, deficiency, or disability.

Does this mean that dogs, like humans, have virtues? Well, yes—although they obviously aren't moral virtues. After all, we do say that dogs do certain things well that other animals don't do. They have a terrific sense of smell, so they're good trackers and hunters. They have a terrific sense of hearing as well. Hey, they're loyal (okay, so they do exercise moral virtue). All these virtues, of course, are relative to their nature. And I hate to say it—but it's true—even when they eat and roll around in indescribably stinky stuff, they're being virtuous according to the standard of dog excellence, which is to conceal their doggy scent from that little squirrel they're hunting!

So Lenny is one really confused dude. He hasn't paid enough attention to the Aristotle book gathering dust on his shelf, because if he had, he'd know that he isn't a dog, and that dog behavior—while truly excellent for dogs—is not so excellent for humans. Whewww! PEEYOO!

One Christian Take on Human Nature

If you went to a Catholic school as a kid, I bet you heard of Saint Thomas Aquinas (1225–1274). He's one of the all-time philosophical heavy-weights, in all senses of the term. He wrote over forty volumes of philosophy, and had such a large tummy that they had to cut a notch out of the table so he could sit there to eat! Anyway, we have to credit St. Thomas for having brought Aristotle to the attention of Europeans who were otherwise living in a pretty dark age.

Basically, St. Thomas added Christianity into the Aristotelian stew. Unlike Aristotle, he held that nature was created by God and reflected His purposes. Although he accepted Aristotle's basic idea of human nature, he tacked on the Christian idea that the ultimate purpose of life was not happiness here on earth but eternal bliss in the hereafter. Oh yeah, he also substituted humility for pride in Aristotle's list of virtues. In short, he accepted the following three Aristotelian principles:

1. In nature everything has a purpose. Lower kinds of nature exist in order to serve higher kinds (cows exist in order to provide food and clothing for people). Each kind strives to develop its own nature as much as possible. Humans strive to develop their distinctive nature, which is reason.

2. Because every living thing has a nature that is appropriate to the kind of thing it is, failure to develop this nature to its fullest extent is an imperfection. Imperfections in turn are bad for those suffering from them and bad, too, for the rest of nature, since the well-being of higher kinds depends on the well-being of lower kinds (sick, stunted, or deformed cows make lousy food and clothing for people). So, each thing in nature ought to develop its natural potential as much as possible. And this "ought" shows that nature is as much a moral, value-laden universe as it is a factual, scientific one.

3. Nature and its moral laws is knowable through common sense and reason. And since every human being naturally possesses common sense and reason, everyone in principle can know nature's moral laws, which are one and the same for all people, no matter who people are or when and where they happen to live.

This last point is very important, because St. Thomas didn't want to say that non-Christians and nonbelievers were necessarily evil—or beyond the pale of moral understanding. The idea that only Christians could be counted on to respect basic moral laws would have made it impossible for Christians to live with anyone else. So St. Thomas insisted that any rational person—even an atheist—could know what nature prescribes in the way of right behavior.

Do the Right Thing!

Because every living thing has a nature that is appropriate to the kind of thing it is, failure to develop this nature to its fullest is an imperfection. Each thing ought to develop its innate potential, including humans. So strive as much as possible to cultivate your distinctive humanity. Fulfill your destiny as a rational being!

St. Thomas's idea—which can also be found in the writings of other philosophers dating as far back as Aristotle himself—is commonly referred to as the *Natural Law doctrine*. The doctrine of Natural Law says that the highest standards for judging right and wrong are not the customs or laws of any particular society, but the universal laws of human nature, as these are known by reason.

Remember Lenny? St. Thomas would say that, by imitating his dog Joey, Lenny violates his own human nature, or the natural law of human beings, which tells us that we should behave in accordance with reason. Now, does anyone out there seriously think that a reasonable person would behave like a dog? Of course not! So what Lenny does is against Natural Law, and therefore immoral.

Ethically Speaking

The doctrine put forth by St. Thomas is commonly referred to as the **Natural Law doctrine.** This doctrine says that the universal laws of human nature are the supreme standards of right and wrong. This doctrine assumes that (a) there is a universal moral nature common to human beings and (b) it can be known through reason, a faculty common to every adult, no matter what society they live in. Is St. Thomas right about this? Do you agree with him that men and women have distinctive moral natures?

Of Suicide and Sex

So knowledge of nature really does tell us what's right and wrong. Take suicide. It's wrong, right? Goes against the rational urge to live. Take killing innocent people. Ditto. Murderers violate other persons' desire to live. And the same applies to stealing, of course, because that endangers the lives of those who have their basic necessities ripped off and, just as worse, destroys the trust necessary for social cooperation—the very ways that humans collectively secure life's necessities in the first place. So far so good. But next we get into more touchy areas, such as sexuality and reproduction.

Let's break this argument down into smaller, easier steps:

1. Procreation is natural to all animal life, including human life, because without it, there would be no life at all.

2. So, procreation is good.

3. Sex organs were made for a purpose. That purpose is procreation.

4. So it follows from 1–3 that procreative sex is both natural and good.

5. Using sexual organs in ways that don't lead to procreation is unnatural and therefore not good.

6. Homosexuality involves using sexual organs in ways that don't lead to procreation.

7. So it follows from 4–6 that homosexuality is unnatural and bad.

Although St. Thomas had homosexuality in mind when talking about immoral sex, many Christians (especially Catholics) as well as persons subscribing to other religions find other forms of nonprocreative sex to be immoral. The Catholic Church, for example, opposes the use of contraception for this very reason. Masturbation and oral sex would likewise be immoral on St. Thomas's view.

> ### Moral Musings
>
> There is practically no form of human conduct that hasn't been considered to be unnatural by some society or other. Some aboriginal peoples regard the idea of private property to be unnatural but think nudity and polygamy to be perfectly healthy.

But what about women who engage in post-menopausal sex? It's clearly not procreative. Does that mean it's wrong, too? Or what about sex between people who, for whatever reason, can't procreate? Then there's the question about abortion. Once sex activates procreation, a process is triggered in which a fertilized egg naturally develops into an adult human being. Aborting that process is tantamount to aborting an innocent life. So does abortion violate natural laws prohibiting, say, the killing of innocent human life? Does it violate the "natural" mothering role of women?

Does Knowing What's Natural Come Naturally?

These are all tough questions, and I won't be able to answer them until we get to later chapters. But the very fact that these questions *are* tough should clue us into something important about the nature of Natural Law that St. Thomas neglected to mention. The idea that nature prescribes what is morally right or wrong might be true even though we might not be able to know with any absolute certainty what nature prescribes.

Take the killing of innocent people. A pretty strong case can be made to show that this kind of behavior is contrary to the well-being of the human species. We know with certainty that human children require parental nurturing for longer periods than do juveniles of other species. We know that parental nurturing is difficult without some kind of social support, be it familial or communal. And common sense tells us that social groups don't stay together long unless there's some basis of mutual trust. So killing innocent people—which is destructive of mutual trust—undermines the conditions by which humans reproduce their kind.

Okay, you say. We know with a pretty high degree of certainty that killing innocent people is contrary to our nature, and so is morally wrong. But what about homosexuality?

One way to go about answering this question is to ask yourself how we know that something is contrary to nature. If something is contrary to the nature of a particular species of animal, then you might reasonably suppose that it's occurrence among members of that species will probably be rare. Like killing innocent people, homosexual behavior is relatively rare among human societies.

But being rare or "abnormal" in this sense is no sure sign that something is contrary to nature. For one thing, some abnormal behaviors, such as being left-handed, are clearly not contrary to nature (unlike murder, being left-handed poses no danger to the survival of the human species). So being abnormal is no sign that homosexual behavior is contrary to nature.

Again, it seems reasonable to say that using something for a purpose for which it was not originally intended is contrary to it's nature, and so is bad. Human arms and hands did not develop in order to kill innocent human beings but in order to get what you need to survive. By the same token, sexual organs originated so that we could procreate, not sowe could have pleasure.

> **CAUTION** **Do the Right Thing**
>
> Something's being abnormal or unusual is no sign that it is contrary to nature (left-handed folks are not at all unnatural). Likewise, something's being used for a purpose for which it was not originally intended is also no sign that it is being used contrary to nature (if it were, then smiling would be an unnatural use of the mouth).

The problem with this line of reasoning is that we often use parts of our body to do things that they weren't originally intended for; and we don't feel that we're doing something wrong. It so happens that I derive great pleasure from using my mouth to make funny faces in the mirror. But I don't think that's why animals like myself originally developed mouths—although I must admit that I like it as a theory!

Maybe the reason why we might think homosexuality is wrong has nothing to do with its infrequency or the inventive use of sexual organs for nonprocreative pleasure. Maybe we think it's wrong because if everyone did it, the human species would most certainly die out. There seems to be a clear parallel here with murder. If everyone murdered, then that would be the end of us.

This seems to have been St. Thomas's thinking. But a closer look will show that it doesn't hold much water. For instance, if everyone in the world decided against having children, that would certainly doom the human species. So does that mean that not having any children is contrary to nature, and therefore wrong? Or suppose in a hundred years that the human population has exploded to the point where the survival of the species is endangered by overpopulation. If everyone decided to have children in such a situation, the earth's population would drown in a sea of pollution, sickness and famine. Would that mean—to reverse the argument—that a couple's having even a single child is morally wrong? And if it did, wouldn't that make homosexuality less dangerous to the welfare of the species—and thus less contrary to nature—than heterosexuality?

The point is that if everyone did too much of one kind of behavior, things would go badly for us as a species. That's because as a species we adapt to our environment by increasing useful behaviors and talents. By dividing different tasks among ourselves we learn to do things more efficiently. But now I'm straying. The real point is this: No one is saying that homosexual behavior should replace heterosexual behavior (and anyway, many people are bisexual). A little homosexual behavior—like a little sexual abstinence—will not doom the human species. So there's no good reason to suppose that some homosexual behavior in humans is contrary to nature.

Okay, you say. But a little murder won't doom the species, either. That doesn't mean that murder isn't contrary to human nature. Point well taken. So why is murder thought to be so much more contrary to human nature than homosexual behavior? Well, look at it this way. Murder is much, much rarer than homosexual behavior, perhaps a thousand times rarer. If the incidence of murder ever even remotely approximated the incidence of homosexual behavior, human society as we know it would be done for. Kaput.

Now, let's try to generalize our findings about what nature says is right and wrong. Common sense tells us that certain behaviors are definitely harmful to human society—and thus go against human nature—even in very small doses. Killing innocent persons is one of them. But there is a range of behavior that is much less harmful—if harmful at all—to the flourishing of the species. And it's with respect to the naturalness or unnaturalness of this behavior that we disagree.

Suicide, like nonprocreative sex, is one of these less obvious cases. On the one hand, it seems to contradict our natural desire to live. On the other hand, it seems wholly in keeping with our natural desire to avoid pain. So which is it? Natural or unnatural?

Things get even more complicated when we recall St. Thomas's claim that reason is the guide to knowing what's natural. Of course, reason is entirely natural to human beings. But human beings use reason to rationalize all sorts of behavior. If human beings rationalize suicide or abortion, who's to say that these actions are contrary to nature? For that matter, who's to say that murder is wrong, if human beings rationalize it as right?

Tried and True _____

We know there are certain forms of behavior that are definitely harmful to human society. But other behaviors are less obviously so. Polygamy, for instance, is practiced in many parts of the world and by some renegade Mormons in the United States. Do you think polygamy is wrong? If so, do you think it's wrong because it's unnatural or because it demeans women?

Looking Ahead to Modern Natural Law

By now you're probably totally confused, right? Well, let's get back on track by changing gears. Remember what I said earlier about the doctrine of Natural Law: It designates a standard of right and wrong that applies to all human beings, simply because they share the same common nature. Human nature is defined by an in-born capacity to reason. And it is reason that defines the Law of Nature.

In the words of John Locke (1632–1704), the great English philosopher: "Reason … teaches all Mankind, who but will consult it, that being all equal and independent, no one ought to harm another in his Life, Liberty, or Possessions." Sound familiar? Well it should, because these very same words inspired the writing of the American Declaration of Independence!

Wow! How did we end up back in America?! Well, in the four hundred years separating St. Thomas from Locke, the Natural Law doctrine somehow morphed into a doctrine of inalienable, or "natural" rights. *Natural rights* are freedoms or rights to things, like property and possessions. Each and every person has them just because they are human beings. Most important, natural rights function as moral limits upon what governments can do to their own citizens.

Natural Law designates a law that is higher than human-made law. It is higher than human-made law because it is based on human nature itself, which is universal to all human society. And because it is higher than human-made law, it can be used as a standard for judging and even resisting that law. For example, if each person has a right to life, but a government violates that right, then we have an obligation to fight the government.

Ethically Speaking

Natural Law designates a law that is higher than human-made law just because it is based on nature itself, which is universal to all human society. Since around the time of Locke, it has been used to justify the idea that some rights (so-called natural rights) are bestowed on each and every one of us solely in virtue of our common humanity. Such natural rights designate basic demands for liberty and life's necessities. They impose absolute limits on what any government can do to its citizens, and even entitle citizens to resist government when it oversteps its proper moral bounds.

The Least You Need to Know

- ◆ Remember that it is natural for different creatures to behave in different ways.
- ◆ Beware! Judgments about what is or is not natural are subject to varying degrees of certainty.
- ◆ Always exercise extreme caution in judging the naturalness or unnaturalness of any behavior.
- ◆ The moral law of nature is higher than human-made law!

Modern Social Contract Theory

In This Chapter

- ◆ Low-Ball ethics: the least you can expect from anyone
- ◆ Thinking of moral rules as business contracts
- ◆ The contractual basis of our obligations to the state
- ◆ When social contracts can be broken

I bet some of you older generation types remember that terrific TV game show *Let's Make a Deal* that was hosted by Monty Hall? Sure you do—it was rated as one the most popular game shows ever! And why not. Contestants would try to pick the most expensive prizes, then Hall would ask them if they wanted to trade the prizes they had for some unknown prize behind a curtain. Ooh, big suspense! Ah, sorry! You just traded your stereo system for a box of hot dogs!

Well, guess what. Life's a lot like that, too. One offer after another, some good deals and some not-so-good deals. The biggest deals are the riskiest ones involving your job and—dare I say it—your marriage! Here you've got to trust the other person to come through with his or her part of the deal. And if he or she doesn't, you're sunk! Come to think of it, you have to rely on your fellow citizens and government to do right by you as well. If government fails to protect your health and welfare, then it's not holding up its end of the bargain, either. And believe me, you can really be in trouble when that happens!

In this chapter we're going to look at the ethical implications of thinking of life as one big contract. We've seen why virtue and natural law ethics seem so appealing. So what's the big deal about the "deal theory" of ethics? Well, to put it rather bluntly, most people, even if they wanted to be virtuous, just can't be. And we can't seem to agree on what nature tells us is right and wrong. So we need a more practical ethical theory that will deal with average people like us—you know, people who put aside virtue for the sake of pursuing the almighty dollar. In short, we need a low-ball, bottom-line ethics that offers just the essential rules—nothing more—for minimal cooperation between diverse, self-interested folk. In the process of working out this ethic, we'll also see why we need laws, police, administrators—the whole government schtick. And we'll see why our duty to obey government depends on government fulfilling its part of the bargain.

Low-Ball Ethics

First, let's get one thing clear: I'm not saying that we shouldn't be virtuous. And I'm not saying that we shouldn't follow nature's dictates. All I'm saying is: Get real! I mean, we're not a bunch of angels right? Just think about all that stuff you learned in Sunday school about original sin. According to those teachings, we're a bunch of selfish, money-grubbing low-lifes.

Okay, I'm overdoing it a bit. But we are motivated to look out for Numero Uno before looking out for Numero Dos and Numero Tres. So maybe virtue ethics and Natural Law doctrine paint a picture of human nature that's a wee bit too rosy. And that's just the problem. How can we ever be certain of what human nature is? When talking about human nature, don't we typically project our own religious and philosophical ideas onto what's natural or unnatural?

That's the problem with moral high-ballers: they have this rosy picture of human nature. We're all supposed to be virtuous and agree on what nature dictates. But this optimistic scenario is really overrated. Several millennia of religious wars should set us straight on that one.

So we need to start over with a low-ball, baseline, minimalist sort of ethic designed for stinkers like us. The social contract theory of ethics fits that bill perfectly. It grants that people are basically self-interested and prone to fighting over the possession of scarce goods. As

> **Moral Musings**
>
> The social contract theory fits our need for a low-ball baseline ethic perfectly. Maybe it's because we live in a business-centered world where we live or die by the dotted line. We do come to a lot of our moral obligations through promise-making and other voluntary agreements. But not all. Just ask anyone who's been in the presence of desperately needy and helpless persons.

Immanuel Kant (the great ethicist you'll be reading about in the next chapter) once said, a minimalist ethic begins with the notion that the human race might not be much different than a "race of devils." Then it shows that even these folks would be compelled out of sheer selfishness—the desire for personal self-preservation—to reach agreement with one another on minimal rules of mutually advantageous cooperation.

Thomas Hobbes

Thomas Hobbes was the first philosopher to have really pushed this idea. Looking around at all the religious civil wars raging in England and abroad during the seventeenth century, and keenly observing how many of his fellow countrymen were behaving like greedy little piggies fighting over a trough of slops, he pooh-poohed virtue, ethics and Christian Natural Law doctrine as so much childish wishful thinking. Then, in one of the most famous images, he laid out what he took to be the real human condition.

Hobbes asks us to imagine, for a moment, that no state or any other artificial, human-made conventions exist. Call this the *state of nature*. Next, consider the fact that the natural condition of humanity is a state of permanent want, or scarcity of goods. In short, our desires are pretty unlimited and there's never quite enough of all the things we desire to go around. For example, can a person ever be satisfied with just so much wealth, so much power, or—what amounts to the same thing—security?

Ethically Speaking

The **state of nature** is an idea used by philosophers to understand how persons would naturally behave if there were no government threatening to punish them if they stepped out of line. According to Hobbes, since what people fear most is death and misery caused by material want and powerlessness, and because wealth and power are scarce resources, people—whose desire for security is unlimited—will naturally fight with one another to get as much wealth and power as they can.

Notice that whereas Natural Law Theory and virtue ethics assume that humans naturally strive to reach a state of peace and spiritual contentment, unfettered by material things, Hobbes assumes just the opposite: because we can never have enough security, we're constantly striving for more wealth and power. A world in which people only strive to achieve inner peace and tranquility with themselves and God is certainly capable of reaching a state of perfect social harmony and brotherly love. Not so a world in which everyone is striving to get more wealth and power to bolster their sense of security.

So the *state of nature* is not peaceable and harmonious. No way, baby! It's dog eat dog. Hey, even if you wanted to be virtuous and let the other guy get ahead of you in line, you'd be foolish to do so. Maybe you have family to support; it's eat or be eaten. To lay it all out in a nice mathematical equation (Hobbes was fond of rigorously logical ways of arguing): Unlimited fear of material insecurity plus scarcity of material things equals "a war of all against all," as Hobbes put it so well.

The State of Nature

Hobbes isn't saying that people in a state of nature (without any government) would actually try to slit each other's throats all the time. No, what he's saying is that people are naturally competitive. If there were no government threatening to punish them if they stepped out of line, enough of them would be sorely tempted to slit some throats. And what about us less rapacious types? Well, we'd have to try to slit the other guy's throat before he slit ours. And worst of all, because we couldn't trust anybody, we'd probably consider slitting the throat of some poor bloke we didn't know, just on the off chance that he might be out to slit our throat.

And notice something else. Even the strongest dude would be quaking in his boots. Sure, he could beat up on any of us weaker and stupider types taken singly. But what if we started ganging up on him? Strength in numbers! That would surely equalize things out.

So Hobbes concludes that people in the state of nature really are pretty much equal. Indeed, each of us thinks our own life is every bit as important and worthwhile as the next guy's. I mean, who is some pompous king or noble to tell me that he's better than me? Nah. I have just as much of a natural right to life's necessities as the next guy. So why shouldn't I have the right to do whatever I can to procure it—even if it means preemptively slitting a few throats along the way?

Hey, I'm beginning to like the way this sounds! Hobbes was sure one heck of a straight-shootin' sort of guy. Especially when you consider the times in which he wrote. I mean, it's pretty progressive for him to say that each and every one of us has an equal right to life—and power and wealth. This business about everyone counting equally will really come in handy later on.

But for the time being, I can't think very straight because I'm trying to dodge daggers aimed at my throat. Gee, this state of nature is sure exhausting and nerve racking. Got to get out of it somehow. But in this scenario the very most I or anyone else could hope for would be to escape all this fighting by crawling into a hole somewhere and staying alive by … hmmm … eating grubs? Come to think of it, this might just be the very worst way to advance my self-preservation. In fact, if everyone else thought the same way I did and withdrew into their own little grub holes, there would be (as Hobbes puts it in his great masterpiece *Leviathan* "no place for industry … no culture of the earth … no commodities … no knowledge … no time, no arts, no letters, no society, and which is worst of all, continual fear and danger of violent death, and the life of man solitary, poor, nasty, brutish, and short."

And grubby, I might add. Well, folks, if human nature in the raw is really this competitive and war-like, I'm heading for the nearest grub hole. Unless there was another solution?

Contracting to Get Out of a Hole

At this point in our narrative we encounter what is commonly referred to as the *Prisoner's Dilemma*. This dilemma shows that when rational people cooperate with one another, they end up with the best possible results. And this might be just the way to get ourselves out of those grub holes.

The Prisoner's Dilemma

The *Prisoner's Dilemma* involves a conflict between two persons, A and B, such that (a) what is in the best interest of A is in the worst interest of B (and vice versa), (b) the second best option for both A and B is to cooperate with one another; and (c) the third best option for both A and B is for A and B to each foil the other's best option. Given that A and B cannot trust each other enough to cooperate because it's too risky, they will each choose so as to stymie the other's best option (which is also their third best option). In this way, both A and B end up worse off than if they had chosen to cooperate with one another. A good example of this dilemma is the nuclear arms race between the former Soviet Union and the United States. Had they trusted each other's declarations of non-aggression, each could have saved itself a bundle of money—and saved the world a lot of anxiety—by stopping the arms race. Just imagine all the starving children whose lives could have been saved by spending that money on famine relief!

Let me illustrate how the dilemma works. Take two prisoners (call them Jenny and Jacky) who have been accused of stealing from Joe. The prosecutor needs a confession from one of them, so he goes to each of them separately with the following plea-bargain deal:

Option A: If you confess, and your partner doesn't, you'll get off with 5 years and your partner will get 15.

Option B: If neither of you confesses, you'll both get off free.

Option C: If both of you confess, you'll get 10 years apiece.

Ethically Speaking

People in the state of nature face what is known as the **Prisoner's Dilemma.** This dilemma shows that when rational people cooperate with one another, they end up with the best possible results.

Obviously, B is the best option for Jenny and Jacky. So if they're rational, they'll pick it, right? Not so fast. Remember, they can't talk to each another, so they have no assurance what their partner will say when presented with the same offer. Suppose what Jenny and Jacky each wants most of all is to avoid spending 15 years in jail—the worst scenario for either of them. Each reasons that if she confesses and her partner doesn't, then she's got only 5 years to serve. That's the second most desirable outcome, but far better than the worst. Furthermore, even if her partner confesses too, she gets at most 10 years. 10 years is not as good as 5 but its better than 15, which is what she'd get if she didn't confess and her partner did.

What to do? Jenny and Jacky will do anything to ensure they don't get the worst sentence. Since they can't talk to each other to find out what the other's really thinking, all they can do is pick the safest course of action. Which is to confess. If both of them are rational, they'll figure that the other one will confess in any case, just to avoid the worst case scenario. So they'll both confess.

But notice what's happened. In acting perfectly rationally, each woman in isolation from the other has picked the next-to-worst outcome for herself—all for the sake of avoiding the worst outcome! If only Jenny and Jacky could have trusted each other, or found some way to cooperate with each other, they might both have elected to shut up, and beat the charge.

Risky Trust

You're probably wondering what the heck this has all got to do with all of us grub-holers in the state of nature. Well, when you think about it, the choice to retreat to a grub-hole is the most viable option for all of us. Because we can't trust each other, and because we each fear for our lives above all else, we'll forgo the two better alternatives—fight and win (the best option) and stay above ground and risk betrayal (the second best option)—for the sake of avoiding the worst possible outcome (fight and get our throats cut).

Actually, for Hobbes the best option is not fighting and winning, because after you win you still have to continue fighting. And eventually you're going to lose an arm or leg, if not your head. So staying and risking betrayal seems like the best option. One way to make it less risky is to ensure against betrayal. But how?

Suppose we grubbers leave our holes and try to trust one another (each knows the other is a grubber, not a fighter, and each suspects that the other wants peace as well; so it's a pretty safe risk to take). We've decided the life of solitary grubbing isn't for us and we want a better life, out in the open, working together for our mutual benefit. So each of us individually agrees with all the others to stop killing and stealing.

But risk remains. Any one of us might be a free loader who takes advantage of the temporary truce—our first contract—to stab the rest of us in the back while we're not looking. Trust is such a fragile thing!

The Social Contract

So we strike another deal: we agree to set up an enforcement mechanism to punish betrayal. Punishment is clearly justified on contractual grounds: If a person breaks a protection agreement with us, then he or she no longer deserves to be protected from us.

At first, we form a vigilante group composed of ourselves. Problem is, we start bickering among ourselves about whether Sally really betrayed the contract of mutual cooperation when she hung out rotten apples to entice all of Sam's juicy grubs to crawl onto her own property, thereby leaving Sam grubless. Also, some of us who think Sally broke the contract aren't sure what to do about it. Do we make Sally spit out all those grubs and hand 'em back to Sam? Or do we slit her throat?

So we take the next step, which is to strike a deal to authorize some third party (possibly from our own group) to interpret, enforce, and apply the terms of our social contract impartially and fairly. Along the way we set up law schools, a criminal justice department, elected officers and judges; the whole nine yards.

And to close the book on Sally, the cooler heads chosen to be the grubbers' legislators and judges decided that she didn't violate the contract for mutual cooperation after all because she was starving and Sam had more grubs than he could eat in a lifetime.

Law and Order

Don't you just love happy endings? Well, hold that hanky, because I think the grubbers just created a government for themselves! That's right, folks. The social contract theory of ethics not only shows why its in the long-term best interest of any rational egoist to agree on basic moral rules—namely, to escape from the inconveniences of a state of nature. But, it also shows why it's in the interests of all rational egoists to have an officially designated umpire to settle disagreements about the proper interpretation, application, and execution of those rules.

Now, rationally enlightened people in a state of nature would eventually see that it was in their long-term best interest to strike a deal with one another. According to this deal, each promises to follow a minimum moral code concerning such basics as life, liberty, and property. True, they might not agree on anything else, morally speaking. Sam might be an atheist who likes to smoke grubs in the privacy of his shack, while Sally might be a converted Hindu who no longer thinks it's right

Tried and True

The social contract theory shows why it's in everyone's best interest to trust one another for purposes of mutually advantageous cooperation. However, its realism consists in arguing for a coercive state that will punish acts of breaking trust (also sometimes known as "free-loading").

to harm, let alone eat, grubs—she now believes that one of them might be her long-departed grandmother.

Oh sure, Sally and Sam don't really like each other, and each has tried to convert the other to his or her way of thinking. But they both remember the old days when people used to fight tooth and nail over grubs, and they want none of that. So they agree to put up with each other's deeper, more private (high-ball) moral convictions for the sake of maintaining peaceful cohabitation founded on shared and public (low-ball) moral convictions.

So what they don't tolerate—and here each totally agrees with the other—is conduct that violates the basic moral terms of the social contract. So important is this code that they don't hesitate to punish those who betray it. And that's why they set up government.

Government Obligations?

Let's see now. How does that work again? Hobbes thought that everyone in the state of nature would agree with one another to hand over all of their power to a government enforcement agency with absolutely no strings attached! The government would be created in order to protect them and their property but, oddly enough, the government wouldn't be contractually bound to do so.

Sound wacky? Well it is—and it isn't. To see why it isn't, let's just examine the way Hobbes reasoned it through. Hobbes thought that government couldn't be party to a social contract between itself and its subjects. If it were party to such a contract, then what would happen if its own commitment to the contract was questioned? Since it is top dog—the supreme authority responsible for interpreting and enforcing the contract—government would have to sit in judgment of itself. But no judge can sit in judgment of a case in which he or she is one of the involved parties. I mean, how could a judge be expected to judge impartially in a case involving itself (lawyers call this a "conflict of interest")?

Hobbes reasoned that the only way to prevent this problem from occurring is by not allowing government to be part of the social contract. By placing government above the law, government would never have to be responsible for judging itself!

Well, by now you've probably figured out what's wrong with this story. John Locke, whom we discussed in the last chapter, did too, and that's why he—not Hobbes—is considered to be the most important social contract ethicist who ever lived. Basically, Locke realized how self-defeating—not to mention dangerous—it would be to give government absolute power to do what it wants without any limits. I mean, if the whole point of leaving the state of nature is to escape from powerful bullies, then why would you voluntarily consent to hand over the security of your life and property to a truly unlimited and all-powerful bully?

You wouldn't, of course. Instead, you and your fellow grubbers would limit the power of the government you created. In other words, you grubbers would make the government sign a contract requiring it to fulfill certain obligations in exchange for receiving your (grubbers') obedience. Because government is created to protect your security—which includes freedom to go about your business as well as your possessions—its failure to do so would immediately release you (grubbers) from your obligation to obey it.

According to Locke, any government that violates the basic natural rights of its subjects goes against the very terms it sets out for citizens. When this happens, subjects can disobey or—under extreme circumstances—even overthrow governments!

But what about Hobbes's concern about making government party to a contract between itself and the people? No problem. In any dispute between government and the people, it's the people—not the government—who are supreme judge. And it's perfectly okay for the judge in this instance to be partial. Just as the buyer of services is the final judge in determining the quality of the services rendered (remember that saying: "the buyer is always right"), the people—who buy governmental services—are the final judge in determining the quality of those services. After all, government only exists to do the bidding of the people.

> ### Moral Musings
>
> Did you know that Thomas Jefferson got the idea—famously memorialized in the American Declaration of Independence (1776)—that all people are created equal, endowed by God with equal rights to life, liberty, and the pursuit of happiness, from Locke's Second treatise of Government (1689)?

Not All Contracts Are Fair

So, now are you happy with the ending of the story? I've totally convinced you that you have a contractual obligation to obey your government, right? Well, maybe not quite right—at least, not just yet. One teensy weensy problem remains. It has to do with the very nature of a "good" contract.

As you know, not all contracts are good, or binding on those who agree to them. Generally, contracts aren't considered legit unless a person voluntarily—with clear mind—enters into one. And almost all valid contracts require the signing of covenants, the swearing of oaths, and other explicit signs of promise-making. But guess what? Unless you're an immigrant who sought citizenship, you never expressly swore allegiance to your government in exchange for future services to be rendered.

And let's face it. Most of us were born in the country where we currently reside. We're not always free to leave the country—it's hard getting permission from would-be host countries to resettle. And sometimes the country where you currently live doesn't allow

Do the Right Thing!

Locke's idea that duty to obey government rests on tacit consent is just an awkward way of saying that we're duty-bound to obey some laws regardless of whether we've explicitly consented to them. Locke himself elsewhere talks about natural duties to others—such as not harming or stealing from them— that stem from our being made equal in the eyes of God.

you to leave. So there's one important sense in which our obedience to government is not at all based on an express, voluntary consent to obey in return for contracted governmental services.

Does that mean that the social contract theory of obedience is all washed up? Not quite. Locke had it right on the money when he observed that some agreements are based on tacit consent (that is, consent that is never explicitly given). I tacitly consent to an arrangement whenever I benefit from it. By benefiting from government services—and not expressly rejecting them—I've tacitly agreed to them; and having agreed to them I'm obligated to contribute taxes to their maintenance.

You Scratch My Back and I'll Scratch Yours

But perhaps consent is really beside the point. The social contract theory presents us with a picture of society as a cooperative undertaking in which burdens and benefits are shared equally. The idea here is really simple: we're all mutually dependent on one another for our well-being, so we have to make sure that the terms of our cooperation are fair for all.

So voluntary consent is not the most important idea for social contract ethicists. Equity— or fairness—is. To repeat, social contract theory invites us to see society as if it were a system designed to benefit everyone fairly, where no one shares more of the burdens—or enjoys more of the benefits—than others.

To begin with, we're all in it together. Business owners need workers and vice versa. The success of great geniuses depends on the little guys who harvest the food on their plate, sew their clothes in dirty sweatshops, and keep their gardens and households neat and clean; and the well-being of everyone depends on the intellectual work of medical scientists and others.

Jean-Jacques Rousseau's Views

As Jean-Jacques Rousseau (1712–1778), another great social contract theorist, observed society is like a living thing in which even the smallest part is essential to the well-being of the whole organism. Because each of us is equally important in contributing to the social good, we must guarantee that our social contracts are as beneficial to the least wealthy and powerful among us as they are to the most wealthy and powerful.

Just think about it. If one part of society is neglected, the other parts eventually feel it, too. In the last 40 years, Americans have begun to realize that problems plaguing the inner cities—drugs, crime, pollution, unemployment, and lack of basic services—can, and often do, spread into the suburbs.

Also, Americans are realizing more and more that changes in the economy that benefit one group of people (as when the Federal Reserve Bank raises interest rates to slow infla-tion and protect earnings and interest payments) hurt another group (those who lose their jobs because of lack of investment and down-sizing). It's almost as if one group is being sacrificed for the sake of another group!

John Rawls's Views

Is it right that some groups should benefit at the expense of others? John Rawls (still liv-ing!), who is often credited with having revived social contract theory in the twentieth century, argues that they shouldn't. He argues, very much in line with Rousseau's think-ing, that in a truly fair society, each person would have an equal opportunity to succeed, as far as he or she can, no matter what kind of life he or she was born into.

According to Rawls, no one deserves the advantages or disadvantages they're born with, because these are simply a matter of luck. Innate abilities (being intelligent) are as unde-served as innate disabilities (being mentally handicapped). The same applies to the social circumstances of your family: It's strictly a matter of luck whether you're born into a poor family of twelve kids or a rich family of two!

Rawls argues that society must be set up to minimize the effects of these accidents as much as possible. That's because inequalities stemming from these accidents really do impact the chances that children have to succeed. So it's especially important, he thinks, that people born into the worst-off circumstances be given the same opportunities to suc-ceed as those born into better-off circumstances. And he thinks that those who are lucky enough to be born into better-off circumstances ought to be willing to give up some of their wealth to help those at the bottom.

Well, you're probably wondering how the social contract model fits in here. Recall what Hobbes had to say about the state of nature? Hobbes said that we have to think of the human condition as one in which there's only so many goodies to go around for equally deserving people. So whether we like or not, we have to think of life as sort of a compe-tition. Now, if the competition is not to be a free-for-all, no-holds-barred, WWF kind of an affair, it has to be regulated—like a game with rules.

Tried and True _____

Next time you feel resentful about having some of your tax dollars go to feeding the poor and indigent, just remind your-self that "there but for the grace of God go I." Truth is, most of what we get out of life—wealth, talents, motivation—is largely a matter of luck, not desert.

And the rules have to be fair. They can't favor some over others. That's the point of the social contract.

Rawls bases his own idea of the social contract on this game model. Society has to be thought of as a game in which people are competing for scarce goodies (jobs, power, prestige, wealth and so on). And the rules governing the game have to be fair, or provide equal opportunity to all. A race that pits world-class runners against disabled runners in wheel chairs would not be a fair race. Neither would a race to enter the best universities and best-paying jobs that pits children from wealthy families against those from poor families. The only way to make the "competitors" equal is to use some of society's wealth to make sure that the unlucky ones at the bottom have health, education, and welfare comparable to those at the top.

Rawls isn't calling for strict equality here, because he knows that inequality can be okay if everyone—including the least well off—benefit from it. To show this, Rawls asks us to imagine a fictional social contract in which all Americans are asked to choose one among several rules for dividing up shares of goodies among themselves. Now, if we let things go at that, our imaginary contractors wouldn't agree on any single rule, because the rich will favor a rule that benefits them ("everyone gets what they already have"), and the poor will favor a rule that benefits them ("soak the rich").

> **Moral Musings**
>
> Are the rules governing the competition for scarce resources (income, jobs, self-respect, etc.) truly fair? Maybe they would be if everyone started out with the same advantages and disadvantages. Since people don't start out with the same opportunities in life, the rules aren't entirely fair—unless, of course, the disadvantages are compensated for by the government.

To get around this problem, Rawls asks us to further imagine that the social contractors have no knowledge of who they are—at least for the time being. Not knowing who you are, you won't know if—in the real world you actually inhabit—you're rich or poor. That way, you'll not be biased in favor of your own class. More importantly, you'll be adopting a moral point of view. You'll be thinking of yourself simply as a human with equal rights. And all the "undeserved" advantages and disadvantages of birth and social standing will play no role in your thinking.

What Would Ideally Rational Persons Do?

What sort of distribution would you choose in this situation? Like Hobbes, Rawls thinks that as a rational contractor, you'll want to avoid the worst possible condition for yourself. So, you'll want to pick a rule that improves the condition of the worst-off. But—you ask—why shouldn't you gamble a bit and pick a rule that favors the wealthy? Because, as far as you know, you might be a poor person. The knowledge of who you really are won't be revealed to you until after you've chosen how to divide the social pie. More important, you know that there are many more poor and lower-middle income folks out there than there are rich folks. So if you're rational, you'll calculate that your chances of being a poor working class Joe are far greater than your chances of being Donald Trump or Bill Gates. So you'll pick a rule that improves the condition of the worst-off.

What rule is that? An equal division might sound good at first, but when you think harder about it, it might discourage persons from working hard (and so encourage free-loaders). Better to have an unequal division in which the worst off are eating hamburgers than an equal division in which everyone's slurpin' down grubs! Likewise, you won't pick a distribution that increases the well-being of most people, because it doesn't offer protection for everyone. So, according to Rawls, you'll pick a rule that allows for inequalities in the distribution of the social pie, but only if such inequalities work to improve the worst-off.

To recap: Rawls uses the thought-experiment of a fictional social contract in order to justify the notion that truly fair rules of mutual cooperation must be to the benefit of the poor as well as the rich. Above all, they require transferring some wealth from rich to poor in order to ensure equal opportunity for all.

Tried and True

Is Rawls right that ideally rational and fair-minded people would choose to improve the condition of the worst off among them? Would it make a difference if the improvement were minuscule and the costs to the better off great?

Broken Contracts

Well, you might not agree with everything Rawls's says (many people don't). But you have to admit, he really makes us think hard about the importance of working against undeserved disadvantages so we can promote equal opportunity for all.

To finish up here, I'd like to suggest that the social contract isn't just an imaginary idea to help us understand our mutual duties as citizens. It's a real, on-going process of negotiation that characterizes any democracy. Just think about. The laws governing our society are the outcome of negotiations between elected legislators and leaders. The election of legislators and leaders are the outcome of other negotiations—between special interest groups, political parties, and the like. Most important, the issues that get put on the agenda are the outcome of debates and other forms of give and take.

If Rawls is right, then all this discussion and deal-making must contain the moral idea of mutual concern for all and equal opportunity. If we thought that democracy was just a free-for-all in which the wealthiest and most powerful got their way, then there would be no morally compelling reason to obey the laws legislators make. I mean, why should I obey laws that were made to help only some people and that hurt me?

One way to clarify this point is to recall what I said about the rules of the game. One reason why we go along with laws that we otherwise disagree with is because we feel that the democratic process was fair. We assume that everyone had a fair shake in getting their candidates elected and had an equal opportunity to influence public opinion, which in turn influences the legislative agenda. In other words, because we believe that the rules governing the democratic game are fair, we think the outcome is fair as well.

But we also know in our heart of hearts that real-life democracy ain't like that. We know that money, money, money buys political influence—and votes. And we know that voter registration lists, malfunctioning voting machines, and confusing ballots deprive many people (at least 6 million during the Presidential Election of 2000) of their right to vote. If that weren't bad enough, we know that millions of Americans are denied equal opportunity education, and so are ill-equipped to participate in political life.

Finally, we have to be concerned about the fact that a disproportionate percentage of Black, Native American, and Latino men are excluded from civil and political life altogether because they're in prison (and when they get out, many are still denied the right to work and vote in elections). Many have been convicted of relatively minor infractions, such as parole violations and drug-related charges involving simple possession, which probably shouldn't be criminalized in the first place. Many have been wrongly convicted, simply because they couldn't afford a decent lawyer. And Racial Profiling on the part of police officers, juries and judges may also have played a role in their conviction. As I noted in Chapter 10, "Middle Age Virtues," the Civil Rights Movement of the '60s aimed at bringing about equal rights for citizens regardless of race and class. But it's not clear that's happened yet. Persons (again, mainly minorities) living in poor inner cities are denied equal opportunity education, equal opportunity employment, and equal opportunity health services. Is it all that surprising that so many of them fall through the cracks?

So I ask you: Have these young men broken their "contract" with America? Or has America broken her contract with them?

The Least You Need to Know

- ◆ Remember, even self-interested people with widely differing religious and philosophical opinions can agree on a low-ball ethic.
- ◆ It's a good idea to think of government as if it were founded on a low-ball social contract.
- ◆ Understand that the most important idea about the social contract is fairness, not voluntary consent.
- ◆ Remember that we're all dependent on one another for our well-being.
- ◆ Remember that inherited advantages and disadvantages undermine equal opportunity and mutual concern for all.

Chapter 12

We Can't Forget Kant

In This Chapter

◆ The importance of duties to leading the moral life

◆ The Golden Rule: Don't use people!

◆ When are there exceptions to the rules?

◆ Do we have a moral obligation to punish criminals?

Consider the following case called *Mrs. Smith Meets Sneaky Pete:*

Kindly old Mrs. Smith is trying to lug home several bags of groceries she picked up at the supermarket. A few blocks from her house she comes across Pete, who seems like a sweet young man. Pete offers to help Mrs. Smith with her heavy bags; he says "I used to help my own grandma with her groceries until she died—please let me help you!" Mrs. Smith gladly hands Pete some of her bags; he follows her toward her house.

As they near the house, Pete formulates his plan: he's going to put down the bags on her doorstep, grab the unsuspecting broad's purse, and hit the road. But just then a police officer comes along. Pete puts Mrs. Smith's bags at her door and leaves; Mrs. Smith thinks "What a nice, helpful fellow!"

Did Pete do the right thing in carrying the groceries for old Mrs. Smith? You might say he did: we should all be helpful to our fellow human beings and, his bad intentions aside, "all's well that ends well." But others might say that Pete did a very bad thing: he carried Mrs. Smith's groceries with the sole intention of ripping her off. That's what we will examine in this chapter: whether your intentions in doing an act affect the ethics of the act.

Do Your Duty!

As you're probably starting to realize, different ethical theories offer different recipes for the moral life. Some tell you that happiness or being virtuous is all that matters; others say that following nature's dictates is best; and still others say that ethics is about self-preservation. This chapter presents yet another recipe for the moral life: *deontological* moral theory. (Don't let this word scare you off!)

I'll focus on one particular philosopher's duty-based theory because it is the most clearly detailed and has had a huge impact on the practice of ethics. That philosopher is Immanuel Kant, a German guy who lived from 1724 to 1804. Now you might wonder "what the heck does some long-dead German guy's theory about duty have to do with me, and this book, and everyday ethics?" Quite a lot, actually, as you'll see in a minute.

Ethically Speaking

The term **deontological** is just a fancy way of saying "duty-based." Any moral theory that is deontological is one that focuses on your duties, whether they be to other people, to animals, or to God. Immanuel Kant's moral theory is this type because it takes duties to other people to be the core of ethics.

Ethically Speaking

You must do your **duty** whether you want to or not. It means that, no matter how you feel about it or what you want to do, you must do an act—whether it's studying for school, keeping promises that you would rather break, or telling a little white lie. Duties are obligations that must be fulfilled.

Kant was one of very few moral philosophers who thought in terms of absolutes: according to him, morality is about following absolute rules. These rules are universal, meaning that they apply to every single person on the face of the earth, and without exception, meaning that you can't make excuses for not following them. Kant didn't appeal to God in saying we had absolute duties; he appealed to our reason alone and left God out of it. This doesn't mean that people who believe in God aren't moral people, though: it's just that Kant wanted duties to be universal and apply to everyone, religious or not. He has a pretty elaborate way of working out what your duties are; but to keep it simple, among our basic duties are …

♦ Always tell the truth.

♦ Always keep your promises.

♦ Never commit suicide.

But before we talk more about these, let's consider what a "duty" is.

A *duty* is something that you are required to do whether you want to or not. It means that, no matter how you feel about it or what you want to do, you must do that act: whether it's taking care of your grouchy father, or giving time for volunteering, or going to a PTA meeting. Duties are obligations that must be fulfilled.

But there's another ingredient to his recipe that you need to know about before we go any further: Kant also believed that the only thing that is totally and completely good without exception is a good will.

Kant didn't mean good will in the Christmasy, "peace on earth," "joy to the world" kind of way. What he meant was that your desires—the things you wish for—must be good. Think about "willing" in the good old-fashioned sense of wanting something really badly: It's like putting every ounce of your being into wishing that something will happen.

Kant believed that only the good will is absolutely good. He pointed out that things we think of as good—being cool and calm, for example—aren't absolute goods, because they can be used for bad purposes. Being cool and calm are "goods" that can turn bad in the hands of a thief. What makes for a really great thief is that she is calm, cool, and collected, even under stress.

Tried and True

You might think being brave is good without qualification, but bravery can result in stupidity (like bungee-jumping!) if put to the wrong purpose. Just go with Kant on this one … the only thing that's absolutely good is the good will—wishing really, really hard for good things.

We already have an example of willing. Think about our friend, Sneaky Pete. He was willing something, all right: willing that Mrs. Smith's loot would end up in his pocket! Kant would say that Sneaky Pete had a bad or evil will because he wanted very bad things. Had he been a decent kind of guy, he would have had a good will, and carried Mrs. Smith's groceries out of a sense of duty, not to serve his own goals!

Let's clear something up right now: given what Kant thinks about a good will, it's not true that "all's well that ends well." Just because an evil act turns out all right doesn't mean that the act becomes good. In Sneaky Pete's case, he didn't steal Mrs. Smith's purse, so the act turned out all right in the end, didn't it? No way! Kant would claim that his act was still wrong, no matter what the consequences, because Pete had evil intentions right from the start.

The moral here is you can't just look at behavior or outcomes to see if an act is right or wrong. A person might look like she did the right thing, even if she had evil intentions; on the other hand, she might look like she did something really bad because an act turned out wrong, even though she had really great intentions. Let's look at an example of this kind of act, using the case of *Jenny Buys Cookies for Grandma*.

Jenny is on her way one Sunday to visit her grandma in the nursing home. She knows how much her grandma loves sweets, and how rarely she gets them in the rest home. She stops at the Best Bakery to pick up some cookies—her grandma's favorite sweet. Jenny's grandma is allergic to nuts, however, and knowing this Jenny asks "Are there any nuts in these cookies?" The baker assures her there aren't; so she buys a dozen cookies to take to her grandma as a surprise.

Grandma is thrilled with Jenny's gift; and after Jenny leaves, she nibbles a couple of cookies. But alas! The baker put the wrong ones in the bag—cookies with nuts—and Jenny's grandma has a severe allergic reaction. In fact, grandma almost dies from the cookies. Jenny finds out afterward, and feels just terrible about the mistake.

What do you think about what Jenny did? Was it a good act, or a bad act? If you look at outcomes, you might say it was a *terrible* act because Jenny's grandma almost died. But there's more to the story than the chain of events—there's also the intentions of the main actor, Jenny. Does the fact that she meant well—she had really great intentions—change our reading of her act? Kant would say it should: Jenny's act is still a good one, despite the screw-ups, because she had a good will. She wasn't like Sneaky Pete, intending all the time to do something bad.

> ### Moral Musings
>
> "Nothing in the world—indeed, nothing even beyond the world—can possibly be conceived which could be called good without qualification except a GOOD WILL."
>
> —Immanuel Kant, *Foundations of the Metaphysics of Morals*, 1785

This is why Kant totally rejected outcomes as a way of judging acts: because things can turn out well even when we don't intend them to, and things can turn out terribly, even when we mean well! (The next chapter will deal with what is called consequentialist theory: It claims, directly against Kant, that what makes an act good or bad is the outcome.)

Okay, we should recap before things get really complicated. Kant's duty-based theory holds the following things:

- Duties are absolute obligations that you must follow through with regardless of your personal feelings or inclinations.
- Duties apply to all of us in the exact same way (no exceptions!).
- The only thing good in itself is a good will; it's the only "good" that can't be used for a bad purpose.
- Your will determines the morality of an act—not the outcome.

Next, we'll see why not all duties are created equally. Kant claimed that some duties are conditional and that others are absolute.

Hypothetical Versus Unconditional Commands

Kant would be asking a lot of us if he was saying that all commands or duties ("Do your homework!" "Eat your brussels sprouts!" or "Walk the dog!") must be fulfilled. That's a lot of orders to have to take! But he wasn't saying that we must obey all commands; some commands we only need to obey if we want a certain result. For example, you only need to obey the command "Do your homework!" if you care about your education or getting to university. You only need to obey the command "Walk the dog!" if you have a dog; and so on. (You'd look pretty silly walking a leash without a dog attached to it, anyway!)

Kant called these kinds of commands *hypothetical imperatives* because you can state them as "if ... then" commands. For example:

◆ *If* you want to go to college, *then* do your homework!

◆ *If* you have a dog, *then* walk it!

◆ *If* you want to be strong like Popeye, *then* eat your brussels sprouts (or was it spinach?)

You should be getting the picture. The idea here is that hypothetical imperatives are not absolute. They only apply if you care about a certain result, or if you have certain desires (like going to college).

Unconditional commands are different, though. They are commands that we must all obey—man, woman, or whoever you are. Remember that Kant believed telling the truth, keeping your promises, and protecting your life are moral commands that we all must obey. He set these three aside as unconditional commands because it follows from reason that you should never, ever, break them. Besides, the absolute wrongness of lying, breaking promises, and killing yourself flow directly from his categorical imperative, which is the test Kant gives us for deciding when and whether we should do an act. Let's consider the Categorical Imperative now, in further detail.

Ethically Speaking

Hypothetical impera-**tives** are commands that are stated in an "If ... then" form. They only apply if you want a certain result. For example: *If you want to know everything about ethics then you must read all this book!"*

Absolute No-No's: The Categorical Imperative

The Categorical Imperative isn't like "if ... then" hypothetical imperatives, which come from our desires and depend on whether we're interested in them or not. The Categorical

Imperative comes from "using our heads" or using our capacity to reason, and is absolute. It was stated by Kant this way:

> Act only according to that maxim by which you can at the same time that it should become a universal law.

It's actually not as difficult as it sounds, and it will help if we use an example to explain what he means. Suppose you're trying to decide whether or not to hop on the back of the bus for free: the doors are open, and the driver isn't looking. Should you do it or not? The way to decide, according to Kant, is to ask something like: "What if everybody did that?" Or "Could I will (or wish) that everybody in the world do it, too?"

Ethically Speaking

A **Categorical Imperative** is a moral obligation that is imposed on us no matter the circumstances or our personal desires. While hypothetical imperatives only apply in cases where you desire a certain end (like "Depart by 1:00 P.M. if you want to be at your meeting by 2:00 P.M."), Categorical Imperatives are absolute obligations that are shared by every single individual in the world.

Moral Musings

Kant says that, when figuring out what our absolute duties are, we must "Act only according to that maxim by which you can at the same time will that it should become a universal law."

Why should you ask these questions? Because as we covered earlier, Kant believes that "what's good for one is good for all." In other words, you're no special exception to the rules, and if you should be free to do something, then so should everyone else! Being a moral person means figuring out what the moral rules are and applying them to everyone, including yourself. So should you take a free ride on the bus or not? Not according to Kant—let's see why.

Kant would say that excusing yourself from paying your bus fare is not something that you could wish everyone to do. That's because you would be logically inconsistent in what you were wishing for if you wished (or willed) to get on the bus for free. You'd be willing at the same time that people both pay and not pay their bus fare. Huh? Well, you'd be willing that everyone pay their bus fare, or else there would be no bus for you to ride since there would be no paying customers; and you'd be willing that no one pay their bus fare, since if you're willing that you don't pay you're willing that nobody should pay. BINGO! You've got a logical inconsistency, and this means you can't rationally will that you should ride the bus for free. End result: get your self to the front of the bus and pay like the rest of us poor slobs!

Thinking from the Standpoint of Everyone Else

All this business about the Categorical Imperative and riding buses comes back to what I said in Chapter 1, "So, What's Your Philosophy of Life?" about taking the moral point of view. The moral point of view is where other people's goals and interests count equally with yours.

Kant is on to something here when he's telling us to think from the standpoint of everyone else: again, it's like saying "What if everyone did that?" It's a really good question to ask, unless you're an ethical egoist and you just don't care about everyone else! But most of us do care about other people; and most of us think that the rules should apply equally to everyone. As soon as you think these thoughts, you're on board with Kant.

Kant gets back to some issues raised in Chapters 6 and 7: If moral reasons are valid at all, they must be valid for all people (including yourself) at all times. What sense is there in saying "people should pay their way" but then acting on a totally different belief by sneaking on the bus for free? You'd be acting immorally (according to your own moral claim), but also irrationally. This is a really important point, since living an ethical life means acting rationally and consistently.

Tried and True

To live a truly moral life, Kant says you must act in rational and consistent ways. This means you can't claim that something is a universal moral obligation and then not act on that obligation yourself. Kant's basic view is "What's good for one is good for all."

Besides, doesn't it really tick you off when people make themselves exceptions to the rule by doing whatever the heck they want? Here's a few examples:

- People who drive on the shoulder of the road in a traffic jam, just so they can get ahead of other drivers.
- People who butt in line at the movies.
- People who run to the front of a new line that opens up at a grocery store, instead of letting other people who came before them take their turn.

People who do these things aren't just rude and arrogant: they're engaging in what Kant would call "inconsistent willing."

Here's why: Because, of course, they are willing that everyone else follow the rules (stay in line in the traffic jam; form a line at the movie theater; wait their turn at the grocery store) and that they should not follow the rules. But because when you're willing for yourself you're willing for everyone else in the world, you can only will one of these options consistently—the one that requires following the rules. You might want to point this out the next time some jerk at the grocery story runs ahead to the start of a new line!

There's another really important part of the Categorical Imperative that Kant mentions, and it also has to do with taking the moral point of view (you know, the view that other people's goals are as important to them as yours are to you). What I'm talking about is Kant's warning that we should never, ever use people.

Don't Use Me

Kant actually had two formulations of the categorical imperative:

1. The first one about "universally willing the maxim of your actions" (or taking the standpoint of everyone else), and this one.

2. "Act so that you treat humanity, whether in your own person or in that of another, always as an end and never as a means only."

Rewind. Play again, only this time in plain English. What he's stating is a version of the Golden Rule: Don't use people. Respect others. Don't treat people like things. Kant is saying: treat all of humanity, yourself and other people, as ends (the main goal), not as means only (don't just use them!). Most people can appreciate this version of the Categorical Imperative, whether they are religious or not.

This idea, "don't use people," falls from the fact that people have two important characteristics:

◆ They can think for themselves.

◆ They have an independent will.

Kant argues that these two things—reason and will—put human beings into their own special kingdom ... what he calls the "kingdom of ends." Unlike things that were created for human use, individuals have their *own* ends, and are not for use like mere things.

Ethically Speaking

Kant emphasizes the importance of **autonomy**, or being in control of your own life. As rational agents with the capacity to choose our own ends, we each have the absolute right to rule our own lives. So we should never ever use people to suit our own ends, because in doing so we violate their autonomy and end up treating them as "things."

What makes it so wrong to use people? It's that doing so fails to respect them as the unique, rational, willing beings that they are. Part of what it means to have reason and will is to be *autonomous*—to be self-governing, or in charge of your own life. By using or manipulating people to suit our own needs, we violate this autonomy that they have, and we treat people as objects or things.

Remember, Kant says we should never treat people "as a means *only*." This "only" is really important: it tells us that while we may use people, we should at the same time recognize their autonomy.

A good example is when you're at a restaurant, and a waitress is serving you. Hey, you might say, aren't I just "using" the waitress as a means to an end? I use her to bring my food to the table and to get what I want. But when you're using the waitress, you don't fail to respect her as a unique individual (at least, I hope not!); you don't treat her as a thing.

Kant's point is that we may use people—to get our cars fixed, bring food to our tables, to take care of our children, etc.—but while we're doing so we shouldn't only be using them. People are distinct from cars and other objects that were created for our use: they are able to think for themselves, and determine their own good. We never have good reasons to decide for others, unless for some reason they can't do it for themselves (like babies or the mentally handicapped).

Kant's ideas about "respect for persons" come up all the time, and are most obvious in health care situations. Walk in to any hospital and you'll see a "Patient Bill of Rights" pasted to the wall. To have any medical procedure done, you have to formally give your informed consent by signing a long, fine-print document. More and more people are encouraged to have an advance directive for health care: these are documents that you fill in and sign, and they indicate what your medical wishes are if you aren't able to speak for yourself in an emergency situation. Advance directives determine things like: do you want CPR? Do you want to be put on a respirator? These practices are all based on the idea of "patient autonomy," and come right back to Kant's notion that people, as rational beings, should be free to choose for themselves. So that's how a dead white guy from Germany has any relevance to ethics today.

Being Your Own Person

Of course, built into this great notion of respect for persons is a lot of heavy-duty responsibilities on your part. For example it means that you have to be your own person. It means that you always have to act as a rational, autonomous chooser. And it means that you have to behave independently of your prejudices, personal preferences, or self-serving motives. In short, if you want the freedom you have to use it wisely—Kant expected nothing less of us. He didn't demand that we be perfect, or that we have IQs of 140—on the contrary, his ethical theory was meant to be based on common sense and reason!

If you think those are heavy responsibilities, try this one on for size: Kant claims that because you have reason and will, your ability to rule your life should be respected even if you might hurt yourself and others in the process. This is all part of what it means to take responsibility: you have choices, and the freedom to choose wrongly.

Do the Right Thing!

If you want freedom you have to use it wisely—Kant expected nothing less of us. This means it's *your* responsibility if you make the wrong choices or do bad things. You can't come crying to us—as the saying goes, "You made your bed ... now lie in it!"

But here's where free will gets really heavy: Kant says you can't come crying to us if you violate the good will by intentionally choosing a bad act. He was so committed to respect for persons that he thought criminals should be respected, too. After all, just because they do bad things doesn't mean they aren't capable of being held responsible. For Kant, to respect criminals we need to hold them responsible for their bad acts just because they could have done otherwise. But they didn't. And so they have to pay!

Getting Your Just Deserts

If you haven't already guessed, Kant's moral theory tells us something about how to treat criminals. He wasn't a bleeding heart, "they can't help themselves" kind of guy: no, Kant took the hard line about people who do wrong. He said those folks deserve whatever they get for their wrongdoing; in short, he supported *retributivism*.

Ethically Speaking

Retributivism is a theory of punishment that is best summed up by the phrase "an eye for an eye." Retributivists claim that criminals should get back in kind what they dish out; this is where killing criminals because they killed other people comes in. Retributivism is often used as a justification for capital punishment.

Moral Musings

"When someone who delights in annoying and vexing peace-loving folk receives at last a right good beating, it is certainly an ill, but everyone approves of it and considers it as good in itself even if nothing further results from it."

—Immanuel Kant, *The Critique of Practical Reason* (1788)

But you might wonder why Kant was a retributivist. Well, it's back to good old reason and will again. Since criminals, like the rest of us, have a free will and the capacity for reason, they have the freedom to decide for themselves what to do. They can't claim that "the devil made me do it" or that they were abused as a child, or didn't have a good upbringing—in short, no excuses! So before the criminal did the bad act, he must have considered doing it from the "what if everyone did that?" perspective. Suppose he robbed a bank, knowing that the consequences are 25 years in prison. In going through with the robbery, the criminal had to will both the bad thing and the penalty. So, according to Kant, in going through with the robbery the criminal has asked to be punished, and it would be morally wrong not to do it!

This might sound strange to you—that criminals will their punishment—but it fits well with Kant's idea of respect for persons. If the ultimate in respecting people means following their will, and the criminal wills both his bad act and his punishment, then we basically owe it to him to give that punishment.

Kant took this view as far as it could go. For example, he said that trying to rehabilitate criminals in prison was a bad thing because rehabilitation comes down to nothing more than trying to make people behave in ways we think is right. "What's wrong with that?" you might ask. It's wrong because it violates the respect for persons that he is so concerned about—"rehabilitation" involves using prisoners as means to social ends. In other words, if a criminal doesn't willfully change her mind based on the use of her reason, then we shouldn't try and force her to change it.

Kant could be a pretty cold guy. Look at what he says about punishing a murderer, even in the case where a society is coming to an end:

> Even if a civil society resolved to dissolve itself with the consent of all its members—as might be supposed in the case of a people inhabiting an island resolving to separate and scatter throughout the whole world—the last murderer lying in prison ought to be executed before the resolution was carried out. This ought to be done in order that every one may realize the desert of his deeds, and that blood-guiltiness may not remain on the people; for otherwise they will all be regarded as participants in the murder as a public violation of justice.

There's a really great lesson in all this, and that is: Be careful what you wish for, you just might get it! According to Kant's theory, if you do the crime, you do the time. And he isn't just talking about prison or capital punishment here: He means that any act you do is an expression of your will, so you'd better be ready to take responsibility for it. Now that gives us all some food for thought!

Finally, consider how seriously Kant took his views about duty and intentions. For this guy, it isn't enough that you do the right thing: You have to do the right thing for the right reasons. The only right reason to ever do anything is to do it for duty's sake. And here's where Kant gets a little weird: he said that kind, friendly, caring people who do good acts because they want to (because they're kind, friendly, and caring) aren't acting morally, but that grouchy, mean people who act begrudgingly out of duty are acting morally. How is this even possible?

It's because the nice person, who is inclined to be friendly and helpful to others, isn't acting on duty alone—she's acting on her inclinations. The old grouch, on the other hand, is acting on duty alone: He doesn't like people, and doesn't really *want* to do whatever it is, but he does it anyway because he must. So the grouch is acting from duty alone, and the nice person isn't—making the grouch morally better. (What a strange world we live in ....)

> **Tried and True**
>
> You might not agree with all aspects of Kant's duty-based theory, but you've got to admit that he's got some good stuff in there. "Respect for persons"—that sounds nice. Thinking "What if everyone did that?"—that's a good move. And recognizing that we all have duties that we are obligated to fulfil ... that's good, too.

A lot of what Kant says might speak to some beliefs you already have. Later in Chapter 15, "There's a Fly in My Recipe," we'll see that there are problems with Kant's theory, but for now we'll give the guy the benefit of the doubt. May he rest in peace.

The Least You Need to Know

- When making a moral choice, ask yourself: "What if everyone did that?"
- Always have respect for other people. It's wrong to force your will upon others, or to use them for your purposes.
- Be careful what you wish for, you just might get it!
- Act from the right intentions: it's not enough that things turn out all right in the end.
- If you think everyone else should follow the rules, then so should you.

Chapter 13

Consequentialist Theories

In This Chapter

- ◆ Why outcomes matter to ethics
- ◆ Thinking about pleasure and pain
- ◆ Is reading philosophy morally better than dining out? Making distinctions between pleasures
- ◆ Setting rules for the best possible outcomes

Imagine yourself in this situation: You're driving to a friend's house to pick him up because you promised to go to a movie with him. To your horror, a little kid on his bicycle suddenly comes into the intersection and gets slammed by an on-coming car. Since you know basic CPR, you would be able to help the little kid until an ambulance can get there. What should you do?

If you answered "I should hit the gas pedal and head on over to my friend's house so we're not late for our movie date," then you failed this particular ethics exam! Most people would say without hesitation that you should stop to help the little kid, even if it means you miss the movie and break your promise to your friend. Why? Because the consequences of not stopping would be horrendous: the little kid could lay there and die without any help.

Did someone say "consequences"? Yep, that's what this chapter is all about. Kant may have thought that you should never, ever break your promises, but in this chapter you're going to consider a totally different view of ethics. We'll consider the view that what counts more than *anything* else is the outcomes of your actions, and that when you're trying to decide what to do you should always choose the act that will have the best possible outcomes. So do your ... uh ... duty (sorry, that was the last chapter!) and give this chapter a read.

Sorry, Kant: Outcomes Matter

Immanuel Kant's duty-based theory commands you to ignore outcomes and always act on your duty. He tells you specifically that you should never lie and never break your promises. And if you remember correctly, Kant had good reasons for claiming these things: Sometimes acts can turn out terribly, even though you meant well, and other times they can work out great, even though you intended very bad outcomes. So according to his theory, you should totally set aside outcomes—they are morally irrelevant to determining right and wrong—and focus only on intentions and duties.

I don't know about you, but I agree with a lot of what Kant has to say. It's true that we don't always judge right and wrong based on outcomes. Remember poor old Jenny and the cookie fiasco? She meant well, and she was doing her duty by visiting her grandma, but—whoops!—things went very wrong. But we don't blame Jenny for that ... we don't say that she did something wrong because her good intentions turned sour. It was just unfortunate, and that's the end of that.

But the case of the kid getting hit with a car? Now that's a different story! In that case, not too many people would set aside the consequences of your action and say that outcomes don't matter ... in fact, if you did drive off to keep your movie date, most people would judge you to be a creep, a sociopath, and other bad things! That's because you have a choice to make, and one option clearly has better outcomes than the other. You choose option one and go to see your movie, you get greasy hands from your popcorn and maybe a little gas. You choose option two and stop to help the little kid, you potentially save a life. It's not hard to do the moral calculations in that case!

Ethically Speaking

Consequentialism is an ethical theory that determines good or bad, right or wrong, based on outcomes. If you're stuck in an ethical dilemma, then consequentialists tell you to choose the act that does the greatest good—or the least amount of harm—for the greatest number of people.

So maybe Kant was wrong to say that consequences never matter. I'm sure you can think of all kinds of examples in your own life where the outcomes of your choices were really important. If you're thinking about those examples, then you've already gone part way down the road to *consequentialism*. Consequentialists claim that what is right or wrong, good or bad, depends on outcomes: specifically, that how much good you do (or how much bad you avoid) is the measuring stick for ethics.

Consequentialism gets at certain intuitions we have about ethics: that "doing good" means not causing unnecessary pain, suffering, or harm to other creatures. Notice I didn't say "other human beings," but "other creatures." This is an important point I'll expand upon shortly—that consequentialists don't exclude animals from their moral theory. Why do animals count, too? Because if we're weighing consequences, and part of what we're concerned about is avoiding causing pain, and animals feel pain, too, then ... I think you can see where consequentialists end up!

But we don't want to get ahead of ourselves here, so let's back up for a second and consider one of the greatest proponents of consequentialism, Mr. Jeremy Bentham.

Jeremy Bentham's Utilitarianism

To get a clear picture of consequentialism, you need to understand Jeremy Bentham's own particular version of it. Bentham lived from 1748 to 1832, and during his lifetime argued strongly for a version of consequentialism that he called *Utilitarianism*. According to his Utilitarian theory, morality has nothing to do with pleasing God or being committed to absolute rules (sorry, Kant!); rather, morality comes down to nothing more than the attempt to create as much happiness in the world as possible.

You're really going to like Bentham's Utilitarian theory, because it's as simple as pie: He was a hedonist who believed that each individual's happiness is based on pleasure and pain. To put it simply, increased pleasure and decreased pain bring about happiness; increased pain and decreased pleasure cause unhappiness. Our moral job, according to this hedonist fellow, is to go about creating as many pleasures and avoiding as many pains as possible—and not just for ourselves, but for others as well.

Ethically Speaking

Utilitarianism is a moral theory that treats pleasure or happiness as the only absolute moral good. According to Utilitarian thinkers, the morality of your actions depends on their results. Acts that bring about an overall increase in happiness or pleasure are morally good; those that result in suffering or pain are morally bad. Happiness and pleasure—sounds good, don't you think?

The Principle of Utility

Bentham's ultimate moral principle is the *Principle of Utility*. Put simply, it states that when we have a choice between alternative actions or social policies, we do the one that has the best overall consequences for everyone concerned. He says:

> By utility is meant that property in any object, whereby it tends to produce benefit, advantage, pleasure, good, or happiness (all this in the present case comes to the

same thing) or (what comes again to the same thing) to prevent the happening of mischief, pain, evil, or unhappiness.

Bentham saw the desire for pleasure and aversion to pain as the great human motivators, and in this he probably wasn't wrong. I mean, who likes pain? Okay, so maybe some of us get off on it, but for the most part we avoid it at all costs! We put off that call to the doctor or dentist for as long as possible; but when it comes to things that give us pleasure, we just can't get enough! Bentham also claimed that each persons' happiness or pleasure was of equal value, and should be weighed equally when determining how you should act.

Bentham's democratic approach to happiness wasn't just saying that we should each go out and "do our thing" to create pleasure for ourselves; we have to consider other people and their pleasure, too. Why? Because of the moral attitude I talked about in Chapter 1, "So, What's Your Philosophy of Life?" where other people's needs matter as much as yours. Hedonism doesn't have to be egoistic, then: it can be social! Bentham said that you should be motivated to act, not just for the sake of your own pleasure, but for the sake of others' pleasure, too. His democratic approach is best reflected in his claim that we should promote "the greatest amount of happiness for the greatest number." Each person's pleasure or pain should count equally when you're trying to make a choice.

Do the Right Thing!

When trying to determine which act results in the greatest amount of pleasure, you can't just consider yourself. You have to be motivated to act for the sake of others' pleasure, too. So if you're ever trying to decide how best to spend your money, you have to consider what kind of expenditure will bring about the most pleasure for the greatest number of people.

So for Bentham, maximizing happiness in society comes down to promoting pleasure and minimizing pain. But get this: He also thought that you could scientifically determine which act promotes the greatest amount of pleasure. Bentham did this by setting up seven categories with seven questions you have to ask yourself:

1. **Intensity:** How intense is the pleasure?
2. **Duration:** How long does the pleasure last?
3. **Certainty:** How certain are you that the pleasure will occur?
4. **Proximity:** How soon will the pleasure be experienced?
5. **Fecundity:** How many more pleasures will happen because of this one?
6. **Purity:** How free from pain is the pleasure?
7. **Extent:** How many of us will experience the pleasure?

Bentham actually thought that by getting out a pen and paper, and giving a "score" for each act you have to choose from, you can scientifically work out which act is morally better. So go grab a pen and paper, and let's try this out.

Rating Our Pleasures

Okay, got them? What you will score is choice A—reading a philosophy book—(hey—reading *this* philosophy book!) versus choice B—having a great dinner out. If you are given the option to do either thing, which one should you choose? Well, let's score each choice based on the 7 questions above and see! We'll use a scale of 1–10, with 1 being no pleasure, 5 being average, and 10 being total pleasure. Here we go!

Choice A—Reading a philosophy book:

1. **Intensity:** Well, unless you're sadistic, you probably don't experience intense pleasure from reading philosophy. You may even find it a little painful sometimes (see #6—purity—on this)! But there may be some pleasure from the experience of learning, so let's give this 5 points.

2. **Duration:** Do you find that the pleasure of reading philosophy—whatever pleasure you get—is long-lasting, or short-lived? Let's score this a little higher, since learning lasts a lifetime: 8 points.

3. **Certainty:** It may not be all that certain that you'll get *any* pleasure out of this or any other philosophy book! So let's give this one only 3 points.

4. **Proximity:** The pleasure isn't likely to come immediately with the experience of reading philosophy … it's more likely to come later. You only really appreciate learning after the fact! So we'll score this kind of low, and give it 3 points, too.

5. **Fecundity:** Here you might want to give a higher score, since the other pleasures that follow from reading philosophy could be great. For example, people might think you're really smart and well-read, which will make you feel really good! A score of 8 points here might be reasonable.

6. **Purity:** Hmmm … it's not clear that reading philosophy is all that free of pain! In fact, while people do it, they usually do it knowing that it ain't always fun. So on the purity score, we'll have to give reading philosophy only 2 points.

7. **Extent:** How many people will experience the pleasure? You're the only one who will directly experience the pleasure of reading a philosophy book; I suppose other people could indirectly experience it from seeing you improve yourself, or by your holding a

Tried and True

When thinking about maximizing pleasure, you've got to include all the possible pleasures and pains that could attach to an act. So if you'll feel guilty for not finishing this book, then that "pain" has got to be included in your calculations about whether to finish it or not. Or if you'll gain weight or get gas from eating that good dinner out (instead of reading this book!) then you've got to include that, too, as pains that are likely to occur.

really intelligent philosophical conversation with them. Then again, you might bore them to death! So unless you go out on the street corner and read out loud from your philosophy book, we'll have to give this one the lowest score: 1 point!

Now for choice B—Having a great dinner out:

1. **Intensity:** Well, most of us derive intense pleasure from eating, and especially when it's really delicious food. Since this is a "great dinner" out, you will probably score it high: 9 points. (We'll give it 9 since some pleasures—like having sex—could still beat it out!)

2. **Duration:** While a good dinner is pleasurable, it's kind of a "fleeting" pleasure, isn't it? I mean, once that porterhouse steak, lobster tail, or vegetarian kebab is gone, it's gone. So let's rate having a great dinner low on the duration scale: 3 points.

3. **Certainty:** Here you'll give a pretty high score again. Knowing that you're going to a great restaurant, and that you'll get to eat what you want, it's pretty certain that the pleasure is going to come, isn't it? Of course, it's possible that your dinner salad may have a bug in it or something, but we'll just assume that all will be tasty: 9 points for certainty.

4. **Proximity:** Knowing that your taste buds will say "yum!" the minute you put that tasty morsel into your mouth, we'll give this a high score, too: 9 points.

5. **Fecundity:** This will have to be rated low. After all, what else follows from a really great dinner? Nothing long-lasting except some gas, or maybe weight gain. So you'll probably want to give 2 points for fecundity.

6. **Purity:** Like I said, there might be some pains associated with your fine dining, like bloat or gas, and possible weight gain (especially if you eat the 20 ounce porterhouse steak!) But still, the dining experience itself will be pretty great: 7 points.

7. **Extent:** How likely is it that many people will experience the pleasure? If you invite a friend along (and I'm sure you wouldn't want to eat at a fine restaurant all by yourself) then at least a couple of people will experience it. But still, it's a limited number, so give it a low score: 2 points.

And the grand totals are: Reading a philosophy book, 30 points. Having a great dinner out, 41 points. Choice B beats out choice A, hands down. So why are you sitting there reading this book?

But you might be thinking, "Hey, this doesn't work! How can you compare reading a book with dining out? They're entirely different things (one involves your mind and the other involves your gut) and it's really hard to compare them!" If you're thinking this, then you're a smart cookie. This is the fly in Bentham's soup.

You Can't Compare Apples and Oranges

Sure, it would be nice if we could scientifically work out the best choice and then go with it: Making ethical choices would be so much easier then! But Bentham's little calculus just doesn't work, because he's asking us to compare apples and oranges. In the exercise you just did, you tried to compare reading and dining out, which aren't that easy to compare, are they? Well, according to Bentham, there's no difference between pleasures: He thought one is as good as another.

In fact, Bentham once said that "pushpin is as good as poetry" (pushpin being a type of bowling). Basically, he thought that bowling and reading poetry are on par. In one way this is nice: it shows he wasn't a snob who put going to the theater above "lowly" things like drinking beer or pigging out. But let's change the examples for a minute: suppose one sicko's pleasure involves kicking cute, fluffy puppies (remember Chapter 7, "'Us First' Ethics"?) and another person's pleasure involves volunteering at the humane society. Do you really want to say that, when comparing those two pleasures, kicking cute, fluffy little puppies is as good as volunteering at the humane society? I think not! So why would Bentham make such a strange claim?

Basically, he was concerned that, if the "elite" decided some pleasures were better than others, they'd be likely to pick *their* pleasures as the better ones. Suppose you're a very rich business person who gets a lot of pleasure out of your wealth: High taxes for the wealthy are very unpleasant because they interfere with the joy you get out of spending your great wads of money. You might decide that, being better than other folks, your pleasures are better than theirs, too. That would mean the pleasure you get out of keeping taxes low for the wealthy would be "better" than the pleasure that the rest of the low-lifes get out of higher taxes for them. But if all pleasures are considered equally—so that your pleasure from having low taxes for the rich is equal to my pleasure from having higher ones—then everyone is considered equally because their pleasures are equally important.

This mattered a lot to Bentham because, in his lifetime, the poor, uneducated, and lower classes had not been counted equally. It was as if the needs, desires, and pleasures of the rich were more important than those of the poor: He saw all kinds of injustices against the poor, like no voting rights, working hours and conditions that caused people to be hurt or killed, and child slave labor. This is why his Utilitarian theory was so revolutionary: Because he argued that the poor, uneducated lower classes should count equally with the rich, educated upper class. And this is also why he emphasized that, when weighing out pleasures and pains, they all count equally and none are better than others.

Bentham was a good guy, because he saw all these injustices going on and, even though he benefited from them (because he was rich, educated, and upper class) he argued for change. He really cared about democracy, and his Utilitarian theory came directly out of his social concerns. Still, you just might want to question Bentham's claim that one pleasure is as good as another. In fact, some people already *have* questioned his claim, including one of his own followers, another great philosopher named John Stuart Mill.

Quality Is Better Than Quantity

John Stuart Mill cut his teeth on Bentham's principles: His father raised him as the next great Utilitarian to follow Bentham's lead. But this doesn't mean that he agreed with every little thing that Bentham said. In fact, Mill disputed some important claims made by Bentham, including his claim that "pushpin is as good as poetry."

Mill's view was that we shouldn't judge the *quantity* of pleasure (how much pleasure you get from an act), but rather the *quality* of it. He disagreed with Bentham that "a pleasure is a pleasure," and said instead that some kinds are of higher quality than others. The pleasure you get from volunteering at the humane society is a higher quality pleasure than the other guy's pleasure from kicking helpless little puppies. The pleasure from reading philosophy is richer in quality than the pleasure from having a great dinner out. And the pleasure of reading Shakespeare is of a higher sort than the pleasure of reading girlie magazines. If we think about quality of pleasure and not just quantity, then we can see that some *are* better than others. As Mill himself once said, it's "better to be a human being dissatisfied than a pig satisfied."

Mill also claimed that when we are trying to decide what to do, and are choosing between options, then we should let people who have experience of both options make the choice. Look at it this way: if you have no experience of reading philosophy, then how can you judge whether you should do that or have a good dinner out? If you have to choose between lower or higher taxes for the rich, then how can you make an informed choice if you don't know what it's like to be poor? I think you get the picture here …. Mill is just pointing out that you need to have experience with both in order to make the choice.

Ethically Speaking

John Stuart Mill distinguished between kinds of pleasures, and thought **quality** was more important than **quantity**. The quality of a pleasure is proportional to the degree to which it contributes to a person's overall intellectual, moral, and aesthetic development. The quantity is just how much pleasure you get out of an act, including how long it lasts, and how good it feels.

Don't think that Mill was just a snob who thought the educated and upper class were better than the poor. That's not why he made this distinction between "higher" and "lower" pleasures. Mill figured that if the average person were given the choice between human pleasures and piggish ones, we'd tend to choose the piggish ones. And this could spell bad news when we're trying to decide between increasing funding for the arts (for example) or giving everyone a big tax rebate. A lot of us would choose the big tax rebate—but this could be really bad for the advancement and enrichment of human beings! So that's why we need people who have experience with *both* "higher" and "lower" pleasures to choose between them … because otherwise we'll be like those piggies, wallowing in the muck and gorging ourselves on piggish delights!

That's why Mill took a different approach to Utilitarianism: instead of focusing on pains and pleasures in each individual case like Bentham, Mill thought about them in the long run. He figured that if we're going to really have the best outcomes (i.e. create the most pleasure/avoid the most pain), then we need to set rules that serve to maximize pleasure and minimize pain. He pointed to our traditions as ways of knowing when pleasures outweigh pains in the long run. Let's consider this point in more detail.

John Stuart Mill's Rule of Utilitarianism

If our ethical goal is to ensure the greatest amount of happiness for the greatest number, then we have to think carefully about how to do this. We could—as Bentham argued— take each case individually and try to determine what will result in the best outcomes. This would mean every time a dilemma or choice comes our way, we'd use Bentham's pleasure calculus to figure out which way to go. But there are problems with doing this.

First of all, imagine how tedious that could be. It means that every time a situation arises, you'd have to start fresh and calculate out pleasures and pains. Talk about ripping your hair out! Who needs this kind of hassle? Second, weighing out consequences in this case-by-case way overlooks the whole history of human trial and error. Why should you go to the trouble of figuring out whether you should kill or steal (or whatever), when the people who came before us have already done that? All we have to do is look at our traditions and laws to see what results in best outcomes.

For Mill, human laws ("don't steal," or "don't kill") are nothing more than rules that have been set out to ensure the best possible outcomes for all of us. Laws against killing have come to pass because, over the ages, human beings figured out that killing has bad consequences in the long run. Someone dies; a family loses a family member; it results in lawlessness—you get the picture. The saying you're probably already familiar with, "crime doesn't pay," makes the point here: It became a social platitude because people figured out over the centuries that it's true!

So Mill's point is simple: let tradition be your guide! It never hurts to set a few little rules to ensure the best consequences in the long run.

Tried and True

You can view human laws as rules that ensure the best possible outcomes for everybody. For example, have you ever wondered why we have the saying "crime doesn't pay"? It's because, after generations of people experiencing the consequences of criminal activity, we know that (for the most part) criminal life just doesn't pay off.

That's what human laws and social taboos are all about: they are guides for us to follow so that we get the best possible outcomes. Let's look at a quick example to see why this is true.

Suppose you're in neighbor John's apple orchard and you're really hungry. You see all the delicious apples that would satisfy your hunger. If you're like Bentham, you'll steal one of John's apples. Why? Because you'll reason that John will not be hurt by missing a few measly apples and you'll be made very happy. But suppose instead you're like Mill: you won't steal the apple because it violates a rule against stealing. And following this rule without exception maximizes the greatest happiness for the greatest number. That's because if anybody tried to make an exception to the rule, then the rule would be weakened, and you wouldn't get the maximal social benefits from it.

So as a general rule, Mill would say, having a rule against stealing is best. Human beings have learned that through trial and error. And since that bit of wisdom is already available to you, instead of reinventing the wheel every time you have to make a decision, you can just appeal to our traditions.

Mill was a really smart guy, because he was on to something that Bentham didn't see: that following tradition is one way of ensuring the best outcomes. Besides being meaningful to us because they link us in community, traditions are bits of wisdom that our ancestors picked up through their experiences, and they're useful tools for maximizing happiness. So the next time you face a moral dilemma, think about our social traditions, our taboos and laws, and you'll already have some good indications of what will result in the best consequences for all!

The Least You Need to Know

- Think about the consequences of your actions.
- Don't be short-sighted when weighing out consequences: sometimes you're better off doing something in the long run that looks less appealing in the short run!
- Consider all creatures' pleasures and pains equally: even animals count!
- When you're making judgments, make sure you have experience on all sides before you make your choice.
- Remember: Not all pleasures are equal. Some are of higher quality than others.

Chapter 14

Using the "F" Word: Feminist Ethics

In This Chapter

- ◆ Are women "natural" caregivers?
- ◆ Women's morality: an ethic of care
- ◆ Egoism for men, altruism for women?
- ◆ Going beyond an ethic of care

Why is it that most caregivers in our society are women? If you look hard, you'll notice that women do most of the care work for babies and children, the elderly, people with disabilities, and the mentally handicapped. Women fill almost all jobs as nursery school, kindergarten and primary school teachers; almost all workers in nursing homes are female; and women occupy most of the jobs as nurses, day care workers, and service workers. What's going on here? Is it that women get off on cleaning up vomit, urine, and feces? Do women's uteruses cramp at the sight of a baby, making them feel a strong urge to care for it?

Our traditional theories about women and care work claim that it's "only natural" to do this work: as the ones who carry and give birth to babies, women are supposedly "naturals" at the whole caregiving thing. They're driven to it.

They melt at the sight of helpless babies or a sick person in need of help. Men bring home the bacon; women fry it up and feed it to the weak and ill.

In this chapter we will consider the caretaking role that women have historically played, and the idea of a "woman's ethic" that derives from their caregiving. This ethic will look really different from the ones that Kant, Mill, Bentham, Hobbes and the gang came up with. This feminist ethic—an ethic of care—denies that we are as independent from others as they say we are. It rejects the kind of high-handed, theoretical ways of thinking about ethics that Kant and the other dead white guys came up with. Let's see what feminist ethics is all about.

Do Women Have a Different Morality?

If you haven't noticed yet, let me point something out to you: All of the ethical theories you've read about so far were dreamed up by men. But not just any men: they were men who had the luxury of time to sit around and think about stuff. Imagine trying to think deep thoughts about ethics and the good life when you've got laundry to worry about, or kids to feed, or a house that needs cleaning, or an elderly mom or dad to take care of! The dead white guys you've read about so far had none of these worries, and why? Because they had someone taking care of all these things for them ... their wives, mothers, sisters, housekeepers—in short, women. Yes, women have done all the care work, from ancient Greece to the present.

> **Moral Musings**
>
> It's not surprising that the moral theories you've read about so far have been thought up by men. It's been mostly men since ancient times who have had the freedom and luxury of time to sit around and think about things. If women's voices are absent in the history of ethics, it's likely because they were kept out of universities and politics and expected to stay at home and raise children.

Of course, since Mrs. Plato and Mrs. Aristotle were busy feeding the kids and doing the laundry, they weren't walking around the streets of Athens or sitting in the Lyceum (the first university ever created) talking about ethics with the guys. This means that ever since ethics started as a theory and practice, women have been left out of it. But, you might say, it doesn't really matter, does it? If ethics is universal and applies to everyone equally, then it shouldn't matter whether men or women come up with the ideas; everyone's included.

But it *does* matter that women have been left out of the conversation, because the conversation has been slanted in a certain direction. Women have been talked about in their absence: and the philosopher guys have said some really nasty things about them! For example, they have said that women are incapable of rational thought; that women are immature; that women are ruled by nature because they menstruate, give birth, and lactate; and that men need to be the "heads of the household" because women aren't capable of the moral and economic sense to run things right. Basically, moral philosophers have painted women as silly, immature, and incompetent.

And if this isn't bad enough, the way ethics has been talked about has also been slanted. Recall Chapter 3, "Convince Me That I'm Wrong," where you considered the scenario of your mother in a burning building. Ethicists have claimed that you shouldn't be partial in your moral consideration of who to drag out of there: You can't have a policy of "mom first!" just because it's your mom. The reason ethicists say this is that ethics has been ruled by objective, universal thinking; thinking that has been dictated by men.

Women and Ethics

Do this thought experiment, though: what if women had been involved in coming up with ethical theories? Is it so likely that we would now be focusing on things like objectivity and universal approaches? Probably not, since women have always been grounded by their particular relationships with their kids, their parents, and their sick and needy neighbors. Women couldn't have their heads in the clouds, because they've usually had their heads in buckets of soapy water, keeping the house clean! It's possible, then, that if women had been given more control over the way philosophy was done, they would have influenced the way we think about ethics.

Guess what? This is exactly what feminist ethicists are now arguing. They claim that the way we do ethics has been overly influenced by men, who have different values and a different focus than women. Because women are—and have been—caregivers, they have a moral perspective that is formed by their relationships with other people. So the idea of women having a "different morality" doesn't necessarily mean that women are biologically different from men in the way they do ethics ... it may just mean that women have been socialized differently and so have a different moral focus!

 Tried and True

In the late 1700s, Mary Wollstonecraft wrote *A Vindication of the Rights of Woman*. In it, she criticizes women's exclusion from educational opportunities and from moral and political life. We should acknowledge and appreciate these early attempts to argue for women's equal right to participate in these areas of life.

A "Woman's Morality"?

And what might that different moral focus be? It is one that rejects the kind of absolute approaches offered by guys like Kant and Mill, where everyone counts absolutely equally and you should use reason alone to figure out what to do. "Baloney!" the feminists say, "What's so bad about letting personal considerations enter into your moral decisions, and what the heck is so bad about being emotional?"

These are good questions. Think about your mom, still burning away in that building. Feminist ethicists would make us question the claim that we should consider impartially who to save from the burning building—you'd be a pretty crummy son/daughter to seriously weigh out who to save. Mom is mom, feminists argue, and rather than being morally questionable, the *only* right thing to do is run in there and get her out! Failing to consider the particular aspects of your moral dilemmas, and the fact that people you really care about are involved, is actually *unethical* according to feminists.

So what we need is a different kind of ethical approach that takes real life seriously; one that includes our relationships with people we love and care about. Feminists claim that we can find that commonsense ethical approach by looking at women's relationships of care. They claim that women have a "different morality"—and a better morality!—than the kind men have offered throughout the ages. It's called an "ethic of care," and comes out of our relationships. So let's feel the love and take a closer look at the ethic of care.

The Ethic of Care

The feminist *ethic of care* came about because modern women pulled off their rubber gloves and came out of the kitchen. They went to universities and, in increasing numbers, started to affect the way we think about things (you go, girls!) And when smart, savvy women started thinking about how ethics is talked about and thought about, they realized that we've only been offered one way—men's way—of doing it.

Ethically Speaking

The **ethic of care** is a different approach to ethics that starts with the importance of relationships. This approach rejects absolutist, objective, impartial approaches to ethics; it argues for the moral value of caring and nurturing, and sees the highest moral good as caring for (and about) others.

So what's been missing from ethics so far, then? How about the most basic ingredients of human life: caring for and about other people, the importance of nurturing, the deep interconnections between human beings, and the way in which our actions can really hurt others that we care about. The ethic of care gets at these things because it understands each and every one of us as being in need of care, nurturance, and love. Maybe The Beatles had it right when they said "All you need is love."

Feminists claim that this ethic of care is a "women's" ethic because we can see it most in women's relationships with people who are dependent on them.

Relationships aren't often voluntary—you can't pick your family!—so the idea of a "social contract" between consenting equals sounds like a joke in real life. Feminists claim that social contract theorists aren't dealing with the real world: it makes no sense to say that a mother and her baby "contract" in some way for mutual benefit. Just imagine it! "Okay, Ma, give me some of that breast milk and I'll give you some cooing and smiles!"

Care and Context

The ethic of care can actually be laid out pretty concretely: it rejects absolute rules like those of Kant ("Always tell the truth!" or "Always keep your promises!") for contextual considerations. Feminists point out that the particular features of our moral dilemmas actually do matter: it's your mother's feelings at risk, or your kid's happiness, and not just anybody's! So when an ethical dilemma comes your way, instead of asking "What if everyone did that?" you figure out what to do under the circumstances you find yourself in. It might require lying or breaking a promise to maintain relationships and to respond to other people's need for caring—and if that's true, then you go ahead and do it! If your best friend is feeling really vulnerable and asks you if her new hair color looks good, you lie and tell her that the shade of pink looks really great on her if that's what it takes to maintain the relationship. To sum up an ethic of care in two words: relationships matter.

Notice a couple of things about this ethic. It comes out of women's caregiving practices, but it doesn't mean you must be a woman to take on an ethic of care. Men can be in on it, too! In fact, feminists argue, men *should* be in on it, since the ethic of care is a far sight better than the traditional ethical theories you've read about. Let's consider why feminists say this.

> ### Moral Musings
>
> "… contractual solutions are increasingly suggested for problems which arise in areas not hitherto thought of in contractual terms, such as in dealing with unruly patients in treatment contexts, in controlling inmates in prisons, and even in bringing up children."
>
> —Virginia Held, *Non-contractual Society: A Feminist View,* 1987

The Ethics of War

The kinds of ethical theories that Kant, Mill, Hobbes, and the boys have come up with have been what you might call ethics of war—they take human beings to be in competition with one another, or at least as being isolated, independent, and self-sufficient. According to their theories, you don't need other people in order to do your moral reasoning and, in fact, these guys think that other people can get in the way of doing it well! It is that kind of ethics, argue feminists, that have led us to war, competition, and destruction. Rather than seeing our shared interests, traditional ethics tends to pit us against one another, thus leading us to behave in ways that encourage fighting, competition, and ultimately destruction. For example, Kant's idea that we only have moral duties to other rational people means that we've destroyed animals and our environment; a more peaceable ethic may be in order if we're going to survive the millennium!

An ethic of care is a "peaceable" ethic because it denies that we're isolated, independent, and self-sufficient. If we need one another—I mean, *really* need one another—then we're unlikely to see each other as competitors for limited resources. We are in relationships of care, and we owe it to one another to nurture and sustain ourselves and our environment. For example, an ethic of care would require us to care about our environment so that we can leave something behind for the people we love—our grandkids and great-grandkids! It means we are required to avoid war, since wars require mothers to send their little boys off to die.

Women have always lived out the ethic of care, and feminists argue that it's high time we take it seriously as a superior moral perspective.

Problems with a Care Ethic

But there are stumbling blocks to the ethic of care. Many men don't take kindly to this kind of namby-pamby ethics, where you consider people in relationships to one another and take the mother-child relationship as your moral ideal. Beyond this problem, there's another one: Why would men want to take on an ethic of care as long as women are responsible for it? Since the care ethic requires men to participate in all the messy caregiving stuff (including the vomit, feces, and urine), men may not be lining up to participate in this "peaceable" ethic. It might be better to leave things the way they are: Let women take care of that stuff—after all, they've been at it longer, and are better at it!—and leave men to the world of work and politics! After all, we wouldn't want men trying to act maternal, and putting diapers on their babies' heads! (Which end is up?)

Tried and True

If we all have an interest in caring about people and being cared for, then this means that men should take up their share of caretaking, too. Besides, it's better for everyone involved if both men and women are involved in care work: Children get more attention that way, and the burden of care gets shared equally.

Okay, men, this can't be the answer. You've got to take some responsibility for caregiving. After all, you contribute to the making of those cute little babies, and you need your wife/girlfriend/partner's income from her full-time job. There aren't too many families who can now afford for mom to stay at home, and besides, women are getting sick and tired (literally!) from their care work.

Do Women Care Too Much?

Especially if you're a female reader, you might be thinking that the ethic of care is the way to go. After all, it's a good thing to share equally in important work like caring for others. In fact, I'm sure some women would be thrilled to have their guys do a fair share of care work. But don't grab the brass ring yet, women! Because there are still some problems to think about that might make the ethic of care less appealing.

First of all, consider this: If you're sick and tired of doing all the care work, and you really want some equality, then the ethic of care isn't going to get it for you. Why? Because the ethic of care glorifies women's caregiving, turning it into a moral ideal and encouraging men to accept it, but it doesn't require any serious social changes. So what you might end up with is women continuing on as they always have, with very little changing except for our appreciation of women's moral perspectives. Recognizing the importance of caregiving doesn't mean that we have to change our ways at all: In fact, someone could argue that if caring is so great and has been women's unique experience, then why deprive them of it?

Second, as other ethicists have argued, what women need in their lives is *less* care and more justice! Let's think about nurses as an example here. In fact, let's look at a case study to see why an ethic of care could be a problem.

> **CAUTION**
>
> ### Do the Right Thing!
>
> As feminist Eva Kittay suggests, when considering how to treat people we should remember that we're all "some mother's child." We've all been cared for at some point in our lives, or we wouldn't still be alive today. And that we've all been mothered at one point or another is the ultimate moral equalizer.

Nurse Ratchett Needs a Holiday

Nurse Ratchett prides herself on being an excellent nurse: Her patients love her because she is kind, caring, and attentive. They are always giving her gifts, like cucumbers from their gardens, plants, or chocolates. What's more, Nurse Ratchett loves her patients right back: She genuinely cares about them and often forms strong bonds with her patients and their families.

But due to hospital cut-backs, Nurse Ratchett is really feeling the squeeze these days. Her patient load has gone way up, so she can't give each patient the kind of personal care she wants to. In fact, she is so busy on the wards now that she can't take much pleasure in her job anymore: There are too many patients ringing their call bells, too many medications to dispense, and too many shifts to be covered. In short, Nurse Ratchett is feeling exhausted and desperate. What's worse, her unit isn't receiving the kind of pay raises that reflect all the hard work she and the other nurses are doing. There is some talk about going on strike if things get any worse, but so far that step hasn't been seriously considered.

> ### Moral Musings
>
> Nursing is a good example of where justice may be required over care. While a nurse's job is entirely about giving care to patients, sometimes the demands of caretaking can become too severe. In such cases, we need to focus on justice for nurses—fair pay, decent work hours, and reasonable patient loads.

Just Caring

So what does an ethic of care have to say about a situation like Nurse Ratchett's? Well, in its original form, the care ethic requires that we put those we care for ahead of all other considerations: remember, the motto at work here is "relationships matter!" Anything that Nurse Ratchett and the others do to interfere with care, or to break relationships, is morally wrong according to this ethic. Demanding their rights or going on strike would damage the care relationship, since patients would be left without nursing care and the patients' need for care and relationship would be violated.

This is why the ethic of care may be problematic: because sometimes women need justice more than care. Justice would require decent salaries for Nurse Ratchett and her colleagues; it would also require reasonable patient loads, and the right to say no to shifts. If we focus only on relationships of care, we can't get at these important issues of justice for nurses. In fact, in order to ensure that nurses are cared for, too, we may need to focus on justice for caregivers rather than focusing on the importance of relationships.

CAUTION

Do the Right Thing!

Don't assume that just because a relationship involves care, it's necessarily a good relationship. Abused women may stay with their abusers because they still care about them, but that's not good. And sometimes care relationships can cause "burn-out" for the caregivers!

Notice, too, that the feminist ethic of care doesn't tell us when to break off relationships, or when caring is not morally good. And I'm sure you know some relationships that just aren't any good, or that may even be harmful to the people involved in them. Some relationships are abusive or completely unequal; some are immoral because the parties involved are doing bad things. In cases like that, the ethic of care may be a bad way to go because it doesn't tell us when to give up on a relationship, or when (like Nurse Ratchett) we can say no to care! If you're a mother and you've ever felt like saying "The kitchen's closed!" or "Do your own darned laundry!" then you know how important it is to be able to "just say no."

We know the following things so far:

◆ Feminists have been critical of traditional ethical theories that have emphasized individualism, independence, and rights.

◆ Women have been left out of the history of ethics; in fact, women have been portrayed in very negative ways by philosophers across the ages.

◆ Caregiving has been mostly "women's work" throughout history, and even now it mostly falls on women to do care work and maintain relationships.

- Women have derived a different ethic or a different moral perspective from their care work: feminists call it an "ethic of care."
- An ethic of care focuses on caring, nurturing, relationships, and our inter-dependencies as human beings.

You might think that Nurse Ratchett's situation spells doom for the ethic of care. But you'd be wrong in thinking that! What I've laid out for you is the ethic of care as it was set out in the 1980s and early 1990s; feminists are now still concerned about promoting caring and relationships, but argue for a "public" ethic of care that makes caring a political, and not just moral, act!

Beyond an Ethic of Care

Did you know that in some countries women are burned alive for not being submissive to their husbands, for not having big enough dowries, or for not providing their husbands with sons? Some countries practice female circumcision, make women cover themselves from head to toe, limit them to one child only, and use ultrasounds to determine if they are carrying female fetuses so that women can abort them and try for boys. The list goes on and on—and what it tells us is that while women are caring for (and about) others, not enough people are caring for (and about) them.

This is why the feminist ethic of care has shifted from focusing solely on caring and the value of relationships to including concerns for justice and rights for women. That doesn't mean that feminists have junked the ethic of care as it was originally conceived, but just that it has been revised to include worries about justice for women. Because while more care *might* help us on a global level to treat women better—since we just might need to care more about them—focusing on caring and relationships might also keep women "in their place," and not be any help in changing the way we view and treat them.

The Least You Need to Know

- When ethical dilemmas come up, think about the implications of your choices for people you love and care about.
- Strive for equality and justice in your relationships, especially if they are caregiving relationships.
- Don't apply social contract theory to all areas of life: it just doesn't work for personal relationships of care!
- Be inclusive: Don't assume that men can't adopt an ethic of care.
- Encourage men to take responsibility for care work, too.

There's a Fly in My Recipe

In This Chapter

♦ Pinpointing problems with ethical theories

♦ Getting the best out of each theory

♦ Should you pick one theory and go with it?

♦ No theory is going to be perfect!

As we near the end of Part 3, your head must be swimming with theories, theories, theories! You've got theories telling you to be virtuous; to follow nature's dictates; to do your duty; to watch out for consequences; and to focus on care and relationships. And you've probably thought to yourself: "I can't do all these at the same time!" Well, you're right … you can't. Number one, it would make you crazy to follow all these dictates; and number two, even if you tried, some of the theories directly contradict one another. You can't at the same time ignore consequences and promote the best consequences for all—so what's a well-intentioned, ethical person like yourself supposed to do?

Well, in order to make the decision about which theory works best, you need to know what's wrong with them. In previous chapters I have outlined different theories, and I've mostly tried to give each of them a straight read. But I'll confess now that each theory has its flaws. But wait! Don't go thinking "Awww … none of them is any good" because that's not true—in fact, you might find that one or two theories are really good, warts and all. So let's look at each theory you've read about so far and get a brief read of its problems.

Limits of Virtue Ethics and Feminist Ethics

I've put virtue ethics and feminist ethics together for a reason: Because, as you might have noticed, the two theories focus on how we ought to behave, and how we should think about relationships, rather than giving us a formula for ethical decision-making. In fact, as you might have noticed, feminist and virtue ethicists are a little vague about what being virtuous or caring requires—you kind of have to make it up as you go along! But this is exactly the point for these theorists: What being caring or brave requires can't be worked out objectively, but depends on the circumstances. Bravery is a great virtue in some circumstances; in others, it's just plain stupid. And caring may be right and good in some situations, but in others it's destructive and leads to injustice.

The main problem with virtue ethics and feminist ethics, then, is that they don't give us much of a guide for action. Think about Kant's duty-based theory for a second: He gives you a way of working out what your duty is, and it applies to every situation you can imagine. Utilitarians also offer ways of calculating how to do the greatest good for the greatest number. But virtue ethicists? Feminist ethicists? They tell you things like "be a good person" or "maintain relationships of care with other people" without giving you a clear idea of how to do it.

This is a problem that philosophers refer to as *contextualism*. Moral theories like Kant's and Bentham's are universalist because they apply to all people in the world at all times: doing your duty or promoting happiness are things we all must do, no matter whether we're living in the United States, Africa, or Japan. But virtue ethics and feminist ethics don't make such universal claims: The ethically right thing to do varies from context to context, from culture to culture, and from relationship to relationship. Does this sound familiar? It should … it's the problem of cultural relativism coming back to haunt us! The same problems for cultural relativists (see Chapter 7, "'Us First' Ethics") arise for virtue and feminist ethicists—when there is no universal right and wrong, there is no objective grounds for absolutely ruling out certain actions and behaviors.

Ethically Speaking

Feminist and virtue ethics suffer from the problem of **contextualism**, or, to use a familiar term, **relativism**. Virtue ethicists and feminist ethicists don't make universal claims: The ethically right thing to do varies from context to context, hence, contextualism. It's the problem of relativism coming back to haunt us!

Rules in Context—Female Circumcision

Let's return to an example I've already used so you can see this contextualist problem more clearly. Remember the mother who lives outside Cairo, and who's trying to figure out whether to allow her daughter to be circumcised? If you were a deontologist like Kant, you could plug in your formula: Ask "What if everyone did that?" and ask "What does respect for persons require?" and you get your answer. It would be pretty hard to justify female circumcision if you take your duties seriously. But a feminist care ethic doesn't offer the same formula for making a decision: the mother has to waffle back and forth about what caring requires in this case. Is it caring to allow your daughter to be potentially maimed or killed from the cutting? Or is it caring to refuse, knowing that the village will turn their backs on your daughter, and that she will probably never be married and never have economic stability? Also, since the context matters, we can't just assume female circumcision is morally wrong because we don't practice it in the United States.

Virtues in Context—Cultural Differences

Next, consider the contextualist problem for virtue ethics. Suppose you're trying to determine what honor requires, and you're Japanese. What might be honorable in Japanese culture—taking your life because you have been publicly shamed or humiliated—would be considered foolish by U.S. standards. People in the United States appear as public buffoons and idiots all the time—remember, one of our vice-presidents couldn't spell "potato," and yet it doesn't bother us. So if you're trying to get a handle on how to be virtuous, on what standards apply, and what you should do … well, virtue ethics doesn't give us a lot of guidance.

So virtue ethics and feminist ethics have their problems. But before you rip the chapters on those theories out of the book, consider flaws with another moral theory: natural law ethics.

 Do the Right Thing!

The right thing to do in a situation will depend on which culture you're in and what the cultural norm dictates. The saying "When in Rome, do as the Romans" twigs us onto this idea. Topless sunbathing may be a morally accepted norm along the French Riviera; but just try it in a public space in Iran or even rural Iowa!

Hitches with Natural Law Ethics

Okay, so we know that virtue ethics and feminist ethics run into relativism problems, and that's bad. But there are some serious hitches with Natural Law ethics, too. Most of the problems come out of its appeal to "nature" and "the natural." Let's take a closer look.

Recall Natural Law theory's main claim that what is morally right is whatever nature dictates. Natural Law theorists appeal to what is natural because if God created nature, and nature works in certain ways, then we should follow nature's dictates because that's what God intended. It's as simple as that.

Claims that homosexuality is morally wrong, that abortion is immoral, that suicide is bad, and that the use of contraceptives is wrong all come out of this appeal to natural law: nature intended men and women to procreate, so homosexuality is unnatural; in the course of things, fetuses develop into full-formed babies, so abortion is unnatural; we have a natural tendency to protect our own life, so taking it is perverted; and preventing human fertilization and conception by using condoms and birth control pills is bad because it, too, interferes with God's intentions.

Well, I hate to tell you, but the main claims of natural law theory are problematic. Why? Because if you pick apart the notion of "nature" and "natural," then you find it pretty hard to maintain that certain practices are "unnatural."

Ethically Speaking

Just because things *are* a certain way doesn't mean that's how they *ought* to be. The idea that "the way things are is the way they ought to be" is a logical mistake. Philosophers call it the **"'is' implies 'ought'" fallacy** (Note: A fallacy is a mistake in your reasoning.)

Tried and True

You'll want to be careful about making claims concerning what is "natural" or what "nature intended." Saying that it is right to do whatever nature dictates is unhelpful, because how do we know what nature dictates? Did nature intend us to cure diseases like tuberculosis, polio, and yellow fever? Did nature intend that human beings send rockets to the Moon?

I'll give you three main reasons why appealing to nature is a problem:

1. Just because things *are* a certain way doesn't mean that's how they *ought* to be.
2. Technology has removed us so far from nature that it's really hard to distinguish what is natural from what is artificial.
3. Whatever human beings do *is* natural just because, to pick up the natural law theorist's main point, God created us human beings to do what we do! Below I'll say more about each of these problems.

You Can't Derive "Ought" from "Is"

The idea that "the way things are is the way they ought to be" is simply a logical mistake. Philosophers call this the "'is' implies 'ought'" fallacy. It's a pretty simple point, actually: just because things are a certain way doesn't mean they have to be or even ought to be that way. Take fighting as an example. We know that, since our earliest times, human beings have fought each other for food, land, and power. Fighting comes naturally to human beings; that's just the way it is. But do you want to say that it therefore *should* be that way? Just because it is the case that human beings fight doesn't mean that it ought to be so. Most people think we should resist our fighting tendencies, and that the human race should work toward peace. So there's an example of the problem: "is" does not imply "ought."

Technology Has Removed Us from Nature

Here's another problem with the natural law theorist's appeal to nature: Technology has taken us so far that we're out of the realm of "the natural." Human beings just aren't living in a state of nature anymore: We don't live naked in the Garden of Eden, where butterflies and birds fly about, and where we live off the land. No, the minute we discovered our nakedness and put on clothing; the minute we picked up a spear to kill our prey; the minute we designed the first building; and the minute we began using herbs to heal sickness, human beings made the turn toward technology. And there's no going back!

That isn't to say that "technology is where it's at," or that if something is high tech it must be good. On the contrary: some technology is not good, and should be avoided. But not because it's "unnatural"—it goes without saying that technology isn't natural! We should avoid it for other reasons, like because it will hurt people, or because it will wreck the environment, or something along those lines.

Think of it this way: we perverted nature a long, long time ago, and we continue to do it every single day. Flying isn't "natural" for human beings—as the saying goes, "if we were supposed to fly, we'd have wings!" Using medicine to kill off bacteria and viruses, provide mechanical support (like respirators and kidney dialysis), and do surgery on fetuses in the uterus is no less "unnatural" than using medicine to abort fetuses. And driving cars down highways at 75 miles an hour is not natural, either, but we gladly do it.

The point here is that you start making empty distinctions when you say that one thing is natural while another thing is not. When you get down to making nitpicky distinctions about what's "natural" for humans to do, then you open up a real can of worms!

What Human Beings Do *Is* Natural

Anyway, we can't make nitpicky distinctions about what's natural for human beings to do, because what human beings do is natural. Natural law tells us that we should behave as nature intended—but simply by using our capacity for reason, and developing human knowledge, we *are* behaving as nature intended! We aren't called *Homo sapiens*—humans as knowers—for nothing. It's in our nature to question, to think, to learn, to know, and to advance ourselves: we've been on the path to human advancement since we first populated the earth. The things we create, the ideas we come up with, and the things we do are all in some sense part of our nature. So science—that's natural for us. Medicine—yep, that's "natural," too. Space technology? Ditto.

> **CAUTION**
> ## Do the Right Thing!
>
> If you think natural law theory is doomed because of its problems, think again. It still has some appeal, especially because it defends the notion of natural rights and the right to life. We still refer to these important goods—even the Constitution protects the basic right to "life, liberty, and the pursuit of happiness."

The flaws with natural law theory should now be obvious to you. People still appeal to what's natural and what isn't when they make moral judgments, but this is problematic. There may be better reasons for saying that something is morally bad than saying it's bad because it goes against nature.

But if you think this spells doom for natural law theory … well, it doesn't. Because as I pointed out in Chapter 10, there are still some very appealing aspects to natural law theory, like the idea that all human beings have inherent value, and that there are natural rights that come directly out of our human nature. We'll have to leave the hitches with natural law theory, in any case, and move on to …

Glitches with Social Contractarian Ethics

Since I'm an equal opportunity critic, let's look at what goes wrong with social contract theory. Because yes, indeedy, it has it's glitches, too!

Let's start with the kind of worries that feminist care ethicists have raised against social contract theory: It takes human relationships to be of no inherent value, but of only instrumental value. In other words, critics have worried that human relationships are only valuable to social contract theorists insofar as they benefit each of us in one way or another. The idea that human relationships are valuable in themselves just doesn't fly for these guys; as you know, they see relationships in terms of "you scratch my back, I'll scratch yours."

> **Moral Musings**
>
> When you think about it, social contract theory probably assumes too much. For example, there are lots of moral relationships that aren't based on mutual benefit or reciprocity. A profoundly mentally handicapped adult cannot "contract" for mutual benefit and those who take care of her will never be reciprocated. Some citizens just aren't in the position to make social contracts or to reciprocate with others.

But what if some of us have no fingernails to scratch with? And who can believe that women "contract" with their babies to care for them; that people "contract" with their families to live together and form a unit; or that prisoners "contract" with wardens and prison guards to behave in certain ways? There are two basic ideas here that cause social contract theory problems:

1. We "contract" with others in any meaningful sense.

2. The parties to these contracts are free and equal.

You Can't Pick Your Families

The idea of a "social contract" is problematic right from the get-go. There may be some cases where you do, indeed, contract with others: you sign contracts with car mechanics, and when buying a car or house. We even sign contracts for surgery. But we sure as heck don't "contract" with family members or friends. In fact, with the exception of explicitly contractual relations (like your relationship with your auto mechanic) not many of our relationships are the way that social contractarians depict them. That's because not too many of us had the opportunity to decide whether we want to be part of our families, or whether we want certain responsibilities and obligations that fall into our laps. A lot of the time they just happen to us, and we're stuck dealing with them.

If someone leaves a baby in a basket on your doorstep, you don't get the chance to accept or decline the "contract." That baby needs you, and whether you agree to it or not, you're stuck! Ditto for families: many people wish they *could* pick their families, or opt out of them! But we can't, and using the social contract model doesn't help us to understand how families should relate. Could you imagine a family unit that ran according to the social contractarian's vision? It would be a pretty cold, hard-nosed family, that's for sure! You usually don't keep a log of what you did for your family members, and what they owe you. So feminist ethicists are right about this: The idea of a social contract has no place in personal relationships.

Who Contracts for What?

The second problem with social contract theory is that it sees people as free and equal. For any contract to be binding, a person has to willingly accept its terms. And it certainly helps if the two parties are socially equal: remember, children don't enter into the social contract model because they are powerless against their parents. A serf who works the land for his king can't be said to "contract," since the serf is seriously unequal to the king, and has no real choice but to do what the king commands.

Well, extend that thinking further and you'll see what else feminists are worried about: That in many cases, people may be vulnerable because they are social unequals, and in no way do they contact to have things the way they are. There are many groups in society—women, children, racial minorities, the elderly—who are viewed and treated as lesser beings because of their age, or

Do the Right Thing!

While it's true that social contract theory is flawed, we shouldn't completely toss out the idea. There are some cases where it's best to see your relationship as contractual. Just imagine acting as though the person trying to sell you life insurance or a used car or an expensive piece of jewelry is someone with whom you're in a relationship of care. Big mistake!

skin color, or gender. It's hard to see how people from these groups contract for the kind of society we live in today. What woman in her right mind would "contract" for a society that pays her 75 cents to every dollar that men earn? What African American would "contract" for a society that treats them as slaves? You get the picture. The problem is that in many cases we're not the free and equal beings that willingly enter into these contracts.

Basically, if a theory doesn't do a good job of explaining why we behave as we do, or if it has only limited application, then it isn't a very good one. Social contract theory has its strong points: it argues that we all *should* see ourselves as free to enter and exit contracts. It tries to explain why human beings come together in community (basically, to maximize benefits to ourselves). But where many of our relationships are concerned, with our children, parents, siblings, friends, lovers, or enemies, social contract theory just can't cut the mustard.

Problems with Duty-Based Ethics

Well, then, maybe it's duty-based ethics to the rescue? If the other theories are flawed, then maybe you should go back to Kant's position about duties and intentions. Well, I wouldn't recommend this until you get the full picture on deontology, because—yes!—it has some tricky spots, too.

There are three main problems with Kant's ethical theory that I'll run past you here. (While there are other ones, you only need to get a general idea of them.)

1. The first difficulty is Kant's claim that outcomes are irrelevant to doing the right thing.
2. The second is his claim that duties are universal and apply without exception.
3. The third problem is that we aren't told what to do when rules come into conflict.

Tried and True

When you're trying to figure out what your duties are, you need to pay attention to interpretation and context. There are often different ways to interpret the same principle. And different duties may apply in different areas of life, so the context you find yourself in makes a difference, too.

Making Predictions

Okay, point 1: Outcomes are irrelevant to doing the right thing. We know this is sometimes true—remember Sneaky Pete and Jenny from Chapter 12, "We Can't Forget Kant"?—but we also know that sometimes Kant is just wrong about this. It isn't irrelevant that the choices you make could harm people. Kant claimed that outcomes are impossible to predict anyway, so trying to achieve the best consequences is a moral mistake. But is he right about this? It's true that sometimes we can't predict outcomes with any certainty—look at Jenny taking those cookies to her grandma—but there *are* times where we can predict pretty accurately what will happen if we do act A versus act B! If you drive off and leave a little boy bleeding at the scene of an accident, you can predict that he's likely to die. So the idea that consequences are always irrelevant is something that's hard to take seriously.

A Duty Is a Duty?

Second, if duties are universal and apply without exception, then we fail to appreciate the many different ways in which a duty can be interpreted. For example, we all have a duty to respect the dead; this applies to everyone in every corner of the world. But how does "respect the dead" get interpreted? Is there only one way of showing that respect? Suppose in one culture respect for the dead requires burying and praying over them, while in another culture, people respect the dead by eating them. They could give you a very sensible story about why eating their dead is respectful: because it recognizes the greatness of the dead person, and lets that greatness enter others' bodies. Unless we want to say that there is only one way to interpret a duty, and that we (that is, North Americans) have the right interpretation, then it's not clear that duties can be applied without any consideration for interpretation and context.

Conflicting Duties

Finally, consider this: our duties may clash, and then we don't always know which one should prevail. An example of *conflicting duties* is where a doctor is treating a terminally ill patient who is in a great deal of pain. We know that doctors have basic duties, like the duty to save lives and the duty to prevent pain and suffering. In this case, if the doctor fulfills the duty to save lives, she will end up prolonging the life of her patient. But if she prolongs the patient's life, she will fail in her duty to prevent the patient's pain! On the other hand, if she is to prevent pain then she must give the patient heavy doses of morphine, which could result in the patient's death.

So if the doctor fulfills her duty to prevent pain, she violates the duty to save lives. Either way, the doctor loses. And since both duties are core to being a good physician, it isn't at all clear what she's supposed to do. Kant's theory offers the doctor no way out ... so it isn't helpful to us at such important times!

Ethically Speaking

Sometimes duty-based ethics may result in **conflicting duties**. This means you have two duties commanding two different things at the same time. Doctors have duties to (1) save lives and (2) prevent pain and suffering. But sometimes to save a life, they have to cause pain; and sometimes to prevent pain and suffering, they have to end a life. See the problem?

These are serious flaws with duty-based ethics; but again, they don't seal the fate of this moral theory. Because sometimes all that matters is that a person did her duty and that she had good intentions. Besides, Kant's notion of "respect for persons" is powerful, and we return to that idea all the time when we talk about ethical issues. So let's not turf this theory out, either.

Issues with Consequentialist Ethics

Finally, we get back to Bentham, Mill, and those other consequentialist types. And, yep, you guessed it! There are problems with this theory, too. In fact, I'm sure you've probably already thought of some of them. But just in case you haven't, let me help you out here.

Justice or Happiness?

Consequentialism suffers from the opposite problem of duty-based ethics: it says that achieving the greatest good for the greatest number is all that matters. Consequences matter. Okay, this is true—but things *other* than consequences matter, too, don't they? For example, to end up with the greatest good for the greatest number you might have to falsely accuse somebody of doing a crime they didn't commit. Or you might have to use one person badly for the sake of others. Better outcomes may come of doing these things, but that doesn't make them morally right.

Why? Because it's morally wrong to stomp all over people's rights, to violate principles of fairness, justice, and equality. So just because something makes a lot of people happy doesn't mean it's necessarily right!

Suppose your best friend is a louse who makes fun of you every time your back is turned (for your sake, I hope this isn't true). The thing is, you're not at all aware of it. You carry on in your little dream world, thinking that you and your friend are best buds, when all the while he is nothing but a big turd. He tells people you're fat. He tells people you're ugly. He tells people you're stupid. But to your face he compliments you and says you're great.

Moral Musings
Not all acts are morally redeemed by good outcomes. Suppose Hitler's Nazi regime had resulted in great good for Germany: even if that were the case, not many people would say it justified his actions. No benefits could ever justify Hitler's treatment of Jewish people in World War II.

According to consequentialists, as long as you don't know about your friend's two-faced behavior, there's no harm done. No bad consequences have resulted from this stinker's behavior because you don't know anything about it. Would you really want to say "well, no harm done" in such a case? Probably not ... because whether you know it or not, whether there are bad outcomes or not, you are being wronged. No unhappiness is created, but still—it's wrong, darn it!

Looking Back

What's more, consequentialists are future-looking people, and don't consider the past. This means that whenever you have to decide between choices, you work out the consequences of each choice and go with the one that achieves the best future outcomes. So you're trying to determine what, in the next five minutes or five years, will be the act that maximizes happiness and minimizes pain. But think about this: sometimes our best reasons for choosing an act are based on the past, not on some future case.

If you have a box of chocolates to give away, consequentialism dictates that you give the chocolates to whoever will benefit the most from them. Everyone gets equal consideration for the box of chocolates. But suppose you have a dear friend (unlike the guy in the last example) who's gone to the ends of the earth to help you out. You have backward-looking reasons for choosing to give the box of chocolates to your friend, even if she won't get the most benefits from them. The backward-looking reasons are that she's been good to you; she's been there for you in the past. Consequentialist calculations don't include these reasons from the past. And there's got to be something wrong with a theory that overlooks obligations we owe to people because of our history with them!

There ... now you have the whole, dirty truth. The ethical theories you've read about so far aren't perfect; heck, each of them is actually pretty flawed! But I don't want you to slam the book shut in frustration and think "Me and ethics ... we're through!" Because there's something important you can get from these theories, even with all their problems. What you can get is an understanding of how complex ethical problems are, and how many different ways there are of solving your dilemmas. You may take an eclectic approach, where you take a little ethic of care and add a dash of duties.

Whatever you do, remember that you shouldn't see any ethical theory as a calculus. Ethics isn't a science, no matter how hard guys like Bentham tried to make it into one!

Also, you just might want to rethink using one theory as your ethical framework, if that's what you had in mind. Different theories are effective for different areas of life: Social contract theory is good for contractual relationships like those with your auto mechanic, but it's less useful for personal relationships. And the ethic of care does much better in working through our personal relationships, but isn't so hot on impersonal ones, like the auto mechanic!

The Least You Need to Know

◆ Remember, ethics isn't a science, and no ethical theory is perfect.

◆ Think about the proper "fit" between ethical theories and your different areas of life.

- Don't doggedly grab on to one theory and run with it. Be aware of flaws with all ethical approaches.
- Avoid moral absolutism and moral relativism: Both approaches can be traps!

Chapter 16

Mixing Recipes

In This Chapter

- ◆ Why all moral recipes need to be mixed
- ◆ Why there has been moral progress
- ◆ Two views about mixing ethics
- ◆ Our ever-expanding moral community

There are purists and then there are people like me. Every morning I eat a big bowl of cereal. I put in bran cereal first. Then I put in oat squares with real crunchy texture that don't get soggy in milk. On top of that I mix in cereal that is 90 percent sugar and has no nutritional value whatsoever, just so I can manage to eat the other tasteless gruel. Finally I add berries, not because they're particularly sweet, but because they look terrific and smell great!

People think I'm nuts. I mean, how can you mix all these different things together and call it food? Don't they all just sort of cancel each other out—the healthy bran gets soggy and cancels out the crunchy oat squares, the sweet stuff rots your teeth and gets diluted by the bran, and the berries just turn the milk this awful blue color. Yech!

Amazingly, despite what you might think, my gruel actually works for me (okay, so I have to close my eyes while I'm eating). Well, the same thing applies to moral recipes. Each recipe looks like it contradicts or cancels out the others. But, as I hope to show you in this chapter, appearances can really be deceiving. Okay, I admit I'm partly to blame for this impression. So now I'm going to set things straight. A fully satisfactory ethical recipe has to mix in all the recipes. After showing you why, I'm going to talk about a couple of ways this might be done. In the end we'll see that humanity hasn't been spinning its wheels in search of moral wisdom. Moral progress is real!

Mixing Moral Recipes

We all know that we gotta have a balanced diet. Well, the lesson from the last chapter should clue you in on the importance of a balanced moral diet. Basically, what we learned from that chapter is that no moral recipe taken by itself can satisfy all of our moral needs. A steady diet of fruit without protein supplements will kill ya. Same thing goes for any one of the ethical theories we've examined. Life is complicated, and no single theory can adequately handle all the myriad life-and-death dilemmas that crop up.

Saying that, of course, doesn't yet show that all the moral recipes we've looked at so far are necessary for living ethically. So that's what I'm going to try to show you now. Let's take each of our recipes and use them as ingredients for a master recipe: a moral goulash combining …

- Natural Law ethics
- virtue ethics
- social contract ethics
- deontological (Kantian) ethics
- consequentialist ethics
- feminist ethics

Tried and True

Morality is human nature. When you think about it, it's pretty much coeval with common sense—the mother of all invention and, in the case of humans, the thing that makes up for the shortcomings of our other senses. Basically, because we're such needy and dependent critters, we have to rely more on complex cooperative schemes than even our primate cousins. And that's where morality comes it.

Human Nature Matters

First off, no moral theory can ignore elemental facts about human nature. If human beings were solitary critters that reproduced by cloning—one adult clone per person, just like cell division—then there would be no need for morality. If people were irrational, instinct-driven psychological egoists like sharks or piranhas, morality would again be useless, despite the fact that we might gather together in groups.

There's an old saying: "Ought" implies "can." You can't be morally obligated to do something you can't do. Insane, compulsive killers are no more morally obligated to desist from killing than are sharks. So, unless you're the sort of animal whose nature allows you to act morally, moral behavior will mean nothing to you.

Natural Law

Natural Law theory understands the importance of beginning with human nature. We may disagree about the particular details regarding what's natural or unnatural. But everyone agrees—and historians, anthropologists, and sociologists confirm—that the human species necessarily reproduces itself in social groupings.

Fact number one: We're social animals.

Fact number two: We're rational animals. And whether God made us that way from the get-go or whether we evolved that way as a way of compensating for deficiencies in our instincts and adapting to our environments through learning is irrelevant. Adding two plus two:

> Social animal plus rational animal = moral animal.

Let me explain by recalling virtue ethics.

Virtue Ethics

Virtue ethics is next on our list because it shows why rational animals do not merely pursue pleasures and avoid pains like other animals. To begin with, being rational means that we can compare and evaluate things in accordance with standards of pain and pleasure. We value things. Because we value things, we can rank things according to the degree of fulfillment and satisfaction—or good—they provide us. For instance, we can put aside our short-term desire to feel good by getting blasted on moonshine and go for long-term, long-lasting happiness, which unfortunately requires sober work!

So being *rational* enables us to break the hold of immediate desire and instinct. We can stand back from the immediacy of life's needs, observe, compare, generalize, value, and—most important—choose between differently valued options! So being rational makes for choice, or freedom—the absolute prerequisite for any kind of moral responsibility whatsoever.

Ethically Speaking

Rational is any behavior, thought, or system that is consistent, efficient, and self-reflective. Someone who held contradictory beliefs (or whose actions contradicted her beliefs) would be irrational. But even a perfectly logical person would still be considered irrational if she didn't harmonize her desires in a way that efficiently promoted the most overall balance of satisfaction or if she couldn't calculate the most efficient means for doing so. And that's not all. Calculating (or prudential) reason is sub-rational if the values and desires so efficiently satisfied conflict with the attainment of larger social goods, such as justice and communal well-being.

What virtue ethics adds to this thought is the idea that we rationally should—and generally do—choose goods that we value as ultimate, such as happiness, or well-being. And, as we've seen, there are biological and psychological prerequisites for achieving happiness. We need food, shelter, clothing, and physical health; and we need other people—their love, recognition, friendship, and care.

Rational choosers will rightly reason that the best way to acquire the biological and psychological goods necessary for achieving complete happiness is by living a virtuous life. Being friendly, considerate, honest, loyal, caring, generous, and fair-minded are, after all, the best character traits to cultivate if you want others to like you and help you out in your quest for the things you want.

So virtue ethics is entirely in keeping with the natural law governing our rational, social nature. A life without virtue would be a lonely life indeed, at least for people who value the association of others for its own sake.

Social Contract Ethics

But suppose you're a misanthrope (one who has a low opinion of humans and a low estimate of the good that comes from having them as friends). Maybe you can live without virtue (or at least most of the virtues). But you can't live without morality! At the very least, reason is a handy tool for calculating the most efficient means for surviving! And the most efficient way to do that is by cooperating with others for the sake of mutual benefit. You don't have to like people or enjoy their company in order to use them for your own benefit. But you do have to get along with them, which requires that you and they agree on basic rules of fair play.

This, of course, is the lesson of social contract ethics. We don't have to be paragons of virtue to see that it's in our long-term selfish interests to live in a human society with basic moral safeguards against killing, stealing, and the like.

Deontological Ethics

But that's not all. Reason is not simply a handy tool for calculating our long-term happiness. It is also a faculty that imposes logical consistency on our thinking. And this is where deontological ethics comes into the picture.

Remember what Kant said about moral reason? He said that we have to be utterly consistent in the way we deal with people. We can't make exceptions for ourselves or others whenever it's convenient to do so. If it's wrong for Suzy to tell Pete a damaging lie, then it's equally wrong for me to tell him that lie. So each of us has to be careful in the way we pursue our ends.

And this gets to another crucial point. We can't just treat others as obstacles preventing—or as means to achieving—our ends. According to social contract ethics, we could decide not to cooperate with people for our mutual benefit and instead merely agree to compete with them for scarce goodies under rules of fair play. That would meet the barest bones requirement for a low-ball ethic. But social contract theorists have all said that fair competition isn't enough. In order to fully attain our personal ends we need the help of others. We need to cooperate with them.

Do the Right Thing! _____

   Social contract ethics stresses the importance of social cooperation for mutual benefit. But it's imporant not to think of this "reciprocity" as simple "payment in return" for services rendered. Sometimes, we pay it forward and not back. For example, each generation pays forward to the next generation the service it received from the previous generation. True, my generation's social security taxes are paying for social security benefits for the previous generation. But can we ever really ever pay back all the blood, sweat and tears shed by mom and dad when we little buggers were growing up?

Social cooperation demands reciprocity—or mutuality (I'll scratch your back if you'll scratch mine). But mutuality only happens when we begin to treat others not only as means for achieving our ends, but as ends in themselves. In other words, as Kant pointed out, we have to see the other person as someone with needs just like us. We have to adopt a higher moral point of view which allows that the other guy's needs are just as worthy of being satisfied as my own.

So full mutuality demands that I treat all human beings as sacred, simply because they're like me—rational evaluators who demand respect as free, responsible moral agents. To respect people in this way, of course, also requires holding them responsible for what they have done. So the idea of desert—rewarding and punishing people for what they've done—is a crucial part of any ethics.

Consequentialist Ethics

Let's recap: We've seen that human nature can't be fulfilled outside of a social context in which virtue, law, moral reciprocity, and desert are absent. Now we'll see that consequences are just as basic to moral life.

If you were to ask someone why any of the above moral recipes should be adopted by a society the only answer could be: It promotes the greatest good for the greatest number of people. Morality, in other words, is good for us—not just you or me taken individually, but all of us.

Tried and True

There are lots of reasons why consequences are important in evaluating the morality of actions. Even if consequences aren't always the only thing that matters (and sometimes aren't even the most important thing that matters), they still count in this minimal sense: The consequences for not behaving morally for whatever reason are bad!

I won't rehearse why consequences matter. That should have become apparent to you while reading Chapter 13, "Consequentialist Theories." Needless to say, there are times when the general welfare counts more than anything else. For instance, quarantining a segment of the population infected with a very deadly virus might be the only way to prevent its spread to society at large, even though doing so puts some members of that population at greater risk.

What I want to emphasize now is something totally different. Saying that morality matters because of consequences is not the same as saying that a particular behavior or action is right or wrong because of its consequences.

Consequences Aren't Everything

The doctrine known as utilitarianism says that a particular action or rule is right or wrong because of its consequences. That's a very limited moral recipe that, while applying to certain situations, does not apply to all of them. For instance, it does not apply to punishment. The moral idea behind punishment is getting your just deserts (which has nothing to do with chocolate pudding, and even less to do with consequences, but which has everything to do with what you deserve, based on your past actions).

A person ought to be punished because he or she deserves it, not because doing so will reduce crime. True, some notoriously nasty governments have reduced crime very effectively by randomly picking innocent people, falsely accusing them of crimes, and then slowly torturing them to death. Personally, I'd rather take my chances with a less effective—but fairer—method of handling crime because—who knows—you just might be one of the falsely accused!

By contrast, when we say that morality in general is good (or ought to be adopted) because of its consequences, we're saying something entirely different. We're not recommending any particular moral recipe as the best one for solving all our problems—which is what utilitarianism does. In fact, as paradoxical as it might sound, it might just be that the most efficient way to bring about the greatest happiness for the greatest number is by *not* trying to bring about the greatest happiness for the greatest number—at least not all the time!

Let me explain. We all know that the easiest way to get to sleep is by *not* trying to get to sleep. The more you try, the less you succeed, because trying keeps your mind active. So the best way to fall asleep is not by directly trying to fall asleep but by *indirectly* falling asleep (personally, I like reading or watching TV because counting sheep requires too much concentration).

Same with bringing about the greatest happiness for the greatest number. Mill, I think, hit upon this idea. In some ways his utilitarianism is indirect rather than direct. For example, when he says that the best way to maximize welfare is by following rigid rules against vio-lating the rights of others, he's saying that a Kantian moral approach—not a Benthamite act-utilitarianism approach—is the best way to make people happy. And come to think of it, he's right! Knowing that we have basic rights that can't be violated simply for the sake of bringing about the greatest happiness for the most number actually makes us more happy than if we didn't have such rights! So we mustn't adopt *only* a utili-tarian recipe in promoting the general welfare, because doing so will definitely not promote the general welfare!

So what I want to suggest is this: Promoting the general welfare is the best reason for being moral.

> **⚠ CAUTION**
>
> ### Do the Right Thing!
> Evaluating particular actions and norms in terms of their promotion of the general welfare is only one of many ways we promote the general welfare. Using deontological, social contractarian, virtue, and natural ethical modes of reason-ing also promotes the general welfare.

Feminist Ethics

Gee, I haven't talked about feminist ethics, have I? Unlike the other moral recipes, femi-nist ethics does not propose a single model of moral deliberation (feminist ethicists can be virtue ethicists, social contract ethicists, or deontological ethicists). Furthermore, although feminist ethics is certainly in accord with human nature, it does not follow directly from human nature in the way that the other recipes do. That's because it addresses a specific problem—the unequal treatment of women in all aspects of life—that is not inherent in human nature. If the unequal treatment of women were eliminated, there would probably be no need for feminist ethics.

Human nature does not demand the unequal treatment of women, because we can easily imagine a fully human society in which men and women were equals. Indeed, we are quickly reaching the point when advances in reproductive technology will make female-only child-bearing a thing of the past. In any case, as things currently stand, men raise children while women work outside the home. This proves that the old gendered division of labor is not at all natural.

So why include feminist ethics as a necessary aspect of moral deliberation? Because gender-based discrimination and oppression has been and continues to be deep and pervasive, especially in less developed and more traditional societies. And because, as a related matter, women have been relegated to the role of caregivers. Caregiving will continue to be the most important aspect of family life as our population ages. And feminists, more than any other ethicists, have helped us understand the ethical implications of it.

Add Some Consequences to a Medley of Duties

All right, I understand why we need different moral recipes. But are there any recipes for ... er ... combining recipes? I mean, how are we supposed to use this important fact about recipes in our daily lives?

Well, in the next couple of sections we're going to be checking out some possible ways of combining recipes.

W.D. Ross

The first recipe for combining moral recipes was suggested by a fellow named W.D. Ross. He was very much drawn to Kant's deontological ethics. But he was unhappy with two features of that ethic.

The first had to do with Kant's insistence that all duties were absolute and unconditional. What Kant meant by this, you'll recall, is that it's wrong to make any exception to your duty. If you have a duty to tell the truth, then you must always tell the truth—even to a would-be murderer who asks you for the whereabouts of his intended victim! Surprisingly, Kant himself justified truth-telling in this instance by saying that you can't predict what good or bad consequences will actually follow from what you say. If you lie, the would-be murderer might be misled into finding his victim by accident; if you tell the truth, the would-be murderer might be caught before he finds his victim.

The second—and related—problem with Kant's ethic is that it puts us in a quandary whenever we find ourselves confronted by two conflicting duties. For example, we could rephrase the situation of the would-be murderer asking for the whereabouts of his intended victim as a conflict between two duties: telling the truth and not killing (the person being asked for the whereabouts of the intended victim could reasonably assume that telling the truth would make him an accessory to murder). According to Kant, we have an absolute obligation to tell the truth and we have an absolute obligation to not tell the truth (that is, to not murder)—and no way to act without being morally damned!

Prima Facie Duties

Ross's solution to this problem preserves Kant's idea that we have duties that can't be overridden for the sake of consequences. But it allows that duties can be overridden by other duties—so that all duties are at best conditional.

To clarify a bit, Ross thought that we could be certain of what our duties were in any given situation without appealing to consequences. Call these duties *prima facie duties*. In the example given above, we have conflicting prima facie duties to tell the truth and to not murder. Next, Ross says that reasoning through the situation will tell us which of the two conflicting duties allows us to fulfill the greatest balance of overall duty. That duty is our actual duty.

Ross himself classified duties into six major kinds: of fidelity (which includes truth-telling), of not causing harm (which includes not killing), of doing good, of justice, of gratitude, and of reparation. According to Ross, we know these duties to be true, independent of their good effects (remember, he's a deontological ethicist).

So we've got all of these duties. How do we know which ones take precedence over others? Well, you might think that Ross would give us a rank ranging from most important to least important. In fact, he seems to have thought that noninfliction of harm takes precedence over doing good. But in general he insists that the determination of which duty takes precedence over another is only revealed to us by reasoning through the particulars of the concrete situation. Like feminist ethicists, he was a contextualist! In some situations, telling the truth takes precedence over not killing—as when the police ask you for the whereabouts of a dangerous, armed criminal. In other situations, the priority is reversed.

But exactly how do we go about reasoning through a situation in determining which among our competing prima facie duties takes precedence? Ross doesn't think that reasoning about consequences will help us much, partly because we'll be faced with having to weigh different types of goods—sort of like weighing apples and oranges. But if we don't reason about consequences, what do we reason about?

Ross never tells us! But in fact, he clearly seems to be mistaken. We *do* appeal to consequences in figuring out which of our competing duties takes precedence in any given situation—at least some of the time.

Ethically Speaking

A **prima facie duty** is any duty that can be overridden by another duty. For example, I have a prima facie duty to protect my family by bombing the terrorists who threaten them, and I also have a prima facie duty to do so in a manner that poses the least risk to innocent life. Sometimes these duties collide. If so, one duty must override the other one.

For instance, when presented with the case of the would-be murderer, most people would say that the would-be informant should lie. Contrary to Kant, it's simply not true that we're uncertain of what the consequences of our action will be in this situation. Our would-be informant might be 100 percent certain that telling the truth will result in the death of the intended victim. Second, there's no doubt that saving an innocent person's life (and not being a willful accomplice to his murder) is a far greater good than making a malicious murderer happy!

So, you *can* combine a deontological theory of prima facie duties with a consequentialist theory of choice!

Add Some Primary Goods to a Casserole of Rights

Okay, we've seen how to combine deontological ethics with consequentialist ethics. Can we combine deontological ethics with a virtue or natural law ethical approach?

Kant thought not. To begin with, he thought that any appeal to human nature in deciding right and wrong was terribly wrong-headed. As far as we know, human nature is more like the way Hobbes described it—piggish—or so thought Kant. Because we have no assurances that human nature is good, morally speaking, we cannot base morality on it. No, we must base morality on rational duty, which very often commands us to do things that go against our natural, piggish desires.

Ditto virtue ethics. Kant thought that happiness was not the end all or be all of goodness. I mean, would we want bad people to be happy? Of course not! No, the only unconditional good worth wishing for is a good, moral will!

Well, Kant has a problem. Remember what I said about "ought" implies "can"? Kant believed that, too. But if he's right that our natures are so piggish and contrary to reason and morality, then how can he reasonably expect us to be moral? Kant tried to get around this problem by saying we had two distinct natures—one divine and otherworldly, the other mortal and this-worldly. But he never explained how two natures inhabiting such utterly different worlds could possibly affect one another!

Not to worry. John Rawls—you remember him—has figured out a way to add a conception of natural goods to Kant's theory. Here's how it works.

John Rawls's Primary Goods

Remember what I said about Rawls's imaginary social contract theory back in Chapter 11, "Modern Socialist Contract Theory"? When you think about it, it's very much like Kant's theory. By asking us to imagine that we—the contractors—are ignorant of who we are, Rawls tries to get us to think impartially, from the standpoint of no one in particular or, if you prefer, of everyone in general. Performing this little thought experiment reminds me that there but for the grace of God, go I. I could have been that unlucky soul! So I will therefore treat her and everyone else with equal respect and equal concern, and insist on equal rights for all.

But rights to what, precisely? Here's where a conception of natural goods comes in. The contractors are assumed to be rational. Rational folks would want goods that sustain their rational lives. As virtue ethics teaches, they would want goods that make possible the pursuit of personal happiness. And they would want goods that make possible their own rational association, which is a just association.

We've already seen what some of the primary goods are that each rational person will want to claim a right to: income and wealth, opportunities and powers, rights and liberties, and a sense of one's own self worth. These are goods that fulfill human nature. So knowledge of human nature—of the goods that are required for human flourishing—is necessary for a deontological theory of rights. Without this knowledge, we wouldn't know what treating everyone equally means. With this knowledge, we know that equal treatment means providing everyone with a fair share of these goods.

Thanks to Rawls's theory of the good, he can take Kant's ethics beyond Kant's own narrow focus on moral no-nos, like killing, stealing, and lying. He can take it in a social and political direction by focusing on the positive goods that just societies need to provide their inhabitants.

There still remains one problem, however. How do we know that Rawls's conception of the human good is the right one?

The only way to confirm Rawls's list would be to ask every person who has ever lived if they agreed with him! Imagine, if you will, a fictional conversation between all past, present, and future generations of people. Suppose further that they are all rational, well-informed, open-minded, and given an equal opportunity to talk. Would they come up with same list of goods as Rawls?

> **Moral Musings**
>
> Rawls agrees with Kant that persons have equal rights. But equal rights to what? Here's where a conception of natural goods comes in. The contractors are assumed to be rational. Rational folks would want goods that sustain their rational lives. As virtue ethics teaches, they would want goods that make possible the pursuit of personal happiness. And they would want goods that make possible their own rational association, which is a just association.

Jurgen Habermas's Discourse Ethics

There's a more practical way to use Rawls's ideas. The contemporary German philosopher Jurgen Habermas (pronounced *YOORgan HAHberMAHS*) calls it discourse ethics, and the idea behind it is very simple. Instead of imaginary social contracts between fictional contractors, we can set up real conversations between real people and let them decide for themselves what goods are important to them.

Really, when it comes right down to it, this is no different than what happens in a free and just democracy! But—you ask—can the average people be trusted to know what's in their own good? I mean, there's a lot of propaganda out there, and some people seem to control the flow of information. Also, lots of people just sit on the sidelines, too busy eking out a living or too unmotivated to inform themselves enough to get involved.

Do the Right Thing!

Instead of letting philosophers do all the thinking for us—speculating on what is good and right from their lofty ivory towers—we should be figuring it out for ourselves. But our understanding will be rational only to the degree that our conversation is truly fair, and everyone has roughly the same opportunities, incentives, and capacities for informed, reasoned discussion!

Habermas has an answer to this problem. Make democracy fairer! To the extent that our democracy is truly fair—allowing all concerned people to participate as equals, unconstrained by ignorance, prejudice, and material need—debate will tend to be rational. We'll check each other's misconceptions, and we'll learn from one another. Why, maybe we'll even end up changing our minds about what's good for our society!

So, instead of letting philosophers do all the thinking for us—speculating on what is good and right from their lofty ivory towers—we should be figuring it out for ourselves. But our understanding will be rational only to the extent that our conversation is truly fair, and everyone has roughly the same opportunities, incentives, and capacities for informed, reasoned discussion!

The Least You Need to Know

- The only adequate moral recipe is one that incorporates all moral recipes.
- Promoting the general welfare might be the best reason for being moral, but being moral doesn't mean you have to always act so as to promote the general welfare.
- There's no reason why you can't obey duties and maximize good consequences at the same time—the best recipes often do both!
- In a free and just democracy, citizens—not philosophers—should take responsibility for deciding what's good and right.
- Have faith in humanity and moral progress—it's a fact!

Part 4

Applied Ethics

If you've followed us this far, you're ready for some slightly more advanced training in ethics. In this part, we'll see just how handy those recipes you learned in the previous part can be in solving some of the most pressing moral dilemmas facing us today. I'm not talking little dilemmas, like: Should I give Mary stinkweeds to tell her I hate her or roses to tell her I love her? No. I'm talking big dilemmas, like: Should I kill this fetus or let it live?

Life and death matters are pretty central to this part. Some of them revolve around abortion, physician-assisted suicide, and killing animals for food and experimentation. Others have to do with measuring the value of environmental preservation, as well as the benefits of work and consumer safety, against the costs of doing business. Hey, who ever said doing the right thing was easy?

Chapter 17

Environmental Ethics

In This Chapter

- Protecting the environment because it's good for us
- Valuing nature for its own sake
- Is cost-benefit analysis morally sufficient?
- Are humans a blight on the planet?

I love to go walking in the forest preserves with my partner and my pug, Ollie. Some Sundays we'll get up, throw on some old hiking clothes, and head out for long walks in the woods. (And despite their reputation, pugs make pretty good hikers ... our fat little guy can handle a three-hour walk just fine!) Anyway, after we've hiked quite a ways into the woods, we find that signs of other human beings fade away, until all we can hear is the twittering of birds or the sigh of the wind in the trees. Those moments are truly sublime ... until we get a little further along the trail to find crushed beer cans, candy wrappers, old lunch bags, and empty cigarette packages thrown on the ground. Then—SCREECH!—the feeling of being alone slams up against reality, and we are reminded again of the human tendency to multiply ourselves and destroy the environment.

Well, that's what this chapter is all about: environmental ethics, or determining the way that we ought to treat our natural environment. We will consider the different ways of valuing the environment (for its own sake, or because it's good for us humans); we will treat the moral appropriateness of using cost-benefit analysis to determine how much harm to the environment is acceptable; and we will consider the rather extreme claim that human beings are blights on the planet and that disease, famine, and war are just the earth's way of keeping us in check! But before we get to pestilence, disease, and death, let's consider the different ways we can think about ethics and the environment.

Determining How to Value Nature

I don't think too many people would deny the value of the environment: it gives us air to breathe, water to drink, rain to help our crops grow, and trees to shade and protect us. But for ethicists, the question isn't just *whether* the environment is valuable, but *how* we ought to value it. For example, some people give *instrumental* reasons for valuing nature: that is, reasons based on the usefulness of nature to supporting human life.

Trees are important, on such an account, because they provide goods for us: we can use them for paper, building houses, and making tables and chairs. But other people reject this human-based system of valuing nature, and argue that the environment is valuable for its own sake, without any reference at all to human needs. If human beings ceased to exist, these ethicists argue, the environment would still have value. Such a view imbues nature with *inherent* worth that has nothing to do with the "goods" that we derive from it.

You might think it doesn't really matter how we value the environment, as long as we do it in some form or another. After all, the goal is to get people to want to protect nature, and their reasons for doing so might seem irrelevant. Whether people stop throwing garbage in the forest preserves that I frequent is all that matters: whether they stop because it makes the hikes ugly for people who want to use the trails, or because nature has inherent value and should not be violated, might not seem to matter.

Ethically Speaking

Some value nature because it's good for us: if we destroy it, we end human life as we know it. Others value nature for its own sake. Those who take a human-centered view apply an **instrumental** value to the environment because they see nature as useful. Those who value nature for its own sake see **inherent** value in it, and reject the instrumental view.

But it does matter. If we value nature because of what's in it for us—the human-centered view—then the environmental policies we support and the steps we're willing to take to protect the ecosystem will always come back to what's good for human beings. We might be willing to allow industry growth, for example, even if it results in destruction to the environment, because industry creates jobs and stimulates the economy. In this case, a human-centered concern for the environment puts humans first and nature second.

But if we see intrinsic value in the environment, then no degree of human good can justify destroying a natural habitat. On the intrinsic view, nature must be free to do its thing, without human intervention. And no arguments in favor of economic stimulation or job creation is going to move the ethicist who sees nature as good in itself!

Feminists Who Love Nature

But there are other important ethical questions surrounding how we value the environment. For example, some feminist environmentalists—called "ecofeminists"—argue that humans have been environmentally destructive because we have acted out a masculinist, imperialist ethic of domination. They point out that, just as men have historically dominated and oppressed women, so they have treated nature in the same way.

According to these ecofeminists, since men have dominated throughout human history, they are largely at fault for the kinds of world-views that have led to war, nuclear disaster, and environmental degradation. The sort of "masculine ethic" that is in question is one of domination and oppression, where men have engaged in a war of "all against all" to dominate and master one another. Given this masculine ethic, it is far less surprising that the environment is in the state we currently find it: Men have used violent means to fight one another for land and power, including land mines, bombs, and nuclear weaponry. Beyond this, say some ecofeminists, men have used notions of modernism and progress to justify destroying nature for human ends.

Moral Musings

"Ecofeminist philosophers ... have shown how the logic of domination is at work in both the domination of nature by humans and the domination of women by men under various forms of patriarchy. In so doing, they have shown that the fights to end both are linked conceptually and therefore politically."

—Victoria Davion, "Is Ecofeminism Feminist?" in Karen Warren, *Ecological Feminism* (Routledge, 1994)

Some ecofeminists have gone further to argue that women are more peace-loving and harmonious, and that a woman-centered ethic is morally preferable to the destructive masculinist one we've seen so far. As mothers, the argument goes, women are more concerned about preserving the environment for future generations; they see the world with a more loving eye. But notice that even this claim is controversial among feminists, since (as feminist critics point out) women, too, are guilty of destroying the environment. They use environmentally harmful cleansers and products; and when it comes to beauty regimes, women have been the culprits in using harmful products like hair spray, perfume, and other cosmetics. So it seems that women, too, have engaged in the same kind of nature domination that men have engaged in, even if it is men that have partly coerced women into engaging in these ecologically unsound practices.

Whether or not you agree with ecofeminists, it's clear that it matters how we value the environment. If the value is anthropocentric—another word for "human-centered"—then we're more likely to accept harm to the environment if it will result in benefits to humans. But then again, we need to break down the kind of anthropocentrism at work: is it a masculinist form, or is there a more peaceable, loving human way to live within our environment? Alternatively, we may altogether want to reject human-centered, instrumental ways of valuing the environment in favor of an ethical approach that sees the inherent value in nature. To begin, let's start with the anthropocentric modes of valuing nature.

People First

Al Gore, a recent vice-president of the United States, is noted for his environmental concerns. As he wrote in 1989 …

> … we are filling the atmosphere with gaseous wastes that threaten changes to the climactic system in the next 75 years as large as those that accompanied the ice ages over hundreds of thousands of years.

Do the Right Thing!

While some ethicists are critical of human-centered views of environmental ethics, others argue that there is no other way to look at the world. As human beings, we can't help but think about the world in terms of how our environment affects us. A "people first" view may not be just a bad kind of egocentrism, then … it may be the only perspective we can have! Think about this when you're wondering about what *kind* of environmental ethics we should support as a community.

Gore's call for change is rooted in concern for the human race: that if we don't change our ways, there will be nothing left for us, because there will be no Earth as we know it. It is a view with which most folks have sympathy since, as humans, we can each relate to the worry that we might kill ourselves off. So this is the first reason that we should investigate taking a "people first" view: because people can understand that perspective, and by seeing ourselves at risk, we may be convinced to protect the environment.

Some ethicists argue that it is virtually impossible to take a nonanthropocentric (or nonperson-centered) view of the environment. After all, we're human beings, and we can't help but see the world from our position as *Homo sapiens*. So the suggestion that we should have a different world-view seems absurd. Since the way we view the world is connected to our place in it, saying that we should have a different perspective on the world—one that doesn't put humans at the center of it—seems ridiculous.

Human-Centered Environmentalism

Whether or not we *can* take a nonperson-centered view of the environment, though, isn't the question. The question here is: should we? Let's assume for now that we could take a nature-centered view of the environment (that nature is good in itself and deserves protection). What reasons might we still have for taking a human-centered view?

Well, first of all, if results are what we want, then appealing to human self-interest may get us there faster. This gets back to the previous claim that we should set aside how people value nature and emphasize getting people to value it at all. For example, it may be a long and circuitous argument to convince someone that wetlands have a good of their own, and that we shouldn't dry them up to build brand new condominiums. You'd have to get into a long-winded explanation about how nature has a "telos"—or an end of its own—and how human beings should not interfere with that.

This whole argument might sound weird to your listener, and not very convincing overall. But put it in terms of self-interest:

> If we dry up all the wetlands and build more condominiums we'll end up with little biotic diversity and this will affect humans directly.

Now you've got people on board right away, assuming, of course, that you can convince them that shrinking bio-diversity upsets the delicate ecological balance necessary for our own survival. In any case, appeals to the instrumental value of a flourishing and balanced environment for human survival seem to be the most effective approach.

Second, since human beings are uniquely rational and moral beings (in ways that nature and animals just can't be), it seems only justified to appeal to those faculties to get us to think about how we want to behave. Again, this puts human beings at the center of the world, but this move seems justified if humans are unique in this respect. Asking questions about what we want as humans, and how we ought to treat nature, may still be rooted in a conception of us as supreme beings, but at the very least it takes seriously our capacity to reason about important moral issues and to work out our duties and obligations.

Finally, instrumental approaches to the natural world seem justified when we're comparing the value of human lives to the nonhuman realm. Sure, a wetland may have a good of it's own—it may be held to have value apart from human lives. But that value is still relative to human beings. When it comes down to it, as some ethicists claim, human life outweighs the value of nonhuman life, hands down. So if ever we have to choose between human lives versus protecting nature, it may seem only right that human lives come first. Even if we have to destroy nature (or animals—see Chapter 20, "Ethics and Animals") to protect human lives, then so be it.

Tried and True _____

Consider the theoretical difference between instrumental and inherent modes of valuing nature. Instrumental modes of valuing line up with a Utilitarian perspective, since you're weighing out the benefits of environmental protection in terms of the good outcomes for humans. Intrinsic modes of valuing are deontological (or duty-based) because they focus on the inherent value of nature, and our moral duties to protect it.

None of what I have said should suggest that the environment lacks value on the instrumental view. Rather, the value of protecting the environment is always balanced against other important goods: like creating jobs for people, creating parks or recreational areas, and using land for farming. The question then becomes: how are we to determine when the value of protecting nature outweighs other human concerns? And the answer? Cost-benefit analysis!

What'll It Cost Me?

This brings us to a pretty standard ethical way of determining how much harm to the environment is justified, and when it is morally called for: *cost-benefit analysis*. Such an approach takes the relative values of different choices, weighs out the likely costs and benefits associated with each choice, and determines which act produces the most benefit with the least amount of costs involved. This sounds reasonable, until you look a little closer at what "costs" are being considered.

For example, cost-benefit analysis includes weighing out how many human lives will be lost in certain actions, and whether the loss of human life is outweighed by other important gains. Notice that it's quite possible—and often happens—that the loss of human life doesn't compare to the greater goods that are produced by a certain act; so according to cost-benefit analysis, nothing has inherent value; not even human life!

Ethically Speaking _____

Cost-benefit analysis involves placing dollar figures on the costs and benefits of doing a variety of acts. The act that is determined morally correct, on this view, is the one that incurs the least amount of costs, and that results in the greatest benefits.

Similarly, on this analysis the environment has no ultimate value, either. According to cost-benefit analysis, a certain amount of environmental pollution (through the dumping of toxins and factory pollutants) is inevitable. Indeed, raw nature itself—in the form of volcanic eruptions, natural forest fires, and animal predation and grazing—was already contributing to pollution and ecological destruction well before people came on the scene. Cost-benefit analysis therefore seems acceptable if the benefits (in terms of job creation, economic stimulation, and capital investment) work to the overall advantage of what is arguably the most important of nature's denizens—us! The government rightly determines that it's better to allow a certain level of pollution and environmental degradation, since this is the natural ecological balance that best suits us.

So we balance out a certain amount of environmental pollution against the good of stimulating the economy through business. Corporations are allowed to trade off with other companies their entitlement to pollute, which is known as "emissions trading." If a corporation wishes to pollute the environment more than its allotted amount, it has one of two options: move south of the border, where environmental protection laws are minimal to nonexistent, or trade other goods with companies in exchange for their "pollution rights." In either case, as you've probably noticed, the result is that corporations pollute our environments with near impunity.

Who Benefits?

Part of what's morally wrong with cost-benefit analysis, however, is that we can allow huge costs to a small number of people for small gains to a large number of people.

For example, companies that have moved south of the border have engaged in such gross environmental pollution that it has resulted in birth defects, disease, and even death for people living close by those companies. Yet we consider these human costs "worth it," and for what? To have another brand of tennis shoes, more cheap clothing, and other such goods that hardly seem to touch the value of human life. So while many people may benefit from having factories produce more stuff for consumption, those benefits pale in comparison to the extreme suffering caused to the concentrated group who suffer serious health problems because of the environmental pollutants. If you add on the loss of the natural environment itself, it's hard to see the case for allowing companies to engage in these practices!

CAUTION

Do the Right Thing!

You might think cost-benefit analysis is an ethical way to determine whether, and how much, environmental pollution is acceptable. But when you think about it a little harder, cost-benefit analysis is hard to swallow. It may involve putting a dollar value on the cost of human lives versus the benefit of having more factories that produce goodies for human consumption. Thus, on this scheme not even human life is deemed to have absolute value. The same is true of the environment: Cost-benefit analysis may justify some serious environmental degradation for some pretty questionable goods. Think carefully about the morality of cost-benefit analysis, and what kinds of "goods" you're willing to put on the auction block!

Given the problems with cost-benefit analysis, perhaps another approach would be preferable. To figure this out, consider the other approach I mentioned earlier: the view that nature is inherently valuable, and that human beings are irrelevant to that value.

Nature First

So far, we've looked in some detail at the anthropocentric way of valuing the environment. On this view, human beings (as living beings) have a good of their own, and we set the value for everything else in the world.

But if *all* living things have a good of their own, we may need to judge the value of non-human life by standards derived from *their* own good. To use only human standards when assessing the moral value of the environment is already to believe that humans are superior to the natural world, which is the whole point in question! Thus, some ethicists claim that the anthropocentric, instrumental way of valuing nature is arrogant and presumptuous, and that to ever behave ethically toward the environment we must respect it for its own sake.

You might be wondering what valuing nature for its own sake means. Essentially, it's an appeal to Immanuel Kant's notion of beings as "ends in themselves" (see Chapter 12, "We Can't Forget Kant"). Of course, if you remember correctly, Kant argued that only rational moral beings are ends in themselves: animals and the environment wouldn't cut it on his account. But contemporary ethicists have extended Kant's idea to include animals (see Chapter 20) and nature. These folks claim that the environment has its own ends that, uninterrupted by human agency, it will pursue. Flowers will bloom and fade; rivers will run (if not dammed up!); entire biotic systems will flourish independently of humans. And by interfering with these natural processes, it is claimed, we wrongfully intervene to thwart nature's ends.

But more than this, treating nature as an "end in itself" involves a moral attitude of appreciating the environment for its beauty and function, without reference to human needs or desires. This attitude has been expressed by environmental activists who argue for the right to continued existence of the ancient mighty California redwood trees. They argue that those trees, some of which have existed for hundreds of years, have a good all their own, and that it is a moral travesty to cut them down. And in making this claim, notice that environmentalists don't appeal to human goods at all;

> ## Moral Musings
>
> It's unsurprising that some environmentalists feel so strongly about protecting the environment that they're sometimes willing to risk their own lives (and those of others) for their cause. Through human actions, we've endangered or rendered extinct a huge number of animal and plant species. Some environmental activist groups you may have heard about include Earth First!, Greenpeace, and the Sierra Club.

it's irrelevant what we need or want, and arguments for human need (for example, to have another highway) don't compete with the trees' rights to continued existence.

Spicing Up Your Life with Biocentrism

To make more sense of the view that human life isn't superior to nature, you need to give more thought to this "biocentric" outlook on nature. The *biocentric approach* goes against the *anthropocentric approach* that puts people first; it teaches us that humans are part of the ecosystem, not above it, and that whatever human beings do has direct impact on the environment. We are members of Earth's community, and as such we are just one part of the interconnected elements. In a strong sense, what we do to Mother Nature we do to ourselves; and in these connections lie our moral obligations to the natural world.

Notice that on this account, the human capacity for reason and morality are not emphasized; rather, what matters is the fact of our being an animal species. This doesn't mean that we deny differences between ourselves and other species: what it does mean, however, is that in connection with nature's ecosystems, we see ourselves as one species among many.

We can do this in two ways. The religious way argues for the sanctity of nature as a divine creation—God's property, as it were. On this model, we are but stewards of nature. Or, we can adopt a scientific outlook. As an animal species, we must recognize our beginnings in the same evolutionary processes that have affected other species; and as animals, we have been equally faced with the evolutionary facts of genetics, natural selection, and adaptation. Since these facts apply as equally to humans as other species, we have no scientific (or moral) grounds for setting humans apart from other species!

Given all this, biocentric approaches that take nature to have inherent value reject the "people first" morality that I mentioned above. This means, ultimately, that human goods don't always "trump" environmental goods; on the contrary, in most cases nature will win out over human needs and desires. So we need yet another highway in California because of traffic congestion? Too bad! Besides, biocentrists argue, people shouldn't be driving so many (and such large) vehicles, anyway. They only pollute the environment and lead to the manufacture of more and more SUVs and other destructive goodies.

Ethically Speaking

Anthropocentric **approaches** to the environment take the "people first" approach, where what counts most is human needs and desires. On this view, the good of nature comes second to us humans. **Biocentric approaches** put the value of the Earth's ecosystem first, and see human beings as only one part of an entire organic system.

And we want more trails opened up in the redwood forests so that human beings can enjoy hiking and backpacking? Tough luck! The forests are doing just fine without us, thank you, and it's immoral to interfere with them just because we want the pleasure of looking at them.

There's one final, radical approach to the environment that is worth considering in this chapter: It's the view that human beings are nothing but a drain on the Earth's resources, and that events that reduce or eliminate human life are morally good because they represent the Earth's attempt to keep us in check. Let's consider this view below.

Radical Deep Ecology: Get Rid of Humans!

To recap, you've considered some different views on how we should value the environment, including ecofeminist views, anthropocentric views, and biocentric views. Each approach highlights a different system of value: One focuses on the male value-system we have in place; another focuses on humans; and the third takes the biosphere itself as the main concern. But there's an even more radical view that has so far been left out of the conversation: the Deep Ecology movement, one that not only displaces humans as the main moral concern, but makes the additional claim that *Homo sapiens* are the whole problem. For example, in 1993 Dave Foreman, Deep Ecologist and founder of Earth First!, claimed that …

Tried and True

While militant environmental activism may seem excessive, consider this: Just as some people believe that protecting the life of the fetus is our moral obligation, so do radical environmentalists think that protecting nature from human destruction is morally obligatory. Almost all movements in human history have had radical factions, from civil rights and anti-war movements, to right to life and environmental ones.

There are far too many human beings on Earth. … Although there is obviously an unconscionable maldistribution of wealth and the basic necessities of life among humans, this fact should not be used … to argue that overpopulation is not the problem. It *is* a large part of the problem. … Even if inequitable distribution could be solved, six billion human beings converting the natural world to material goods and human food would devastate natural diversity.

Some Deep Ecologists have been so radical that they've argued that disastrous events like the AIDS epidemic, Third World famine, and war are necessary solutions to the population problem. According to Deep Ecology, then, anthropocentric environmental views are too shallow to be of any moral value; so Deep Ecology represents a radical form of biocentrism.

How Deep Is Deep Ecology?

And what are the moral implications of the Deep Ecology platform? Well, Deep Ecologists claim that we must find humane ways to restrict and lower the human population. But unlike Malthusians, who make a similar claim (see Chapter 23, "Economic Justice"), Deep Ecologists argue that reducing the human population ought to be done not for our own sake, but simply for the sake of the environment. They even support what some folks provocatively call "bioterrorism," or what is less polemically known as militant activism. The Deep Ecology movement is linked to Earth First!, a radical environmental activist group that has typically used "monkeywrenching" techniques to save the environment from destruction. For example, Earth First! activists will chain themselves to trees to prevent bulldozing; put metal spikes in trees to prevent their being cut down; and cement their feet in the path of construction sites where forests are being clear-cut for housing developments. These tactics are intended to prevent the destruction of our ever-shrinking forests by foiling developers' construction plans. As a result, such groups are highly controversial and draw media attention to their causes.

While you may not agree with the actions of militant groups like Earth First!, you have to agree that environmental issues are a pressing concern. The hole in the ozone layer continues to grow; the northern ice caps continue to melt; and an increasing number of animal and plant species are becoming extinct. It's also clear that the Earth can only support so many human beings, especially where we live such high-impact, technological lives in the western world.

Sharing the Burden

This leads to another final point worth considering: that not all human beings have an equal moral debt to right the wrongs of environmental destruction. For example, studies show that western people are far more destructive to the natural environment than are people from the non-western world. We use up more land, take up more space, and destroy more natural resources to support our modern lifestyles than do people in less-developed countries. As some feminists have argued, it may be the case that people from different classes, cultures, and genders have different moral roles to play in reducing the human population. So whereas some critics argue that our overpopulation is caused by people who continue to have large families in Third World countries, others point out that we shouldn't look at numbers of people, but at the amount of resources and space that each individual takes up. On this view, populations in the United States, Canada, Great Britain, and other "first world" countries are far more to blame for environmental degradation than are people having large families in undeveloped countries. It may be technology and capitalism that lead to the most destruction, and not numbers of people!

This chapter has considered some pressing and difficult issues involving human life and the environment. Clearly, not all environmental ethicists agree on what we need to do to protect the environment, how we should go about doing it, or even what kind of environmental ethic we want to apply.

I have run through some of the main streams of thought concerning ethics and the environment: ecofeminist, anthropocentric, and biocentric. As you have learned, not even *within* these ethical approaches do people agree. Some ecofeminists, for example, think that women have been more virtuous than men, and that a masculinist ethic has led to environmental destruction; other ecofeminists reject the idea that women have lived more lightly on the planet than men. Some anthropocentrists are willing to risk the environment more than others to support human goods. And some biocentrists are far more radical than others.

Do the Right Thing!
We each need to take a hard look at the lifestyles we lead to consider the impact we're having on our environment. In taking environmental concerns seriously, we're required to ask hard questions like: Do I really need that shiny new SUV? Do the products I use lead to unnecessary pollution and waste? Am I living the least environmentally destructive life that I can?

Indeed, it may well be that there never has been such a thing as a pristine, pollution-free, ecologically balanced environment. If the ecological balance is constantly shifting and naturally causing species to evolve and diversify or die off (there have been many mass extinctions in the history of our planet), then saving nature from itself will become a highly selective process—in which case we're back to using some kind of cost-benefit analysis. But now that the stakes are higher—the next mass extinction may involve our own species—we have to be extremely judicious in our analysis, and factor in costs and benefits that exceed the economic bottom line, narrowly understood.

The Least You Need to Know

- There isn't just one way of "doing" environmental ethics: there are widely differing views on the subject!
- Instead of writing off militant environmental activists as mere "extremists," or "bioterrorists," think about their reasons for their actions.
- Don't assume that people in Third World countries are the most environmentally destructive: Large families may not be the real problem.
- Consider the way you live your life, and try to think of ways to "live lightly" on the planet.

Chapter 18

Biomedical Ethics

- ◆ Understanding the principles of health care ethics
- ◆ The ethics of abortion
- ◆ Is it ever right to help patients end their lives?
- ◆ When using people is ethically acceptable

In 1991 Dr. Timothy Quill, a medical doctor, published a now-famous article in the *New England Journal of Medicine*. His article was controversial because in it he admitted to participating in physician-assisted suicide. Dr. Quill gave one of his cancer patients, Diane, a prescription for pills that he knew she would use to take her life when she felt it was appropriate. Quill says that, when he gave her the prescription, "I made sure that she knew how to use the barbiturates for sleep, and also that she knew the amount needed to commit suicide."

Were Dr. Quill's actions justified? His admission certainly raised questions about what a doctor's role should be in helping patients to end their lives. Biomedical ethics raises this ethical question plus many, many others. Is it morally acceptable to allow doctors to perform abortions? Should patients ever be used for research purposes? And should we pursue things like cloning and genetic technology? These are the issues that you will read about in this chapter. So let's get going, stat!

From Principles to Practice

Biomedical ethics makes up its own huge area of study in ethics: people now treat the ethical issues in health care as a separate area of ethics. Health-care ethicists serve on hospital ethics committees, on research ethics boards, and work as clinical ethicists (ethics consultants in hospitals). There have now been so many books and articles written on ethical issues in health care that they couldn't all be listed.

Ethically Speaking

Biomedical ethics is the application of moral philosophy to the medical arena. Since ethical issues in medicine and health care delivery include everything from A–Z (abortion to xenotransplantation … okay, A–X!) the broad term "biomedical ethics" is often used. But you might also see some ethicists talking about "medical ethics" and "health-care ethics." All these terms point to the same field of study.

The branch of ethics called biomedical ethics really got its start in the early 1970s, when two guys named Tom Beauchamp and James Childress wrote a book called *The Principles of Biomedical Ethics.* These two pointed out that ethical theories (of the sort we outlined in Part 3, "General Recipes for Guiding Ethical Decision-Making") aren't useful when thinking about ethics in health-care situations. Why? Because you can just imagine a doctor who has to work and think fast, scratching her head and pondering virtues versus duties versus consequences as her patient bleeds to death. Ha! Doctors don't always have time to sit down as philosophers and determine what is the ethically right thing to do; they need fast answers. So Beauchamp and Childress came up with a list of four principles that are core to the ethical practice of medicine:

- Autonomy (the right to make choices for yourself)
- Justice (being fair)
- Beneficence (doing good)
- Nonmaleficence (avoiding harm)

I'll say more about each of them in a minute.

These principles are meant to be handy because they don't carry any heavy duty theories along with them. Why do we need theories when we can just turn to principles, pick one, and act quickly?

For example, if a patient's wishes seem most important in a situation, then you pick the principle of autonomy and act on that. If you can't do good for a patient because he's too ill to be saved, then you pick the principle of nonmaleficence and at least try not to harm him. And if you get two people in need of emergency medical care and you can only treat one right away, you'd appeal to the principle of justice to help you out. It's supposed to be that simple!

Health-care ethics as a field of study really expanded after the four principles model was proposed. But not everyone buys into it—some people still prefer ethical theories for practicing health care ethics. Here's why: It's often not clear in medicine which principle is most important, or how to apply your chosen principle.

Imagine a situation where two patients are brought to a hospital emergency room in need of immediate attention. One is an alcoholic drunk driver who hit another driver; the other patient is the victim whose car was hit. Both patients are in danger of dying without immediate care, but the emergency room is on a skeleton staff so they can't operate on both patients. Suppose the drunk driver arrived by ambulance shortly before the other patient: How should the staff determine who to operate on first? Should they appeal to the principle of justice? And if they do so, should they take a "first come, first served" approach to justice and treat the drunk driver first, or should they put the other patient ahead of him? Is it morally right to put the other patient ahead of the drunk driver based on a value judgment about drunk drivers? Maybe the staff should focus on beneficence instead. But then what does it mean to "do good" for either of these patients?

Clearly, the principles don't always help us out of difficult moral situations in health care. But still, the four principles of health care ethics are appealed to all the time. Let's look at each of them in a little more detail.

Autonomy

The principle of patient autonomy tells you that each rational, competent person has the right to make medical decisions that affect his life. Since each individual knows his or her own values, beliefs, and preferences best, we must let each person decide for himself. For several reasons, this principle is now considered essential to the good practice of medicine. First, there's a long history of *paternalism* in medicine. Paternalism literally means "rule by the father," and in health care, it resulted in doctors making decisions for their patients without consulting them. Doctors used to withhold information from patients, lie to them, dictate treatment—it was basically "doctor knows best."

Second, respecting autonomy ensures that patients have given their free, informed consent for treatment. Health-care professionals are now so concerned about patient autonomy that patients have to sign consent forms before staff

Ethically Speaking

The practice of paternalism in medicine is now considered a bad thing. **Medical paternalism** involves making choices for (or forcing choices on) patients who are capable of choosing for themselves. It directly violates patient autonomy. But there was a time not so long ago when a physician's paternalistic treatment of his patients was considered to be justified, and even morally good.

will do anything to them (you know ... those long, fine print forms that you never read, but sign your name to the bottom of).

Finally, the possibility of lawsuits now lays heavily on the minds of health-care providers. Especially in the United States, where health care is run for profit, caregivers don't want to do anything to patients (or deny patients any treatment) that could result in caregivers being hauled into court! By focusing on patient autonomy, patients get what they want, and staff are way less likely to be sued for something.

Justice

The principle of justice speaks to other ethical worries in medicine: that people should be treated justly, fairly, and equally, and that when patients are in similar medical situations, we should treat their cases the same. Beauchamp and Childress were right that justice matters to health care: We need to always be sure that medicine is practiced fairly, with equal concern for all patients.

Issues of justice mostly arise in health care when we get down to questions about rationing care. If you don't already know—but most of us do!—health care is a scarce resource. It's expensive, and eats up a huge part of our federal budget. So when we're deciding how to distribute health-care resources, or, on a more personal level, which patients should get medical resources and which ones should not, we need a principle of justice to help us figure out how to ration in a way that is fair, respectful, but that also makes sense. The principle of justice leads us to ask things like: Should 90-year-olds get scarce heart transplants? Should we spend more research money on AIDS or cancer? If we have time to operate on only one patient, but two require emergency care, which one should we choose?

Tried and True

Medical staff are supposed to practice beneficence—doing good—for patients. But it's getting harder now that patient autonomy reigns supreme. It's hard to "do good" if you don't know a patient well, and have no idea of her beliefs, values, or preferences; or for a patient from a culture you're totally unfamiliar with. Be careful when making decisions about what is "good" for others.

Some Americans get the best care in the world, and some get no health care at all! If we all have equal need of it, and health care is basic to living a half-way decent life, then it's unjust that people go without it. Some ethicists appeal to the principle of justice to argue for a universal system of health care.

Beneficence

The principle of beneficence—to "do good" for patients—gets at an idea that's basic to health care—that it's whole purpose is to make lives better, to improve patients' situations, and to make people well again. The principle of beneficence is what motivated the kind of medical paternalism I talked about earlier: Physicians wanted to do good for their patients, and really thought that it sometimes required lying to them, or withholding medical information, or dictating the one right kind of treatment. So the principle of beneficence runs into problems because health care professionals are now worried that doing good may violate patient autonomy.

Bear in mind, then, that beneficence is a problematic, though necessary, principle of health care ethics. As patients, we want more than to not be harmed by doctors; we want to be helped by them.

Nonmaleficence

The principle of nonmaleficence is kind of a fall-back position for health-care providers: It tells them that, if they can't do good for patients, they should at least not harm them. Who'd argue with that? Bear in mind that this doesn't mean doctors shouldn't cut us open, or stick needles in us, or give us painful treatments: Those things hurt us, but in the long run they benefit us! No, the principle of nonmaleficence is a caution against taking serious risks with patients, or doing things that have no immediate or long term benefits for them. A sensible, good principle to apply, don't you think?

There are problems of interpreting what it means to "harm" someone, though. As a doctor I may refuse to do abortions because I don't want to harm a woman or her fetus; but the woman might not see abortion as a "harm" at all! (More on this later in the chapter.) Or a patient might demand a treatment that a doctor sees as no benefit at all—is it harming the patient to let her have it?

So now you've got the run-down on the four principles of health care ethics. Let's take a quick look at some issues in biomedical ethics that have been real hot button topics!

Death Be Not Proud

Let's look at the difference between *euthanasia* and *physician-assisted suicide*. In the case of euthanasia—literally meaning "the good death"—doctors are in charge of ending patients' lives: they turn off respirators, or give lethal injections, or stop tube feeding patients. But in the case of physician-assisted suicide, doctors like Timothy Quill give patients the means to end their *own* lives (for example, by writing a prescription for a lethal injection). This means patients can go off on their own with the proper means to commit suicide.

Ethically Speaking

The tenth edition of Webster's dictionary defines **euthanasia** as "killing a hopelessly sick or injured person in a relatively painless way for reasons of mercy." This differs from physician-assisted suicide, where doctors don't do the actual killing, but provide terminally ill patients with the means to go off and commit suicide.

There are things you should know right away before you get into moral judgments about euthanasia and physician-assisted suicide (from now on, I'll call it PAS for short). The first is that euthanasia is already practiced by doctors, and is an accepted practice in hospitals. The real euthanasia dispute isn't about the ethics of turning off respirators, deciding to not treat patients, or stopping their tube feedings: these are *passive* forms of euthanasia, and are now almost universally accepted. They're called "passive" euthanasia because the doctor supposedly doesn't do anything to cause the patient's death: The doctor "lets nature take its course" by stopping the medical intervention.

The real dispute concerns the ethics of *active* euthanasia: that is, when doctors take direct action to end patients' lives, like giving them lethal injections. Many (but not all) ethicists make a moral distinction between killing—active euthanasia—and letting die—passive euthanasia. The active form is said to go against the doctor's role of saving lives. We know at least one guy who's in jail for practicing active euthanasia, Dr. Jack Kevorkian, who I'll say more about later in this chapter.

The other thing to know is that PAS is already practiced—usually quietly—in the United States and Canada. It's not always "quiet," though: Consider our famous friend, Kevorkian, who publicized the fact that he practiced PAS on people who asked for his help. Kevorkian created the "mercitron" machine, which was set up to administer lethal doses of medication. All his clients had to do was pull the paper clip off the tube, and the machine delivered the lethal dose. Kevorkian publicized his participation in PAS, but was never prosecuted for it. (He was finally jailed for practicing active euthanasia, not PAS.) But other physicians also practice PAS quietly and with anonymity, because they worry about the consequences of getting caught.

So now for the big question: Should active euthanasia and PAS be allowed? Is it always wrong for doctors to end lives? Some ethicists sure think so, and argue that both active euthanasia and PAS are no-no's; others think both practices are legit, and should be allowed by law. Let's look at the arguments on both sides!

Ethicists opposed to active euthanasia and PAS make the following claims (I'll lump them in together to keep it brief):

1. Helping patients to die violates the doctor's duty to save lives.
2. Human beings don't have the right to take their own lives—it's playing God.
3. The consequences of allowing active euthanasia and PAS would be very bad for society: patients would no longer trust doctors, and we might end up killing patients who don't want to die.
4. We need to keep a distinction between killing patients and letting them die: if we cross the line between passive and active euthanasia, we go too far.

5. Active euthanasia and PAS are most likely to be practiced on society's "undesirables"—the disabled, mentally handicapped, elderly, and poor.

6. Doctors should not be making value judgments about which lives are worth living and which ones aren't.

Tried and True

Physician-assisted suicide is legal in the Netherlands, under very specific conditions. Patients must be terminally ill, have a prognosis of six months or less, and have psychological evaluations by at least two doctors. So ask yourself: could Canada and the United States set similar conditions for the practice of PAS and active euthanasia? Do individuals have a right to it?

Ethicists in favor of active euthanasia and PAS offer the following arguments:

1. Doctors have a duty to prevent pain and suffering, and helping patients to die is just an extension of that duty.

2. Each individual should have the right to die, and should have help by doctors in exercising that right.

3. The consequences of policies against active euthanasia and PAS are bad for patients: They end up experiencing a slow, painful death.

4. If we allow passive euthanasia, where doctors stop treatment, remove respirators, etc., then we should allow active euthanasia. Why? Because in both cases, the intention (that the patient will die) and the outcome (the patient's death) are the same, whether you remove a respirator or give a lethal injection.

5. We can no longer distinguish a "natural" death from an "unnatural" one: Medicine has been used to extend lives way beyond what nature intended, so we can't appeal to just "letting nature take its course."

6. Interfering with a patient's wish to die is unwarranted medical paternalism, and it is wrong.

It's your job to go through each list of reasons and see which ones you agree with and why. We could spend a whole book talking just about these issues, but we don't have the space here. What you should keep in mind is that reasons for and against active euthanasia and PAS come in the form of deontological, consequentialist, natural law, feminist, and social contract arguments. These positions are used to argue *both* for and against these practices.

For example, consequentialists take different stances—some claim that the likely outcomes of these practices will be so bad that we shouldn't allow it, and others claim that we'll do the greatest good for the greatest number if we allow it. And people use duty-based arguments both for and against active euthanasia and PAS (i.e. some say doctors have the highest duty to save lives; other say doctors have the highest duty to prevent pain and suffering).

One last thing to think about: even if we agreed that PAS is morally acceptable, we have to think about how issues of poverty, loneliness, and lack of health care coverage can lead terminally ill patients to wish they were dead. In a country like the United States, where approximately 45 million people lack health care insurance, we might be jumping the gun (so to speak) in legally supporting PAS. It's possible that, with decent medical care, those who currently ask for help in terminating their lives might want to continue living. If PAS is every morally justified, it shouldn't be based on a lack of medical coverage for patients at the end of their lives.

Murder or Killing? Issues in Abortion

Abortion has been one of the biggest hot button issues in the United States, and it still is. Politicians' political careers are often staked on the abortion debate, because voters feel so strongly about it one way or the other. For the purposes of practicing ethics, though, you need to get beyond any emotional reactions you might have so you can clearly consider the ethical issues involved. One of the problems with the abortion debate is that it results in mud-slinging and name calling: pro-choicers are often called "baby killers" and "murderers" while pro-lifers are named "Bible thumpers" and "woman haters." This is un-philosophical and, anyway, doesn't get at the deep and important ethical issues involved in the abortion debate.

Consider this list of ethical questions that are core to abortion:

> **CAUTION**
>
> ## Do the Right Thing!
>
> When discussing extremely controversial topics like abortion, you shouldn't engage in the unhelpful and unphilosophical practice of verbally attacking your opponents. To let yourself get sidetracked by emotional "gut" responses is to lose sight of the important moral questions and to close off debate. So leave the sticks and stones behind when you think about emotional and divisive issues like abortion.

1. Are fetuses "persons" in the moral and legal sense? (No one denies that the fetus is human—it's made up of human genetic material. The disagreement is about whether fetuses are persons like you and me, worthy of the same kinds of legal protection.)

2. Even if fetuses aren't now persons, should their *potential* to be persons give them the right to life?

3. Should women have the absolute right to determine what happens in and to their bodies?

4. Anti-abortionists say that abortion is killing. But is killing always wrong? We talk about cases of "just killing"—in times of war, and in self-defense. Is abortion "just killing"?

5. Does a fetus gain rights the closer it gets to birth? Should we allow abortion in early stages (months 1–3), but make it illegal in later stages (months 7–9)?

6. Should women who get pregnant through rape or incest have the right to abortion? Is this different from women who get pregnant because of contraceptive failure or refusal to use contraceptives?

7. Is the health of the pregnant woman a factor in abortion? If continuing a pregnancy will kill the pregnant woman, is it ethical for her to abort it?

Whew! I think you've got enough ethical questions to keep you puzzling for a year!

In the U.S. context, abortion is legal up until a certain point. This is so because of the 1973 *Roe* v. *Wade* abortion decision. The decision decriminalized abortion, which had until that point been illegal unless the pregnancy directly threatened the pregnant woman's life. *Roe* v. *Wade* recognized that during her first three months of pregnancy, a woman's constitutional right to privacy outweighs the state's interest in protecting the fetus. During the first trimester, women have unlimited rights to access abortion; but after the third month, the state's interest in protecting the woman or fetus override abortion rights. In the second trimester, states may restrict abortion to protect the pregnant woman's health; in the third trimester, because the fetus is so far developed, states may limit abortion to cases where the woman's life is in danger. This is why women find it difficult if not impossible to get an abortion after the 26th week of their pregnancies.

People in the United States just don't agree about *Roe* v. *Wade:* Some think it went too far because it allows women to have early abortions; others think that it is too strict because women are denied abortions at later stages of their pregnancies. So you can see why Americans take such strong views on this!

There are other serious ethical issues that relate to abortion, and they come out of the reproductive technologies we now have available to us. If you didn't already know, there are techniques like in vitro fertilization (IVF) and embryo freezing that are now used to help couples have babies. The problem is, folks who think fetuses are persons and deserve the same rights and respect as the rest of us are opposed to IVF and embryo freezing, because both of them often result in the death of the embryo.

IVF involves taking sperm and egg outside the uterus, putting them together in a petri dish, and allowing fertilization to occur outside the woman's body. Some resulting embryos are stronger than others, and the "strong" ones are implanted in the woman's uterus, while the "weak" ones are thrown out. And, since IVF is really expensive and hard on women's bodies, doctors freeze the extra "strong" embryos just in case the woman doesn't get pregnant on the first try. Embryos end up in a state of frozen animation, waiting to be unthawed and used for another cycle. But since embryos are the early stages of human life, and from embryos come fetuses and then babies, the practice of these reproductive technologies is also a moral problem; the same issues arise here as in the abortion debate. People violently disagree about what ethics requires in these cases!

Dr. Frankenstein Revisited

To understand the big stink about human research and experimentation, you need to know about our sad history of using, abusing, and killing people for the sake of scientific research. In some cases, the research has been of totally questionable scientific value.

◆ In Nazi Germany, Jewish people in concentration camps were used by Nazi doctors as research subjects. These prisoners had no choice, and were given no information about what was being done to them or why. "Scientific" experiments included breaking children's bones to see how they would heal, putting people in ice baths to see how long it takes for hypothermia to set in, and injecting subjects with things like window washer fluid to see its effects on the human body.

◆ In the 1930s, an experiment was done in Tuskegee, Mississippi, that used 400 African American men to study the progression of syphilis, a sexually transmitted disease. The men were all told that they had "bad blood" and that they would receive free treatment from the government if they went to the local medical clinic. The men were never treated, but were studied without their knowledge as the disease advanced. Even after penicillin was developed as a treatment for syphilis, steps were taken to keep the diseased men from receiving it. The research trial ended in 1972; all the infected men had died by then.

We now have strict guidelines for human research that require the subjects' full, informed consent to participate; they must be free to exit the research program at any time; and the research must be of real human value. In cases of children and the mentally handicapped, we generally require that the research be of direct benefit to the individuals themselves, since they aren't capable of consent.

Consider these important ethical questions about experimentation on human subjects:

1. Should we ever experiment on people who can't give free, informed consent (children, the mentally handicapped, prisoners, the poor)?

2. If a person is dying, should she be allowed to participate in very risky experiments on new drugs that could save others' lives?

3. How much information do people need in order to give informed consent? (And if it's highly technical medical information, can the average Joe or Jill really understand the risks?)

4. Is "proxy" consent ethical (for example, allowing a wife to consent for her incompetent husband)?

5. In randomized clinical trials, participants aren't told whether they're getting the "sugar pill" instead of the experimental drug. Is this ethical? Can people *really* give consent in such cases?

You can think about these issues from the perspective of duty-based, consequentialist, care, or social contract ethics.

Carbon Copies: Cloning and Genetic Technology

Ahhh ... at last we come to the cutting edge of medical technology. More and more the media trumpets things like cloning (remember Dolly, the sheep that was recently cloned in England?), stem cell research, and the human genome project. From the sounds of it, the Brave New World isn't just a future possibility—it's here! But what do these technologies involve, and what are some of the real ethical issues tied up with them? You have to watch out, because if you take cloning as an example, folks have come up with some pretty silly ethical worries: that people who are cloned won't have souls; that, should your kidneys or heart ever fail, you might use your clone to harvest organs for yourself; and that we'll use armies of clones to go to war for us.

> **Moral Musings**
>
> What's morally wrong with cloning? It isn't that we're likely to use armies of clones to go to war for us, or that we may end up using our clones to harvest organs for ourselves—that's just silly! Rather, cloning challenges the moral idea that human reproduction is dictated by nature and that it's not natural for humans to come into existence in this way.

Creating a "Mini-Me"?

To keep it simple, cloning involves taking your genetic material and using it to create another human being exactly like you. No sexual reproduction is involved at all, so the clone has no biological parents (except you, if it's your clone). But beyond looking frighteningly like you at various stages of life, clones aren't likely to be much like you at all; they aren't going to be blank-eyed copies that have no personalities of their own.

Look at it this way: while part of who you are comes down to genes (your brown hair, green eyes, dimple, etc.), a huge part of who you are is socially created. This means that your clone is likely to be a very distinct person, with her own characteristics and personality. Even if clones look just like us, unless we exactly replicate our life conditions for them, they aren't likely to *be* like us at all! This kills questions about whether they will be used as organ banks, or whether we'll use them to create armies. We're no more likely to use clones for such things than we would any other human being—unless our moral sensibilities totally leave us!

The more likely ethical issues raised by cloning come out of natural law worries: that it's not natural for people to be created in this way. Do you think it offends the dignity of the individual to come into being like this? Do we have a moral duty to *not* create human beings in this way? What should we do with the products of cloning technology? Who should "parent" the beings that we clone?

Stem Cell Research: Abortion Revisited?

Next, consider another issue in genetic technology: stem cell research. It's highly controversial right now—President Bush is being pressured from different groups to either shut it down or accelerate it! On the plus side: Stem cell research may provide solutions to awful things like Parkinson's and Alzheimer's Disease. On the minus side: The most responsive, adaptable stem cells come from embryos and … well, I'm sure you can see the problem already!

So far researchers have been using spare human embryos—ones that have been frozen, and that couples donate to science because they no longer need them. This gets folks who are opposed to abortion and in vitro fertilization upset enough—because it means we're using human beings as "things" in the service of others. But now researchers are claiming that the best stem cells come from fresh embryos; researchers think that cryopreservation (freezing) may affect the usefulness of the embryos. Because fresh embryos are even more alive than frozen ones—and thus have even greater potential for life—opponents of abortion are especially opposed to this kind of research.

In general, you can think about issues in cloning and genetic technology either from the perspective of consequences or of moral obligations that we have to not do certain things. For example, we may one day be able to splice the genetic material of human beings with apes to create ape-human hybrids. Such technology may even have some good consequences for human beings: they'd be dexterous creatures, maybe useful for space exploration. But ask yourself: Should we even go down a road like that? We may have moral duties, both to ourselves and the beings we could someday create—to not do it at all. That's where we need ethics the most … and why we need to remember that just because we can do something doesn't mean that we should!

The Least You Need to Know

- ◆ Use the four principles of health care ethics—autonomy, beneficence, nonmaleficence, and justice—to help you think through ethical issues in medicine.
- ◆ Make sure you think about bioethical issues in a philosophical way; don't just respond from your gut!
- ◆ Remember: Just because we have the medical technology to do certain things doesn't mean we ought to do them.
- ◆ Be sure to see the connections between bioethical issues: ethical issues in stem cell research and cloning are related to abortion.

Chapter 19

Business Ethics

In This Chapter

♦ Is caveat emptor—"let the buyer beware"—ethical?

♦ How do we make businesses be ethically responsible?

♦ Should businesspeople be encouraged to "squeal" on each other?

♦ When does advertising go too far?

The Case of the Exploding Ford Pinto: Do you remember this case from the 1970s? The Ford Pinto was a sub-compact car that was marketed to average folks as an affordable new car. Lee Iacocca came up with the idea, demanding that the Pinto weigh no more than 2,000 pounds and cost no more than $2,000. During design and production, however, crash tests showed that the gas tank ruptured, even at lower speeds of 25 miles per hour. Fixing the Pinto would have required changes to the car's design.

Iacocca did not want to invest money in changes, and by lobbying the government, managed to convince them to delay regulations on gas tanks for eight years. One argument Ford used was based on cost-benefit analysis: according to their estimates, the rupturing tanks would cause 180 burn deaths, 180 serious burn injuries, and 2,100 burned cars each year. Ford determined it would have to pay $200,000 per death, $67,000 per injury, and $700 per car for a total of $49.5 million. But it would cost more than that to make the cars safe for people to drive: changes to the car would cost $11 each, which comes to $137 million per year. Ford's argument to the government was basically that it would be cheaper to let people burn!

This is just one case that makes us think about ethics and business. What the heck is going on? It sounds like the business world needs a little ethics. This chapter will consider some important issues in business ethics, like whether *caveat emptor* ("let the buyer beware") is a fair way to treat customers, whether business people should blow the whistle on one another when they discover wrong-doing, and whether corporations have moral obligations to society beyond making lots of money.

Let the Buyer Beware

There's an idea floating around out there that you may or may not be familiar with: in fact, maybe you've run up against it in your life as a consumer. It's the idea of *caveat emptor*, "let the buyer beware," and basically requires that we be smart, savvy consumers. So if you buy that red, shiny, used car without doing your research, and you later find out that the engine is toast—well, tough luck! Or if you buy those magic weight loss pills that promise you'll lose 30 pounds in a month, and you gain 3 pounds—sorry, Charlie! And if (God forbid!) you get a cute little puppy from a puppy mill, and it turns out to be a sick little puppy—you foot the bill, baby!

The principle of "let the buyer beware" puts consumers in the position of having to research purchases so they know what the heck they're buying before they take it home and it falls apart. Classic example: I bought a great looking record player at a church sale a couple of weeks ago; the tag said "It works!" But did I plug it in and check it out before I bought it? Nope. Did it work when I got it home? Nope. Good thing I was only out five bucks on that one—but just imagine, false advertising in a church!

Ethically Speaking

Caveat emptor is a Latin phrase that means "Let the buyer beware." It basically requires that we be smart, savvy consumers: if we buy things without knowing what we're getting, and it turns out to be junk—well, tough luck! It puts responsibility on each of us as consumers to research our purchases or live with the consequences.

You might think this idea is really unfair—I mean, why should we have to be the ones who "beware"? Why don't those stinkers who produce the widgets and other junk that gets put on the market have to follow certain guidelines? The answer is—they do. But the government doesn't oversee every minute detail of each product that comes to market. We could spend billions of dollars on monitoring manufacturers alone! The truth is, we don't want to commit huge portions of our federal budget to this kind of vigilance.

Besides, some people are offended by the idea that the government should protect us from manufacturers who are just waiting to prey on us naive little simpletons. Part of what it means to be a free citizen is to have the freedom to make choices, to take risks, and to get a bum deal now and again. If the government were too heavy-handed in protecting us from our own stupidity, it'd be a pretty bad case of paternalism.

Paternalism Again

Remember paternalism? It came up in the chapter on biomedical ethics, too. Paternalism comes into the consumer world when the government does things to either benefit us or protect us from hurting ourselves. It's like saying, "Here, Johnny, I know what's best for you, even if you don't, so I'll go ahead and do it." The problem with this kind of paternalism is this: How likely is it that the government will really know what's best for you, and do a good job of protecting you from bad things? Maybe you could even accept someone who knows you really well trying to do what's best for you … but the government? They know nothing about you!

This isn't to say that the state takes a totally "hands off" approach to products that make it to market. On the contrary, in order for something to *get* to the market, it has to pass safety inspections, and meet industry regulations. There are different regulations for different products—so new cars have to meet certain standards for the car industry, toys have to meet different standards, and so, too, do food and drugs that get put on the market. We don't want just any old thing getting put out there for us to consume. (Especially not cars with exploding gas tanks!)

Tried and True

One way of figuring out when paternalism for consumers is justified is to apply a "reasonable person" standard. This standard asks us: What could a reasonable person be expected to know about a particular product? In some cases, through a little research, we can know quite a bit. In others, we couldn't expect a reasonable person to be able to know much

Avoiding Booby Traps

So the ethical issues here are: how much regulation is called for? How much can the average consumer be expected to know before they buy something? Should certain things be kept off the market because they're too dangerous for us? And where does the manufacturer's responsibility come in?

Here's a good example of why *caveat emptor* is a problem for consumers: the manufacturing of silicone breast implants. There was a huge stink in the 1990s over these gelatinous blobs that women were buying in droves and having implanted in their chests. The implants, as it turned out, were prone to leakage—in some cases after their cosmetic surgeries, women found the silicone had seeped out of their implants and migrated into other parts of their bodies! Class action suits against implant manufacturers resulted, and some women even claimed that their implants caused serious illnesses, like lupus or cancer.

Should we apply "buyer beware" thinking to such a case? Bear in mind that, even if the women had done serious research before having the implants done, they wouldn't have found any studies available about the likelihood of seepage. Why? Because manufacturers hadn't done any such studies prior to marketing them. Besides, it's hard for us average folks to read technical medical or scientific reports on products and interpret their meaning. I mean, have you ever read the names of ingredients on your pill bottles? Ack! The words are unpronounceable!

So you should keep this in mind: *Caveat emptor* works in some areas of consumer life, but not others. You have the obligation to make sure that the car or boat you are buying works properly (test drive it), and that the new pajamas you want to buy don't have rips in them (try them on). We even have consumer magazines to help us out on these purchases. But it's much more difficult to "test drive" your breast implants, research the 10-syllable drug that your doctor is recommending, or find out whether psychotherapy will work for you. So in some areas of consumer life, a *laissez-faire* approach is morally acceptable; in other areas it isn't. While saying "what you see is what you get" might be fair with the car, boat, or pajamas, it sure as heck isn't fair for the Hydroxpropyl Methylcellulose that's in your ibuprofen! Enough said.

Ethically Speaking

Some people take a **laissez-faire** approach to the market. "Laissez-faire" means allowing people to engage in buying and selling without interference. The idea is that the market will control and stabilize itself, without the government getting involved.

Payback Time

The preceding issues lead us to ask whether businesses owe something to us, not just as consumers, but as a society. Some business ethicists claim that the only moral obligations businesses have is to make lots of money—beyond that, there's nothing more. Why? Because once we start requiring businesses to do more—to be run in certain ways, to hire certain people, to meet certain costly environmental standards—then we interfere with the whole point of business, which is profits. The ethically best businesses, on this view, are those that are doing their job well: making lots of money, creating jobs, stimulating the economy—that kind of thing.

But there's business and then there's business. Some corporations are hugely profitable because they hire people at near-slave wages. They keep their overheads low by not spending anything on the workplace, so workers are stuck in dilapidated buildings with no running water and no bathrooms. Or they keep overhead low by not doing research before putting products on the market (like the silicone implant fiasco), by violating environmental standards, or by going against fair business practices. So ethicists who claim that businesses only have a moral responsibility to make money aren't factoring in all these issues.

CAUTION **Do the Right Thing!** _____

Remember: We the people (the common schmoes, the taxpayers) subsidize businesses, so they *do* owe us something! If you think that businesses are self-started, without the help of some serious government cash, then think again. Even where businesspeople *do* open their own businesses—with their own start-up funds—they benefit from certain tax shelters, deductibles, and other perks that they get on the backs of us taxpayers.

You know that saying "No man is an island"? Well, no business is an island, either! Even so-called private corporations have benefited from public funding. Think of it this way: the state funds researchers to do studies on all kinds of things, from soup to nuts, and these studies are fair game for corporations to use, too. These researchers are paid out of public funds: so in a real sense, businesses take a free ride on the studies paid for by taxpayers.

Corporate Debts to Society?

In short, businesses are social entities. They rely on societies to support them, on consumers to buy stuff, and they have the capacity to help or harm citizens. So saying businesses only have the moral obligation to make big bucks overlooks some pretty basic social responsibilities that they owe to all of us.

But should there be limits on corporations' social responsibilities? After all, it's good for us if businesses show a profit. When profits are down, bad things happen: People lose jobs, and then they have no money to buy things with. That means more people lose their jobs, because consumers aren't buying stuff. That can lead to the worst thing— a depression—which is bad for everybody. So if we hold businesses to a really high standard of ethical behavior, we could seriously affect their profits, resulting in very bad things for us. What to do?

The answer is to balance concern for profits with social responsibility. If profitability is a business's sole bottom line, then we end up with situations like the exploding Ford Pinto or leaking breast implants—unhappy situations, to say the least! This doesn't mean that corporations should ignore profits, though; it just means that we will all have to constantly ask ourselves "What is it worth to us?" Do we want to risk women's safety for the sake of big breasts? Do we want affordable new cars so badly that we'll take the risk of blowing up on the highway? These aren't questions for corporations only: they're questions you should put to yourself, too. Because corporations won't market things if people won't buy them!

What's a Life Worth?

One final point about profits versus social responsibility. In order to figure out whether a product is "worth it" or not, we have to do something that looks ethically ugly: *cost-benefit analysis*. Cost-benefit analysis involves working out the "pluses" of having a certain good or technology versus its "minuses"—lost lives, environmental harms, exploiting people and animals, and so on.

Cost-benefit analysis is "ethically ugly" because it might just seem wrong to balance things like human lives or the environment against "goods" like driving cars or having big breasts. If you're a Kantian-type, you'll take respect for persons really seriously, and think that no human life should be calculated against social goodies ... human life, after all, is invaluable. Cost-benefit analysis requires us to put a price on human life—literally a monetary value, as Ford did in the Pinto case—and determine whether the benefits outweigh that human cost. If cost-benefit analysis makes you uncomfortable, then that's a good thing: it means you are an ethical, thinking person.

 Ethically Speaking

Cost-benefit analysis is a way for businesses to figure out whether a product is "worth it" or not: they work out the "pluses" of having a certain good or technology versus its "minuses"—lost lives, environmental harms, or exploiting people and animals. Cost-benefit analysis requires us to put a price on human life—literally a monetary value, as Ford did with the Pinto—and determine whether the financial benefits outweigh that cost.

But cost-benefit analysis is a common part of all our lives: we do it all the time. It's a form of consequentialism, since it requires you to weigh out the consequences of different options. For example, every time you get in your car and drive down a highway at 75 miles per hour, you engage in cost-benefit analysis. You've basically asked yourself: do the benefits of a slow trip to your destination (arriving alive by horse and buggy, for example) outweigh the costs involved in driving 75 miles an hour down the highway? Knowing the number of highway fatalities, is it worth taking the chance with your life (and others' lives) to get where you're going faster? Apparently it is, since we do this all the time!

Similarly, a company asks itself: should we market this widget, knowing that the likely outcomes will be X and Y, or should we not market it, knowing the likely outcomes will be A and B? What are the benefits? What are the costs?

The company figures out which action will maximize outcomes, and it goes with that choice. What we have to watch out for with corporate cost-benefit analysis, however, is that companies don't put such a high value on the widget they want to produce that human life pales in comparison to the likely profits they'll make!

Imagine cost-benefit analysis concerning a new baby toy going like this: "Well, we know babies could choke on this widget, since it's small enough for some kids to put in their mouths. But parents will love these things! They'll sell like hotcakes! And if, on average, 1 out of every 100,000 babies chokes and dies, and only 1 out of a 1,000,000 parents sues, we'll make a fortune, even paying out damages and funeral costs for the babies." Yech!

You're Busted! Whistleblowing

Business ethicists have wrung their hands over another ethical question that involves business relationships: Should businesspeople "squeal" when they find their bosses or co-workers engaged in corporate wrong-doing? Look at this list of "wrongs" for a second:

- You look over your cubicle to find a co-worker downloading pornography off a website.

- You know your boss has pirated software—copied it without paying for it—and wonder if you should report it.

- You know a colleague has fudged some data to make the figures come out right.

- You find out that your friend is sleeping with the boss and was recently promoted.

- You discover that a colleague is cheating on his time card.

- You overhear a co-worker's phone conversations: Every day she's been calling her boyfriend in Greece from her office phone.

Tried and True

When considering the ethics of whistleblowing—whether or not to squeal on your co-worker or boss—you can think about it from different perspectives. You could use a consequentialist, deontological, feminist, or social contract approach to determine what is morally right.

Okay, these are enough to start with. You might have your own scenario that you can add. I've mixed together what I take to be mundane and serious ethical problems. The question is, in any or all of these cases, is it morally right to "blow the whistle" on the corporate wrong-doer? How do you go about figuring this out?

Well, one way to go is to look at the consequences of squealing in each separate case; another would be to consider the duties that you owe to yourself, others, or the business itself. Let's consider each of these approaches in turn.

Thinking 'Bout Consequences

First, the consequentialist approach (see? I told you those theories would come in handy). In each of the cases, you could ask yourself what the likely outcomes are of each act, consider alternatives, and come up with the course of action that will result in the best overall consequences. When figuring out whether to "rat" or not, you'd have to consider the happiness and unhappiness from everyone's perspective.

For example, take the first case of the guy who's downloading porn off the Internet: do you tell on him or not? In trying to decide, you'd have to include your own happiness/unhappiness, your co-worker's (he'll likely be out of a job), and the outcomes for all the other people you work with. Suppose our porn freak is a real slacker who doesn't do his job and whom no one really likes. If you squeal on him, he'll likely lose his job—this creates unhappiness for him. But that means someone else will get his job, and it's likely to be someone better since a worse job couldn't be done! So that means the business will benefit. In addition, since no one likes porn boy anyway, everyone else will be thrilled that he's gone. Putting the scenario this way, it looks like you should blow the whistle to achieve the best outcomes.

The Duty Thing

You could approach the dilemma from another perspective, of course—the deontological one. Then, instead of weighing out consequences you'd consider what duties and obligations you owe—whether to the company, your co-workers, or this particular guy. For example, if you figure out that you have obligations to your company, then it might be your duty to blow the whistle on this guy as part of that corporate obligation. Or, if you work it out that you have an overriding duty to your co-workers, then it might be your moral responsibility to squeal on him. But if you have an absolute moral obligation to the fellow himself—suppose you caught him doing this before, and you promised you'd never tell on him—then that duty might outweigh all the others.

The same thing applies to each of the scenarios I listed above. With the moral theories in hand, you have ways of deciding what you should do. And there are more than just consequentialist or deontological ways: you could also use a feminist relational approach (which act will be most caring/least disruptive of relationships?), a social contract approach (is the guy violating his agreement with the company?), and so on.

But let's get back to a Kantian point: when deciding in any one of these cases what you should do, should your motivations matter? Remember that Kant thinks they do: You should only blow the whistle if it's for the right reasons. But what are those reasons? It shouldn't be that you're ticked off at your boss because he didn't give you a raise, or that you don't like your co-worker, or that you're vindictive. Those, if you remember, are crummy reasons for squealing on people. No, the right reason would be because you've reasoned things through and worked out that it's your duty to tell.

Do the Right Thing!

In a recent ad campaign against software piracy, billboards pictured a tie nailed to a wall; the caption read: "NAIL YOUR BOSS! 1-800-BUSTHIM." Millions of dollars are lost each year because businesspeople don't pay for software. Although it's illegal (and unethical) to copy software without paying for it, the ad encourages squealing to get back at your boss. Is this a good ethical reason to do it?

Ethics in Advertising: A Contradiction in Terms?

I've taught business ethics before, and each time the same joke comes up: someone always says "Business ethics? Isn't that a contradiction in terms?" Ha ha. In any case, some people *do* think that talking about ethics in advertising is contradictory, since the very purpose of advertising is to trick us into buying things we don't need, or to make us want things we didn't want before. And it's true that some forms of advertising have been and continue to be less than ethical. Consider the case of subliminal advertising: it appeals to our subconscious, and gets us to desire the manufacturer's product. Let's take an actual example, and call it *The Mysterious Desire for Popcorn* case.

In 1957, a researcher named James Vicary claimed that he used sneaky advertising in a New Jersey movie theater to get people to buy more goodies at the concession stands. During the films, he said he flashed messages like "Eat popcorn" and "Drink Coke" on the screen. The images appeared so quickly that the moviegoers didn't actually perceive it; but it worked, since the sales went up. Vicary claimed that popcorn sales increased by 58 percent and coke sales by 18 percent because of these messages. When this little trick—called *subliminal advertising*—was discovered, the theaters were told to stop using it, since this kind of advertising is considered unethical.

The example of subliminal advertising should lead you to ask: just what is ethical in advertising? Should advertising be done on the model of "no holds barred"—or is it justified to have strict regulations surrounding what (and how) companies advertise?

Some libertarian-types (that is, people who think that no government intervention is ever justified) would argue for the "no holds barred" approach to advertising. After all, you could argue, we should be free to watch, hear, and read what we want, and it's up to each of us to determine whether or not there's truth in advertising.

Ethically Speaking

Subliminal advertising usually involves flashing images on the television or movie screen. The images appear so briefly— for less than a split second—that viewers aren't even aware that they saw it. Such advertising appeals to the consumers' subconscious, and gets them to buy the manufacturer's product.

This takes us right back to the issue of *caveat emptor* that was raised at the beginning of this chapter. If we were to take an "anything goes" approach to advertising, then we'd have to be pretty hip to the advertisers' claims, and we'd have to do a heck of a lot of research to know what's what. Few of us have the time, money, or energy to engage in the kind of super-sleuthing it would take to distinguish the truth from lies in advertising, and most reasonable people think the state should play some role in regulating advertisements.

Protecting the Vulnerable

Let's take an easy example of why advertising needs to be regulated: the case of children. Maybe you have kids of your own. If not, let me tell you this: kids are gullible. They'll believe things they're told by people who appear to be in positions of authority, and they're very easily suggestible.

My daughter is constantly coming up with new things that she wants, and most of the ideas come from ads she sees on television when she's watching cartoons. Darn that TV set! If we didn't set any rules about advertising on television, then little kids would be told all kinds of lies about different toys and products, and they'd believe every one of them.

And most parents know that even with standards for advertising, things are bad enough. Kids get the gimmies, and the advertisers make it really hard for us parents to say no!

You can see why we need to protect kids from advertisers: Our little ones can be great little consumers, and companies make gobs of money off them. But more than this, kids need to be protected, since some lies in advertising can actually harm children, and not just make them want our money. It's one thing if an ad tells kids that buying the newest doll that poops will provide them with endless hours of entertainment (when in fact, most kids will actually toss the doll aside after five minutes); it's another thing if an ad tells them that the newest zit cream will make them social stars and end all their teenage anxiety!

And going beyond television ads, think about tobacco advertisements that have explicitly been targeted to youths. Thank goodness for regulations that stopped these ads from appearing on billboards: otherwise, kids might believe that they're cool if they smoke, and that smoking will make them popular.

Marketing Designer Drugs

Kids aside, there's another problem with advertising that concerns adults, too. It's that as viewers and consumers, we often aren't in the position to verify or falsify claims made by advertisers. How am I supposed to know if it's true that a certain face cream will make my skin look 10 years younger? I could try it out, but it'd take quite a while to find out if the claim is true or not (by then I could go through a lot of face cream). Or to take a more dangerous example, how can I judge the pharmaceutical ads that have recently been legalized for television?

You know those new pharmaceutical ads—the ones that tell us to ask for "the little purple pill"; that advertise drugs for incontinence, obesity, arthritis, impotence, hair loss, heartburn, and depression. This kind of direct-to-consumer advertising, previously not allowed by the Food and Drug Administration, has really paid off for drug companies: The ads have turned certain medications into "designer" drugs that consumers are asking for by name.

Defenders of such advertising claim that they're only providing information to viewers, and in this way should be seen as educators for the public. I might not know that the burning in my chest is heartburn, and that there's something out there to treat it. So, as one ad exec has said about these ads, because of them "patients have been more easily able to diagnose symptoms that went ignored for many years. Our whole goal is just to encourage a conversation with your health-care provider."

Whether or not pharmaceutical ads should be aired on television is a moot point now that they *are* being aired. But what about other kinds of television advertising that are currently illegal? Ever notice that tobacco and alcohol companies don't advertise on TV? Ever wonder why? It's because

Do the Right Thing!

Don't be fooled! When they market designer drugs, advertisers play on your fears and uncertainties regarding your health. And in addition, they aren't encouraging consumers to buy generic, cheaper versions of certain drugs and pills—they are encouraging us to go for the brand names.

they aren't allowed to—they are government-controlled substances and, because they're addictive and bad for your health, the FDA has ruled them out. How does that grab you? These companies can advertise in magazines, pubs, on the walls of bus shelters and on billboards, but they can't come into your home through the boob tube. Not now, at least. You can think these questions through on your own. It's a really interesting set of ethical issues. But for now, let's consider one last ethical issue in advertising: the problem of puffery.

Puffery occurs when advertisers make exaggerated claims about their products: "It's a mind-blowing experience!" or "It'll make you orgasm!" or "It'll change your life!" As the saying goes, there's lies and damned lies … and puffery is the former. Advertisers blow the benefits of their products way out of proportion, and make claims that can't really be substantiated. I mean, maybe some people do have orgasms when washing their hair with certain products … who knows? Just don't you be disappointed if it doesn't happen for you!

Puffery is borderline legally acceptable, because as long as advertisers don't out-and-out lie (that is, knowingly make claims that just aren't true), they're still within their rights. So notice on the bottles of weight loss pills—"Lose 30 pounds in a month!"—there's a teensy weensy warning that says "These claims have not been substantiated by the FDA." Watch out for these little disclaimers. They point you toward puffery, and could save you a few bucks. The question here isn't about the legality of puffery, but the ethics of it. Should companies be free to make such exaggerated claims about their products? Is it harmful to people that they do so?

Ethically Speaking

Puffery is a term used in connection with advertising. Those who engage in puffery (meaning all advertisers!) make exaggerated claims about their products: "It's a mind-blowing experience!" or "It'll make your orgasm!" or "It'll change your life!" There's nothing illegal about it: As long as the advertiser isn't making false claims about the product, puffery is not against the law.

This is an arguable point, since most people are aware of the lengths advertisers will go to in order to get us to buy stuff. Exaggerating the value of products may be legally acceptable, but it isn't necessarily ethical!

One thing I hope you take from this chapter is that government paternalism isn't always bad: We consumers are vulnerable, sometimes ignorant, and may require protection. Citizens may argue about how much protection we require, and we may never all agree on that particular point; but we should be glad for regulations, standards, and laws that keep businesses in line.

The Least You Need to Know

◆ Remember: *caveat emptor!* Always research products before you buy them.

◆ Don't assume that ads must always tell the truth: puffery is a common practice in advertising.

- If you have to decide whether to blow the whistle on someone in the workplace, make sure you do it for ethical reasons, not as "payback."

- Hold businesses to reasonable ethical standards: if they engage in unfair business practices or exploit their workers, don't buy their stuff.

- Know your limits as a consumer: If you can't pronounce the name of the drug you're buying, you might not know enough about it.

20

Ethics and Animals

In This Chapter

- ◆ What do we owe animals?
- ◆ Moral arguments for vegetarianism
- ◆ Determining when research on animals is justified
- ◆ The ethics of wearing animals

In the 1600s, philosopher René Descartes was busy learning about the sciences, and asking all kinds of important philosophical questions. Descartes is considered to be one of the greatest modern philosophers of all time, but this fellow took a very dim view of animals. He thought that animals are little more than machines, conscious automata that don't have the capacity to think. So the story goes that Descartes threw a cat out the window just to prove his point!

Now for most of us doing such a thing seems pretty morally disgusting. I don't know anyone these days who makes the controversial claim that animals can't even feel, let alone think. Most of us are willing to grant that animals are "sentient"—they can feel pains and pleasures—and most think it's wrong to unnecessarily cause harm to them. But most folks don't agree on what it means to "unnecessarily" cause harm to animals: does this mean we shouldn't use them to test cosmetic products or perfumes? Does it mean that we shouldn't eat them or use them for furs? And what about using animals for medical testing—is it justifiable to cause animals pain if it can result in great advances for human medicine?

This chapter will consider all of these issues. You will consider the claim made by more extreme animal rights activists that animals are our moral equals, and that they have rights equal to human beings. And while you might not change your mind about where you stand on ethics and animals, this chapter just might make you reconsider that thick steak that you were going to have for dinner tonight!

What Do We Owe Animals?

First, you need to consider the most basic question of what, if anything, we owe to animals. You can't very well decide whether it's right to eat meat, wear furs, or test on animals if you don't first determine whether animals have rights to any particular kind of treatment. In what follows you will see that some people think animals deserve no protections whatsoever: They're here for human use, and there's no limits on what we are entitled to do with them. But as you will also discover, others think that animals have rights that must be respected; some radical animal rights defenders even claim that an animal's life is of equal value to (and is sometimes *more* valuable than) human life! Let's start with the traditional view: That animals are here for our use, and that there are no moral limits on what we may do with them.

The Traditional View: Dissect 'Em and Eat 'Em

You don't have to go back very far in human history to find the radical view that animals are of no moral value. Zippo. Nada. Zilch. As I already mentioned, early modern philosophers like Descartes thought that animals were more like machines. But even those who recognized that animals could feel pain, like our friend Immanuel Kant, didn't necessarily think we had any moral duty to avoid causing pain and suffering to animals. Why? Because animals aren't rational creatures like us human types. Sure, we can do things to them that cause untold agony—like setting leg-hold traps—but animals aren't able to reason, to form a rational life plan, or to get beyond their innate drives. If you remember correctly, Kant believed that we human beings belong to a special kingdom all of our own, the "kingdom of ends," meaning that we must never be used by others. But Kant didn't include animals in this kingdom because they can't reason and they lack a moral will.

Tried and True

You don't have to believe that animals have rights to justify protecting them from harm. Immanuel Kant and St. Thomas Aquinas claimed that people who treat animals cruelly are likely to do the same with other humans. This means we have a moral obligation to not treat animals in ways that will likely lead to abuse of human beings, too.

This theme of "reason and will" is a common one. The Natural Law philosophers, like St. Thomas Aquinas, were concerned about it, too. According to these guys, human beings have the God-given right to use animals as they see fit because God created the heavens and the earth (and everything within it) for our use. Heck, God even gave Adam the authority to name the animals: what more evidence than that do we need of our moral superiority? According to Natural Law theorists, it's part of the natural order of things than human beings should hunt, kill, and eat animals. We're bigger, we're stronger, and we're smarter (okay, most of us are). On this world view, it makes no sense to talk about "animal rights," since to have a right you must be able to claim it, and animals just can't do that.

So with a few notable exceptions in the history of human thought, animals just haven't rated very high. Part of the reason is because of the supposed superiority of human beings. But another reason is that we haven't always had the time (or luxury) to question our relationship to animals. For the most part, human beings have been too busy using animals to plough the earth, put food on their tables, and provide warm clothing to question whether we *should* be doing it. Only in our modern world, with synthetic fibers to keep us warm and with all sorts of animals as pets (including ferrets and pot-bellied pigs) does the question of animal rights come up. Remember, "'ought' implies 'can,'" meaning that we can't be morally required to do something that is virtually impossible. Well, 150 years ago it was *possible* to make the moral claim that people shouldn't use animals, but it was pretty much impossible to avoid doing it.

But even now, some folks reject the view that we owe anything to animals. Some ethicists, for example, have claimed that it's morally acceptable to use animals for any human purpose we deem necessary, even if it's for frivolous things like testing cosmetics and perfumes. Since human beings come so far above animals on the scale of moral importance, an animal's life is second to even the most foolish of human desires. Still others take a more cautious approach, claiming that some uses of animals are immoral if they serve no real human purpose. Kicking a cute, fluffy little puppy because it relieves stress is just one example. People who take this view tend to think that most of our uses of animals are justified: they put their foot down, though, where no real good will come from the use (or abuse) of the animal. Many people, then, even those who have pets, think that when it comes to researching and consuming animals, we should "dissect 'em and eat 'em" without feeling guilty about it.

The Radical View: Animals as Our Equals

Contrast the "dissect 'em and eat 'em" view with the radical one: that animals are our moral equals. According to this idea, we have no business doing most of the things that we do to animals; our treatment is based on the wrongful belief that humans are "better" than animals.

But if you think about what really counts—the ability to feel pain and pleasure—then animals rate way up there with the rest of us. Recall Chapter 13, "Consequentialist Theories," where I presented the Utilitarian approach to ethics. According to famous Utilitarians like Jeremy Bentham and John Stuart Mill, what really matters is creating as much happiness as possible in the world, and minimizing pain and suffering. Bentham and Mill weren't particular about *whose* pains and pleasures we are talking about: Any living being that can be harmed or helped in a situation—any sentient being—is deserving of moral consideration. So if we're deciding whether we should kill a seal pup to make a fur coat, Utilitarians would argue that the pup's pain and suffering, or conversely, its happiness, should count in the ethical equation.

While John Stuart Mill and Jeremy Bentham died a long time ago, there have been more contemporary ethicists who make similar arguments based on animals' capacity for pain and suffering. Most famously, Peter Singer has claimed that it is almost always wrong to use animals in service of human beings. As a modern Utilitarian, Singer points out that the capacity for pains and pleasures is a prerequisite for any creature to have interests at all. As he puts it …

> A stone does not have interests because it cannot suffer. Nothing that we can do to it could possibly make any difference to its welfare. A mouse, on the other hand, does have an interest in not being kicked along the road, because it will suffer if it is.

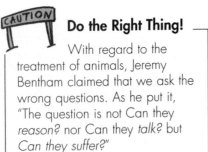

Do the Right Thing!

With regard to the treatment of animals, Jeremy Bentham claimed that we ask the wrong questions. As he put it, "The question is not Can they *reason*? nor Can they *talk*? but Can they *suffer*?"

But the fact that animals have interests (say, a basic interest in continued existence) doesn't settle the case about animal rights. Utilitarians are always in the position to judge that one being's pain is justifiable if the good that will come of it outweighs the "badness" of it's suffering. Kicking a mouse along the road wouldn't pass the Utilitarian calculus of happiness versus pain: whatever pleasure you might get from kicking a mouse certainly couldn't measure up to the pain you cause the poor little creature by doing it. Notice that the size of the creature matters not one bit: even a little mouse's pain is sizable, especially when the rationale for causing that pain (because I like to kick it) is so poor.

What about really noble reasons for causing pain to animals, then? Could you justify causing a mouse pain and suffering if the goals are truly noble ones (like learning how to reverse paralysis in human beings)? Here Utilitarians have to admit that it might be morally acceptable to harm an animal if a much greater good will come of it. We'll get into that issue in a later section of this chapter. The important thing to remember so far is that philosophers who see animals as our equals usually do so on the grounds that we all equally experience pleasures and pains. And guess what? There's an even stronger position that's been argued; a position claiming that favoring humans over animals in all cases is just a different form of racism.

Favoring Humans: Another Form of Racism?

That it's a kind of "racism" to favor humans over animals may seem like a startling claim. But hear out the argument before you decide that it's just a flaky idea! Philosophers who believe this make a comparison between the way women and African Americans have been treated in the past and the way we currently treat animals. Let's look a little more closely at this idea.

If you think about the history of racism and sexism in the United States, then you get a good idea of what animal rights activists are concerned about. Take, for example, the historical view that African Americans are inferior to whites. Most people now agree that such a notion was based on really bad reasoning, and really bad science. Or, similarly, it was once commonly held that women are "naturally" inferior to men in every way that matters: it was believed that women couldn't reason, and because of that "bare fact" they were prevented from voting, seeking an education, and holding jobs.

Most people now recognize that those ideas about women and nonwhites are just wrong. But how did they come about in the first place? By looking at differences between people—some are black, some female—the assumption was somehow made that those differences make people unequal. If people are unequal, then there's nothing wrong with treating them different. And so we came to the practice of holding some human beings as slaves and domestic servants, allowing others to dominate over them.

But just because people look different doesn't mean there is any important moral difference between them. And if we treat some people better than others, such preferential treatment is based on nasty things like prejudice and hatred. Well, the same argument can be made for animals. Yes, animals are different from human beings. They look different, they think different, and they don't even show the same mental capacity as human beings. But guess what? Radical animal rights activists claim that treating animals as objects just because they are different from human beings is just like treating African Americans and women like objects just because they're different from white men.

Tried and True

Just as human beings can be racists and sexists in their dealings with one another, so can they be "speciesists" in the way they think about and treat animals. The mistake in behaving as a speciesist is that, in the most important ways, human beings and animals are the same. We feel pain and we feel pleasures. Kick a human being, and it hurts her. Kick a mouse, and it hurts the mouse. Case closed.

Valuing Animals Above Humans

There's an even more radical claim to be considered, too, and this one has caused a lot of outrage. It's the idea that, in some cases, animals may have a stronger right to life than human beings. Consider an anencephalic baby, for example (that is, a baby born without a brain). Some ethicists argue that the anencephalic baby may be of the human species, but it will never develop into a fully functioning human person. Without a brain, you can't breathe on your own, and if enough of the brain stem is missing, there isn't even the capacity to feel pain. In cases like that, it may be morally justified to save an intelligent animal's life—a chimpanzee, for example—over the life of the baby. Why? Because the chimpanzee has the capacity to lead a flourishing chimp life, and certainly has the capacity to feel pleasure and pain. To automatically prefer the baby's life over the chimp's is just what some critics would call another example of speciesism: treating one being as "better" than another just because it is a different species.

Whichever way you go on this issue of what we owe animals—whether you hold the "dissect 'em and eat 'em" view or the "animals as our equals" view—one thing is for certain. We are no longer justified in assuming that we can do any old thing that we want to with animals. Nowadays, anyone who wants to do harm to an animal is expected to have a reason; and we can (and do) deny people the right to hurt animals if we think their reasons are bad.

So let's look at this in a little more detail. Because some people think that our reasons for eating animals just aren't good ones, and that if we were truly moral people, we'd give up eating them altogether! Tofu, anyone?

You Are What You Eat: Moral Arguments for Vegetarianism

You probably know people who are vegetarians. Heck, you might even know people who are vegans. *Veganism* is a more radical version of vegetarianism, where one not only refuses to eat meat, but any product that comes from animals.

Ethically Speaking

Veganism is a more radical version of vegetarianism, where one not only refuses to eat meat, but any product that comes from animals. So eggs? No touchy. Food products with lard? Nope. And milk? Sorry, Charlie. Vegans take a principled stance against using animals in any way, shape, or form.

You may have met people who are vegetarian or vegan, but you may still wonder why they think it's wrong to eat meat. Unless you're a vegetarian or vegan yourself, you might not understand the rationale for it. The reasons, I hate to tell you, are actually pretty good ones. Let's look at them now.

The simplest reason vegetarians give as to why it's wrong to eat meat is because it hurts animals when we eat them. In order to eat them, we've got to kill them first, and that can get really ugly. (If you've ever lived near or worked in an abattoir—a slaughterhouse—then you have first-hand experience with the ugliness of killing cattle for meat.) We generally think that unnecessary killing is morally bad. Well, according to vegetarians, killing animals for food is unnecessary because we can get along just fine without relying on meat. So killing animals to eat them is unnecessary killing and is morally wrong.

Beyond this, though, there are other important moral considerations. Take the problem of factory farming, for example. Another objection vegetarians and vegans have to eating meat is that almost all our meat now comes out of factory farming. What this means is that animals that appear in packages in the grocery store had a miserable, horrible life leading up to their slaughter. So we can't even make the argument that eating animals isn't so bad because they suffer a quick death and it's over. No, animals spend a long time in factory farms before they are slaughtered; farmers need to fatten them up, ensure good product, and squeeze as many cattle, chickens, or pigs as they can into a small enclosure in order to keep costs down.

> **Do the Right Thing!**
>
> If you're not convinced that you shouldn't eat meat, consider this: Factory farms are like concentration camps for animals. Animals are penned up and maimed in preparing them for slaughter. If you are going to eat meat, you need to deal with the moral implications of the practice.

Accessory to Murder? The Ethics of Wearing Animals

When I talk about "wearing" animals, I'm thinking about anything from leather belts, boots and shoes, to fur coats and cosmetics. We "wear" animals any time we put a product on our bodies that comes from one of our four-legged friends (and yes, this includes wearing wool, even though we don't kill sheep to get it). The question is, is it always wrong to wear animals? Is wearing some things (like leather belts or shoes) morally acceptable, while wearing other things (like furs), not?

If you apply the same reasoning against eating animals here, then it's hard to make a distinction between wearing a leather belt and wearing a fox-fur coat. Animals died for it, and that's that. But our intuitions might lead us in the opposite direction: they tell us that the wrongness of wearing animals is in direct proportion to the degree of human need. For example, humans need to wear shoes, and leather makes particularly well-wearing, long-lasting shoes. So you could argue that there is some degree of "need" to wearing leather shoes. But a glorious fox-fur coat?

> **Moral Musings**
>
> Is it always wrong to wear animals? Is wearing some things (like leather belts or shoes) morally acceptable, while wearing other things (like furs), not? One way to answer this question is to determine whether the use fulfills any real human need. For example, we may "need" leather shoes in a way that we don't "need" fox-fur coats!

It's not clear that there's a "need" to wear such a coat, especially when so many artificial fibers are available that are warm and don't require animal bloodshed!

Another distinction could be made between using cows and using foxes: using cowhides to make leather is good use of the animal, since we also use cows for food. But foxes? The *only* reason we kill foxes is to get their coats. The rest of the poor animal gets thrown away. The same is true of clobbering seal pups to make fancy, seal-skin coats. We use the fur off the pups and toss the rest away. So you could argue that wearing leather is less heinous than wearing fur, simply because we use the whole animal in one case and not the other.

But what about other uses of animals, like wearing cosmetics and perfumes? These products either come directly from animals, or are marketed after experimentation on animals to test the safety of the products. Either way, animals are killed so that we can wear them.

Again, there are a couple of possible views here. One view is that it's immoral to use and abuse animals for human purposes, period. Another view is the "gradualist" one I've already mentioned: that we can determine the morality of wearing animals by trying to figure out how serious and pressing the need is. Using animals for cosmetics and perfumes doesn't seem to match up with the leather shoe example because, again, we're talking about using animals for pretty frivolous purposes. Wearing lipstick and rouge? Smelling good because we buy outrageously expensive perfume? These "needs" hardly seem to pass the litmus test of meeting human needs!

Animal rights activists who belong to organizations like Greenpeace and PETA aren't often seen going after people who are wearing leather shoes or belts—their concern seems to be with the less justified, more frivolous uses of animals for fur coats and cosmetics. Maybe that alone tells us something.

Research on Animals Ever Justified?

Speaking of perfume, we need to consider one more issue in our brief survey of ethics and animals: experimentation and research on animals. Here you can bring to bear all the things I have talked about so far, including sentience and human needs. In fact, animal sentience and human needs are the two "biggie" issues when it comes to the morality of experimenting on animals.

We use animals to test everything from cologne to cancer. For example, rabbits have been used to test the harms of hairspray by spraying it into their eyes to see what damage is caused. The rationale is that, by finding out if it damages bunny eyes, we can prevent it from hurting *human* eyes.

On the other end of the spectrum, we do experiments on animals to test the effectiveness of certain treatments for cancer, AIDS, and Alzheimer's disease. In cases like this, researchers claim that the potential benefits to human beings are so great that the harm to animals is justified.

So how do we distinguish between these two kinds of experimentation on animals? Well, as I'm sure you're starting to guess, the answer is a little complex.

The Need for Good Reasons

Some ethicists take the view that almost no experimentation and research on animals is morally justified. This is because it's often the case that the human ends that such experimentation is serving aren't important enough to justify abuse of animals. Let's consider the hairspray example again. Would you really want to say that the

Tried and True

Generally speaking, philosophers determine the morality of animal experimentation by appealing to two important considerations: animal sentience and human needs. The greater the pain caused by the experiment, the greater the rationale we need for doing it. Causing animals untold amounts of pain to test a new line of hairspray would be immoral; causing animals great amounts of pain to advance research on Alzheimer's disease might not be.

human good served—a nice coiffure that doesn't get blown in the wind—is important enough to justify spray-ing a toxic substance into a rabbit's eyes? And even in the nobler cases of cancer and Alzheimer's disease, it's not always clear that the research or experimentation is going to have a direct positive outcome that will really advance our understanding of these things.

Remember, if we're going to justify using animals, we have to have darn good reasons, and the good outcomes from the experimentation have to be pretty predictable. Suppose I'm a researcher doing an extremely painful experiment on animals, and I'm doing it because I think a certain result *might* occur. The less certain I am of my hypothesis, the less justified I am in harming the animal to test it out.

Reasons, Schmeasons

On the opposite extreme, philosophers have argued that any scientific purpose that we use animals for is morally justified just because we're human beings and they're not. As rational, higher-order beings, we should not concern ourselves about harming animals; it's all in the order of things. Anyway, these folks argue, it's ridiculous to suggest that we should put human beings at risk in doing research and experimentation: we need to start with animals and, once we're certain that a drug or treatment is beneficial, only then should we attempt it in human beings. Without the use of animals, some researchers have pointed out, medical science would still be in the Dark Ages!

As you can see, we have to decide what it is that really matters. Does it matter most that human beings are rational, higher-order creatures, or that human beings and animals can *all* experience pains and pleasures, which makes us similar in the most important ways? Here's a hint: if you take the former view, you're defending a Kantian idea of rationality; if you take the latter view, you're a Utilitarian who places emphasis on our capacity to feel.

Our examination of the ethics of animal research/experimentation is necessarily brief. There's a lot more that could be said about it. But the idea here is to get you thinking about some of the broader issues surrounding animal experimentation. And one of the big bones of contention between ethicists is whether the human capacity for reason makes human beings better than animals, so that we can do what we want with them, or whether the shared capacity for pain and suffering makes us all equal, so that the harms we do to animals must be seriously weighted against human desires.

Agreeing to Disagree

There's one last thing to bear in mind, and it has more to do with how we treat one another when we differ on our views of ethics and animals. It's this: Iindividuals who make a moral commitment to vegetarianism, and to eliminating as much as possible the use of animals from their lives, are making a *personal* commitment. You shouldn't automatically assume that just because your office mate, or best friend, or family member chooses to go vegetarian, that she or he is making a moral judgment of *you*.

It's important to remember this, because otherwise vegetarians might be mistaken as taking the moral high ground. We sometimes assume that they're saying something like "It's too bad you're such a lowly, immoral person that you're still eating meat. You should become a better person and act like me!" People who reject the turkey on Thanksgiving Day aren't just party-poopers, then: They're acting on a strong moral belief that is deserving of respect.

So the tactic of easing *our* consciences about eating meat by attacking vegetarians is misguided. Vegetarian friends have reported to me that they've been at parties or dinners

Tried and True

People who come to the decision to stop eating meat or wearing animals aren't necessarily doing it to show you that you're immoral: They are doing it because they have had a change of heart, and they feel uncomfortable continuing on as meat-eaters.

where their vegetarianism becomes an issue; people will inevitably engage them in conversation about it. And sometimes, nonvegetarians will get defensive about their own meat-eating and say things like "Hey ... you're vegetarian but you're wearing suede shoes. What gives?" This is the kind of moral challenge that isn't productive, since it makes both parties defensive and leads to hard feelings.

People usually have strong feelings one way or the other about animal rights; it's not the kind of thing that we can be casual or dismissive about. But you might not have given a lot of personal thought about your stance on ethics and animals. Hopefully this chapter will start your thinking about this, and lead you to some deeper consideration about where *you* stand on these issues.

The Least You Need to Know

- Even if you don't think animals have rights, you should think about the way we treat them and how that impacts our treatment of other human beings.
- Remember that animals are sentient, too. We must have really good reasons for inflicting pain upon them.
- When determining whether animal experimentation is morally justified, consider the human need that is being served.
- Avoid challenging others on their vegetarianism. It's not a judgment of your moral choices, but an expression of their own values and beliefs about animals.

Part 5

Beyond the Personal: The Ethics of Social Justice

So you think that ethics is just about doing the right thing on a personal, individual basis. Think again, kiddo! There's only so much nastiness you can eliminate, and only so much benevolence you can promote acting on your own. Even if everyone were to become morally upright overnight—which, frankly, is about as likely as the cow jumping over the Moon—there'd still be lots of bad stuff going on.

This part will tell you why. A lot of injustice is caused by bad laws and government policies. The rules of the game governing economic and political life leave a lot to be desired. Even rules that are fair on the surface sometimes end up being unfair in light of the background conditions—of past (and present) racial and gender discrimination—under which they're followed. We're going to look at the justice (or injustice) of policies aimed at promoting affirmative action and multiculturalism. Before we get there, we're going to have a pretty thorough understanding about the justice (or injustice) of social welfare, capitalism, socialism, current forms of democracy, and equal pay for equal worth. Hey, it's a heady bit of stew to offer up, but you're ready for it, right? Right.

We're Talking Social Justice!

In This Chapter

- ◆ Social justice as distinct from personal morality
- ◆ Bad luck and social injustice
- ◆ Injustice and vulnerable groups
- ◆ Political activism

I used to think that if people were good and just in their personal moral conduct, all would be well with the world. Change people's hearts and you change the world! Well, there are lots of heartless and otherwise immoral people out there who make things miserable for everyone. So changing hearts and reforming personal morality is a good place to start.

But over the years I've come to realize that lots of bad things happen to people—injustices that no amount of personal morality and heartfelt charity will make right. Take poverty. In many (perhaps most) cases, it isn't the fault of the poor, but of unlucky circumstances and an economic system that rewards those who possess capital or talents that are in demand. Behaving morally toward people who are economically vulnerable by not exploiting them or taking advantage of their disadvantage is what moral decency minimally demands. Also demanded is providing food, clothing, and other forms of charitable assistance to the extremely needy, so long as you have the resources to do it.

But all the charity in the world will not eliminate the injustice of poverty, which includes the insult of not being self-sufficient and independent. Nor will it even get at the root causes of poverty, which are sustained, in part, by bad or nonexistent laws, bad or nonexistent government, and bad or nonexistent economic regulations.

We're talking social injustice, folks. The kind of injustice that can be lessened only through concerted efforts at social reform. In this chapter we'll learn why social injustice is different from more personal forms of moral injustice and why it is different from just plain bad luck. We'll examine different kinds of social injustice, domination and oppression, as well as different causes of social injustice. Finally, we'll learn why allowing people to suffer from undeserved disadvantages is unjust.

When Moral Decency Just Isn't Enough

Remember what I said in Chapter 2, "The Inevitability of Ethical Dilemmas," about morality and norms? A lot of what we consider to be good and right is a matter of following social norms. Sometimes the norms in question are laws. Even if we happen to find some laws immoral or bad, most of us think that we should be law-abiding.

Of course, there are times when we have an obligation to disobey laws that require us to do things that are deeply immoral, such as discriminating against people simply because of their race. Moral decency demands that we treat others fairly, and fairness requires treating others as equal human beings, regardless of their skin color.

Now, suppose we lived in a society where the law required that black people sit in the back of buses, patronize black-only businesses, and use separate and inferior accommodations. This is the situation that existed in many parts of the South prior to the Civil Rights Act of 1964. Suppose further that virtually everyone—blacks and nonblacks—found the law immoral and deliberately refused to obey it. These people would be fulfilling their moral obligation. They would be behaving justly toward one another. Yet something would still be wrong. The state and its laws would still be treating blacks as inferiors. As long as the racist law remained in effect, society would be unjust, even if almost all the people in it were morally decent.

Do the Right Thing!

Being fair to others in your personal conduct is not enough. So long as the state is discriminating against others in your name, you have an additional obligation to change it. For it's social institutions that limit and define the extent and quality of our moral community.

Here's another reason why moral decency isn't enough. Sometimes bad social institutions make it impossible to be morally decent. At the very least, they place morally decent persons in dilemmas in which, no matter how they decide, moral evil will result. Take our white Southerner who wants to do the morally decent thing and offer his bus seat to a black person. He'll think twice about it, knowing that any violation of the race code will endanger himself, his family, and his friends.

It's Not Just Bad Luck

So being a good person isn't enough. We have to try to make our society just as well. But what is social justice?

Boy, you got me there. Trying to define social justice is a little bit like trying to glimpse into heaven. Perfection in whatever form is often hard to imagine, especially when you and I and the society we live in are so imperfect. But, hey, look at it this way: At least we know we're imperfect. And we know our society is imperfect as well—and unjust. So let's start by asking the easier question: What is social *in*justice?

Sometimes when I talk about the social injustice of poverty in my classes, a student will demand to know why poverty is an injustice. In most cases, a person's poverty is not caused by personal injustice—say, the vicious behavior of some particular individual. In fact, a lot of it has to do with simple bad luck.

Now there are many kinds of bad luck. The first has to do with the genetic lottery. Some people are born with healthy genes, others not. The second concerns the familial lottery. Some of us are born into rich families, others into poor ones. Some kids have loving parents, others mean and abusive ones; some have educated parents as role models, others have uneducated parents as role models. A third kind of bad luck consists in the various accidents that happen to us, such as being hit by a car or losing your job because your company went out of business.

Taken by itself, bad luck is not injustice. Sure, we sometimes blame God for being unfair to the unlucky, but who are we to challenge God's justice? So no one is to blame for bad luck. And bad luck is not, as such, injustice. It's just bad luck.

Moral Musings

When trying to locate social (in)justice, the notion of "moral luck" can be helpful. This idea points out that the kind of situation we're born into is the result of a crap shoot, and not anything we did or didn't do. It's a kind of "there but for the grace of God, go I" perspective that makes us think carefully about how the life circumstances we're born into—through no action on our part—affect our opportunities. This isn't to say that any of us who are born lucky should beat ourselves up for it, but it does mean that we can't congratulate ourselves on our moral luck. After all, whether we're born into the Rockefeller family or a poor family in India is totally beyond our control.

Does that mean that poverty that is caused by bad luck is just—or at least, not unjust? Well, not exactly. But before we see why, let's examine the concept of injustice a bit more closely. To say that something is unjust is to imply that some human agency is to blame for it. John's being hit by a car driven by a homicidal nut is more than just bad luck. It's an injustice—an outrage—of a personal sort. Because the driver willfully takes something valuable from John—the use of his body—the driver owes him compensation.

Personal injury is an obvious example of an injustice because it is caused by the negligent or vicious behavior of an individual. But what about social injustice? Take the case of our racist state. In this case, the state and its laws are to blame for the social injustice inflicted on blacks. More precisely, because the state acts in the name of its nonblack citizens, they are partly to blame. The agent of social injustice is not just a person, but a group of persons—the nonblack majority.

Clear enough. But how does this example bear on the social injustice of poverty? In countries like the United States, poverty isn't deliberately willed by the state as was racial discrimination in the South. Rather, poverty is allowed to happen; the state stands back and allows fortune or misfortune to play itself out.

Tried and True

There are different ways that each of us can be accomplices to social injustice. One way is to ignore social problems like poverty and unemployment. Another is to allow others to get away with racist or other hurtful remarks that directly impact the life prospects of other people. But sometimes challenging these problems requires a lot of moral courage.

So, can the state and its citizens be blamed for allowing poverty to exist? Maybe. Because sometimes standing back and doing nothing is tantamount to giving approval. It's like being an accomplice or at least an accessory to crime. Take racial discrimination in this country. When the federal government outlawed racial discrimination and segregation in the Armed Forces following World War II, it stopped intentionally discriminating against blacks. But it continued to allow whites to discriminate against blacks in employment and access to private and public accommodations; and it continued to allow Southern states to impose mandatory racial segregation.

Since 1964, the federal government has legally prohibited segregation and intentional discrimination in education, employment, and public access. Had it not done so, it could have been blamed for allowing such discrimination to happen. Likewise, had it not ordered private and public establishments to provide access to the disabled, it could have been held blameworthy on that account. So the state and its citizens can be blamed for allowing bad things to happen, even when they don't actively promote them.

When Bad Luck Becomes Social Injustice

We are now beginning to see how poverty might be a social injustice. At least, we can see how the state and its citizens can be held responsible for allowing unjust things to happen.

But how can something that is caused by bad luck—poverty say—also be a social injustice? Sure, the state allows poverty to exist, but what's unjust about that?

Maybe social contract theory can help us out here. You'll recall that social contract theorists aim for a low-ball ethic that lays out the minimal moral rules for living together peaceably. They assume, first, that social cooperation for mutual advantage is in everyone's interest, and second, that getting people to cooperate peaceably can only happen if everyone voluntarily agrees to abide by common rules of fair play.

Here's the kicker: In order for each person to agree to the rules, each would have to see that it was in her interest to do so. Knowing that fact, we could not expect everyone to voluntarily agree unless the rules were in everyone's interest, and so treated everyone equally. Equal treatment means giving everyone equal rights. But having equal rights means nothing without equal opportunities to exercise them. You can't give a child born into life-threatening poverty a right to life that is equal to the right to life of a child born into affluent circumstances unless you provide that child with the food, clothing, shelter, medical care, and education necessary for having an equal opportunity to succeed in life.

> **Moral Musings**
>
> Another way of saying that social cooperation should be mutually advantageous for each person without exception is to say that each person should have rights that are equal to those possessed by any other person. But equal rights mean nothing unless they come with equal opportunities to be exercised.

Who Deserves What?

How does bad luck fit into all this? Children who are born into life-threatening poverty are unlucky through no fault of their own. Their poverty is undeserved. Ditto the honest hard worker who loses his job because the company he works for unpredictably goes out of business (perhaps due to mismanagement or declining demand for the company's product). But what about the person who brings bad luck upon himself due to reckless behavior? It's hard to feel that society owes anything to the millionaire who recklessly squanders away his savings on what he knew to be risky investments.

So where does this leave us? Society, it seems, owes little or nothing in the way of material support to people who start out with equal (or greater than equal) opportunities and then fall into poverty through deliberate recklessness. There seems to be no social injustice in allowing persons to suffer from diminished opportunities that they have brought upon themselves. However, society does owe something—as a matter of right—to persons born with diminished opportunities. And it owes something to persons who are born with full opportunities and who then lose them because of accidents that are beyond their control, including those stemming from arbitrary fluctuations in the economy. So when the state fails to compensate people for these forms of bad luck—through unemployment insurance, disability insurance, welfare assistance, medical insurance, and so on—it becomes an accomplice in maintaining social injustice.

Let me elaborate a bit on this last point. A person might deny that society owes anything to people who lose their jobs or who can't find jobs. After all, haven't people who have lost their jobs voluntarily assumed a risk in taking the job? And haven't people who can't find jobs voluntarily assumed a risk by not learning the right skills and by not living in the right places?

Yes and no. The important question is not whether people have voluntarily assumed risks in life, but whether the risks they have voluntarily assumed are reasonable. It is reasonable to assume the risk that you might lose a job once you've obtained it, because obtaining a job is itself the best way to lower the risk of poverty. You're helping society and yourself by getting a job, so society owes you something when you lose it due to no fault of your own.

> ### Moral Musings
>
> The important question is not whether people have voluntarily assumed risks, but whether the risks they've assumed are reasonable. It's reasonable to assume the risks of losing a job once obtained, because obtaining a job is itself an insurance policy against risk.

The case of the person who can't find a job is a little trickier. If people have learned skills that they reasonably thought would be marketable in their location, then they have taken a reasonable risk that is entirely in keeping with their good intention to contribute to society. The market is to blame for their bad luck, and society should compensate them for it. The duty to compensate is just as strong (if not stronger), if society has not provided the job seeker with the education necessary for acquiring decent-paying marketable skills and jobs in which those skills are needed.

Do People Ever Deserve Their Bad Luck?

Before leaving the topic of bad luck and social injustice, let me raise a few serious complications. So far I've assumed that there's an important moral difference between deserved bad luck and undeserved bad luck. Society ought to compensate for undeserved bad luck. If it doesn't, it violates the principle of equal rights and commits a social injustice. No such violation occurs in the case of deserved bad luck—at least on social contract grounds.

But is there a sharp difference between deserved and undeserved bad luck? More precisely, is there a sharp line marking off what we've voluntarily assumed responsibility for in our lives and what we haven't? Take our reckless millionaire. Perhaps he suffers from a psycho-pathological form of gambling compulsion caused by depression, which in turn is caused by poor upbringing. Maybe he's aware of his condition and has even sought medical treatment, but experiences a sudden, uncontrollable relapse and gambles away his entire assets in one sitting.

Our gambler is not fully responsible for what he did. He didn't choose the upbringing that made him compulsive.

So his bad luck is not entirely deserved. If so, maybe society should partly compensate him for part of his loss. Again, take the case of someone who is so depressed that she no longer feels motivated to work. Perhaps she was raised by parents (and perhaps grandparents) who were unemployed as well, due to lack of education and lack of jobs. Surely, she was not responsible for being born into social circumstances into which she could not, as a child or adult, acquire a strong motivation to succeed. Is her lack of motivation a case of undeserved bad luck that ought to be compensated for by the state?

See how complicated social justice is? And we're not even talking about the most difficult and controversial problem: deciding on the best way to compensate for bad luck! Do you provide the compulsive gambler with psychotherapy and a supportive environment until he breaks his bad habit? Do you provide the chronically depressed and undermotivated unemployed some combination of welfare, counseling, medication, job-training, and guaranteed employment in a decent-paying occupation? Do you go further in eradicating the cycle of poverty through massive economic reform?

People with Disabilities

Just in case you thought things couldn't get more complicated, here's another consideration to think about. People born with severe physical and mental impairments may not be able to contribute much to society in the way of productive work. But the social contract theory says that equal rights should be bestowed upon those who either are, have been, or will be mutual contributors. It's because (1) we depend on others for our well being and (2) dependency is risky, because susceptible to bad luck, that we accept the justice of a social safety net. But in the case of severely (especially mentally) handicapped people, the relationship of economic support and dependency is

CAUTION

Do the Right Thing!

How should we treat people who aren't capable of being the ideal, productive citizens in society? Surely those citizens shouldn't lose their basic rights just because they can't be equal contributors. Here's where we need to appeal to our basic, shared humanity: That, as human beings, we all deserve a fair share of resources to ensure that we each have a decent life.

not mutual, but one way: The profoundly disabled are entirely dependent on a society that supports them.

Here, I think, we need to appeal to Kantian ethical theory. No one ought to forfeit their basic rights simply because they are incapable of being an equal contributor to the social contract. This applies in an obvious way to people who, though not contributing now, once contributed in the past or will contribute in the future. But it also applies to persons who could never have contributed, because they have been born with a seriously disabling and irreversible handicap. People with profound physical and mental impairments who require institutional care fit this profile. If society ought to provide these unlucky people with the resources necessary for sustaining their lives, it is only because of their basic humanity.

To continue with our ever-expanding list of complications, notice that these Kantian considerations about the intrinsic value of human life also prevent us from allowing people to suffer the extreme consequences of their own reckless decisions. A person who becomes paralyzed from the neck down because of an injury sustained while driving drunk shouldn't be allowed to die from his newly acquired disability. He is still a part of society and, more importantly, he is a human being with a basic right to life.

Are We Our Brother's Keeper?

Let's backtrack a bit. We've seen that social injustices come in many varieties. Some happen when the state deliberately discriminates against persons (as when the state legally mandates the enslavement, segregation, and discriminatory treatment of certain groups of persons). Others happen when the state permits such discrimination without expressly prohibiting it. But most social injustices happen when the state doesn't adequately compensate for the bad luck borne by its own citizens.

The state has an obligation to compensate in these instances because, in many cases, the source of the bad luck is the economic and social system maintained by the state. Earlier I mentioned bad luck associated with the genetic lottery. We tend to think of this sort of bad luck as something the state bears no responsibility for. But think again! Not only are people who live on the economic margins of society more susceptible to occupational accidents (unskilled, lower-paying, and predominantly physical jobs are more dangerous than office jobs) and crime (lower-income neighborhoods are breeding grounds for gangs), but they are also more susceptible to poor health. Lacking decent access to hospitals, women who live in low-income neighborhoods receive poor prenatal care and are often exposed to more toxic substances in their environment. Exposure to toxic waste dumps and other toxic hazards (such as lead paint) increases their risk of having children who are born with developmental disabilities.

Getting the State Involved

Why is the state responsible for this bad luck, if the source of the bad luck is the economy? Well, the state decides to promote stable economic growth by controlling inflation (the rising cost of goods and services). Because inflation is caused when consumers demand more of a limited supply of goods and services (thereby raising the price of goods and services), the state undertakes to decrease the demand, or buying power, of consumers. It does this by discouraging businesses from hiring more workers (or even by encouraging them to lay off workers). Raising the interest rates at which money is borrowed discourages businesses from borrowing and investing money in jobs. So raising interest rates (by decreasing the supply of available money) results in less investment, less employment, less consumption, and lower inflation. It's good news for all of us employed consumers, but it's bad news for those whose jobs are cut—very often the marginally employed poor, who are typically (as the saying goes) last hired and first fired.

On social contractarian grounds, we all should benefit from the economic system that we help contribute to. If the economy's good functioning depends on workers getting fired as the result of government policy, then it seems only fair that the government should compensate them with unemployment insurance, welfare, or—better yet—new jobs.

If the state acts in our name (as it should in any democracy), then we—that is, all of us citizens—are our brothers' keepers. Those of us who benefit from a policy of lower inflation have an obligation to compensate those who suffer from that policy. But what are limits of this obligation? How far do they extend?

Tried and True

Arguably, the government has a moral obligation to support its citizens through programs like unemployment insurance, welfare, job creation programs, and social security. In fact, some ethicists claim that you can tell the moral quality of a government and its people by the support that is given for social programs.

Thinking Beyond Borders

As we shall see in Chapter 27, "Getting Our Just Des(s)erts," they might extend globally. That's because the economic system is a global economic system. The social contract theory is not limited in its application to persons who happen to belong to one geopolitical unit—be it city, province, or state. Its application extends as far as the system of social cooperation for mutual benefit extends. And that system is global. We are all dependent on people of other countries to provide us with clothing (if you don't believe me, just look at your clothing labels), oil (where do you think all that "crude" that fuels our economic system comes from?), labor (from migrant agricultural field workers to computer specialists), and a host of other goods and services. What people living abroad do directly impacts our lives—and vice versa.

This becomes even more obvious when we realize that the global economy is but part of a bigger one that includes our global ecosystem. There is now widespread agreement among scientists that temperatures are rising around the globe (the so-called greenhouse effect), which in turn causes the melting of the polar ice caps and the reduction of rainfall in parts of the world. The consequences of such warming, scientists warn, could be disastrous by the end of this century, bringing in their wake massive coastal flooding and desertification of once-fertile land.

Global warming is caused by the release of carbon dioxide into the atmosphere. The increased emission of carbon dioxide, in turn, is caused by the burning of fossil fuels and other energy sources. The latter, of course, is one of the effects of global economic growth, which in turn is partly fueled by global population growth. However, the leading producer of carbon dioxide is not the country with the biggest population, but the country with the biggest economy—the United States. Although the United States comprises only 4 percent of the world's total population, it produces about 30 percent of the world's total carbon emissions.

So we live in a *global community*, where the benefits and costs are shared by the population of the entire world—albeit unequally. As in the case of the domestic economy, benefits enjoyed by some are purchased at the cost of burdens imposed on others. The privilege of buying inexpensive clothing made abroad almost always depends on the low wages and poor working conditions of those who make the clothing. In turn, by maintaining these sweatshops—for example, by preventing workers in these "sweatshops' from organizing into labor unions—clothing manufacturers in other parts of the world that provide higher wages and better working conditions are forced to close down or re-establish themselves abroad—as sweatshops.

Ethically Speaking

A **global economy** is but a worldwide community in which the benefits and costs are shared by the entire world—albeit unequally. Assuming that social contract applies as well here as in the domestic situation, those who are most benefited by the system have a duty to distribute the benefits as well as the burdens more equitably.

If the social contract theory applies to the global as well as the domestic market, and if the theory requires compensating those who, through no fault of their own, are made to shoulder the burdens without deriving the benefits of the global system, then it follows that those who benefit from the system—no matter where they live—have a social justice duty to raise the living conditions and life prospects of those who mainly shoulder the burdens. And it follows that everyone has an obligation to do what they can to lower the emission of carbon dioxide. This obligation, it seems, requires more from those who contribute most to the problem and who are, incidentally, those who can best afford to do so.

As we shall see, the most effective means for combating social injustices like the ones described above is through social and political means. Getting governments to pass—and enforce—laws protecting workers and lowering emissions is the only way to correct or compensate for the harms of a global economy that should benefit everyone.

What's in a Right?

I'm going to close our discussion about the extent of our social justice duties by defining that extent a little more precisely. I've already mentioned that Kantian ethical theory extends basic rights to persons regardless of whether they are (1) capable of cooperating with others for mutual benefit or (2) members of our own society. But what does it mean to have a right to something?

If someone says they have a right to speak freely, then they're saying that they can and should be permitted to speak freely by others. *Rights*, then, are demands we impose on others. Furthermore, because demands that cannot be enforced are empty demands, there is the expectation (or at least the hope) implicit in every rights-based demand that others should not only heed the demand but be ready and willing to enforce it.

The notion that rights are enforceable demands placed on others is very important. But it's also difficult to bring about completely in all cases. For example, Kantian ethics demands that individuals have a right to life simply because of their humanity. But take the case of a lonely starving farmer who happens to live in a very poor, famine-stricken and undeveloped state—a state so undeveloped and poor that it lacks resources and enforcement powers to make good her right to life. Clearly, if the state she lived in had the resources and the enforcement capability to provide her with food, then it would be primarily responsible for doing so. If it failed to do so, it would be guilty of allowing social injustice.

Ethically Speaking

Rights are demands we impose on others. Furthermore, because demands that cannot be enforced are empty demands, there is the expectation (or at least the hope) implicit in every rights-based demand that others should not only heed the demand but be ready and willing to enforce it.

Because the state and its inhabitants are all impoverished and powerless, the responsibility for making good her right to life falls elsewhere. Maybe we could say that the responsibility falls on the rest of the world and whatever global famine relief agencies happen to exist. Here again, famine-relief agencies can be held responsible for her life only to the degree that they actually have the resources and powers to intervene on her behalf.

If they don't, then the blame for failing to save her life falls on those wealthier, more capable governments. More precisely, because it is we who elect our government's leaders, it is we who indirectly bear responsibility for her life. If we fail to encourage our government to act effectively on her behalf, then we, too, are guilty of perpetrating a social injustice.

In a nutshell, opportunities for social injustice increase to the extent that the world becomes a global community of social cooperation and mutual dependency. Opportunities for social injustice also increase as the world becomes richer in resources and capabilities. For, as our wealth and capabilities increase, so increases our responsibility for enforcing basic rights.

What Causes Discrimination?

Okay, now that we know what social injustice is, let's find out what causes it. I've already let the cat out of the bag in my discussion of social injustice and bad luck. Some forms of social injustice are caused by intentional discrimination against particular groups, as when the state requires or allows racism in employment, education, accommodation, and political participation. This kind of injustice singles out members of particular groups—based on gender, race, nationality, sexual preference, religious affiliation, age, or physical (or mental) condition. The intention underlying such discrimination is often bad—to harm and degrade—but sometimes not. Old laws that forbade women from holding certain jobs (e.g., bartending) were usually aimed at "protecting" them from bad men. Unfortunately, such paternalistic measures also treated women as children who needed the protection of men.

Sometimes groups suffer discrimination that is not intentional, but institutional. Institutional discrimination, however, typically has its origins in intentional discrimination. One example of *institutional discrimination* is the disadvantage blacks have in finding and keeping jobs. Because of past intentional discrimination, most blacks still live in job-poor segregated communities. But many jobs in predominantly white suburbs are advertised through word of mouth, and to get these you normally have to live in the community that has them and interact with the people responsible for filling them. Also, small business owners prefer to hire people they know and trust. So even without intending to discriminate against blacks, they will most likely hire someone they know, or someone who lives in their community. As for keeping jobs, blacks who find themselves entering fields that were once forbidden to them now encounter another obstacle: the seniority system. Being last hired, they are often first fired.

Ethically Speaking

Institutional discrimination is maintained by institutions that are racially neutral on the surface, such as local hiring and seniority retention.

People of the World, Unite!

Now that we have a better understanding of social injustice and its causes, what can we as individuals do about it? Well, remember what I said earlier about the shortcomings of personal morality in dealing with social injustice. Doing the right thing morally—even contributing time and money to providing charitable relief—is not enough to eliminate social injustice. To do that, we need to encourage our leaders to pass better laws and adopt better policies.

It makes sense. Laws and policies often directly contribute to social injustice. Anyway, problems of social injustice are usually too large for individuals to tackle on their own. States have the powers and resources as well as the coordinating mechanisms needed to effect large-scale social changes efficiently. Furthermore, people are often more willing to contribute resources for change if they know that others are doing so as well.

Of course, saying that we have a duty to lobby the government doesn't tell us anything about how to make change happen. Sometimes the problems of social injustice are so serious and urgent that they call for swift and radical change. Sometimes it takes a civil war to eliminate a great evil like slavery. Then again, sometimes the ultimate solution to social injustice requires radical changes that can at best be implemented gradually. I suspect that reforming the global economy will proceed by many halting steps over the course of many years, and will be propelled by struggles between rich and poor as well as by environmental crises. Whatever form the just world takes—assuming that it takes form at all—one thing is certain: social and moral progress won't happen unless we make it happen!

Do the Right Thing!

Your job, as an ethical person who cares about social justice, is to keep your political representatives on their toes. Drive them nuts by engaging in annoying letter-writing campaigns; send in petitions signed by you and other constituents. Besides irritating the heck out of them, it might just encourage them to pass better laws and policies.

The Least You Need to Know

- Fulfilling your personal moral duty involves fighting social injustice.
- When left uncorrected, bad luck can be just as much a source of social injustice as discrimination.
- The extent of social injustice depends on our capacity to correct it.
- Our social justice duties are global as well as domestic.
- Fighting social injustice requires political action.

The Immigration Controversy

In This Chapter

- ♦ Immigration and lifeboat ethics
- ♦ Thinking about immigration from the community standpoint
- ♦ Liberalism and immigration policy
- ♦ Immigration policy and the real world

You'll recall from Chapter 2, "The Inevitability of Ethical Dilemmas," that I used to help migrant farm workers in their struggle to form a union. These folks put up with atrocious working conditions, miserable wages, and zero benefits. Part of the problem was that there were too many of them. Swelled by the ranks of immigrants who were willing to work for peanuts to survive, they were competing with one another to see who could get scarce jobs at any wage. I thought that cutting off the flow of immigrants would solve the farm worker plight until I learned more about the immigrants. Many were starving. Fleeing from bad governments in Mexico and Central America that neglected, uprooted, or killed them, these people were simply asserting their God-given right to live just like the rest of us.

What should the United States government do—protect its domestic workers or save these foreigners from starvation and death? Tough question, especially when I considered that the government's own policies in that area—from supporting oppressive military regimes to supporting free-trade agreements—might have contributed to the starvation and death! The question is tough for another reason, too. It makes us think hard about the rights of individuals as individuals, and how they might conflict with the rights of groups and communities. Does the individual's right to live outweigh the nation's right to protect its own members? In this chapter we will see how two important theories of social justice—liberalism and communitarianism—answer this question.

Lifeboat Ethics: Trying to Stay Afloat

The moral issues bound up with immigration have been referred to as *lifeboat ethics*. Why? Because worries about how much immigration a country can tolerate without "going under" is similar to questions about how many people a lifeboat can hold without being sunk. Let's look at this a little closer.

Ethically Speaking

When talking about immigration issues, some ethicists appeal to "lifeboat ethics." **Lifeboat ethics** refers to any situation where we cannot possibly save everyone. If we put 120 people in a boat designed for 50, the boat will swamp and everyone will drown. Similarly, some argue, if we were to open the floodgates and allow unlimited immigration, everyone in the United States would suffer.

Moral Musings

"Without a true world government to control reproduction and the use of available resources, the sharing ethic ... is impossible. For the foreseeable future, our survival demands that we govern our actions by the ethics of a lifeboat, harsh though they may be. Posterity will be satisfied with nothing less."

—Garrett Hardin, "The Case Against Helping the Poor," *Psychology Today*, 1974

Suppose you're one person out of 120 who survive a shipwreck. There's one boat to save you all, but it's only supposed to hold 50 people. There are a number of ways to decide who should get in the boat. For example, you could take an "everyone for themselves" approach and allow people to fight each other for entry; you could take an egalitarian approach, which means that each individual's interest in getting into the boat is treated equally; or you could take a need-based approach, where you give priority to pregnant women, people with children, and those who will be most useful to the group.

Whatever choice you make about filling up the lifeboat, one thing's for sure: It can only hold 50 people, and if you allow more than that number in, the whole boat will capsize. So there's clearly a problem because, if you take an egalitarian approach and let everyone in, it's likely that no one will survive the shipwreck.

As you can imagine, the lifeboat scenario is likened to immigration policies. According to a lifeboat ethics approach to immigration, we are faced with the same kind of problem—we have far more people who want to enter the United States than we could ever reasonably sustain. This means that we need to be clear about what our limits are, who we can allow in to the country and under what conditions, and how that number of immigrants is going to affect the country as a whole.

Protecting Individual Rights

The lifeboat viewpoint clashes with another perspective that emphasizes each individual's right to pursue his or her own good. Clearly if you're living in a country that is wartorn, where your civil rights are unprotected, and where drought and natural disaster are causing starvation and dehydration, you have a personal interest in leaving. If we take seriously the view that each individual human life is of equal moral value, it's hard to see why some human beings should be prevented from seeking decent life circumstances that folks in other, richer countries enjoy. Given what I said in Chapter 21, "We're Talking Social Justice!" about "moral luck"—that none of us has control over where we are born or what circumstances we are born into—we certainly can't claim that we are entitled to a good life while people in Third World countries are not.

If we take the individual rights approach to immigration, then it seems as if we're committed to having an open immigration policy where the United States allows all comers entrance into the country. Why? Because if we block people from entering "our country," then we directly interfere with their rights to pursue their own good. People must be free to move elsewhere to seek a better life; restrictive immigration policies deny them this right. In addition, while an open immigration policy may seem extreme, remember that it's not only immigrants who are benefiting from living in America: Employers have a strong desire for cheap labor, and many immigrants take on jobs that no American-born individuals are willing to do.

But still, as I noted with the farm workers, if we let unlimited numbers of people enter the United States, new problems are created. We end up with

> **Tried and True**
>
> When thinking about what kind of immigration policies you want to support, remember that immigration helps us and not just would-be immigrants. There are many jobs that Americans just can't do or don't want to do. Immigrants who take these jobs aren't moving in and taking jobs away from American citizens, then—rather, they are supporting the market.

extremely depressed wages, terrible working conditions, and harsh competition for very few jobs. Being too open in our immigration policy, then, could have the opposite impact of what we intend: It could condemn people to living a life of poverty and deprivation here in the United States. So rather than encouraging respect for persons, this approach could end up violating it.

Moral Theories to the Rescue

Remember those ethical theories you learned about in Part 3, "General Recipes for Guiding Ethical Decision-Making"? Here's where they come in handy! Because, generally speaking, lifeboat ethicists are taking a kind of Utilitarian position on immigration, while those who focus on individual rights are taking a Kantian approach. It makes sense: If you're worried about not overfilling the lifeboat, you're basically focusing on the consequences of allowing too many people in. Creating the greatest happiness for the greatest number of people may require saying "no" to some people who want to immigrate to the United States, but who could serve to topple the economy by putting undue pressure on our social and economic resources. But if you're concerned with individuals' rights to pursue their own good, you're really a type of Kantian, since Kant's moral theory focuses on the rights of individuals to pursue their own ends and our moral obligation to respect those rights. If that's what matters most, you won't be so concerned about the consequences of immigration—you'll be more worried about respecting human beings as moral equals.

Do the Right Thing!

Remember, our moral position on immigration can't come from an "us versus them" morality. Ultimately, all Americans came from some other place to seek a better life; individuals in our family histories decided at some point to make the move. This means that any moral stance we take on immigration mustn't assume that immigration is morally bad because we don't want "those people" coming into our country.

It's more than likely that you take one of these two positions on the immigration debate: Either you're more concerned about the consequences of it, or you're more concerned about people's rights to seek their own good. But there's another way of looking at the tension between ethicists who argue about the morality of immigration, and this is a difference in their commitments to liberalism versus communitarianism. Let's consider these two viewpoints now.

Liberalism Versus Communitarianism

As it turns out, there's another way of looking at the dispute over immigration. Some people take a liberal view of the issue, focusing on individual rights and freedoms (again, very much like Kantian moral theory), while others take a communitarian approach, concerning themselves with the good of the community. According to communitarians, individual rights can be dangerous if they serve to destroy the fabric of a community. But let's not get ahead of ourselves here: We'll start with liberalism.

Defending Individual Rights

Probably the single most important social and political doctrine circulating today is liberalism. We hear talk about liberalism and liberals all the time. Democrats in the United States like to be called liberals; Republicans, by contrast, reject the label, and instead prefer to call themselves conservatives. Truth is, liberalism comes in many varieties. And almost everyone, including most conservative Republicans, would probably consider themselves liberal on at least some issues.

Liberalism traces its roots back to the seventeenth and eighteenth centuries. Philosophers like John Locke, whose own writings deeply influenced Thomas Jefferson and our other Founding Fathers, defended the natural right of individuals to seek their self-preservation as they saw fit, free from interference by the state.

The stress here is on the word "natural." As you'll recall from Chapter 11, "Modern Social Contact Theory," Locke was a believer in natural law and natural rights. He believed that individuals are free by nature, apart from any membership in society, and that they have rights reflecting that freedom. These rights include the right to hold or give away property and to defend against aggressors. As natural and God-given, these rights were superior to any right that state and society might claim against individuals. In fact, Locke, like most social contract theorists, saw state and society as mere tools existing solely for the benefit of protecting individuals' rights.

> **Ethically Speaking**
>
> In its basic form, **liberalism** upholds the natural freedom and equality of all people. It demands that we tolerate people's different beliefs and values, and that each individual has the right to go about their business without interference from others. In the immigration context, this might just mean the freedom to exit and enter countries without interference by governments.

Liberalism and Immigration Laws

What does liberalism tell us about the immigration debate? Well, as you have probably noticed, the kind of classical liberalism that Locke defended is concerned with respect for individual rights. A classical liberal might argue for unrestricted immigration: That individuals possess natural rights to pursue their self-preservation as they see fit. As natural and God-given, these rights are superior to any rights that a state might claim against them. For example, states rightly exercise their power only when they uphold individuals' natural rights. So, the state has no right to prevent American farmers from hiring foreign laborers, since both employer and employee are merely seeking to exercise their God-given right to life and property. Individuals, according to this view, have the natural right to move about and pursue their own good.

However, a classical liberal could argue the opposite point as well. Suppose it turns out that the would-be immigrant's natural right to life clashes with the same right of the domestic worker; for instance, by threatening to deprive the domestic worker of his or her job. Assuming there is no other way to resolve this clash, a classical liberal might well support restricted immigration.

Moral Musings

"There but for the grace of God go I"—that's the thought an American should have when considering the right of a starving Guatemalan to enter the country. To regard citizenship as a birthright bestowed on a select few is really no different than the kind of thinking that reigned in the days of oppressive monarchies. Power that is undeserved is no basis for claiming an exclusive privileged right, so why should citizenship by birth be any different?

There isn't one simple answer if you take a liberal approach to immigration. But whatever answer you do get will be based on a concern for the rights of individuals.

Ethically Speaking

Communitarianism is the view that human beings are, first and foremost, social creatures. It rejects the liberal notion that society is nothing more than the coming together of individuals for mutual benefit. Communitarians hold the warm and fuzzy view that communities are what make us human—it isn't that individuals make up communities. Without communities to participate in, the argument goes, we wouldn't be human at all.

Communitarianism

Liberalism places the rights of individuals ahead of community welfare. But there are several strands of ethical thought, sometimes lumped together under the heading of *communitarianism*, that reject this priority. Communitarianism begins by rejecting the liberal view that individuals possess freedom and rights in some natural way, prior to society and state. There are at least four main reasons for believing this to be the case:

- Humans are essentially, not accidentally, social animals. We have no concept of ourselves as individuals—of who and what we are—apart from belonging to human community; it is community that gives us the languages, meanings, and values by which we understand ourselves and our world.

♦ Humans are essentially, not accidentally, social animals because we cannot reproduce our species apart from living together in families and other long-term cooperative communal arrangements.

♦ Individual freedom and rights are meaningless apart from being collectively agreed upon in some specific way. No rights and freedoms are absolute. To take a well-known example, your freedom of speech doesn't extend so far that it entitles you to recklessly endanger people's lives by crying "Fire!" in a crowded auditorium. Even our very right to life is not absolutely binding: You are entitled to kill me if I deliberately try to kill you. However, specifying the precise extent of our lawful freedom is the business of the community and its rightfully appointed lawmakers.

♦ Individual freedom and rights are empty demands unless backed by a social enforcement mechanism. Freedom exists only where it is protected, and it is protected only in society.

Tried and True

Communitarianism explains why loyalty to friends and family often overrides respect for more distant and abstract duties. In some cases, we have a greater responsibility and duty toward those we identify as belonging to our community than we have to outsiders and strangers. Thus, communitarians are often cautious about immigration—obligations to people currently in the community are more pressing than obligations to distant others who are "outsiders." Sometimes conservative communitarians appeal to our patriotic duty to larger communities, such as the state. That "loyalty" is sometimes interpreted as protecting our community against the invasion of immigrants. Be cautious about what kind of communitarianism is being presented and whether you agree with it or not.

The previous reasons explain why we belong to society before we belong to ourselves, why we are social beings before becoming individuals. But these reasons don't yet explain why we live in distinct communities, as opposed to one global community. Communitarians give the following additional reasons for communal diversity:

♦ We need to feel secure about who we are, and that self-certainty can only be provided by persons who know us intimately and care deeply about us. Strangers cannot provide this recognition. However, family, friends, neighbors, co-workers, co-worshippers, and significant others care about us, and vice versa.

♦ The circle of those who know us intimately and care about us deeply cannot be indefinitely large. Our knowledge of others and our concern about them diminish to the extent that we are removed from them. My knowledge of and care for complete strangers are virtually nil.

◆ It follows that the circle of those who know each other intimately and who care about each other deeply must be conceived as a relatively closed, distinct community. There's only so much intimate contact and mutually deep concern to share, and the wider we extend it, the more diluted and worthless it becomes. By the same token, the more we focus our intimate contact and mutual concern, the stronger our loyalty and commitment to those on whom we focus.

◆ Consequently, we have a greater responsibility and duty toward those we identify as belonging to our community than we have to outsiders and strangers. Duties to members of the community outweigh duties to individuals taken simply as individuals.

Communitarianism and Immigration

As I've described it, traditional communitarianism would most certainly support restricted immigration, because it places the rights of our national community ahead of the rights of individual foreigners. By its very nature, unrestricted immigration would permit people from many different cultural backgrounds to mix with the domestic population. Such an influx of strangers could weaken intimate and stable bonds. The sheer open-endedness of the association could also destroy any sense of mutual concern and commitment. The clash of cultures might provoke social conflict or, at the very least, encourage people to question tradition and authority. It would certainly change the identity of the community, perhaps to the point of destroying it altogether.

Do the Right Thing

CAUTION

Since social justice requires diminishment of undeserved suffering, we might adopt a policy that compensates would-be immigrants who are denied entry. One such policy would be to improve the economic and political lives of immigrants in their native countries. If we provide economic aid and pressure their governments to respect rights, would-be immigrants would no longer have as strong an incentive to leave their native lands.

Ethics of Immigration in the Real World

We've now abstractly examined how liberalism and communitarianism might respond to the social justice of (un)restricted immigration. Now let's see how well these theories fare in the real world.

Immigration as Righting Wrongs

First, we know that we live in a global community in which the policies adopted by our government affect the lives of strangers living thousands of miles away. If our government's policies directly or indirectly contribute to the political repression and economic destitution of would-be immigrants, then it would appear that our government has a duty to reverse these policies and compensate those who have been damaged by them. The idea of compensation is in keeping with the classical liberal notion that any violation of rights and freedoms must be rectified. One way to do that might be to allow the immigration of would-be immigrants who have had their rights violated because of our government's policies.

The Importance of Families

Second, we know that some members of our community immigrated in order to help us as much as help themselves. There are many jobs that Americans can't do or don't want to do. It would be wrong, on communitarian grounds, to prohibit immigrants living here from reuniting with children and parents who live abroad. Families are an important part of who we are. That's why communitarians make such a big fuss about family values and the importance of stable families in maintaining a vital workforce and community. Consequently, we should walk the talk and allow those who have immigrated the same right to enjoy their families as the rest of us.

> ### Moral Musings
>
> If families are important to communitarians, they should support immigration policies that are targeted at reuniting families. It would be wrong for communitarians to prohibit immigrants who are living and working in the United States from reuniting with their children and parents who live abroad. If being part of a family is a basic human good, having immigrant status shouldn't deny people the enjoyment of that good.

Respect for Cultural Identity

Third, some countries have a distinctive religious and cultural identity that ought to be respected. The state of Israel, for instance, was created as a refuge for Jews following World War II. Although Native American reservations have a complex origin based on treaty and forced concentration, they today serve as something of a refuge for Native Americans who wish to practice their aboriginal religions and lifestyles. Traditional communitarianism allows nations like these to take would-be immigrants' cultural identities into account in deciding whether or not to admit them.

Does communitarianism also allow nations like the United States to do the same? Only recently (since the '60s) has the American government stopped using racial and ethnic criteria in choosing its immigrants. For most of its history, America saw itself as overwhelmingly culturally English and, to a lesser extent, Western European. Only gradually did it open itself up to Mediterranean and Eastern Europeans while immigration from China, Japan, and the Philippines was virtually cut off during long periods beginning in the late nineteenth century. Today, the United States is thoroughly multicultural and becoming more so day by day, largely thanks to immigration. Given its constitutional embodiment of liberal toleration and freedom, it would be inappropriate for it to engage in the kind of cultural and religious selectivity that otherwise seems justifiable for Israel and America's indigenous peoples.

The Inevitability of Immigration

Fourth, given the fact that we live in a global economy that seems almost inevitably to generate increasing inequalities between rich and poor nations, we can probably expect immigration—legal and illegal—to increase. The more transient populations become—and labor mobility seems virtually synonymous with a global capitalist economy—the less stable our communities become. This raises an interesting question. Are we becoming the sort of impersonal, open-ended network of flexible and impermanent voluntary associations that classical liberalism spoke about? If so, should we resign ourselves to this fact by opening up our borders?

But what about problems of national security and overpopulation? The world we inhabit today, with increasing risks of epidemics, terrorist attacks, and ecological destruction, gives us reason to reject unrestricted immigration. Even if states became economically porous, local communities would still fight to control the integrity of their territory. A borderless mega-state like the United States would simply be replaced by many smaller mini-states with borders.

Last but not least, once we've allowed people to become members of our community, how should we treat them? Once they've been contributing members for a sufficient amount of time, there doesn't seem much to distinguish them from native-born citizens. On both liberal and communitarian grounds, it seems only fair to extend them full rights of citizenship. After all, what concerns all should be decided by all.

But then immigrants should be treated with equal respect and dignity. Singling them out for discriminatory and punitive treatment—for instance, by denying them benefits accorded to citizens—seems unjust. Likewise, unjust is changing in midstream the rules of their association with us. Immigrants who have lived in the United States for many years have developed reasonable expectations about the benefits they will receive and the burdens they will bear. To suddenly overturn these expectations amounts to violating our contract with them.

The Least You Need to Know

- The social justice of (un)restricted immigration varies depending on which theory we adopt.
- Immigrants should be treated with equal respect and dignity.
- A lifeboat ethics approach to immigration policies makes us question what degree of immigration a society can withstand.
- All American families, in some sense, can be said to be immigrant families. American culture is built on people who came to America in search of a better life.

Chapter 23

Economic Justice

In This Chapter

- ◆ Justice as distinct from efficiency
- ◆ The right to subsistence
- ◆ Ethical arguments for and against capitalism
- ◆ Alternatives to capitalism
- ◆ The global economy and the problem of the Third-World debt

"All that is solid melts into air." That's my favorite quote from Karl Marx. He was talking about the industrial form of capitalism that existed during his time—the late nineteenth century. How much truer it seems in today's faster paced cybernetic capitalism!

Today, millions of shares of stock are traded every day by computers; the value of world currencies fluctuates depending on computerized trading as well, and credits and debts are accumulated faster than you can blink an eye.

And all that "virtual money" can melt away just as fast. Those of you who are old enough might remember what happened on October 19, 1987—also known as "the market melt-down," or simply "black Monday"—when the market lost more than a quarter of its value. Those of you who are truly ancient might even remember further back, to the famous crash of 1929 that inaugurated the Great Depression. There's no denying it. Capitalism is utterly unprecedented in its capacity to build up and melt down fortunes. Nothing remains constant in the wake of its path; its scope is virtually all-encompassing, penetrating and transforming every aspect of our lives.

So it's important for us to stand back and ask whether capitalism is a force for good. In this chapter, we're going to learn what capitalism is and why it has been heralded as a great moral force. We will also see why some people find it unjust and inefficient. After examining some alternative economic systems, we'll turn our analytic gaze on a very serious problem of economic oppression: the problem of Third-World debt, which in turn raises questions about the social justice of free market globalization.

How Big Is Our Pie and Who Gets Which Slice?

Before we get started, it's important to distinguish justice from efficiency. When philosophers of economics talk about *justice*, they mean the rightness of how benefits and costs get distributed. It's a matter of deciding who should get what. When they talk about *efficiency*, they mean the greatest overall ratio of benefits to costs. Here, it's a matter of deciding which option will yield the biggest pie or the greatest overall value for everyone.

Ethically Speaking

Justice means the rightness of how benefits and costs get distributed. **Efficiency** means the greatest overall ratio of benefits to costs.

Let's illustrate with a simple example. Suppose you're giving a birthday party for your twin daughters. You take them to the bakery and ask them which of two cakes they would prefer. Cake A is small, but is evenly sliced in half, so each daughter will get the same sized slice. Cake B is bigger, but is sliced unevenly, so that one daughter will get a much bigger slice than the other. To complicate matters just a bit, suppose that the smaller of the two slices in cake B is the same size as either of the slices in cake A.

As a parent, which cake would you choose? Well, you might opt for fairness, and pick cake A. But knowing that your daughters have big appetites, you might figure that its better to pick cake B on the assumption that the one who gets the big slice will be fully satisfied and the other will at least be no less satisfied than if you had picked cake A. You're thinking: better to have greater overall satisfaction (efficiency) than equal but less satisfaction (justice).

Of course, when you think really hard about it, it's not so obvious that picking cake B really is more efficient, or more totally satisfying. If you stick to a narrow standard of efficiency—say, filling up stomachs—it is. But if you broaden your standard of satisfaction to include seemingly external considerations, like feelings of resentment on the part of the daughter who gets the smaller slice and feelings of guilt on the part of the daughter who gets the bigger slice, then it might not be! All of which just goes to show that standards of efficiency are no more obvious than standards of justice.

Everyone Deserves at Least Some Pie

We're going to talk more about efficiency below. For now let's begin by asking a simple question about justice:

> Does each of us have a positive right to basic resources, capacities, and opportunities necessary for living a minimally decent life?

Leaving aside the difficulty of deciding what counts as a minimally decent life, we can answer this question affirmatively.

Recall our discussion of negative and positive rights in Chapter 22, "The Immigration Controversy." We begin with Locke's belief that each of us as a human being has a natural right to life. Minimally, this means that each of us should be permitted to do what we need in order to live, free from interference. However, as we saw, this permission (or negative right) means nothing unless we have the capacities, resources, and opportunities to take advantage of this permission. Locke, for instance, thought that either land or paid work should be made available to each of us.

Furthermore, we saw that there had to be something—a state, say—that could interpret and enforce this provision for resources, capacities, and opportunities. So, if we assume that everyone ought to have a right to life (just because they are a human being), then we must conclude that everyone ought to have an enforceable right to the provisions necessary for life. The enforceable right to provisions assumes that there are responsible agencies—governments or relief organizations—that can in fact enforce the right. If no governments or organizations exist that can provide the needed provisions—because doing so would seriously deprive others of these provisions or because the provisions simply don't exist—then the right, in effect, doesn't exist.

In fact, we do live in a world in which there are plenty of provisions for everyone. So there's no reason why anyone's right to get by should not be honored. Sometimes simply stopping from doing something—such as selling arms to a government that is starving some portion of its own population—suffices to honor the right. Generally, the best way to secure people's subsistence rights is to secure their political and civil rights. Allow people the civil freedom to freely associate and speak out and you enable them to figure out for themselves what is to be done. Allow them the political freedom to form unions, cooperatives, and political parties—and allow them the right to elect their leaders—and you allow them to remove many of the governmental obstacles preventing them from finding sustainable land and decent-paying work.

The Virtues of Capitalism

Saying that everyone ought to have their subsistence right satisfied doesn't tell us much about how best to do it. Capitalism and its socialistic counterparts are all quite capable of accomplishing it. The main question is: Which does it most fairly and efficiently?

The proper place to begin answering this question is by examining capitalism, which today stands virtually unchallenged as the world's dominant economic system. But what is capitalism?

Well, it's a system in which the major part of production and distribution is in private hands, operating under what is termed a profit or market system. By contrast, socialism is characterized by public ownership of productive property, coupled with a public mechanism for distributing goods. Some socialist economies are almost entirely planned by the state, dispensing almost entirely with markets, while other socialist economies use markets instead of centralized plans.

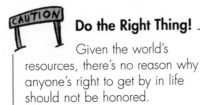

Do the Right Thing!

Given the world's resources, there's no reason why anyone's right to get by in life should not be honored.

Ethically Speaking

Four key features define **capitalism:** the existence of companies, profit motive, competition, and private property.

Most economies of the world (including that of the United States) combine elements of socialism and capitalism in varying degrees. Countries that have social welfare safety nets (which the United States all but eliminated in 1996) designate some productive property as public property and also provide for the public redistribution of tax revenues targeted toward benefiting a variety of private interests, from large corporations to people on welfare.

Companies

Companies are special kinds of businesses in which profits and risks—if not control and ownership—are dispersed among many stockholders. Most likely, if you have a pension, you also have a stake in some stock. Legally, companies have rights and obligations just as if they were persons. They may even do things—under guidance of management (such as enter into contracts and lawsuits)—that the majority of their stockholders disapprove of!

Profit Motive

Capitalism is based on the assumption that people are primarily driven by a profit motive to amass property and consume. As surprising as it might sound to you, the profit motive was not the dominant motive ordering people's lives for most of human history. Prior to capitalism, most people wanted (and expected) to just get by. In Europe during the Middle Ages the pursuit of profit was considered a sinful distraction from the proper Christian pursuit of spiritual salvation. Usury—lending money with interest added—was even punishable by death in some quarters!

Competition

What keeps self-interested profit-seeking in check is competition. Unrestrained self-interest counsels the would-be profit-seeker to price gouge her customers and starve her employees. Only competition from other profit-seekers, who are more than willing to grab a slice of the action—by attracting more customers with lower prices and by attracting more employees with higher salaries—keeps her honest.

Most important, competition encourages an efficient satisfaction of wants by encouraging an efficient production of goods. Producers who waste scarce resources by producing more of a product than can be sold suffer the consequences of unsold or sold-below-cost products. To stay profitable, they must cut back on the production of their product and divert resources to the production of more saleable products. Ideally, the law of supply and demand that regulates competition would result in there being just enough and no more of available stocks of commodities to satisfy existing demand—a maximally efficient use of resources.

Privately Owned Productive Property

Capitalism presupposes private property—or more precisely, a special kind of private property: productive property. In any economic system some things will always be consumed and owned by individual persons as their private property—like the food on your plate or the clothing you wear. But only in capitalism are the means of productive property privately owned, such as farms, factories, warehouses, and machinery (in the Middle Ages, land was held by nobles as a trust to monarchs, the church or to other nobles, and couldn't be sold; craft tools were passed down from father to son, and couldn't be sold either).

This means that decisions about what gets produced, how (and how much of) it is produced, and the way it gets produced is in private hands. The laboring power of workers is also their private property. Capitalism is premised on the idea that workers are free to sell their laboring power to the highest bidder—a freedom denied most workers in the Middle Ages.

Now that we have a better idea of what capitalism is, let's examine its virtues.

Capitalism and Its Virtues

To begin with, it allows more freedom than its Medieval predecessor did—people are free to earn their living however they want to, and they can dispose of their property as they see fit. Furthermore, it certainly encourages vastly higher levels of productivity and consumption. But leaving aside this comparison, what else might be said in its favor?

- ◆ Capitalism is just. It gives people what they deserve. That is, it rewards hard work, skill, thrift, and creativity. All other things being equal, the harder you work, the more skillful you ply your trade, the more you save for the future, and the more inventive you are in coming up with useful ideas, the more you should be rewarded. Need and virtue? Capitalism doesn't reward need and virtue, because being needy and virtuous isn't as such productive. True, it also rewards sheer luck. But who's to say the person who stumbles upon the occasional nickel on the pavement doesn't deserve it? As they say, finders keepers.

- ◆ Capitalism is efficient. Private property holders generally take special pride in caring for their property. Commonly held (or public) property is often abused or destroyed because no one feels especially attached to it. Also, competition geared toward profit leads to ever efficient and cheaper ways of producing things. The end result is greater prosperity for all. Even if the prosperity may benefit some more than others, it's ultimately good for everybody. As the old saying goes, a rising tide raises all boats.

- ◆ Capitalism is human nature. Like Ayn Rand said way back in Chapter 6, "'Me First' Ethics," people are basically self-interested and acquisitive. Why mess with it?

> **Moral Musings**
>
> Compared to the economic system that existed in Europe during the Middle Ages, capitalism is both fairer and more efficient.

Capitalism and Its Vices

Now that we've looked at what capitalism's defenders say, let's see what the other side thinks. Here is a list of complaints.

Inequality

Capitalism is unfair because it generates tremendous inequalities in wealth that deeply affect the life prospects of the poor. You need money in order to make money. So, while people who have lots of bucks can invest it in high interest-yielding CD accounts, stocks and bonds, those who have spare change can only stand back and watch their piddling savings being eaten away by inflation. True, big differences in wealth that would otherwise condemn the poor to a very miserable existence (and early death) can be partly offset by state-subsidized welfare payments and jobs, but such a redistribution of wealth operates outside of (and limits) the mechanism of a capitalist market. Finally, as I noted in Chapter 21, "We're Talking Social Justice!" the inevitable economic downturns that are inherent in capitalism generally hurt the poor more than the rich.

Exploitation

Capitalism is unjust because it exploits workers. This criticism—one of Marx's favorites—goes something like this. Profits are the difference between what the capitalist pays to produce his product (the cost of raw machinery, materials, and labor) and what he sells it for. In order for the capitalist to justify his profit, we must assume that, somewhere along the way, extra value was added to the final product in the course of being made. Since machines and resources are lifeless and add nothing apart from living labor, we have to conclude that the extra value that justifies the capitalist's profit margin was added by the worker. So the capitalist is pocketing as his profit the extra-value created by the worker—in essence, ripping the worker off.

Tried and True

Marx criticized capitalism on Kantian grounds: He thought that capitalists used workers mainly as means for generating profits. Instead of regarding them as ends in themselves, capitalists, he noted, worked their workers to death, no doubt figuring that they, like any other piece of productive equipment, were expendable and replaceable.

Neglect of the Needy

Capitalism is unjust because it neglects the needy. Those who can't produce in a capitalist system— the very old, the very young, the infirm, the profoundly disabled, the unneeded, the unlucky—are left out in the cold. The state can save them, but only by taxing and redistributing profits.

Inefficiency

Capitalism is inefficient. The growing gap between rich and poor is mirrored in the concentration of corporate wealth and economic power. When corporations become monopolies, markets cease to be competitive and you have price gouging and labor exploitation. Furthermore, the concentration of wealth in fewer and fewer hands leads to recurrent crises of overproduction. With fewer consumers at the bottom end possessing enough purchasing power to buy all the goods being produced, businesses have to scale back production and lay off workers, thereby worsening the crisis. If we're lucky, it's only a recession; if we're not, it's a depression. But even under the best of circumstances, there's a lot of stuff being produced that seems wasteful—for example, the billions upon billions of dollars spent on getting us to spend more money!

If you broaden the category of efficiency to include costs that are not factored into business calculations (such as wages and the like), capitalism fares even worse. Take the environment. Capitalism thrives only by growing, growing, growing. All that growth in production and consumption requires a growth in energy expenditures—typically in the form of carbon-dioxide releasing combustion. The exponential increase in factories, gas combustion vehicles, fire-cleared land—you name it—comes with a steep price, and it's called global warming!

And let's not forget pollution and overdevelopment of the environment—the destruction of our ecological balance with nature. Mirroring overdevelopment is the underdevelopment of unprofitable areas. Underdevelopment in the United States exacts a terrible price in inner cities and rural areas, which record a significantly higher incidence of crime, drug addiction, unemployment, and family breakdown than other areas.

But some of the most devastating side effects of capitalism might well be political and geopolitical. Along with the concentration of wealth we have the concentration of political power—surely not a good thing for societies that proclaim themselves to be democratic. Government elected by the rich generally tends to be government for the rich. The result is class warfare and, when things really get out of hand, civil war. And when countries start seriously competing with each other for scarce markets and resources … oh boy, look out!

Moral Musings

One of the hidden costs of global capitalism is the price for admission to the game. The International Monetary Fund (IMF), the World Bank (WB), and other global lending institutions often insist that, in order to receive loans, poor developing countries "restructure" their economies by downsizing government (welfare, education, and health) and opening up domestic markets to foreign trade. These measures often put these countries at the mercy of rapacious multinational companies, whose take-over of local economies often results in greater unemployment, poverty, and ecological degradation for the native population.

Alienation

Finally, capitalism might not conform well to human nature. As I noted earlier, people have not always been profit motivated and materialistic. Even today there are still aboriginal peoples who live simpler, communal, noncompetitive lives. But perhaps the question about human nature should focus less on the way people are than on the way they should be.

For example, while observing that people in capitalism were in fact self-interested and competitive, Marx wondered whether they were really free and fulfilled. He wondered about this because he saw around him lots of rich people who led spiritually empty lives. Money apparently can't buy everything, and the pursuit of the all-mighty dollar at the cost of other human pursuits can be deadly. Marx also felt that the very nature of work under capitalism was unfulfilling and that people had lost control of their lives.

The complaint about unfulfilling work (or as Marx put it, alienated labor) is not simply a complaint about how workers feel—although many people do complain about their jobs—but about how they are in comparison to how they should be. According to Marx, what determines how people should be is their human nature, and what distinguishes this nature from animal nature is productive activity that is …

- Free rather than forced
- Social rather than individual
- Conscious of meaning, value, and beauty
- Infinitely creative and inventive
- Complex and self-enhancing

Wow! Now that's a lot to digest in one swallow! One way to try is by noting that, for Marx, capitalism both realizes human nature (in comparison to the economy of the Middle Ages) and frustrates it. Capitalism frees people from servitude to nobles and guilds; but it abandons them to the demands of the market and the mechanical process of assembly-line production. It brings persons together in great factories, but pits them in competition with one another. It creates refined and sophisticated products while imposing dirty, unhealthy, and mind-numbing working conditions on workers. It brings novelty and wonder into our lives but also repetitive routine and boredom. It unleashes the greatest all-around development of productive forces the world has ever seen, but condemns many people to stultifying, one-dimensional, unskilled jobs (like tightening a screw on an assembly-line).

Now it seems to me that the decisive question is whether capitalism must impose alienated labor on its workforce and, if so, whether any other efficient mode of production would likely do the same. Is the intensive division of mental and

Tried and True

Capitalism requires a highly efficient organization of the labor process that must have seemed strange and oppressive to farming folk accustomed to the freer and more flexible work habits of seasonal agricultural labor. Just think of the discipline required to adjust one's bodily movements to the unforgiving mechanical motion of machines and the relentless pace of assembly line production. Even punching in time clocks must have seemed like a very unnatural thing to do!

manual labor characteristic of capitalism necessitated by standards of economic efficiency? If not, then why is it so characteristic of capitalism?

Common wisdom says that specialization is the key to efficiency; therefore, the more intensive the division of labor, the more efficient it should be. But common wisdom is contradicted by experience, which shows that when businesses have broken down the division of labor—by introducing job rotation, team work, and worker management and planning—productivity increases.

> ### Moral Musings
>
> History shows many instances in which companies were willing to sacrifice productivity for the sake of ensuring management's control over the workplace. At the end of World War II, for instance, the aircraft industry replaced skilled machinists with less efficient machines run by less skilled operatives, partly in order to eliminate the control that skilled workers and their unions exercised over the machine shop.

We might conclude from this that unalienated work is inefficient. And because it is inefficient, some businesses have sought to eliminate it. Can we also conclude that, as companies become more enlightened, capitalism as a whole will become more labor fulfilling?

Not necessarily. Although companies have an incentive to become more productive, top- and middle-level managers have a deep stake in maintaining power over their workers. That power, however, is premised on the intensive division of mental and manual, skilled and unskilled labor. By keeping workers unskilled—or by introducing machines that replace skilled workers with unskilled workers—CEOs can always argue that they need separate managers to coordinate the many detailed, marginally skilled jobs.

Virtues and Vices of Noncapitalist Economies

The biggest complaint against the justice of capitalism is that the free market fails to reward those who deserve it most. Noncapitalist economies seek to ensure that those who deserve it most get it—as a matter of government policy. For the sake of simplicity, let's lump all these government-driven economies under the heading of "socialism."

For instance, suppose you think that capitalism rewards those who don't work—say, those who sit back and live off their inheritance. You might think it would be fairer if the state owned all productive property and rewarded people on the number of work hours they put in (or, to maintain a stress on efficiency, the number of articles they produced).

The problem is: How do you compare and weigh such incomparable factors as the danger, difficulty, and degree of skill required in performing a job? All things being equal, it seems that jobs that are more dangerous, difficult, or just plain disgusting should be rewarded more on an hourly basis than other jobs. But how do you assess danger in comparison with the difficulty? How do you compare apples and oranges?

CAUTION **Do the Right Thing!**

One modest attempt to by-pass the market in assessing fair salaries and wages is comparable worth. Comparable worth involves evaluating the worth of a particular line of employment to a company in terms of the effort, skill, risk, responsibility, and difficulty of the job in comparison to other jobs within the company. Many companies already evaluate jobs in accordance with this criterion or worth. The Equal Pay Act of 1963 requires equal pay for work of equal skill, effort, and responsibility performed under similar circumstances. Comparable worth goes beyond this in requiring equal pay for dissimilar jobs of comparable worth.

Marx, for one, thought that an ideal affluent society would reward need rather than work. His motto was:

> From each according to his ability, to each according to his need.

One way to reward need would be to improve the condition of the worst off—the position defended by John Rawls, whom we discussed in Chapter 11, "Modern Social Contract Theory." This "maximin" (maximize the welfare of the minimum group)approach also be justified on Utilitarian grounds, as being maximally efficient, or maximally satisfying.

The principle of marginal utility teaches that receiving more of any good beyond what is necessary for minimally benefiting from it yields smaller and smaller additional benefit. For instance, giving a little more bread to a starving person might make the difference between life and death, whereas giving it to a well-fed patron of Spago's restaurant would probably be wasteful (our patron is doubtless busy gobbling down Lobster Neuberg as we're speaking). In general, the principle of marginal utility favors an equal distribution of goods.

Applying this "maximize the worst off" pattern of distribution is very problematic, however. How do we identify, compare and rank different classes of needy persons: the disabled, the sick, the poor, the racially oppressed? If increasing the income of the worst off by just a dollar costs the well-off $1,000,000 each, should we still do it? Wouldn't guaranteeing everyone basic incomes encourage the lazy to freeload on the hard working?

Perhaps besides efficiency we should also work virtue into our need-based distribution. For instance, we could target only those needy who are morally deserving—because they came by their neediness through bad luck rather than through their own reckless behavior. In that case, we would have a three-pronged rule for providing assistance: All things being equal, a person deserves more welfare assistance than another if he is (a) more likely to benefit from it (efficiency criterion), (b) needier, and (c) less responsible for causing the need (virtue criterion).

Robert Nozick

As you can see, different preset formulas for doling out goodies have different strengths and weaknesses. However, all such patterns suffer from one serious defect: after they've been put into practice, who's to say people won't mess them up by switching things around? As social philosopher Robert Nozick once pointed out, you could give 1,000 people equal shares of $100 each and they might all decide to pay Wilt Chamberlain (the late basketball great) a buck a piece to razzle and dazzle them. The only way to stop Wilt from becoming ten times richer than everyone else would be to "prohibit capitalist acts between consenting adults."

Another problem with preset formulas is that they presuppose that those implementing them have nearly perfect knowledge about assessing needs, balancing costs and benefits, and so on. But as recent experience has shown (witness, for instance, the collapse of the Soviet Union), such "command" economies are notoriously inefficient. It's one thing when businesses miscalculate the demand for their product—that is a relatively small waste of resources in the grand scheme of things, and easily corrected by the market. It's another thing when the state—as sole producer and distributor—screws up!

> ### Tried and True
>
> The collapse of the Soviet Union in 1991 was due in part to massive economic failure. The country had become so economically inefficient—as a combination of corruption, mismanagement, excessive military spending, and poor planning—that only a massive infusion of market-based reforms could get it back on track. These reforms were never fully implemented, and the selling off of state-owned enterprises—the most viable ones at that—sadly amounted to robbing the Soviet people of their birthright. Crony capitalism has not turned out to be much better than the old bureaucratic socialism!

Finally, there's the nagging problem of incentives. If people know in advance that they're going to receive a decent income from the state no matter whether they work hard or not, they might be tempted to become slackers and parasites. There's a Catch-22 here: if the safety net is truly humane and affords the recipient a decent standard of living, it competes with the job market. If it is not, then it is probably not humane.

Where does all this leave us? Both capitalist and socialist economies are plagued by different sorts of inefficiencies and social injustices. What should be done?

Combining Systems

The obvious answer is to combine the best features of both systems. In fact, most existing capitalist and socialist economies do just that. Western welfare states like the United States allow for government-sponsored intervention in what is otherwise a capitalist economy. The unemployed needy can take advantage of a host of public allowances, ranging from food stamps to Medicaid (with states providing welfare or workfare). Likewise, most socialist economies (including those found in Cuba, China, and Vietnam) take advantage of the efficiency provided by profit-driven markets.

Of the major industrial democracies in the world today, the United States is undoubtedly the most capitalistic. While American economists criticize European and Japanese economies for being too socialistic—and by American standards, inefficient—European and Japanese economists criticize the American economy for being too capitalistic—and by their standards, unjust. Most Europeans and Japanese are amazed that the United States lacks decent universal healthcare for all its citizens. They are often appalled at the level of urban and rural poverty that exists here, as well as the general lack of real equal opportunity education.

Americans, too, often complain about these injustices. Who knows—maybe universal health insurance and education reform are waiting around the corner for them. Perhaps America's capitalism would be fairer if everyone born in America started out with roughly equal opportunities and resources. But that would require heavily taxing—and then redistributing the proceeds from—the estates bequeathed by the wealthy to their heirs. It might also require that the government employ those who are capable of working but are currently jobless. Most people prefer decent work to welfare, because our sense of self-respect is closely tied to our sense of being needed by others.

Moral Musings

To cite John Rawls, only societies that "disperse the ownership of wealth and capital, and thus prevent a small part of society from controlling the economy and indirectly political life itself" allow for the full flourishing of democracy. For the aim of justice is not simply to redistribute income to those with less, which, after all, is compatible with very large and inherited inequalities of wealth but to "put all citizens in a position to manage their own affairs and to take part in social cooperation on a footing of mutual respect.

—John Rawls, Preface to the Revised Edition of *A Theory of Justice*

A more radical solution to injustice—sometimes known as worker control socialism—envisages workers setting up their own businesses (with loans from government banks) and competing with one another in a market economy. The government owns all productive assets, but leases them to entrepreneurial workers, who then pay a tax for the privilege of using the assets. One advantage of this system is that the government can encourage entrepreneurs to invest in underdeveloped areas. Another is that workers who control their own workplace are highly motivated and efficient producers. Yet another is that worker-controlled businesses have a somewhat less pressing need to grow than their capitalist counterparts, since the profit motive is not the only motive directing workers' decisions. Thus, worker-controlled socialism might be less wasteful, less energy-consuming, and less polluting than capitalism. Just as important, with breaking down the division between mental (managerial) and manual labor comes greater equality in wages and profit-sharing between those at the top and those at the bottom.

The Global Economy

Now that we've examined the issue of economic justice from a theoretical point of view, let's look at some pressing global applications: malnutrition, sweatshops, and the income gap between the rich and the poor.

Malnutrition

Malnutrition continues to be a serious problem throughout the world (including the United States). Economists have suggested two approaches for dealing with it: neo-Malthusianism and developmentalism. Neo-Malthusians (named after eighteenth-century British economist Thomas Malthus) argue that malnutrition is caused by overpopulation. Since they believe that famine relief and other forms of developmental assistance encourage people to have large families, they advise against assisting the starving poor. In effect, they defend an extreme market-based solution: if the supply of workers outstrips the demand for labor (or if the demand for food outstrips food supply), then nothing should be done. Wages will drop below subsistence—thereby reducing the number of workers to a level that meets market demand; and the starving poor will die off to a level that meets available food supply.

Developmentalists, by contrast, argue that providing relief and developmental assistance actually discourages population growth. Their reasoning is this: If you live in an undeveloped region of the world, having large families is rational (because there's no government social security to take care of you in old age); also children produce much more than they initially consume. However, if you provide jobs and education for the adult population—including women, who then must work rather than spend time raising children—their savings and pensions will save them in old age.

The debate between neo-Malthusians and developmentalists today has been decided in favor of the developmentalists. If malnutrition exists, it's not because there's not enough food, but because it can't get to where it's needed most (often for political reasons). Also, evidence pretty conclusively confirms the developmentalist theory: Rising levels of education and job opportunities across the board encourage smaller families.

The only question remaining today is whether free-market capitalism is the best way to bring about this development. Defenders of globalization (the global extension of capitalism) argue that by lowering tariffs and opening up markets, the demand for goods will increase worldwide, which will then increase the demand for labor worldwide, which will then raise the wages and standards of living for workers worldwide.

Sweatshops

The critics aren't so sure. The demand for labor has indeed increased, but at what benefit to whom? Sweatshops here and abroad in which workers (often children and young women) work long hours under dangerous and degrading conditions for very low wages and zero benefits have lowered the cost of many imported goods. But flooding the domestic market with cheaper goods has driven many domestic manufacturers out of business, caused them to relocate abroad (thereby costing domestic workers thousands of jobs), or caused them to slash wages and benefits at home in order to remain competitive.

Gap Between Rich and Poor

And then there's the growing gap between rich and poor. Economic development in the Third World depends on foreign investors (banks and companies based in rich industrial nations) who expect a return that is anywhere from two to four times their capital outlay. The net drain of wealth from poor to rich is partly explained by the fact that developed countries purchase cheap raw materials from undeveloped countries in exchange for expensive technologies and other finished products. As undeveloped countries become poorer—and increasingly indebted to developed countries—their governments are forced to cut spending on health, education, and welfare in order to pay off the debt. They're also forced to replace labor-intensive production aimed at satisfying local subsistence needs with machine-intensive production aimed at satisfying the luxury needs of a global export market. The result is increasing underdevelopment: loss of jobs and government services, scarcity of basic food staples, and environmental degradation.

What Is to Be Done?

One thing that can be done—within the current framework of globalization—is for banks and governments in developed countries to forgive Third-World debt, and to do so without requiring—as the International Monetary Fund (IMF) and World Bank (WB) currently do—government downsizing, currency devaluation, and other forms of economic austerity. Doing so is a matter of simple justice, for the following reasons:

- The Third-World debt is crushing. Forty-one heavily indebted poor countries (HIPCs)—thirty-three in Africa—owe $220 billion dollars in foreign debts. To gauge the impact of this debt, consider that a child in Nicaragua is born owing over $2,000 in foreign debt, while the average yearly income there is only $390.

- Most HIPC debt was accrued during the Cold War, when the United States and its allies encouraged the governments of many HIPCs to borrow money from them for purposes of building up their defense capabilities. The low-interest rates at which the loans were initially made later skyrocketed during the Seventies (the loans had to be repaid in U.S. dollars, the value of which had collapsed).

- Much of the money borrowed by HIPCs ended up in the pockets of corrupt leaders—often with full knowledge of the governments and banking institutions making the loans. Very little of the money ever trickled down to the masses.

- Many of the HIPCs who took out the loans were headed by self-appointed dictators who were not accountable to the people they governed. These people and their descendants should not be held accountable for sins committed by past rulers.

- Persons who declare bankruptcy have their debts forgiven so that their lives aren't permanently ruined. Simple justice urges similar debt forgiveness for bankrupt nations (Germany, Poland, and Egypt have all had substantial portions of their past debt forgiven by the United States).

One final thought. You might think that forgiving HIPC debt is too costly for banks and governments in the developed world. Fact is, because HIPC debt will never be repaid in full, its market value is a piddling fraction of its official value (for example, the market value of Haiti's $8.3 billion debt is just $377,000—a mere drop in the bucket). Forgiving the debt will not hurt banks and lending governments; rather, it will free up HIPC countries from payment obligations that prevent them from buying goods abroad and developing!

The Least You Need to Know

- Governments of the world should ensure that everyone has their basic subsistence needs met.

- In considering economic justice and efficiency, capitalism and socialism both have unique strengths and weaknesses.

- The fairest and most efficient economic system will combine market mechanisms with government policies targeting the needy.

- Globalization has both good and bad effects.

- Wealthy countries ought to forgive the Third-World debt.

Chapter 24

Political Justice

In This Chapter

- ◆ Democracy, good laws, and civil disobedience
- ◆ Democracy with and without representatives
- ◆ Ethical arguments for and against democracy
- ◆ Democracy in the workplace and beyond

The presidential campaign of 2000 was a powerful lesson in civics. Many Americans were surprised and dismayed to discover that a candidate who won most of the popular votes (by over half a million) could still lose the election. But that was perhaps the least upsetting news. More disturbing were revelations about hundreds of thousands of votes being thrown out due to faulty voting machines and confusing ballots.

To top it off, in Florida—the state that ultimately decided the election by a mere 537 votes—there were allegations that voters in predominantly black precincts were being wrongfully turned away from voting booths. In fact, many people with previous felony convictions were denied the right to vote, as well as many who were mistakenly thought to have such convictions. Finally, to top it all off, the methods for recounting mail-in ballots and machine-rejected under-marked (so called "dimpled" ballots) were ultimately decided in courts of law, whose own judgments struck many as highly arbitrary and partisan.

Given the enormous complexities and severe time constraints, it may well be that there was no way to decide the election in a manner that would have been fair to all. But looking back, we can at least pinpoint ways to improve the fairness of the next election. All of which raises an important question: what does fairness demand of us in the area of politics and power-sharing? In this chapter we're going to examine why democracy has been thought to be the fairest system of power-sharing. We're going to examine different types of democracy and the moral arguments for and against them. We'll then conclude by asking whether and, if so how, democracy might be extended to the workplace and the rest of the world.

To Obey or Not to Obey?

Democracy got its big start in ancient Greece over 2,500 years ago because people needed a way to convince themselves to stop fighting with each other and voluntarily agree to some common rules. Sounds a little bit like the old social contract theory, doesn't it? Well, in way it was. You see, the rule of law is more secure if people freely obey it because they see it is in their best interest to do so and not because some tyrant is going to crush them if they don't.

Now there are two ways in which people can be persuaded to freely obey the law.

- First, the law itself may be in everyone's interest (for example, laws against killing and stealing). If tyrants are wise, they'll be sure all their laws make everyone happy!

- Second, even if the law might not be in everyone's interest equally (for example, tax codes are seldom thought to be perfectly fair to everyone), it's still considered to be the result of a fair process (procedure) that we've all agreed to. Think of games. Losers accept the fairness of the results because they've accepted the rules of the game by which the results were obtained. As long as the rules are fair for everybody—favoring none of the players—so are the results.

> **Moral Musings**
>
> This form of democratic decision-making, sometimes referred to as "decision by unanimous consent," was sometimes used by Native American tribes in North America (the Iroquois Federation used a form of democratic decision-making that may have inspired some of our Founding Fathers). Its biggest advantage is that no one is left holding the short end of the stick; its biggest disadvantage is that it's hard to get almost 100 million voters to unanimously agree on anything!

Democracy—not even-handed dictatorial consultation—struck the Greeks as an eminently fairer procedure for deciding things (after all, dictators are never perfectly impartial and wise). The Greeks used democracy to decide who gets to make laws, serve on juries, collect taxes—and do all the things we associate with government. Many such offices were filled by a random lottery of all citizens (term limits applied in some cases). Others were filled by election. The main point, however, is that these democratic procedures were impartial, favoring no one above anyone else. For this reason, Greeks had a very high respect for their laws and government officials.

We have a duty to obey even laws we disagree with, so long as they were arrived at by a fair, democratic procedure. The basic idea is that if each of us has an equal opportunity to cast an equally weighted ballot (in which your vote counts the same as mine) in electing government officials, we have no reason to complain about the justice of the outcome, regardless of whether we happen to disagree with it. Of course, we could insist that *everyone* has to agree on a decision in order for it to be ratified.

Civil Disobedience

Democratic justice also explains the limits of our obedience. As the John Locke (see Chapter 11, "Modern Social Contract Theory") counseled and as scores of reformers since him have repeated, those who are arbitrarily denied the right to participate in democratic governance are under no obligation to obey laws that discriminate against them. Rev. Martin Luther King Jr. gave this reason in justifying his refusal to obey the racial segregation laws in the South, where blacks were denied the vote.

Civil disobedience involves a peaceful and public refusal to obey a law that is deeply unjust and that the majority refuses to change. Civil disobedience may be a legitimate response even when those protesting are not excluded from political participation, so long as those protesting think the law is deeply unjust. Because civil disobedience is a public form of moral protest and not a private act of criminal behavior, it should be treated differently (the proportionately milder sentences imposed on perpetrators of civil disobedience are not regarded by them as punishment but as a continuation of their public witnessing).

Why Democracy?

Would democracy be preferable to benevolent and wise dictatorship? Many have thought so. Here are some of their reasons:

♦ No one is perfectly wise and all-knowing. Given our human limitations, two heads are better than one. (pragmatic argument)

♦ When it comes to running an organization, the aim is to maximize the happiness of the membership. What better way to know what the membership wants than to let everyone have an equal vote in the matter? (Utilitarian argument)

♦ We need a way to protect ourselves from those who exercise power over us. Give us the vote so we can vote the B.S. out of office! (self-defense argument)

- No self-respecting adult would allow another to control his or her fate. Paternalism, however benevolent and wise, is for children, not adults. (liberal argument)
- Only in collective deliberation and decision-making do we fulfill our natures as free, rational, and social beings. (communitarian argument)

Critics, of course, haven't taken these arguments lying down. Take the first argument. Plato argued that two heads are not always better than one. If the two heads are misinformed and easily swayed by prejudice and the one head is truly knowledgeable and reasonable, then why not favor government by one head? Hey, isn't our Supreme Court based on just this idea—that a few wise judges should have the right to overturn what the less wise majority of Americans want?

The second argument also has problems. Who says the aim of government policy should be to bring about the greatest happiness for the greatest number? What if bringing about the greatest happiness requires oppressing a minority? Also, should everyone's (including the Nazi's) preferences be counted equally? And how do you know what John Q Public really wants? Just because candidate X got elected doesn't mean that everyone who voted for X supports everything X supports.

Tried and True

Two heads aren't always better than one. In 1933 Hitler was elected Chancellor of Germany in a democratic election but kept his campaign promise by abolishing democracy! In the American South, the white majority used its numerical advantage to elect white leaders who passed laws ensuring that the black minority would be denied the right to vote, along with being denied equal treatment across the board.

The third and fourth arguments—defending democracy on grounds of self-defense and individual freedom— seem odd, too. The best way to defend individual rights is to lay down a bill of rights that can't be overturned by any democratic majority.

The final argument—that democracy promotes communitarian virtue—doesn't seem to wash either. Hey, just take a gander at our own democracy. What do you see? Lot's of people selfishly voting for their pocketbooks, that's what. All democracy really boils down to is a big power grab by those who have the money and influence.

The American Experiment

Well folks, when it comes to democracy, the truth lies somewhere in between. James Madison and other Founding Fathers who designed the American Constitution appreciated both sides of the argument. They were going against prevailing currents in supporting even limited democracy. In fact, no one before had ever seriously considered extending democracy over such a broad expanse of land.

America's fledgling democracy was very different from the one we know today. People without substantial property were not allowed to vote (each state imposed its own property qualifications); and, of course, women and slaves were not allowed to vote, either. Not only was voting limited, but the Founding Fathers were really concerned about the tyranny of the poor over the rich, the tyranny of big, populous states over small, rural states, and the tyranny of Protestants over Catholics. They wanted to limit democracy as much as extend it.

And they did, too. The Bill of Rights limited the power of the federal government over the states and, after the Civil War, limited the power of state governments over their own citizens. The Founding Fathers set up a Supreme Court for interpreting and upholding these rights against wayward majorities.

Contrary to what many Americans think, the U.S. Constitution establishes that the president be elected indirectly, by persons who make up the *Electoral College*. Today, the composition of the college is determined by which states each candidate happens to carry in the popular election (each state is assigned a number of electoral votes that is roughly proportional to its percentage of the overall American population). A candidate who gets the highest percentage of votes in a state normally gets all of that states electoral votes. These votes, however, really elect a slate of electors that have been chosen by the candidate's political party. Although members of the electoral college are nominally free to vote for anyone they want to, most states bind them to the candidate to which they were originally committed. If no candidate wins a majority of electoral votes nationwide, the election goes to the House of Representatives.

 Ethically Speaking

The **Electoral College** was designed to ensure that the President would be elected by a broad base covering many states—weak as well as strong—even if this didn't accord with the overall popular vote (sorry, Al Gore). It was also designed as a stop-gap measure preventing the masses from electing a truly bad candidate (the assumption being that members of the Electoral College would be more knowledgeable and virtuous than the average citizen). Until the twentieth century, U.S. senators were also elected indirectly, by state legislatures, and for much the same reason.

Speaking of senators, the U.S. Constitution established a bicameral legislature consisting of a lower chamber (the House of Representatives) and an upper chamber (the Senate). This setup was also designed to protect small states from big ones. Although states are awarded a number of House seats proportional to their percentage of the U.S. population, they each get just two senatorial seats. Because all legislation has to pass through both chambers, the power of a sparsely populated state like Wyoming (under 1 million) is virtually equal to that of a big state like California (over 30 million).

Is This Fair?

It all depends. On one hand, it protects the citizens of rural states like Wyoming from being dominated by the more numerous citizens of urban states like California. On the other hand, it violates the principle that everyone's vote counts equally. Given the difference in population between Wyoming and California, the vote of your average Wyomingite in the Senate counts more than thirty times as much as the vote of your average Californian. It's as if we erased all the legal boundaries separating states and gave thirty votes to individual voters living in Wyoming for every single vote given to individual voters in California!

Letting Someone Else Make the Decisions

One of the most basic procedural decisions supporters of democracy have to make is whether to elect representatives or not. As I noted above, the Greeks took the idea of democracy literally: rule by the people (demos) meant that average citizens held public offices, so that there weren't any professional politicians worth speaking of (think of how club members rotate the offices of secretary, president, and vice-president). This is called *direct participatory democracy*—where the people rule themselves directly rather than elect or appoint others to do so.

We've all belonged to small clubs where democracy consists in people talking to one another and resolving disagreements by a simple show of hands (with the majority carrying the day). Let's call this direct voting democracy. Now as our club grows in numbers we reach a critical mass—say, when the club divides into different chapters—where it becomes difficult for all club members to decide all the important issues in one gathering. Also, coordinating club activities now becomes quite difficult, and much more detailed planning is required. So members from one chapter delegate by election some of their own to represent them in planning meetings with delegates from other chapters. This is known as representative democracy, and it's the system most modern, large-scale governments of the world have.

Has our club now suddenly become less democratic by electing people to act on behalf of its membership? Jean-Jacques Rousseau (see Chapter 11) certainly thought so. For him, dictators are dictators, elected or not. Here's another way to look at it: When representatives aren't being tyrannical, they're doing exactly what we—John Q Public—want them to do. So why do we need them? Many states allow average citizens to draw up propositions, collect signatures to put them on ballots, and vote directly on them.

The short response to this objection is that our society has changed since the days of ancient Greece (whose largest democracies numbered perhaps 30,000 citizens). Society is complex, so you need specialists trained in technical areas of the law to draw up statutes governing everything from toxic waste disposal to Medicare disbursement. The Greeks had slaves to do lots of the work so they could attend to public affairs, but John Q Public can't spend all of its time on politics.

Ethically Speaking

Direct participatory democracy means direct rule by the people themselves, often without the use of elected leaders. For instance, the male citizens of Athens voted directly on laws, even though they also elected a Council of Five Hundred to deliberate and propose laws. (Today, many states also provide for popular referenda of this sort.) Furthermore, there were few if any professional politicians or government officials (except perhaps a few military leaders); most government posts were filled by lottery, and civil and criminal suits and were decided by a simple majority of jurors (often numbering up to five hundred or more) without judges or lawyers.

Furthermore, representative democracy isn't really a step back from direct democracy. Sure, we've given up some decision-making power to others, which has freed us to spend time with our families, earn a living, and just escape from political life if we want to. But there's also a sense in which we haven't given up any decision-making power. First, we participate directly in local civic affairs that are squarely in our domain of concern and competence—witness, for instance, the vitality of New England town hall meetings. Second, what we delegate to elected representatives is less decision-making power than deliberation-power, and deliberation-power is something we never give up.

Deliberating or Governing?

Let me explain. The laws that our elected representatives decide on are often very general in their formulation. Their meaning is often just a summary of arguments given in committee meetings and the like. In other words, statutory laws are just summaries of debates that guide judges and administrators in their decision-making.

As Mill argued in his essay *Considerations on Representative Government* (1861), elected representatives are delegated the task of deliberating, not governing. But they don't deliberate for us. Rather, they take up the concerns and opinions of John Q Public and reformulate them at a somewhat more sophisticated—and hopefully more

Do the Right Thing!

Representatives shouldn't just repeat what their constituents say. They should reformulate public opinion in a more balanced way. For example, this could be done by compromising with legislators who represent the interests of their constituents.

balanced—register. That's why it's important to elect representatives who are both more knowledgeable than the average citizen and perhaps more publicly minded as well.

If representatives seek to reformulate what John Q Public is saying and thinking at a somewhat more precise, informed, and balanced register, then shouldn't they be reproducing what John Q Public is saying more or less exactly? Yes and No. The word "representation" is a bit confusing because it can mean three very different things.

- Representing can be "repeating." This can't be the meaning of democratic representation. First, representatives typically represent diverse peoples with differing interests and perspectives. The persons they represent seldom speak in one voice, and so can't be represented as one voice. Second, representatives not only reformulate public opinion, but they do so in dialogue with other representatives. Modifying and compromising opinions is the essence of democratic dialogue, so that the public opinion that gets represented is always represented differently, rather than being exactly reproduced.

- Representing can be simple delegating, where one person is authorized to stand in for another, as when a parent acts as trustee for his or her child. This can't be the meaning of democratic representation, either, since it entirely subordinates the public's voice to that of its representatives. Of course, we should expect our representatives to exercise some independent judgment, even if that means occasionally voting against the wishes of their constituents. But representation stops being accountable to the public when it becomes detached from it.

- Representing can be communicating with others in a relationship of mutual accountability and trust. Falling somewhere between the extremes of repeating and delegating, this conception of representing captures the transformative and interactive relationship that exists between representatives, on one side, and between representatives and their constituents, on the other.

What Gets Represented

Now that we have a better understanding of what democratic representation involves, let's examine what gets represented: interests, values, and perspectives. Interests refer to particular policy preferences: such as whether there should be a local tax on beer, or an affirmative action guideline for public hiring. Values refer to the moral and religious principles that govern our choice of preferences, such as: freedom, family, equality, etc. Perspectives, by contrast, refer to one's outlook on the world as determined by one's experiences, such as having experienced racial discrimination, having lived with a disability, and so on.

Generally speaking, when people think of representation they have in mind interests. The idea that interest-groups ought to be represented seems uncontroversial enough—that's why we give Wyomingites an equal voice in the Senate. But what about African Americans? They're geographically spread out and their members don't seem to share any interests that would distinguish them from members of other racial groups (their support for anti-discrimination laws is shared by other racial groups). Not being a distinctive interest group, they don't seem to merit special representation.

However, they do seem to merit representation if you include perspectives among the things that ought to be represented. All African Americans have experienced at least racial insensitivity and discrimination in their lives. So maybe our society should ensure that their perspective gets represented in legislatures—and preferably by people who have the relevant experiences.

Who Gets Represented?

The idea that racial minorities should be represented along with interest groups takes us to the question of who should get represented and how much. Mill thought that representative democracy should ensure something like proportional representation among all major political groups.

First, he argued that every adult should have the right to vote. This helps protect and promote their interests, recognizes their contribution to the community, and nurtures their rational development and sense of self-respect (he also thought that persons who had higher levels of education should be allowed to cast more ballots). Second, he thought that the winner-take-all method of electing representatives should be replaced by a system of proportional representation, since this would lessen the problem of majorities tyrannizing over minorities.

The United States uses the winner-take-all system for electing members of congress. Whoever wins the most votes in a congressional race wins. Suppose the Republican candidates in each congressional race win 51 percent of the vote while Democratic candidates win 49 percent. Republicans would win all the seats. But that result wouldn't accurately represent the wishes of the American population as a whole, 49 percent of which voted Democratic.

To avoid this tyrannical result, Mill recommended eliminating single-seat, winner-take-all districts and replacing them with a nationwide system of voting. Suppose you have 100 seats up for grabs nation-wide and 200 candidates competing for them. Any candidate who receives at least $\frac{1}{100}$ of all votes cast nationwide is elected. Each voter ranks the 200 candidates according to his or her preferences. First preferences are counted first. If a voter's most preferred candidate has already received $\frac{1}{100}$ of the vote, then that voter's second preference is counted—and so on down the line.

CAUTION

Do the Right Thing!

Maybe we should replace our current winner-take-all method of electing representatives with a system that would permit a more proportional representation of interests, values, and perspectives. If we adopted Mill's system, minority groups would have a better chance of electing representatives that would articulate their unique perspectives.

A system like Mill's would more likely guarantee a congressional representation comprising 51 percent Republicans and 49 percent Democrats. It might also make it easier for smaller minorities to get their candidates elected. Under the single-seat, winner-take-all system, a minority group that composed just $\frac{1}{100}$ of the American electorate would normally be unable to elect a candidate representing its perspective. Under Mill's system—and taking the above example as our reference case—it would, so long as every member of this group ranked its preferred candidates the same way, because doing so would guarantee that its most preferred candidate got $\frac{1}{100}$ of the first-rank votes necessary for election.

There are other methods that might be used to guarantee proportional representation. Sometimes by redesigning the shapes of districts you can ensure that a relatively concentrated minority can elect a representative of its choice. But which minority ought to be so favored in this manner? And who should be given responsibility for redesigning the districts? Other methods that have been used in the United States strike a compromise between our current system of electing congressional representatives and Mill's system. Implemented at state and local levels, these involve setting up large, multi-seat districts where, in some instances, voters are allowed to cast two or more ballots for one or more candidates.

Cultivating Democracy in Our Everyday Lives

Democracy is more than just voting in elections. It's a way of life. Here the communitarians (see Chapter 22, "The Immigration Controversy") got it right. No amount of procedural tinkering will make the public want to put the good of everyone ahead of narrow partisan self-interest. But unless the public can see its way to doing what's good for everyone and not just for the many and powerful, democracy will always mean the rule of the stronger over the weaker.

Sure, we can limit even more than we currently do the amount of money that candidates can spend on their own campaigns as well as the amount that others can give to campaigns, political parties and advocacy groups. We can limit the access of lobbyists to politicians and impose term limits. All of these rule changes might make elections fairer and encourage candidates to think more about their constituents' needs rather than the needs of wealthy patrons.

But politicians are only as good as the people who elect them. And the people who elect them are only as good as the culture that nurtures them. So the key to democratic justice is cultivating virtuous citizens. How do we do that?

Active Participation

First, we have to understand that as a way of life democracy requires active participation on the part of citizens. Citizens are the watchdogs who hold elected officials accountable for their actions. To the extent that we allow these officials to set the legislative agenda according to their own whims—instead of doing it ourselves—we become the passive subjects of their dictates. So representative democracy requires direct, participatory democracy at the grass-roots level. I'm talking PTA meetings, writing your representatives, demonstrating out in the streets—whatever it takes to get your voice heard amid the din of public opinion.

Tried and True

Democracy is only as good as its citizens are virtuous. Fair procedures won't protect against tyranny—what's needed is a society whose culture nurtures equal respect and concern for all.

Second, participation isn't fair unless everyone has roughly equal opportunities, capacities, and resources for participating. Above all, the poor should be provided economic and educational opportunities for informed and effective participation.

Third, the formation of public opinion should itself be democratic and well-informed by the mass media. The mass media, in turn, should reflect a full range of opinion, free from domination by corporate-sponsored publicity.

Fourth, citizens should be educated in civic virtue. They should ...

♦ Imagine what it's like to be someone differently situated

♦ Debate issues with an open mind

♦ Be willing to change their personal lifestyles for the sake of promoting the general good

Does civic virtue then demand that we put aside our differences in talking to one another? No. To ask, for instance, that African Americans leave behind their particular grievances as African Americans and speak only as American citizens would be grossly unfair to them and would deny others the benefit of learning from their unique perspectives.

Does civic virtue demand that we refrain from arguing in ways that will undermine the effort at reaching agreement with others who disagree with us? Perhaps. In the company of fellow citizens who do not—and will not—share our particular beliefs, it is proper not to refer exclusively to these beliefs in trying to convince them to change their minds. So pro-life activists shouldn't appeal exclusively to the divine sanctity of fetal life when arguing with pro-choice atheists, who in turn shouldn't insist on the nonpersonhood of the fetus in their response to religious pro-lifers.

Again, we have to keep an open mind about what counts as a civil conversation. Almost all people agree that hate speech is wrong. But during the sixties, peaceful demonstration was often viewed by government authorities as disorderly conduct rather than as political argumentation. In suppressing peaceful demonstration, the government denied the participants—some of whom lacked formal education and the kind of cool, intellectual politeness we associate with academic discussions and televised political debates—a public space in which to be heard.

Lack of Bias

Last but not least, care should be taken to ensure that the terms of political dialogue are not slanted in favor of one of the parties. For example, because Native Americans were forced to defend their territorial claims in what was for them the alien legal language of private property and contract, they were prevented from genuinely and convincingly defending their belief that their land meant something else to them, something spiritual and communal.

Expanding Democracy

Talk about the ethical culture of democracy takes me to one final point. People who are used to being told what to do by others at work are more likely to passively accept the dictates of their elected officials. By contrast, those who exercise greater control over their working lives are more likely to be active questioners of authority at all levels.

Ethically Speaking

Workplace democracy requires allowing workers to control how they work and, in some cases, what they make. For example, in Germany unions and management work together in designing workplace policies, and in the former Yugoslavia, workers' self-managed enterprises allowed all employees to vote on policies.

If Democracy is so good for working things out in informal clubs and federal, state, and local governments, then why not extend the principal to the workplace? In fact, most of the arguments that justify democracy at the level of political life also apply to our work-a-day lives. Take the knowledge argument. As I mentioned in Chapter 23, "Economic Justice," businesses that have experimented with *workplace democracy* experience higher worker satisfaction and higher productivity. An important part of that higher productivity comes from having workers—who often know the details of their work better than their bosses—share their knowledge with management.

Another important argument has to do with contribution: what concerns everyone should be decided by everyone. Work is such an important part of lives—for many people, the most important part—that it concerns them more deeply than almost anything else.

One objection to workplace democracy is that in a capitalist society private ownership of productive property gives total control over the workplace to owners. If someone owns something, shouldn't they—not the employees—call all the shots?

Not necessarily. First, when talking about stockholding companies, ownership is often scattered over thousands of stockholders, who delegate decision-making to managers. So, when it comes to controlling their property, owners don't call all the shots. Second, managers don't call all the shots either. The public—in the form of government oversight—dictates standards of workplace safety and collective bargaining (and sometimes wage and price controls as well).

Finally, we have plenty of examples where those who own the property have less control over the property than those who inhabit it. Owners of apartment buildings aren't allowed to dictate the interior decor and furnishings—let alone behavior—of their tenants. Cities are in some sense privately owned—by people who purchase the municipal bonds that keep them running. But these people have no right to dictate how the city should be run, which after all is a matter for citizens to decide!

Beyond Our Borders

Now let's turn the focus in another direction and ask about extending democracy beyond the borders of the nation state to include, if not a global state, then a global democratic federation of states. We've got something of a dilemma on our hands. On one hand, the principle that what concerns everyone ought to be decided by everyone pushes us in the direction of some sort of global democracy—after all, we live in one global community in which what goes on here has powerful repercussions over there. We are mutually dependent on other nations economically, environmentally, financially, and in many other ways as well. On the other hand, you'll recall what I said about global states in Chapter 22: The danger of oppression and domination increases as states become bigger and more centralized.

What to do? As the experience of the United States shows, large size is no absolute obstacle to local control. Federalism involves a form of power sharing in which some areas of life—defense, say—are more efficiently placed under federal control while other areas of life are more efficiently placed under local (state, county, and municipal) control. States are no longer sovereign, or free to do whatever they want to inside their borders (e.g., states are not free to enslave, segregate, or otherwise discriminate against any portion of their citizens). However, all states have some representation at the national level.

Do the Right Thing!

Respect for human rights pushes us in the direction of a global democratic federation of states. Such a federation would be like the United States, where each state has some—but not total—sovereignty over its own domestic affairs. So, think global and act local!

Can federalism work at the global level? Environmental, economic, health, and security problems have become global problems whose solution calls for a global response. All nations must work together in solving these problems. Communitarians rightly point out that nations must be allowed to govern themselves. But this right should not protect nations against outside interference from other states if the nations in question violate the basic rights of their own citizens or endanger the well-being of other nations. Independent states have a right not to be dominated by other states, but they shouldn't have a right to do whatever they want to. Furthermore, any state that insists on going it alone—pursuing its own self-interest at the expense of the interests of other nations—places itself in an awkward position should it someday need assistance from other states.

Recognizing that all states should be bound by a universal respect for enforceable human rights points us in the direction of some kind of a global democratic federation of states. Nations, global financial institutions, and multi-national companies must be made more accountable to the world—and should probably be encouraged to become more democratic and open in their internal governance as well.

The Least You Need to Know

- Democracy is more than a political system; it's a way of life.
- Democracy only flourishes among people who respect one another as free and equal, and who are in fact free and equal.
- Democratic tyranny can be avoided only if all vulnerable groups are represented.
- A democracy is only as good and just as its citizens are.
- Justice may well require implementing democracy in the workplace and in global structures of governance.

Chapter 25

Gender Justice

In This Chapter

♦ Identifying the wrongs of sexual harassment
♦ Giving women equal pay for equal work
♦ What's wrong with prostitution and pornography?
♦ Making gender irrelevant

A friend of mine once told me about a conversation that took place between her son and daughter when they were little kids. This friend is a committed feminist, and was careful to raise her children as equals, which makes what happened even more surprising. Riding the bus one day, her daughter was looking out the window at a group of construction workers; she turned to her mother and commented: "Mom, I want to be a construction worker one day!" "You can't," her brother retorted, "You're a girl, and only boys can be construction workers!" My friend was upset that her son said this, and claimed that at that moment she was struck by the absolute power of gender role socialization.

Gender roles cut across every aspect of human life, and have a strong impact on the lives we lead as men and women. In the not-too-distant past, women were assigned rigid feminine roles that denied them the same basic freedoms as men: they weren't allowed to get an education, vote, hold public office, be property-owners, inherit property, or divorce abusive husbands. Since then, as a recent cigarette advertising campaign tells us, "You've come a long way, baby."

But have women come such a long way? While it's true that the rigid structures that limited women's lives are no longer in place (women can vote, get educated, hold office, divorce, etc.), we don't yet live in a gender utopia. Women still earn about 75 cents to each dollar earned by a man; the number of women in politics is still minuscule; and sexist views of women are still evident in things like pornography, prostitution, and the sexual harassment of women. This chapter will consider some of the legacies of gender injustice, and what it is that feminists are complaining about when they talk about "patriarchy" and "sexism."

Sexual Harassment

Let's start with a continuing problem that was only recently given a name: sexual harassment. For decades women put up with bad treatment by men that was viewed as "just a joke." You know the behaviors I'm talking about: when men pat women on the bum, comment on their looks, stare at their breasts, tell filthy jokes that involve a naked woman and her mailman, put naked pin-up girls on the office walls, etc., etc., etc.! The reason these behaviors had no name is because they weren't seen as connected in any way: after all, nothing was meant by them but a little horsing around, and women were told not to be hypersensitive.

Ethically Speaking

The United States Equal Employment Opportunity Commission (EEOC) says that "Unwelcome sexual advances, requests for sexual favors, and other verbal or physical conduct of a sexual nature constitutes **sexual harassment** when submission to or rejection of this conduct explicitly or implicitly affects an individual's employment, unreasonably interferes with an individual's work performance or creates an intimidating, hostile or offensive work environment."

But as women grew in numbers in the workplace, the "old boys' network" was challenged, and feminists began to call for an end to such sexist and humiliating treatment. For the first time, discussions about the "hostile environment" to which women were subjected at work and elsewhere was taken seriously. And the behaviors I noted above were finally recognized as the common experience of women's *sexual harassment*.

As things now stand, sexual harassment is a form of sex discrimination that violates Title VII of the Civil Rights Act of 1964. Any behaviors that suggest that a person's continued employment is dependent on her acceptance of unwanted sexual attention, or any actions that create a hostile work environment (like naked pin-up girls, for example), fall under this act. And while sexual harassment is at least being dealt with as a legal issue, it is still a problematic moral one.

Some critics claim that turning harmless jokes into a violation of people's civil rights is political correctness spinning out of control. For those who are no longer free to enjoy their discrimination against, and degradation of, women, the new legal rules seem like a hideous moral mistake. Indeed, some people blame bad-tempered, humorless feminists for starting these problems in the first place. These folks claim that, if women are going to participate in the public sphere, they need to learn to "take it like a man" and get a sense of humor.

But feminists have pointed out that this is the very problem: women are expected to be like men both in the workplace and beyond, accommodating themselves to male-dominated spaces and attitudes. Feminist critics argue that the sexual harassment of women is just a small part of a bigger system of domination that puts women at the mercy of men. Since men hold power over women through their sexual domination of them, it is unsurprising that women have experienced sexual discrimination in the workplace. In fact, such discrimination is everywhere, from pornography to prostitution, to domestic violence and rape. So those little "behaviors," taken individually, may appear harmless. But if you take the big picture into account, they amount to a lot more than a hill of beans!

It's important to understand that sexual harassment isn't an isolated problem: it's part of a broader system of sexual discrimination against women. This is why women who complain of being sexually harassed, and feminists who push for laws against such treatment, aren't just being "whiners"; they experience this treatment as a direct hit against themselves as individuals or against women as a group.

Keeping this system of domination in mind, let's look at another important issue concerning gender justice: women's demand that they be paid equally when they do the same work as men. While you may think women have broken all the barriers to their equal participation in the workplace, when you look at pay scales you quickly realize that we still have a way to go!

> **Moral Musings**
>
> Feminist legal theorist Catharine MacKinnon has claimed that, by its very nature, men's domination of women (and society) is sexual. She says: "Male dominance is sexual. Meaning: Men in particular, if not men alone, sexualize hierarchy; gender is one … male power takes the social form of what men as a gender want sexually, which centers on power itself, as socially defined."
>
> (*Toward a Feminist Theory of the State*, Harvard University Press, Cambridge, 1989)

Equal Pay for Equal Work

Did you know that in 1999 women earned only 72 cents to every dollar men received? To put this figure into perspective, this means that, for every $100 earned, women have $28 less to spend on things like food and housing. This 28 cents per dollar really adds up when you consider that, over her working lifetime, a 25-year-old woman is going to lose more than $523,000 to unequal pay!

Tried and True _____

If you want to figure out whether pay differentials between men and women are morally justified, you need to take into account things like years of work, and level of education. But even these factors don't go deep enough: Jobs are segregated according to sex such that women earn far less for their types of work than men earn for the types of work they do!

Things are even worse for African American and Latina women, though. Studies show that African American women earn only 65 cents and Latinos 52 cents for every dollar that men earn. So not only is gender an issue in pay equity, but so is race.

There are some important moral questions to be posed here: First, is this pay differential morally justified? And second, how are we to ensure that women are paid and treated fairly? Some folks respond that such pay differentials can be written off to women's entering the job market at a much later point than men, meaning that it will take time for them to "catch up." But this doesn't account for the fact that, with the same degree of education and the same number of years working at a job, women *still* earn less than men on average.

Determining Comparable Worth

Here's another problem with the demand for equal pay for equal work: Oftentimes, women just don't do the "same" work as men. For example, the service industries are dominated by women: in jobs such as nurse, day care worker, primary school teacher, nursing home aide, and restaurant staff, women overwhelmingly outnumber men. By contrast, in the trade industries, like carpentry, masonry, roofing, and electrical work, men dominate over women. So while we may be able to compare men and women's salaries where they're doing the same job, this doesn't work so well where jobs are segregated according to sex. How can we determine whether day care workers should earn as much as roofers? What's the value of a waitress' work versus that of an electrician?

One response to leveling the "paying field" between men and women has been an appeal to comparable worth. Determining comparable worth involves applying objective categories in evaluating the relative value of jobs by focusing on the "worth points" for the four elements found in most jobs—something, by the way, that many companies already do:

- ◆ Knowledge and skills: the total amount of education, information, or skill needed to perform the job
- ◆ Mental demands: the degree to which the job involves individual decision-making
- ◆ Accountability: the amount of supervision the worker requires in doing the job
- ◆ Working conditions: taking into account how safe the job site is

By using these four categories, advocates of comparable worth argue, we can try to objectively determine the "worth" of different kinds of jobs. By doing calculations on a point-scale, employers can figure out what the "point-value" is for any given job. This means that waitressing jobs can be given a point-value that can be compared with the point-value of a truckers' job. And while the jobs are different, by determining things like how much education is required to do it, how much supervision is required, and how risky the job is, we can come up with an account of the comparable worth of waitressing versus trucking.

While this may seem like an odd way to determine the worth of various jobs, look at it this way: Employing a comparable worth standard can get at issues of gender justice by addressing what has been called the "feminization of poverty," and by assessing the value of work.

The fact that more than half of all poor families in the United States are headed by single women, and that women are the primary recipients of Medicaid, food stamps, and legal aid, has led to discussions of the way that poverty is experienced by far more women than men. But if wage-earning women were being paid what their jobs were worth, far more women would be able to adequately support themselves and their families.

> **Do the Right Thing!**
>
> If you think that there are no real gender-based inequalities that we need to worry about, think again! Studies indicate that more than half of all families living in poverty have single female heads-of-household. Since many men don't pay their child support, and working mothers are often stuck in job ghettos, this means that women and children are unnecessarily plunged into poverty.

Value of Comparable Worth

Second, a comparable worth standard may actually account for the value of women's work, so that women are no longer exploited by giving them little pay for what is sometimes demanding and difficult work. Another "perk" to doing comparable worth evaluations is that, as we raise the pay for jobs dominated by women, it is more likely that men will want to participate in them, thus hopefully ending job segregation based on sex.

Criticism of Comparable Worth

One final note. Critics of comparable worth charge that it violates the law of supply and demand. According to this law, low wages—say, in the female-dominated home health-care industry—reflect the oversupply of labor in that area, not gender discrimination. They argue that if you try to artificially raise wages in this area using comparable worth guidelines, you'll only create new problems. Either you'll create labor shortages in other areas or—what's more likely—you'll end up forcing companies to lay off a lot of costly "overpaid" home health-care providers. So comparable worth is either economically inefficient or self-defeating, since it causes harm to the women it's supposed to be helping.

Interestingly, this argument—against setting wage levels through nonmarket criteria—is also trotted out against minimum wage laws, which most Americans support. Although high minimum wage levels (around $11.00 per hour—over twice the American minimum) may have contributed to higher unemployment in European countries, there is no evidence that they generally do so, since increased labor costs are passed along to the consumers, who seldom notice minuscule price increases spread over a large number of commodities. Anyway, as we saw in Chapter 23, "Economic Justice," the market is not always the most efficient or the most just mechanism for distributing burdens and benefits.

This brief review of the "equal pay for equal work" issue indicates that some serious thought still needs to be put into questions about gender and pay equity. But for now, let's leave this issue to consider the controversial issue of pornography.

Pornography: It's More Than Skin Deep

Let's be clear about this from the very start: there is no single position, feminist or otherwise, on the *pornography* debate. Many different groups have weighed in on the morality or immorality of pornography, including feminists, conservative Christian women, religious groups, lesbians, libertarians, and even animal rights activists (since sometimes animals are used and abused in the making of pornographic materials). So even though what I will present here will try to cover different perspectives on pornography, I can't possibly detail all the different arguments for and against it.

But more specifically as an issue of gender justice, pornography has received a great deal of attention. Why? Because while some "soft" porn is relatively harmless and silly, other forms are extremely explicit, "hard core," and arguably degrading to women. Again, you should note that not all feminists, let alone all women, agree that pornography is degrading: Some women even celebrate porn for freeing women from the old Victorian morality that used to confine women and deny their sexuality.

So pornography can be viewed in morally opposing ways: as a degrading, offensive, and harmful way of depicting and stereotyping women, or as a breaking free of oppressive patriarchal morality. Let's briefly consider the reasons for taking either perspective.

Ethically Speaking

Pornography can be defined as the explicit depiction of men, women, and/or children in degrading sexual contexts. But whether material degrades or objectifies the people portrayed is a matter of opinion. So any definition of pornography is bound to be controversial.

Arguing Against Pornography

Those who are morally opposed to pornography as a form of gender injustice focus on the ways that women are used and abused in the pornography industry. Since women have historically been associated with their bodies and their sexuality, and since men have used these as the grounds for dominating them, pornography may be seen as just another form of the sexual domination of women by men.

Pornographic depictions of women exploit their sexuality, reducing women to body parts that are to be penetrated and defiled by men. Furthermore, the porn industry is male dominated: very few of the videos, books, magazines, or websites are run by women, and relatively little of the pornography that gets consumed is consumed by women. So, as some critics argue, pornography is just another way by which men exploit and subjugate women for the sake of their own pleasure.

Think back to the issue of sexual harassment, and the claim that it is tied to a system of sexual control and domination of women. You could see pornography as yet another part of that system. In fact, sexual harassment and pornography aren't really separate problems at all, according to more radical feminists: they are part of a system of interlocking barriers that prevent women from being seen as men's moral equals. This is because both pornography and sexual harassment—along with rape, prostitution, and domestic violence— treat women as sexual objects.

Ethically Speaking

When feminists refer to **patriarchy,** or to patriarchal power, they are referring to a social system within which men dominate women. Patriarchy literally means "rule of the father"; so patriarchal cultures are those where men are dominant and women, subordinate. Usually feminists are concerned about the way that patriarchal power results in the *sexual* domination of women by men.

Worse still, some feminists argue that pornography leads to the rape and abuse of women. How? By depicting women as weak, passive objects, and by sexualizing violence against women, porn makes rape and violence seem exciting and somehow acceptable. And while there is still no demonstrated statistical link between rapists and the consumption of pornography, some critics still hold that a pornographic, *patriarchal* society makes the abuse of women easy and acceptable.

Arguing for Pornography

Now consider the opposite argument: that, rather than oppressing women, pornography liberates them from conservative, Victorian-style sexual mores. We know that well into the twentieth century, women's sexuality was seen as dangerous and evil; it was something to be hidden and controlled. The Women's Liberation Movement that began in the 1960s had a direct impact on those mores, revealing the sexism behind ideas of women as sexually dangerous. So, argue some feminists, the participation of women in the porn industry is not an expression of sexism and hatred of women: it can also be seen as women reveling in sex and sexuality, and as the chance (finally) for women to reject repressive ideas about their sexuality.

Feminists who argue for the moral acceptability of pornography also point to the dangers of censorship. If porn is considered immoral and degrading to women, then the likely response is to attempt to censor it. But, as we know, censorship can be highly problematic in a culture that emphasizes freedom of speech and expression. Furthermore, as some critics point out, pornography is a matter of taste, and, as the saying goes, "There's no accounting for taste." Besides, if there are women active in the porn industry who claim that they *enjoy* making films and pictures, then who are we to deny them?

So, depending on your point of view, pornography is degrading to women and threatens gender justice; or pornography symbolizes women's rejection of a repressive Victorian morality. You decide!

Sex Work: Beyond a Labor of Love

The debate surrounding gender justice and pornography leads nicely into a discussion of gender justice and prostitution, or what I'll also call "sex work." This is because the two are connected—women who are involved in sex work are often involved in the pornography industry, too—and because the same arguments are made for and against the morality of prostitution. Let's see how the two issues are connected.

First of all, return to the disagreement about whether porn symbolizes women's degradation or their sexual freedom. The same disagreement arises concerning women's sex work: some critics claim that it degrades women by reducing them to a sex object for men's pleasure; others (including some sex worker activists!) claim that it's empowering, and that giving pleasure to others is a legitimate form of work.

It all comes down to a dispute between whether anti-prostitution politics reflect a kind of sexual repression or whether sex workers are just suffering "false consciousness" in thinking that they really *choose* to be sex workers. Some feminists criticize prostitutes who claim they enjoy sex work by arguing that they are simply kidding themselves: What appears to be a life choice is really the product of a sexist society that makes selling their bodies highly profitable for women. For women who have little education, job training, or life prospects, prostitution hardly seems like a "choice" in the same way that women choose to be a doctor, lawyer, politician, or teacher.

Censorship and Pornography

So, like the porn industry, sex work raises questions about choice and freedom in a patriarchal society. But, also like pornography, prostitution raises questions about censorship: whether legally preventing situations of paid sex is morally appropriate. If we assume that people engaged in sex work—prostitutes and their johns—are rational adults with the capacity to choose for themselves, then it's hard to argue that we should interfere in these sexual arrangements that are based on mutual consent.

> **Tried and True** _____
>
> No matter what you may think about the morality of prostitution, you might be in favor of government regulation of the sex work industry. If sex workers are viewed as legitimate employees, they will be required to meet industry standards: free from disease (like AIDS, Hepatitis B, and other communicable diseases); decent working conditions; protection from abuse by johns. Furthermore, government regulation of the prostitution industry could add to the number of taxpaying citizens, since sex workers would pay tax out of their earnings like everyone else. These measures are being tried in countries like Holland and Brazil and are proving to be effective in "cleaning up" the sex work industry.

Yet, as anti-prostitution feminists argue, the prevalence of female sex workers sends out a strong message that women are available for men's use, and that the primary "good" of women is their sexuality. As you can imagine, some women strongly object to prostitution because it implicates *all* women, not just sex workers, as "sluts" and "whores."

Sex worker activists argue for the regulation of the sex work industry, not for shutting it down. As they point out, men will seek out women for paid sex whether the state makes it legal or not. By regulating the industry, governments can ensure women's health and safety by providing regular medical check-ups, by eliminating the need for pimps (who are notorious for abusing and dominating sex workers against their will!), by ensuring that brothels meet certain health and safety standards, and by allowing sex workers to organize for benefits like health care, sick leave, paid vacation, and so on. This not only better protects sex workers, but their children, too.

Pros and Cons

Again, there are compelling arguments on both sides of the prostitution debate. On the "pro" side, advocates argue that women can and do choose the life of a sex worker, and that it can be liberating for women to provide sexual services without the expectation that love will be attached to it. Women have traditionally been associated with love, not sex, so mixing up these categories may just lead to new ways of viewing women's sexuality. On the other hand, if prostitution is just another piece in the patriarchal puzzle, then there isn't much room for women's free choice to enter the sex work industry.

Whatever you think about the issue after reading this, one thing's for sure: there is no simple way of figuring out what gender justice demands. If we ban things like pornography and prostitution, some folks argue, we eliminate women's choices in these areas and treat them like children, denying them the adult right to make personal life choices. If we don't take a moral stand against these practices, other people argue, we end up continuing a patriarchal system that serves to degrade and sexually dominate women. Neither option is all that pleasing, is it?

Should Gender Matter in a Just World?

We'll wrap up with a more general issue concerning the very existence of gender roles. To return to the story I started with, consider those kids on the bus, one who is thinking about being a construction worker, the other telling her "You can't because you're a girl!" You might wonder if, in an ideal world, we shouldn't have gender roles at all. That way, no individual would face the limitations caused by the strong gender roles that are imposed on us. Imagine the human possibilities that have been denied because our system of gender roles has prevented them from happening: female presidents, male nurses, an equitable sharing of child-rearing duties. If girls and boys weren't pushed into their roles, we might end up with a far more open and just world.

> ### Moral Musings
>
> Try this thought experiment: Suppose gender didn't exist as a social category at all. What might our social world be like without these strictly defined roles? What are people apt to look like, how do you think they would behave, and how would we relate to one another? Sometimes by thinking about how we use categories, we get a clear idea of what purpose they serve.

So to answer the earlier question, some critics claim that gender should *not* matter in a just world. Since gender roles aren't "natural" at all, but are socially constructed, and since they lead to men and women being denied the full range of human emotions and possibilities, an ideal world might not include gender roles at all. As some utopian thinkers depict it, this would mean that instead of having two gender roles, male and female, we'd have any variety of human appearances, behaviors, and career choices, none of which have anything to do with having a penis or vagina! This means you couldn't automatically pick out a male or female person on the street; it would also mean that you couldn't discriminate against someone on the job because you suspect that the person is female and likely to take maternity leave.

But we should be careful to distinguish the claim that gender *shouldn't* matter in an ideal world from the claim that gender *doesn't* matter in this world. Because it does matter, as things stand, whether you're a male or female person. If you have a uterus, for example, that means you're of the female gender, so you're a high-risk job candidate for employers. Why? Because as a female person with a female gender, you're likely to become pregnant at some point and, because of the way our social world is constructed, to take a long time off work to care for your baby!

Given the fact of gender in our social world, it would be foolish to pretend that gender doesn't matter, and to try and move toward treating men and women as equals. Because in the current context, treating women as men's "equals" means that women will be treated like men, and that women must compete with men on *their* turf. This isn't the kind of "equality" that feminists have in mind when they dream of an ideal world. While some women just want the right to compete equally with men in the board room, the bedroom, and on the sports field, most want a more egalitarian world, where men must do their part in being more like women, too.

In short, to make sure that women are treated justly in our current cultural climate, we may need to focus on affirmative action strategies that "level the playing field," as they say, and give women a real chance to compete for social goods. How can women compete fairly and equally for jobs if employers are allowed to discriminate against them because they have a uterus? How are women supposed to enter nontraditional fields of work, and succeed, if men are resistant to having women as co-workers, and if they "haze" women on the job and treat them badly?

By simply telling women to "get out there and try," we don't do enough. Given our history of denying women the right to vote (which they didn't get until 1920), and the right to hold office, seek an education, and hold property, modern women have inherited the vestiges of a highly repressive, patriarchal culture.

In Chapter 26, "Affirmative Action and Multi-culturalism," I will discuss affirmative action strategies in more detail, but here it is worth noting that such strategies aren't attempting to "keep men down," but rather to "bring women up" to an equal starting position.

So while equality between men and women may be the long-term goal, we may have to pay attention to the way women's differences from men

Do the Right Thing!

When thinking about issues of employment, it may be morally right to give hiring preference to women, all things being equal. This is because, in many industries, women are a decided minority. For example, when we hire in philosophy departments there is usually an affirmative action approach taken, since women traditionally have been discriminated against in this area.

have led to discrimination against them. Like racial justice, gender justice can only be achieved through a long and committed battle against sexist stereotypes and expectations.

But as I will argue in the next chapter, there's one major difference between race and gender: While race has recently been understood to be a false category that isn't based on any biological fact, gender differences are deeply connected to the biological differences between men and women. So it might be the case that gender differences are even harder to eliminate, if it can be done at all, because they appeal back to biological differences between men and women. Our task will be to figure out which differences between us (if any) are biologically given, and which gender differences are socially constructed.

The Least You Need to Know

◆ Patriarchy is at the root of many practices that harm and degrade women. When considering issues like prostitution, pornography, and equal pay for equal work, remember that these problems are connected by this system of patriarchy.

◆ Remember that there is no broad agreement on whether pornography and prostitution threaten gender justice for women.

◆ Be committed to women's equal treatment in the workplace. Making inappropriate comments and hanging up posters of "pin-up girls" make the work environment hostile for women!

◆ Don't assume that gender differences are naturally given. Since gender is socially constructed, we need to think critically about the idea of "man's" and "woman's" role.

Chapter 26

Affirmative Action and Multiculturalism

In This Chapter

- ◆ What is race and why does it matter?
- ◆ Multiculturalism and anti-racism as two aims of social justice
- ◆ Arguments for and against affirmative action
- ◆ Cultural recognition for the deaf

I still get misty-eyed when I read Martin Luther King Jr.'s famous "I Have a Dream" speech, which he delivered in front of the Lincoln Memorial on August 28, 1963, at the height of the Civil Rights Movement. Here's King, dreaming about the day when people in America "will not be judged by the color of their skin but by the content of their character"; when "the jangling discords of our nation [will be transformed] into a beautiful symphony of brotherhood"; when "black men and white men, Jews and Gentiles, Catholics and Protestants, will be able to join hands and to sing in the words of the old Negro spiritual, 'Free at last, free at last; thank God Almighty, we are free at last.'"

We've come a long way since King delivered those mighty words. We've outlawed segregation and legal discrimination and our society has made tremendous strieds in racial healing. But I wonder whether we've gone far enough in eradicating racial injustice and bringing about equal opportunity for all. Blacks as a whole lag far behind whites economically (the typical black family has one tenth of the assets of a typical white family); they continue to be underrepresented in legislatures and on corporate boards; they have a lower life expectancy and suffer a higher rate of infant mortality; they are incarcerated at a much higher rate than whites (mostly on drug-related violations); and they continue to face discrimination at all levels of life, from police profiling to discrimination in securing loans and real estate "red-lining."

In this chapter we'll examine what our society has done to eliminate this racial injustice. We'll see why affirmative action came into being and what the arguments are, both for and against it. We'll also look at the ethical value of multicultural diversity as well as claims that American Sign Language constitutes a distinct deaf culture worth preserving. Finally, we'll try to imagine how an ideally just society would treat race and ethnicity. However, before we start, I'd like to say a few things about race and racism.

It's Just Skin-Deep After All

In Census 2000, the U.S. Government tried to take a nose count of all Americans, including asking each of us to identify what race and ethnicity we belong to. Persons were asked if they are Hispanic or not, and then they were invited to pick one or more (up to six) racial categories that best described them. What was remarkable about this approach was that it recognized that racial identification is not an all-or-nothing affair—none of us, in fact, is racially pure when it comes right down to it. Furthermore, it tacitly recognized that race itself is largely a matter of personal preference. As for me, just call me mixed up!

Not so long ago Americans thought that race was an all-or-nothing affair—something fixed in nature, having to do with the blood you inherited from your parents. For example, among whites it was assumed that if you inherited even a drop of "black" blood from, say, a great-great-grandparent, then you were totally black. It also meant that you were mentally as well as physically inferior.

Modern genetics has totally refuted this biological notion of race.

- First, there is no scientific connection whatsoever linking physical and mental traits.
- Second, a person's racial features express his genetic make-up, which in turn is the product of recombining the genes he inherited from his parents.

Depending on how their genes are recombined, persons may or may not look very much like their parents. Genetically speaking, persons who look racially alike are as different or more different from each other than persons who don't look racially alike. Finally, what gets designated as a racial feature is a matter of arbitrariness. Among persons who live in relatively closed breeding populations, height might be less variable than skin color.

So, while physical characteristics have a genetic basis, there's no biological reality that corresponds to "racial kind" in the way that there is a biological reality that corresponds to "species kind." In some sense, given our species' common roots in Africa, we could say that there's just one human race—or, if you prefer to retain talk about racial features, that we are all mixed up—I mean, mixed race! So the idea behind Census 2000—that your racial identity is more a question of how you feel about yourself than what you are—accords with the facts of modern biology.

Which raises another good question. If race doesn't exist in any biological sense, should people still think of themselves racially? Perhaps in an ideal society they wouldn't. Racial distinctions are a modern invention. Prior to the European conquest of the New World, people divided themselves mainly on the basis of religion and culture. Religious and cultural conversion on the part of the heathen/barbarian was almost always possible. The only differences that were regarded as natural were differences between the sexes and, to a far lesser extent, differences between nobles and commoners.

> **Moral Musings**
>
> Your racial identity is really determined by social conventions and increasingly by how you feel about yourself. The famous golfer Tiger Woods, for instance, prefers to designate himself a "Cablasian," because he has Caucasian, black, and Asian ancestry!

So you see, we didn't always divide the world along racial lines. Racial distinctions were invented to justify the enslavement of Africans and Native Americans by Europeans. Perhaps in an ideal world, differences in skin pigmentation would matter about as much as differences in eye pigmentation.

Is there a good reason for people to identify themselves racially? That's a hard question. We still live in a racist society. Blacks rightly band together as blacks in fighting racism. Expressing pride in being black protects against negative social stereotypes of blackness. Expression of white pride by whites, however, is inappropriate, since it's not intended to combat negative stereotypes but to reinforce white superiority. That doesn't mean that whites shouldn't be proud of who they are as individuals, but it does mean that pride in being white may be inappropriate.

It also doesn't mean that whites should stop identifying themselves as "white" on census forms. Identifying yourself as white in this context merely helps the government to provide every group its fair share of services and representation.

We're One Big Family

Recently, some high schools have formed European-American clubs. Some critics have argued that these clubs don't just express pride (or interest in) European cultures, but express pride in being white—as a kind of racist reaction to the formation of various non-white ethnic clubs. But national culture and race intertwine.

We often think of cultural differences as forming the basis for ethnic identifications and biological differences as forming the basis for racial identifications. Reality is more complicated than this. Members of the same *ethnic group* often share overlapping physical features; and members of the same racial group often share overlapping cultural traits. This isn't surprising, since both physical and cultural traits are passed down from generation to generation, the former through genes, the latter through socialization. In fact, at various times in America's history ethnic nationalities—such as the Irish—were once regarded as racially distinct and even inferior.

Ethically Speaking

Ethnic groups are national cultural groups; they often have distinctive racial characteristics, just as racial groups often have distinctive cultural characteristics.

Distinctive characteristics—racial or cultural—are not shared by all members of a group. For example, people who immigrate from South and Central America to the United States are lumped together as Latinos—something they would never have thought of identifying themselves as prior to immigrating to the United States. There's a good reason for this, of course. Immigrants mainly identify themselves by nationality, and "Latino" is not a nationality. Furthermore, there is no one thing that all "Latinos" share in common. Brazilians speak Portuguese, not Spanish; and some second-generation American Latinos speak only English. Most, but not all, Latinos have some Native American or black slave ancestry. Most but not all are Catholic. Yet, there are often significant overlaps between people lumped together as Latino; and the fact that deviations from the mainstream Anglo culture—in language, skin color, and culture—often result in discrimination, it's hardly surprising that Latinos come to accept their common Latino identity, in much the same way that blacks come to accept their common black identity.

If race and ethnicity are so closely linked together, then it seems that what applies to one ought to apply to the other. For instance, if we think that an ideal world would be a world without racial distinctions, then it seems that we should also think that an ideal world would be a world without ethnic differences. In fact, if you consider some of the changes that would have to happen in order for racial thinking to disappear—such as complete residential and occupational integration of all races—it becomes clear that these changes would have deep cultural repercussions as well. For many aspects of ethnic culture are also cultivated in relatively tight-knit and geographically bounded racial communities.

This takes us to another very hard question. Is complete racial and ethnic integration a desirable ideal to strive for? We think that racial integration is desirable for fighting racism. However, even after the elimination of legal segregation we see that many blacks prefer to live in black communities because they feel more welcome there. Even after all traces of racism are gone, some blacks may still prefer to live among blacks for cultural reasons. For example, although certain aspects of the African American spiritual tradition can be (and have been) transported into all cultures, the black church as the bedrock of a distinctive black identity can't be. Some blacks might still prefer to live in predominantly black communities in order to preserve this identity.

The problem of integration suggests two ways of fighting discrimination against religious, ethnic, and racial groups:

◆ anti-racism

◆ multiculturalism

Anti-racism targets racial segregation, and so promotes the aim of racial integration at all levels of life. It reminds us of our common humanity, and the universal rights we share with all others. It's ideal is that of a raceless society, where physical differences between people are as insignificant as differences in eye color.

Multiculturalism, by contrast, targets cultural domination—or the attempt by a dominant culture to eradicate, assimilate, or otherwise integrate subordinate cultures to the point where they no longer exist as distinct and independent. As a positive agenda, multiculturalism encourages us to respect all cultures as equals. Unlike anti-racism, it sees positive value in preserving and promoting differences, even if this requires granting special exemptions and privileges to minority cultures that are endangered.

Tried and True

Anti-racism and multiculturalism are different ways of combating discrimination. The former stresses our common humanity; the latter the cultural differences among us that deserve mutual respect.

Let a Hundred Flowers Bloom

I will have more to say about anti-racism below. First, let's look at multiculturalism more closely. What sorts of policies do people have in mind when talking about multiculturalism?

◆ Throughout the world, practitioners of certain minority religions receive exemptions from military service, dress codes, and mandatory workdays. In one extreme case, Hasidic Jews living in New York were granted their own separate school district in order to shield their children from harassment.

◆ Universities in the United States and elsewhere have introduced area-studies programs focusing on the cultures and societies of different regions of the world. They have also set up programs focusing on ethnic Americans, women, and gays and lesbians. Some public schools have experimented with Afro-centric accounts of history and literature. Most schools offer some instruction in the contributions that different peoples have made to America.

◆ Some states and municipalities have promoted bi- or multilingualism in schools and other public institutions. In Canada, the provincial government of Quebec passed language laws protecting the distinctly French nature of Quebecois life.

◆ Native Americans living on tribal reservations are exempt from many federal and state laws. Tribal councils are granted wide-ranging jurisdiction over lawsuits and other legal matters.

Do the Right Thing!

We ought to respect people's individuality; so we ought to respect the cultural identifications that are apart of their identity.

Now that we have an idea about the many different forms that multiculturalism takes, let's look at the ethical arguments that have been used to support it. Although some people have defended multiculturalism on the grounds that it is good—noting that cultures comprise different kinds of knowledge that can be tapped for problem-solving—most have defended it for social justice reasons. This argument runs as follows:

◆ Our sense of self extends beyond our sense of belonging to the human species to include our particular identity as a unique individual.

◆ An important part of our particular identity as an individual is our belonging to particular groups—including religious and cultural groups.

◆ We ought to respect people in their particular individuality as well as in their universal humanity.

◆ Therefore, we ought to respect the particular religious and cultural groups that give people their particular identity.

◆ A society that demands that people refrain from publicly expressing their religion, culture, or language does not treat them with equal respect and so violates their rights.

◆ A society that does not provide all civil religions and cultures fair opportunities for expression is unjust.

◆ A society that does not encourage its members to appreciate different faiths and cultures is insensitive.

Multiculturalism sounds pretty compelling, but like many methods for achieving justice, it's hard to put into practice. It tries to protect smaller cultures from being dominated by bigger ones. But what happens when practitioners of smaller cultures freely choose to assimilate into bigger cultures?

Deaf Culture

Most people who are born deaf view themselves as belonging to a distinct cultural community whose language (in the United States) is American Sign Language (ASL). Many of them now want to preserve that culture by discouraging parents of congenitally deaf babies from inserting cochlear implants in their babies' ears so that they can hear like other children. Deaf culture activists fear that implanted children will prefer hearing culture over deaf culture, thereby killing off deaf culture through disuse. Some of these activists even go so far as to compare parents who want their deaf children to "be normal like everyone else" with those blacks who lightened their skin in order to "pass" as white!

Now both blacks and deaf people feel that their handicaps are caused by social discrimination rather than by natural incapacity. But here the similarity ends. Blacks suffered—and continue to suffer—a degree of intentional discrimination, dehumanization, and segregation that was never the same for the deaf. More importantly, there is a clear sense in which being born deaf is a natural—and not merely social—handicap. In order for the deaf not to be handicapped outside of their very small communities, society would have to do far more than end discrimination against them by providing them with visual cues. Everyone would have to learn ASL (and, to be fair, everyone would also have to learn the languages of all other citizens who can't learn English fluently)!

So, it's not always unjust to allow the assimilation of a small culture into a bigger one. A cure for deafness would probably result in the demise of deaf cultures and deaf communities over time. That would eliminate a handicap whose causes are not entirely the result of unjust societal discrimination. And when the handicap is a result of societal discrimination—as in the case of racial segregation—ending the discrimination will also lead to greater cultural integration, if not assimilation.

Leveling the Playing Field or Reverse Discrimination?

We've talked a lot about multiculturalism but what about anti-racism? Anti-racism says that racial discrimination in housing, employment, education, finance, and public and private accommodation is unjust. Ending discrimination means allowing everyone to compete equally for scarce positions and resources. The standard of fairness is this: those who are best qualified should get the position or resource, regardless of their race. Over time, a level playing field should spread positions and resources evenly across the population.

Racial minorities that were previously segregated off from society and denied access to jobs and resources should be integrated into society and be allowed to compete for their fair share of the goodies, just like everybody else.

The problem with this goal is in getting there. Anti-discrimination laws only target intentional or deliberate discrimination. Now, any racist employer with half a brain won't advertise his racism to a black job applicant. When turning down the applicant, he'll say something like: "So sorry, but you're not quite what we're looking for." Suppose you, the applicant, suspect something's fishy. In order to win a lawsuit against our racist employer you'd have to hire a lawyer and pray that some incriminating evidence will materialize proving that you've been ripped off. In the end, chances are you'll still be out of a job—and your pocketbook will be a little smaller to boot!

Ethically Speaking

Institutional discrimination is not deliberately intended, but merely reflects the continuing effects of past discrimination. When this kind of discrimination occurs, then, it isn't the result of an individual's intentional actions, but is rather the outcome of a system that was set in place hundreds of years ago.

Then there's unintended, *institutional discrimination*. Let's suppose there are no racists out there. Nevertheless, because of the history of past discrimination, you and your family find yourself living in an impoverished segregated black community that has poor schools and few jobs. When our good-intentioned white employer interviews you for a job, he finds that your schooling inadequately prepared you for the job. You're still the victim of discrimination—but not intentional discrimination. Oh yeah, there are some unskilled jobs available out in the white suburbs. But these jobs are advertised by word of mouth. Since you're not well connected with folks in that neck of the woods, you're out of luck. You got it—more institutional discrimination.

Affirmative Action

Affirmative action initially meant actively recruiting qualified minorities—mainly blacks. Good faith recruitment policies didn't work very well, so the government asked businesses to set deadlines for hiring a certain number of blacks. This didn't work very well either, so the government started imposing quotas—a set number or percentage of jobs—that had to be filled by blacks. Along the way, women and other minorities were added to the list of protected classes. Courts have since ruled that the use of affirmative action quotas in college admissions is unconstitutional and that their use in government contracting is highly suspect.

In order to see what went wrong with affirmative action we need to first look at the arguments given in support of it. Some of these arguments are consequentialist in nature.

Affirmative action is supposed to bring about racial harmony, expand the pool of qualified applicants so as to create a more competitive and efficient labor market, ensure a wider distribution of professional services, and increase wages for all classes of workers. These arguments are very speculative and controversial, and are certainly beyond my capacity to assess.

The social justice arguments, by contrast, are easier to assess. To simplify matters a bit, let's assume that they apply most strongly to affirmative action for African Americans.

Ethically Speaking

Affirmative action is the practice of showing preference in hiring, promoting, contracting, and admitting people to institutions of higher education and professional schools. It can take a variety of different forms, such as quotas or tie-breaker affirmative action, where, all things being equal, you give preference to the woman or minority candidate.

◆ The distributive justice argument says that affirmative action is necessary in order to ensure that black communities have equal access to professional services. Since blacks are more willing than nonblacks to service black communities, justice for black communities requires the education and licensing of an adequate number of qualified black professionals—something that won't happen in today's society without the help of affirmative action.

◆ The level-playing-field argument says that blacks are unfairly disadvantaged by poor schools and discrimination. In order to ensure that they have a fair chance to compete with whites for scarce positions in employment and higher education, they must sometimes be hired or admitted ahead of nonblacks who seem somewhat better qualified, based on test scores and the like.

◆ The compensatory justice argument says that black families have suffered irreparable harm because of centuries of legalized slavery, segregation, and discrimination. Recent studies estimate that slavery ripped off black families to the tune of 4.7 trillion dollars in unpaid labor and that from 1929 to 1969 they were underpaid by 1.6 trillion dollars. Now that's a lot of dough, especially when you consider that upward to two thirds of the improved fortune of each succeeding generation comes directly or indirectly from inherited wealth.

Do the Right Thing!

Blacks ought to have equal access to professions, compete on an even footing with others, and be compensated for past harms. The best way to achieve all three aims might be affirmative action.

◆ The idea that blacks should be given some monetary reparation for this robbery—in the form of one-time cash settlements divided among families, university scholarships, or massive community development grants—is one form compensatory justice might take, and is not without precedent (the U.S. Government has provided monetary reparation to Native Americans and Japanese Americans for the government's wrongful seizure of their property). Affirmative action, too, can be understood as a kind of compensation for past job discrimination.

Affirmative Action and Role Models

Let's take a closer look at these arguments. Some have objected that the argument for redistributing social goods is just too speculative. Do you really need to have more black doctors and lawyers to ensure blacks equitable access to medical and legal resources? If this argument applies to anyone, it applies to certain non–English-speaking immigrant groups, who need access to professionals fluent in their language.

However, the argument can be rephrased to apply more strongly to blacks. If justice requires that all children have an equal chance to develop a sense of self-respect and confidence in their abilities, and if that chance depends upon the existence of appropriate role models, then black children will have fewer chances to develop a sense of self-respect and self-confidence the fewer number of black professional role models there are. Without affirmative action influencing higher education admissions policies, there might not be enough blacks admitted to professional schools and, consequently, not enough future black role models.

The argument from leveling the playing field seems pretty solid. There's plenty of evidence showing that blacks continue to suffer the effects of past and present discrimination. Many blacks are (or were) poorly served by the public schools they attended (many of which were segregated), and so were denied the right to an equal opportunity education that would have enabled them to compete with whites on an equal footing.

Moral Musings

Affirmative action now effectively protects most of the American population. In 1996 the Clinton administration expanded the list of affirmative action beneficiaries of federal contracts to include small businesses owned by women, the disabled, and the socially disadvantaged, in addition to those owned by blacks, Latinos, Indians, Asians, Eskimos, and Native Hawaiians.

Problem is, this argument applies to nonblacks as well. Poor whites growing up in rural poverty also faced undeserved economic disadvantages. Even if white workers benefited from white racism, they were sometimes indirectly harmed by it, since low-paid black laborers were often used as strike-breakers against white unions. And, of course, many ethnic groups and women have experienced discrimination (which explains why they, too, have been protected by anti-discrimination statutes). The demand contained in the Americans With Disabilities Act (ADA) that businesses and other establishments provide reasonable accommodations for disabled workers and clients is in fact an affirmative action demand.

Comparing Discriminations

Clearly, in order for affirmative action to be an effective tool for leveling the playing field it must be administered in a way that is sensitive to individual differences in comparative disadvantage. This will be difficult to do, although not entirely impossible. For example, being a woman today is much less of a disadvantage than it was thirty years ago (in fact, women have made the greatest strieds in educational and economic advancement of any group, and now comprise a solid majority of all students attending institutions of higher education). Being a Native American resident of an impoverished reservation, by contrast, is still (at least in most cases) a very serious disadvantage.

Because it is often very difficult, if not impossible, to compare different types of disadvantage and discrimination, it may well be that, in some cases, the aims of affirmative action might be accomplished better using other means. Bringing about equal opportunity education for all as well as sharply reducing the effects of poverty, disability and other forms of disadvantage might be the fairest thing to do, but it will come with a very hefty price tag.

A cheaper but less fair method for determining admission to public universities that recognizes the unequal quality of education provided by different high schools involves admitting the top percent of each high school's graduating class. States like California and Texas now use this method instead of affirmative action. Because the schools in California and Texas concentrate together students of one race, the hope is that this method will ensure that the most deserving students from all races will be adequately represented.

Like the level-playing-field argument, the compensation argument for affirmative action sounds better in theory than in practice. Many groups besides blacks can claim that they deserve compensation from past wrongs done to them by the government. Ranking which groups have been harmed the most—and therefore have first claim to compensatory affirmative action—will be daunting, to say the least. More challenging still is the fact that individuals within different groups have not all suffered (or benefited) equally from past discrimination.

Tried and True

Because it is often very difficult, if not impossible, to compare different types of disadvantage and discrimination, it may well be that, in some cases, the aims of affirmative action might be accomplished better using other means.

For instance, those who benefit the most from affirmative action—the current generation of black youth—are not obviously the ones most harmed by past discrimination. Reversing the tables, those who have the most to lose from affirmative action—the current generation of white men who will be denied placement, employment, or promotion for the sake of helping others—are not obviously the ones who benefited the most from past discrimination.

I used the word "obviously" because if you recall what I said above about how each succeeding generation is advantaged or disadvantaged by what it inherits from the previous generation, it might be that the current generation of blacks has been harmed more by past discrimination than their forebears, who directly suffered the worst discrimination. Likewise, it might be that the current generation of white men has benefited more from past discrimination than their forebears, who more actively supported or went along with it. But no matter how you slice it, the fact is that not all blacks suffered equally—and not all whites benefited equally—from past discrimination. So once again, any fully just application of affirmative action for purposes of compensation would have to look closely at individual cases.

Is Affirmative Action Reverse Discrimination?

So far we've looked at some of the arguments in favor of affirmative action. Affirmative action sounds good in theory, but perhaps not so good in practice. In many respects, it seems like a rather crude method for tackling a problem of social injustice that requires more radical and costly solutions. But there's more to it than that. Some people have argued that affirmative action has bad consequences and is deeply unfair to white men.

The bad consequences that affirmative action allegedly produces are the following:

- ◆ It fuels racism by making whites resentful of blacks.
- ◆ It stigmatizes blacks as inferior.
- ◆ It elevates the less qualified over the better qualified.

> **Moral Musings**
>
> Critics charge that affirmative action harms blacks by stigmatizing them as inferior. Although some blacks oppose affirmative action for this very reason, studies show that 75 percent of black college students strongly endorse race-sensitive policies to increase racial diversity.

Now it's unclear whether affirmative action fuels a white racist backlash. Suppose it does. That doesn't mean we should get rid of it (you'll recall that forty years ago many people opposed civil rights laws for the same reason). As my dear granny used to say, you can't fry eggs without cracking shells (or, doing the right thing isn't going to please everybody). Of course, if you could bring about racial justice using less divisive methods—and we have mentioned some of them—then of course we should; but then again these other methods might well be costlier in other ways.

It's also true that some black beneficiaries have reported feeling stigmatized as inferior by their white school and office mates (however, recent studies show that the vast majority of such beneficiaries report no such feelings). What should be done? If affirmative action were eliminated, blacks might still feel the stigma of inferiority, since there would be fewer of them represented in the professions. Also, maybe the blame for the stigma should fall on the whites who make blacks feel inferior.

Does affirmative action elevate the less qualified over the better qualified? Yes, if you think that the only relevant qualifications for measuring future job performance are things like where you went to school, what grades you got, and how well you performed on standardized tests. Surely these qualifications matter. The question is, how much?

Pronounced differences in test scores and grades may sometimes predict different levels of job performance. But admissions officers and prospective employers using affirmative action guidelines are not required to admit or hire unqualified candidates who fall below a minimum grade level or test score. Anyway, grades and test scores are not always a reliable predictor of job performance—that's why businesses and professional schools interview prospective applicants. (Incidentally, recent studies conducted by the University of California-Davis School of Medicine and by Derek Bok and William Bowen, the former presidents of Harvard and Princeton, show that there is no difference between affirmative action and regular admission students regarding rates of graduation, completion of residency training, obtaining board certification, and job placement.)

In some cases, grades and test scores might be irrelevant—you don't need to be a literary genius or mathematics whiz to be a damned good electrician. In other cases, high test scores and advanced degrees might be a disqualification (a teacher with a B.A. in history can probably teach a sixth-grade course on American history as well as—if not better than—a person with a Ph.D. who has spent her life doing research and teaching graduate students).

Other kinds of qualifications—such as speech, appearance, friendliness, and so on—are more subjective, and therefore more prone to racial biases. Experience is an important qualification, but it, too, can sometimes mask true ability. And let's not forget that some qualifications are not at all related to future performance. Princeton University admits 40 percent of all admissions applicants whose parents were former students of the university in comparison to just 15 percent of the regular applicant pool. Last but not least, race itself might be a relevant qualification when filling a high-profile post in a Black Studies Program at a university; for typically, such positions involve role modeling and mentoring as well as teaching and research.

Is Affirmative Action Fair?

Now that we've examined some consequentialist objections to affirmative action, let's look at the fairness objection. This objection is very straightforward. It asks: Why should qualified white males be penalized (i.e., bumped from positions in favor of qualified blacks)

Tried and True

Affirmative action is indeed a strategy for "leveling the playing field." But unlike past forms of racial discrimination, it doesn't try to accomplish this by dragging white men down to the level of oppressed women and minorities. Rather, its aim is positive: to compensate for the continuing effects of sexual and racial discrimination. In other words, its aim is to elevate women and minorities to the current, privileged status enjoyed by white men.

simply because of their skin color? Doesn't this amount to reversing the sort of discrimination that was visited upon blacks?

To begin with, regardless of whether it is fair or not to white men, affirmative action doesn't impose on white men the kind of discrimination that white men imposed on blacks. Affirmative action isn't intended to demean white men, and it's certainly isn't intended to "keep them in their place" (white men still control most of the wealth and power in this country and throughout the world).

Second, if the argument says that people should not be favored or disfavored for jobs because of qualities over which they have no control (such as race), then it's still too sweeping. A very small person will be fairly disadvantaged when applying for a job in the National Basketball Association, just as any man will be fairly disadvantaged applying for a job in a rape counseling clinic. We are all judged by personal attributes over which we have no control. The question is, are these attributes relevant to the goal or task against which they're being judged? Race is certainly relevant to the goal of promoting racial justice.

Finally, if the argument says that it's wrong to penalize innocent people for wrongs committed by others, then the proper response is that even innocent persons have no right to reap the benefits of social injustice. White men aren't being penalized for past injustice; they're being prevented from cashing in on an unfair advantage.

The Least You Need to Know

- Racial and ethnic categories are social conventions, not biological realities.
- Anti-racism and multiculturalism promote justice through racial integration and respect for cultural differences.
- Affirmative action is fair in theory, but perhaps less fair in practice.
- Bringing about racial justice will probably require far-ranging solutions to poverty and educational inequality.

27

Getting Our Just Des(s)erts

In This Chapter

◆ The importance of thinking for yourself
◆ Dealing with moral evil
◆ Moral responsibility: who owes what to whom?
◆ The up-side of ethics

Duties, obligations, consequences, relationships: this book has given you a lot of things to consider. As you put together your recipe for a good moral life, you might just wonder what you're supposed to do with all the ingredients! Especially if you're concerned about using the recipe to ensure just des(s)erts, you'll want it to have just the right blend of justice with care, adding a dash of consequences and duties.

This final chapter is what I hope will be a fond farewell to ethics. This doesn't mean that, after you close the cover on this book, you're finished with it. As I'm sure you already know, ethics isn't something that is simply "book learned." It's an open-ended process of checking and re-checking your moral beliefs, values, and actions to ensure they line up with your moral point of view. As you spend your life perfecting your moral recipe, there are a few standard ingredients that you will probably want to fold in: thinking for your-self, being a person for others, and taking responsibility for your actions while holding others responsible for theirs.

We will consider these aspects of moral life and end on a positive note. For while it's true that doing ethics, and leading an ethical life, can be pretty heavy-duty, there is reason to think positively. Because—hey!—things might not be hopeless after all. So put on your chef's hat, and let's start putting the final recipe together.

For Further Consideration ...

First, let's give a little more thought to some of the issues I have treated in this book. Most of Part 3, "General Recipes for Guiding Ethical Decision-Making," has focused on different ethical theories, and what they have to say about living the moral life. Recall that ...

- Deontologists instruct you to do your duty.

- Consequentialists require you to consider the likely outcomes of your actions.

- Virtue theorists argue that being a person of excellence is what most matters.

- Feminist ethicists claim that you should do your moral thinking in terms of relationships and care.

As I pointed out, each of these theories has something to offer: we need to develop them and be aware of what we're committed to if we're going to use any one approach.

Do the Right Thing!

If you care about doing ethics well, you'll want to deliberate from the best possible position. This means having a wealth of background information to help you in your decision-making. For remember this: It's very easy to criticize other's actions from a birds-eye, objective point of view. But knowing more about that person and her situation makes it much harder to make harsh moral judgments!

But theories and principles are limited because we need context in order to make accurate determinations of right and wrong. So this is the first point for your further consideration: That you need details, information, and a rich background within which to make moral judgments. Otherwise, you risk making harsh assessments of others' actions based on the little information you have.

What this amounts to is avoiding things like jumping to conclusions, making "snap" judgments, and assuming the person in question is just "like those" people. When we do these things, we assume that there is only one good perspective on a moral situation: our own! Critics of that view—that there's one, objective moral perspective—have argued that we need a situated approach to ethics, a moral perspective that is known as standpoint theory.

Taking a Stand: Standpoint Theory

Standpoint theorists point out that, rather than one "objective" moral perspective, there are many perspectives or standpoints from which to make moral judgments. For example, it matters whether the standpoint you're doing ethics from is that of a white wealthy person or a poor person of color. As the white, wealthy person, there are certain features of the moral situation that will stand out for you; and there are other aspects of it that you will miss. This is also true, of course, of the poor person of color: her moral perspective will come from her own experiences in the world. So, you might ask, how are we supposed to figure out which "standpoint" is the best one to use? If we have no objective moral perspective, how do we choose the best one?

Standpoint theorists claim that you should always try to adopt or listen to the standpoint of the most marginalized persons. That means you should give greater weight to the perspectives of individuals who lack the social privileges enjoyed by others.

For example, suppose you're considering the ethics of putting homeless people in jail for panhandling. Since pedestrians sometimes feel threatened by homeless panhandlers, and the constant request for money can be annoying and offensive, it might be best to support policies and bylaws that eliminate the problem. Should you support a bylaw that puts homeless people in jail for this bothersome activity? How do you decide?

Standpoint theory states that, in order to decide what is morally right in such a situation, you need to consider the problem from the perspective of the homeless person. This is especially important given that homeless people in our society are hardly a blip on our radar screens. We often don't notice them (unless they come up to us and ask for money!), and we certainly don't hear their voices weighing in on questions of law and public policy.

Consider my home city. Chicago has a large population of homeless people; and for the most part, they live under the city streets where it is warmer and protected. Remember, Chicago is a bloody cold city! So other than seeing homeless folk on the streets where they're panhandling, we don't often have reason to think about why they're there, how they got there, what their needs are, or how they view things. But by adopting their marginalized perspective, you take them seriously as moral agents.

The problem is ensuring that we fairly and accurately represent their standpoints. I could use my imagination and try to "walk in the shoes" of a

Ethically Speaking

When trying to make moral decisions, you need to adopt a standpoint approach. **Standpoint theory** requires you to consider a moral issue from the perspectives of individuals who are least privileged. That way we ensure that the voices of people who lack social privilege get heard. And we avoid making snap judgments about others' actions.

homeless person (if he has any!), but after doing this I could hardly say I've "been there." I'd be pretty arrogant to suppose that my little thought experiment about homelessness would give me a clear understanding of that perspective. Anyway, there are many "homeless" perspectives, and not just one, so it's also arrogant to think that chatting with a homeless woman on the street for a minute makes me an expert on homelessness!

So what to do? Why bring up standpoint theory in the first place if it's so darned complicated? The answer is: Standpoint theory requires a certain amount of humility and moral honesty when we're making moral deliberations. It denies us the arrogant, "I've got the right answer" mentality. This is a good, desirable thing in our ethical lives, since standpoint theory reminds us to consider the plight of other people. And how do you avoid taking an arrogant approach to different standpoints? By doing your research! Read the writing of experts in the field (there's lots of good books on homelessness, and qualitative studies on the homeless community). Engage with homeless people in your community—you might be surprised to hear their stories. And educate yourself about the causes of homelessness. If you do your homework on this issue, you will probably find it much more difficult to make objective claims about the moral wrongness of panhandling.

> **Tried and True**
>
> Your thinking about other people's standpoints should extend beyond a consideration of panhandling and homeless people. That was just an example of the kind of difference that our standpoints make. In just about *any* moral situation you will be faced with, you need to consider what the various standpoints are, and which ones are marginalized or privileged. You should ask yourself: Are some perspectives silenced because the people holding them lack power and social prestige? How does this silencing impact their place in the world? By asking these questions, you link up ethics and social justice in a fundamental way.

The Personal Is Political

The second point for your consideration is this: Ethics isn't just a personal or individual activity. Your actions and choices can directly or even indirectly impact the lives and interests of other people. There's a saying that was popularized by feminists some years ago: "the personal is political." This means that, though you have a private life as a citizen, your personal choices have social and political impact. It also means that ethics requires a commitment to political, social action, since what you do in the public sphere (or don't do, as the case may be—like not voting!) has an impact on the kind of society we all live in.

It should be kind of comforting to know that your personal little problems aren't so unimportant after all—and that we aren't little insignificant peons in the grand scheme of things! What we each do as individuals certainly does matter to social and political life. And when a bunch of us little peons get together on an ethical issue, some real change can occur. It just takes political will and ethical commitment to do it.

Think of it this way: whatever moral stance you take on a subject indicates something important about you. When you take a moral position, you stand for something in an important way. For example, consider an exchange that happened between my daughter and our vegetarian friends. My 10-year-old daughter was engaging them in a conversation about the ethics of meat-eating: My friends talked about their love of animals, and why they feel they can't be morally consistent as animal-lovers if they eat meat. Sabina took their arguments very seriously; it became clear that my friends' "standing for" vegetarianism caused her to think seriously about her own love of meat (especially bacon!). I'm not saying that Sabina changed her mind about meat-eating right then, but the fact that people she cares about stood for something had a real impact on her own thinking. This is one example of how your personal moral choices speak volumes, and how others can be affected by them.

> **Tried and True**
>
> The next time you are talking with a child about a moral matter, think about the way your moral stance affects her. Though our own personal moral choices may seem like "private" matters, they often have broader impact. When we take a moral position we stand for something in an important way; and it's important to remember that you may be influencing others.

Social Institutions and Personal Choice

A third point for your consideration concerns our social institutions. Choices are structured by institutions that may act as hindrances to actions you think are morally right. Indeed, most people experience times where they want to do what they think is "the right thing," but they can't because of the way our social institutions are set up.

For example, consider a couple who discovers through genetic testing that they are going to give birth to a baby with spina bifida. Suppose that this couple truly wants to have their child, spina bifida or not. But they have low-paying jobs, little income, and three other children to care for. This couple knows that there is little monetary, educational, and medical support for disabled children, so the choice that they think is morally right is hindered by the lack of broad social support for people with disabilities. They may decide against continuing with the pregnancy just because of the way our social institutions are set up.

This problem—that society sometimes makes difficult or impossible our own moral choices—is one of the more tragic features of moral life. There are times when, despite your best efforts to make something happen, your social and political world defies you. Things just will not change.

There's another aspect to the tragic nature of life: Not only can our moral choices be blocked by social structures and social institutions, but so can many of our life opportunities. Opportunities are often determined by circumstances beyond our control: whether we're born into rich or poor families, whether we're educated or not, whether we're black or white, and so on.

If you take seriously this tragic aspect of human life, then it's much more difficult to apply a "bootstrapping" mentality to our treatment of others. Instead of asking why others don't pull themselves up by their bootstraps (as my grandpa used to say) and improve their own lives, we must consider the social and political barriers that block their ability to do so. It might also require us to take a "there but for the grace of God, go I" approach to our dealings with others. In other words: that unfortunate person could have been you, since fortune and misfortune is beyond human control.

Tried and True

I can write and talk about the importance of providing good care for members of society, but without the economic and political commitment of our major social institutions, it may seem like a lost cause. While we need to be realistic about our goals, we also need to avoid the kind of cynicism that prevents us from standing for something that matters to us.

Ethically Speaking

The **theodicy problem,** or the "problem of evil," occurs when bad things happen to good people. It makes us wonder: would an all-powerful, all-loving God really allow innocent people to suffer and die? We have only two possible responses: that God's ways are mysterious, and we can't know His ultimate plan, or that there's no reconciling the evil that occurs in the world.

Dealing with Moral Evil

Speaking of fortune and misfortune, there's one more "downer" point to consider: It's what some philosophers call the *theodicy problem*, or, in plain English, the problem of evil. This is a moral issue that troubles both theists and atheists alike, and can be devastating. The problem of evil arises when bad things happen to good people—a loved one dies of cancer; an innocent child is killed in a car crash; or thousands of people are killed in events like September 11. In such cases, the deaths appear senseless, inexplicable, and downright evil: there seems to be no rhyme or reason for them.

I experience this theodicy problem whenever I read in the paper about the children who are killed in the crossfire of gang wars. In one recent case, a little boy was killed by a bullet that came through his living room window—the bullet was intended for someone else, but hit him by mistake. When such senseless things happen, we ask ourselves: How could there be an all-good, all-knowing God who could allow such evil to happen to innocent people? If God is all-powerful, can't He use his power to prevent the evil that is done in this world?

There are only a couple of answers to this problem, and neither of them are satisfactory.

1. The first goes like this: These awful, inexplicable, horrible things that happen to innocent people must ultimately be good, or God wouldn't let them happen. We can't know God's ultimate plan, so we can't judge His goodness. But this response may be little comfort to those who are mourning the loss of their loved ones in the senseless World Trade Center crash. Even for those of deep faith, such evil is hard to reconcile with the concept of an all-powerful God.

2. The other response to the problem of evil isn't much better. It's to accept that, yes, bad things *do* happen to good people, and there's no denying that fact. We can't appeal to God's ultimate plan, and we can't pretend that all evil is reconcilable in the end. The world can be a cold, harsh, and scary place—especially these days, as we wonder at people mailing anthrax to others, threatening to bomb bridges and blow up malls.

So God's mysterious ways, or reconciling yourself to evil—those are the basic options. I don't know about you, but neither answer inspires confidence in the possibility for goodness in the world or in the ultimate goodness of human beings. All we can do in such cases is remember that, for every evil act that occurs, there are good ones that follow in its wake. Think about the firefighters and others who risked their lives to save others after September 11; and the outpouring of support for families who lost loved ones.

Okay, so you've given consideration to some of the heavier aspects of moral life. When you dwell on these moral questions, things may start to get pretty heavy. But let's dispel the doom and gloom and look at the up-side of ethics—what it means to live the good life. Ahhh, the good life! But I don't mean sun and sand here—no, the "good life" in moral terms involves acquiring some important moral capacities and perspectives.

Living the Good Life

This book has already considered what it means to live the good life. If you passed over earlier chapters, you may want to return to them to consider in detail what "the good life" involves. Here I just want to offer a few parting shots on the subject: that, at the very least, you must be able to think for yourself, and take responsibility for your actions while holding others responsible for theirs.

Thinking for Yourself

"Oh no, not this again!" you may be saying. Yes, I covered this ground earlier—but it's so important to the ethical enterprise that it bears repeating. Think for yourself. Be an individual. As our buddy John Stuart Mill says, "He who does anything because it is the custom makes no choice." Since ethics involves making choices for yourself, if you're not thinking for yourself, then you're not living the ethical life. Heck, some philosophers would claim you're failing to be human if you're not doing this, since what differentiates humans from animals is our capacity to think as individuals!

Moral Musings

The requirement that you think for yourself can be the most difficult aspect of moral life. Consider the recent events of September 11: Not only is it unclear what is the morally right thing to do, but there is strong moral censure of people who express "unpatriotic" views. For example, people who choose not to hang an American flag may be charged with being anti-American; and those who don't support the way the U.S. Government is reacting to the events of 9/11 face harsh criticism. With the understandably strong patriotic sentiment, thinking for yourself is difficult and takes a certain degree of moral courage.

The reason I bring this up again is because the call to think for yourself is sometimes the hardest part of ethical life. Let me give you an example. Given the events of September 11, it's hard to know *what* is the right thing to do. Should we be bombing Afghanistan? Should we support economic sanctions against countries that support the Taliban? What makes things worse is the understandably strong sense of patriotism that some Americans are expressing as a response to the September 11 attacks. Part of the patriotic sentiment includes an intolerance of different viewpoints, and an expectation that everyone act in solidarity. And while solidarity is important, it must not be achieved through the violation of independent thought.

So, while Mill thinks that custom and tradition should be used as guides to the ethical life, he also thinks they can't stand in for individual thought and opinion. This is brought home by the events of September 11: We need to be able to think through this tragedy, and our moral responses to it, without being limited by the opinions of others.

Beyond thinking for yourself, there's another aspect of living the good life, and it involves taking responsibility for your actions and holding others responsible for theirs. While this may seem like a pretty straightforward issue—if you choose to act and someone gets hurt, you are responsible for his harm!—it's actually quite complicated. Let's consider some hard questions about responsibility.

Taking Responsibility and Holding Others Responsible

Another important aspect of the "good life"—since we're on the subject!—is knowing when to take responsibility and when to hold others responsible. This may seem like a simple issue, but it's actually quite complex. For example, it's clear that if I choose to do something that causes harm to others, I am responsible for that harm. If I recklessly run a red light when I'm driving my car, and I hit a pedestrian crossing the street, then I am inarguably responsible for the harm I caused.

But in other cases, my moral responsibility for my actions might not be so clear. To take a simple case, if I am brainwashed by a cult into a certain action, can we really say that I am responsible for what I do? We'd probably say in such a case that I am *compelled* by the cult to act. But compulsion can take on a variety of forms, including social ones. If you're a young mother without income, and you have a starving toddler on your hands, then you might take the risk of getting caught in order to steal food for your child. People might say you're responsible for your act in that case—you chose to steal, and you must suffer the penalty. But another reading of your action suggests that you were compelled to act out of necessity.

Let's consider an even more contentious case of moral responsibility: drug-addicted pregnant women. On some moral accounts, women who use drugs or drink alcohol during pregnancy are moral monsters because they are failing in their basic responsibility to their fetuses. Most women, when they choose to get pregnant and carry a fetus to term, go out of their way to take good care of themselves during pregnancy: They get exercise, eat well, avoid harmful substances (like cigarettes, alcohol, drugs) and avoid risks that would endanger their pregnancies. Given this, the harms that addicted pregnant women do to their fetuses seem even more monstrous.

Do the Right Thing!

You need to be careful in your thinking about moral responsibility. It's not always true that people are responsible for their actions: They may act out of hunger, addiction, poverty, or some other kind of external compulsion. Some people's lives are so deeply affected by poverty and need that their array of choices don't come close to those of other, more privileged, people!

But if you look a little harder at the addicted pregnant woman's situation, it's not so clear that we can hold her entirely responsible for the potential harm done to her fetus. By virtue of her addiction, it isn't that she "chooses" to do harm to her fetus. She isn't making choices in the way we normally mean. So to hold her responsible for choosing to harm her fetus may be a mistake. This isn't to say that having an addiction clears you of any and all moral responsibility for your actions: But it does mean that the addiction makes it difficult to assign responsibility through choice.

What this means is that punishing these women after they give birth to addicted babies may not be the most moral choice. Getting them treatment for their drug or alcohol addiction makes sense; even having them do community work in a neonatal clinic where they can see the effects on babies of drugs and alcohol—that makes sense. But putting them in prison for willfully causing harm to their babies? That's arguably an improper response based on a thin notion of "choice."

When you add in the earlier point that many of our life opportunities are determined by circumstances beyond our control, then the drug-addicted pregnant women's personal responsibility is even more questionable. When people are born into negative life circumstances—poverty, abusive homes, poor family structure, and poor educational opportunities—it's even harder to see how people "choose" the way that their lives turn out. So this is another aspect to consider in assigning responsibility: what are (and were) the life circumstances of the persons under consideration? Is society also at fault for the moral condition of the person's life?

> ### Moral Musings
>
> Some people argue that we should implement "Good Samaritan" laws. These laws would require that, where citizens are in the position to help others whose lives are at risk, they have a moral and *legal* obligation to do so. Critics of good Samaritan laws argue that you can't legislate morality. What do you think?

I'll give you this much: the question about when, where, and how much responsibility to assign to individual wrong-doers is a tough one. People who criticize the "soft" approach I've outlined—that we shouldn't assign moral responsibility where people have no control over their lives—argue that we don't treat people with respect when we fail to hold them to the same standards as the rest of us. If I say that we shouldn't hold substance-addicted pregnant women responsible for harming their fetuses, I may be denying their free agency, and taking away their capacity for free choice. Just think about Immanuel Kant's account of retributivism outlined in Chapter 12, "We Can't Forget Kant"—he argues that people deserve to be punished because they *will* their punishment!

But I do think that, where the issue of responsibility is concerned, we have to think carefully about what it means to make a free and informed choice. As I mentioned in Chapter 18, "Biomedical Ethics," it's sometimes hard to see how a person has the necessary information and the freedom to make informed choices. If you are an AIDS patient, for example, and you are desperate for a cure, is your choice to participate in an extremely dangerous drug trial really unconstrained? Mightn't even the slightest bit of hope make you willing to subject yourself to any drug, no matter how risky?

Whichever way you go on this question of responsibility, one thing's for sure: It's not as simple and straightforward as it initially may have appeared! In just about every moral situation we need to ask the question: How do we assign responsibility in a way that is fair-minded and appropriate?

Thinking Positively: Hey, It's Not So Hopeless!

It's really important to finish this book on a positive note: First, because if you leave with the impression that ethics is all about gut-wrenching doom and gloom, then it might scare you off for good. But second, it's important to think positively, because, really, things aren't so hopeless after all! The ethical life is about good things, too: As you're aware after reading this book, the Greeks thought that the ethical life was the best life lived, and the Utilitarians think ethics is about bringing as much happiness into the world as possible.

Consider the up-side to ethics in the following ways:

- There's meaning in ethical life even if, in your lifetime, you don't see progress or change. As I mentioned earlier, it may frustrate and make you cynical about ethics when, despite your greatest efforts, nothing ever seems to change. And when you think about great people who died for their ideals—like Dr. Martin Luther King Jr.—and how the problems they were fighting against persist, it may seem like a lost cause. But don't despair. Your life touches people on a local level, and that's important, too.

- Appealing to virtue ethics also gives your life meaning. When you consider some of the truly excellent people you know, both famous and not, you probably realize that there are good people who are worthy of your respect. This makes life meaningful, and reminds us that there is good to be found, even in flawed human beings.

- The fact that you bought this book in the first place is a good sign: It means that you aren't so cynical about ethics that you have totally given up thinking about it. So that's a good thing!

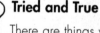 **Tried and True**

There are things you can do that express the "up-side" to ethical life. For example, you can join a service-oriented club that helps people in your community; you can get involved in a charity; give a hand at animal shelters; or participate in grass-roots political organizations that lobby on behalf of the environment.

And remember this important point: Even though we may not have completely eliminated the moral evils that occur in the world, we've certainly been moving in the right direction. Over the course of centuries, we've made progress with issues like slavery, women's rights, animal rights, democracy, and social welfare.

You've come a long way if you've read this book from cover to cover. While it only offers a brief treatment of many ethical theories and issues, you're well on your way to leading a thoughtful, reflective, moral life. This isn't to say you weren't always a good, ethical person: But none of us can be fully responsible or responsive adults without thinking about the deeper reasons underlying our actions and institutions.

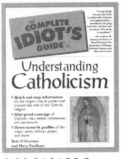

Glossary

affirmative action   The practice of showing preference in hiring, promoting, contracting, and admitting people to institutions of higher education and professional schools.

autonomy   The capacity to be self-governing, or in charge of your own life.

capitalism   An economic system defined by the existence of companies, profit motive, competition, wage labor, and private property.

care ethics   An approach to ethics that starts with the importance of relationships. It sees the highest moral good as caring for (and about) others.

caveat emptor   A Latin phrase that means "Let the buyer beware."

circular reasoning   Any reasoning in which the conclusion of an argument merely restates a premise of the argument, and has the form "C (some statement) because of C." Good arguments support conclusions with independent reasons (evidence) and have the form "C because of E" (where "E" is some statement other than "C").

communitarianism   The social and political doctrine that rejects the liberal view that individuals possess freedom and rights in some natural way, prior to duties owed the community.

conflicting duties   Whenever two duties command two different things at the same time. For example, fulfilling the duty to save life by means of a painful treatment conflicts with the duty to prevent pain and suffering.

consequentialism   An ethical theory that determines good or bad, right or wrong, based on outcomes. Famous defenders included Jeremy Bentham and John Stuart Mill.

contextualism   The ethical doctrine that the rightness and wrongness of actions depends entirely on the particular contexts in which they occur, so that lying is right in one context but wrong in another.

cost-benefit analysis   A method of doing consequentialist ethics that involves calculating the costs and benefits of an action and choosing actions that maximize benefits relative to costs.

deontological ethics   An ethical approach that focuses on duties and not consequences in determining right conduct. Famously identified with the philosophy of Immanuel Kant.

determinism   The view that nothing happens without a cause. It's just a high-fallutin' way of saying that there's no such thing as free will.

direct democracy   A kind of democracy in which people rule themselves directly rather than elect representatives to do so for them. One variant is workplace democracy, in which workers control how they work and, in some cases, what they make.

discrimination   Any way of distinguishing persons that has the effect of stigmatizing some group of persons as inferior to another group. Discrimination need not be intentional; institutional discrimination is caused by mechanisms and procedures that are otherwise quite neutral and nondiscriminatory, such as local hiring and seniority retention.

Divine Command theory   The ethical theory that says that something is right or good just because God commands it and that something is wrong or bad just because God condemns it.

dogmatism   The stubborn refusal to consider challenges to your own ethical point-of-view.

egoism   The theory that people always act out self-interest (psychological egoism) or that they should act out of self-interest (ethical egoism).

ethical dilemma   Any situation that forces us to choose in a way that involves breaking some ethical norm or contradicting some ethical value.

ethics   The philosophical discipline or aspect of life that involves questions about right and wrong conduct, good and bad values.

ethnic groups   National cultural groups (in North America, typically immigrant groups).

euthanasia   A Greek word meaning "the good death." It involves physician-assisted mercy killing or physician-assisted suicide, as when doctors give patients the means to end their *own* lives.

hedonism   The consequentialist ethical doctrine that what is good and right is what promotes pleasure.

imperatives   Moral commands that are either hypothetical (stated in an "If you want something … then do this" form) or categorical (stated in a "Do this, and don't give me any ifs, ands, or buts" form).

integrity   The uncompromising commitment to a code of ethics or values that are consistent with one another.

"'Is' implies 'ought'" fallacy   An error in reasoning that involves supposing that just because things *are* a certain way that they *ought* to be that way.

laissez-faire   The economic doctrine that holds that people should be allowed to engage in buying and selling without interference.

liberalism   The political doctrine that upholds the natural freedom and equality of all persons. Its main pillars of faith are toleration of differing creeds and the right to pursue one's own good as one sees fit without interference from others or the state.

lifeboat ethics   The view that, given limited economic and environmental resources, immigration must be limited to prevent the destruction of a society.

Malthusianism   The doctrine, named after British economist Thomas Malthus (1766–1834), that holds that malnutrition is caused by overpopulation, the only cure for which is death by starvation.

Natural Law doctrine   A doctrine that says the highest standards for judging right and wrong are not the customs and laws of any particular society, but the universal laws of human nature, as these are known by reason.

nihilism   A term, which comes from the Latin word *nihil*, or *nothing*. For Friedrich Nietzsche, ethical codes are nihilistic destructive and unhealthy, because they deny what is most vital about life.

norms   Regular ways of doing things that everybody agrees on. Unlike other conventions, ethical norms regulate all aspects of our lives in ways that are crucial for the existence of society.

Nuremberg code   An international code of ethics that governs human research and experimentation. It was set in place after the Nazi medical atrocities of World War II were discovered. The code requires that human subjects give fully informed consent, that the study yield "fruitful results for the good of society" and that subjects not be put at risk of death or disablement.

objectivism   The belief that morality is based on some universal, eternal, and unchanging fact. For example, murder is always wrong, for all times and places.

paternalism A doctrine that literally means "rule by the father"; in health care, it resulted in doctors making decisions for their patients without consulting them, in total violation of their autonomy as an adult.

patriarchy A term that literally means "rule of the father." Patriarchal cultures are those where men are dominant and women are subordinate. Feminists are concerned about the way that patriarchal power results in the *sexual* domination of women by men.

pornography Can be defined as the explicit depiction of men, women, and/or children in degrading sexual contexts.

prima facie duty A duty that applies to a given situation such that it can be overridden by another duty that applies to that situation.

Prisoner's Dilemma A dilemma that arises between two persons who find themselves in an competitive or conflicting relationship with one another, such that their most rational decision results in each achieving a less optimal outcome than if they could have cooperated with one another.

quality The quality of a pleasure is proportional to the degree to which it contributes to a person's overall intellectual, moral, and aesthetic development.

quantity Refers to how much pleasure you get out of an act, including how long it lasts, and how good it feels.

rationality A term that designates the capacity to think logically and consistently and to order one's ends and means efficiently so as to achieve the greatest success possible. Moral rationality further involves critically examining the compatibility of one's action vis-à-vis the actions of others as well as the preferences and motivations that underlie it.

relativism The belief that morality is relative to each individual culture, and that we can't make universal moral claims like "murder is always wrong."

retributivism A theory of punishment that is best summed up by the phrase "an eye for an eye."

right Any claim against (demand imposed on) another person or some governing body to be guaranteed some good, such as freedom, security, welfare, etc.

sexual harassment Defined by the United States Equal Employment Opportunity Commission (EEOC) as "unwelcome sexual advances, requests for sexual favors, and other verbal or physical conduct of a sexual nature whose submission to or rejection explicitly or implicitly affects an individual's employment, unreasonably interferes with an individual's work performance or creates an intimidating, hostile or offensive work environment."

skepticism An attitude of doubting the truth of some claim.

standpoint theory   A theory that requires you to consider a moral issue from the perspectives of individuals who are least privileged.

state of nature   An idea used by philosophers to understand how persons would naturally behave if there were no government threatening to punish them if they stepped out of line.

subjectivism   A doctrine that says that moral judgments are nothing more than expressions of personal preference.

subliminal advertising   A form of advertising that appeals to the consumer's subconscious in order to get them to buy the manufacturer's product.

theodicy problem   A problem, also known as the "problem of evil," that occurs when bad things happen to good people. It makes us wonder if an all-powerful, all-loving God really would allow innocent people to suffer and die? We have only two possible responses: that God's ways are mysterious, and we can't know His ultimate plan, or that there's no reconciling the evil that occurs in the world.

Utilitarianism   A moral theory that treats pleasure or happiness as the only absolute moral good. According to Utilitarian thinkers, the morality of your actions depends on their results. Acts that bring about an overall increase in happiness or pleasure are morally good; those that result in suffering or pain are morally bad.

value   Any standard for judging the worth of some thing or some action. Intrinsic values are goods we want because they are valuable in their own right, apart from anything else. Instrumental values are goods we want because they help us achieve some other good(s).

veganism   A more radical version of vegetarianism, where one not only refuses to eat meat, but to use any product that comes from animals. This includes clothing, cosmetics, leathers, and furs.

virtues   Character traits that refer to specific sorts of human excellence. Exercising them contributes both to one's own well-being and to the good of society.

Appendix B

For Future Reference

Selected Primary Texts (Classics for Those Who Like Being Challenged)

Aquinas, St. Thomas. *The Summa Theologica* (excerpts). In *The Political Ideas of St. Thomas Aquinas*, edited with an introduction by Dino Bigongiari (New York: Hafner Publishing, 1953).

Aristotle. *Nichomachean Ethics*. Translation and introduction by Terence Irwin (Indianapolis: Hackett Publishing, 1985).

Gilligan, Carol. *In a Different Voice: Psychological Theory and Women's Development* (Cambridge: Harvard University Press, 1982).

Hobbes, Thomas. *Leviathan*. Edited with an introduction by Edwin Curley (Indianapolis: Hackett Publishing, 1994).

Kant, Immanuel. *Grounding for the Metaphysics of Morals*. Translation by James W. Ellington (Indianapolis, Hackett Publishing, 1993).

Locke, John. *Second Treatise of Government*. Edited by C.B. MacPherson (Indianapolis: Hackett Publishing, 1980).

Marx, Karl. *Selected Writings*. Edited by Lawrence Simon (Indianapolis: Hackett Publishing, 1994).

Mill, John Stuart. "On Liberty" and "Utilitarianism." In *The Utilitarians/Bentham/Mill* (Garden City, NJ: Anchor Books, 1973).

Nietzsche, Friedrich. *On the Genealogy of Morality*. Translation by Maudemarie Clark and Allen J. Swensen (Indianapolis: Hackett Publishing, 1998).

Plato. *Republic*. Translation by G.M.A. Grube (with introduction by C.D.C. Reeve) (Indianapolis, Hackett Publishing, 1992).

Rawls, John. *A Theory of Justice* (Cambridge: Harvard University Press, 1971).

Rousseau, Jean-Jacques. *On the Social Contract and Discourses*. Translation and introduction by Donald Cress (Indianapolis: Hackett, 1983).

Selected Commentaries and Applications (Less Challenging)

Beauchamp, Tom L., and James F. Childress. *Principles of Biomedical Ethics* (Oxford: Oxford University Press, 1994).

Kittay, Eva Feder and Diana T. Meyers, (eds.). *Women and Moral Theory* (Totowa, NJ: Rowman and Littlefield, 1987).

May, Larry, Shari Collins-Chobanian, and Kai Wong. *Applied Ethics: A Multicultural Approach* (Upper Saddle River, NJ: Prentice Hall, 1998).

Palmer, Donald. *Looking at Philosophy: The Unbearable Heaviness of Philosophy Made Lighter* (Mountain View, CA: Mayfield, 1988).

Rachels, James. *The Elements of Moral Philosophy* (Boston: McGraw-Hill, 1999).

Singer, Peter. *Animal Liberation* (New York: Random House, 1990).

Westphal, Dale, and Fred Westphal. *Planet in Peril: Essays in Environmental Ethics* (Orlando: Harcourt Brace, 1994).

Selected Websites

Philosophy Coffee Houses and Chat Clubs

dir.clubs.yahoo.com/Entertainment__Arts/Humanities/Philosophy/

Philosophy Links

www.cwru.edu/275730/artsci/phil/links.html

Other Useful Links

www.academicintegrity.org/links/asp

Miscellaneous Applied Ethics Resources (Popular and Academic)

www.ethics.ubc.ca/resources/misc/topics.html

www.lib.utk.edu/reds/phil

Index